The Racial Politics of Bodies, Nations and Knowledges

The Racial Politics of Bodies, Nations and Knowledges

Edited by

Barbara Baird and Damien W. Riggs

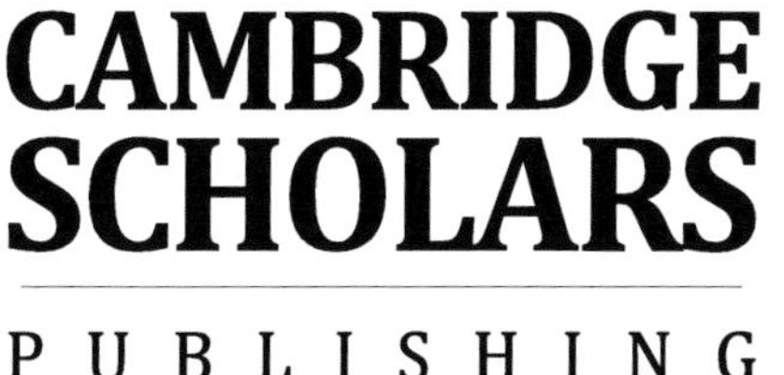

The Racial Politics of Bodies, Nations and Knowledges,
Edited by Barbara Baird and Damien W. Riggs

This book first published 2009

Cambridge Scholars Publishing

12 Back Chapman Street, Newcastle upon Tyne, NE6 2XX, UK

British Library Cataloguing in Publication Data
A catalogue record for this book is available from the British Library

ISBN (10): 1-4438-0326-X, ISBN (13): 978-1-4438-0326-7

TABLE OF CONTENTS

LIST OF ILLUSTRATIONS

List of Tables

CONTRIBUTORS

Barbara Baird is head of the Department of Women's Studies at Flinders University in Adelaide. Her research interests focus on the history and cultural politics of sexuality and reproduction and their intersection with discourses of race and nation. She has recently been guest editor for a special issue of *Australian Feminist Studies* concerning "the child".

Anne Brewster teaches at the University of New South Wales. Her books include *Literary Formations: Postcoloniality, Nationalism, Globalism* (1996), *Aboriginal Women's Autobiography* (1995), *Towards a Semiotic of Post-colonial Discourse: University Writing in Singapore and Malaysia 1949-1964* (1988) and *Notes on Catherine Lim's Little Ironies: Stories of Singapore,* with Kirpal Singh (1987). She co-edited, with Angeline O'Neill and Rosemary van den Berg, an anthology of Australian Indigenous Writing, *Those Who Remain Will Always Remember* (2000).

Kathleen Connellan lectures in art and design history at the University of South Australia. Her research connects art and design with issues of social accountability in race. Currently she is portfolio leader of research in the South Australian School of Art where she is working towards linking an understanding of art/design with ethical issues in visual representation.

Prof. Silvo Devetak is the Director of the European Centre for Ethnic and Regional Studies at the University of Maribor, Slovenia. He is a full professor for international public law and the Head of Department of International Law and International Relations at the Faculty of Law, University of Maribor, Slovenia. For two mandates he was a member of the UN CERD (1976-84) and has acted as a coordinator of several international projects on discrimination. In 1997 he was awarded by the Slovenian government with the title "Ambassador of Science of the Republic Slovenia".

Originally from Finland, **Dr. Johan R. Edelheim** worked in the hotel industry in Europe and the United States for ten years before taking up a career in education in the late 1990s. He has postgraduate qualifications from the fields of business administration, education, philosophy, tourism management and cultural studies and has lectured in HE institutions in Finland, China and Australia. Johan's research interests are divided between critical investigations of tourism enlightened by cultural studies methodologies on the one hand, and practical hospitality management issues on the other. He has published and presented his work extensively at international conferences, as well as in peer-reviewed journals, and in the popular media.

Vikki Fraser is a PhD candidate at the University of Western Sydney. Her research interests include queer subjectivity, cyber cultures, and the intersections of space.

Bronwyn Fredericks is an Aboriginal woman originally from South-east Queensland, Australia. She is acknowledged as a writer, educator and activist and has been actively engaged with Indigenous community controlled organisations for over 25 years. Bronwyn writes poetry, socio-political prose, essays and academic papers and has been published within Australia, Ireland, Canada, England and the United States. She is currently a National Health and Medical Research Council (NH&MRC) Post-Doctoral Research Fellow with Monash University and the Queensland Aboriginal and Islander Health Council (QAIHC). QAIHC is the peak body agency for the Aboriginal and Torres Strait Islander community controlled health service sector in the Australian State of Queensland. She is also a Visiting Fellow with the Indigenous Studies Research Network, Queensland University of Technology (QUT).

Ron Hoenig is a PhD student in journalism and cultural studies focusing on the Australian media's depiction of asylum seekers. Born of Hungarian Jewish refugee parents, he has a background in the arts and multiculturalism, having worked as a teacher, playwright, actor, community arts administrator and arts bureaucrat. Since 1996, he has worked as an editor and journalist in the South Australian education department. He is Co-Chair of the South Australia Council for Christians and Jews. His PhD study brings together his passions about writing, multiculturalism and the depiction and treatment of ethnic and other Others.

Catherine Koerner is currently completing her PhD in Development Studies at Flinders University. She has worked in various non-government organisations and community development positions over the past 15 years. Her research interests include critical race and whiteness, identities, community development and education.

James Lovell graduated from St Ignatius' College, Athelstone, in 2002. He completed a Bachelor of Arts, majoring in psychology and literature, at the University of Adelaide in 2006. In the following year James completed his honours degree in psychology, again at the University of Adelaide. James is currently working as a Level Four Family Support Worker for Mission Australia in Mansfield Park, where he provides support to families that are homeless or at risk of homelessness.

Fiona McAllan is currently researching indigenous/settler interrelations with regard to law, language, subjectivity, ethics, belonging. Her PhD thesis explores the repression of indigenous voices in these relations. Recent publications include 'Customary Appropriations' in *borderlands ejournal,* Vol. 6, Issue 3, and 'What Sovereign Rights for Indigenous Australians?' in *The International Journal of Diversity in Organisations, Communities and Nations*, Vol. 8, Issue 3.

Damien W. Riggs is an ARC postdoctoral fellow in the School of Psychology at the University of Adelaide. His research interests encompass critical race and whiteness studies, lesbian and gay psychology and parenting and family studies. He is the editor of *Taking up the challenge: Critical race and whiteness studies in a postcolonising nation* (Crawford Publishers, 2007) and author of *Priscilla, (white) queen of the desert: Queer rights/race privilege.* Damien lectures in gender and sexuality studies and social research methods, and is the editor of the Australian Psychological Society's *Gay and Lesbian Issues and Psychology Review.*

Colin Salter is a Social Scientist and Environmental Engineer with a special interest in the social implications of science and technology. He has been an active member of environmental and social justice campaigns for more than a decade, participating in actions across Australia, Canada and the United States. Participation in social justice movements spurred an interest in how whiteness manifests itself in the good-intentioned actions of white supporters of First Peoples struggles for respect and recognition. He has presented research findings throughout Australian and Canada and will be awarded his PhD early in 2009.

Anna Szorenyi lectures in the Department of Gender, Work and Social Inquiry at the University of Adelaide. She completed her PhD with the Centre for Women's Studies and Gender Research at Monash University on representations of refugees in popular culture. Her current research interests converge generally on representations of suffering, addressed from feminist, critical race and postcolonial perspectives. Anna serves on the Editorial Board of the *Australian Feminist Law Journal* and is currently Treasurer of the Australian Critical Race and Whiteness Studies Association.

Alice Te Punga Somerville (Te Atiawa) is a Lecturer at Victoria University of Wellington, with specialisation in Maori, Pacific and Indigenous writing in English. Born and raised in Aotearoa New Zealand, she received her PhD at Cornell University, and spent time at the University of Hawaii at Manoa during her doctoral studies. She is in the process of completing her first book, *Once Were Pacific*, which explores Maori articulations of connection with the Pacific. She also writes the occasional poem.

Simone Ulalka Tur is a Senior Lecturer at Yunggorendi, First Nations Centre for Higher Education and Research, where she has served since 1998. Simone Ulalka is from the Yankunytjatjara community, located in the Anangu Pitjantjatjara Yankunytjatjara (APY) lands, more than 103,000 square kilometres of arid land in the far northwest of South Australia. Simone Ulalka is a recent recipient of an ARC Indigenous Discovery Grant.

Chris Wilson is an Academic Advisor/Associate Lecturer at Yunggorendi First Nations Centre at Flinders University who is currently undertaking a PhD in Archaeology. As an early career academic Chris' primary research interests have included Indigenous archaeology, cultural heritage management, Indigenous youth and identity and was instrumental in assisting in the repatriation of Ngarrindjeri Old People (human remains) from Museum Victoria and the UK. More recently Chris has been delivering cultural education training for universities, government agencies and the private sector as well as developed a cultural education training manual for the *Inspire* Peer Mentor program. As an Academic Advisor, Chris provides one-on-one academic support, advice and advocacy for Indigenous students at Flinders University.

ACKNOWLEDGEMENTS

We would like to begin by thanking all of the contributors for engaging with reviews, undertaking revisions in short time frames, and for generally helping to produce such an excellent collection. Thanks must also go to our 2007 conference co-convenors: Tracey Bunda, Alia Imtoual, Catherine Koerner, Sharon Gollan and Kathleen Connellan. We would also like to thank all of the people who kindly reviewed chapters for the book. Many thanks are due to Mary Lyons for editorial assistance in bringing the book to completion, and to Amy Patterson for her wonderful artwork that was both the conference logo and now appears on the cover of this collection. Barbara acknowledges the support of funding from an Australian Research Council Discovery grant in the preparation of this book. Damien and Barbara thank each other for making this such an enjoyable experience and for the always enthusiastic and engaging collegial relationship that has resulted from this.

INTRODUCTION

THE RACIAL POLITICS OF BODIES, NATIONS AND KNOWLEDGES

DAMIEN W. RIGGS AND BARBARA BAIRD

In the spirit of the conference at which the chapters in this book were originally presented, and as recognition of the racial politics of living as two white academics in a colonial nation, we begin this introduction by acknowledging the sovereignty of the Kaurna people, the First Nations people upon whose land we live in Adelaide, South Australia. We also acknowledge that prior to colonisation more than 200 Indigenous nations existed in Australia and we recognise the sovereignty of these nations and pay our respects to elders both past and present. By emphasising the relationship we as two white academics have to the fact of Indigenous sovereignty, our point is not to overwrite the multiple relationships between individuals living within Australia and beyond, nor is it to suggest that only Indigenous and white relations require attention. Rather, our point is that by opening with an acknowledgement of our location, it is of central importance that we engage with our relationship as white Australians to ongoing histories of colonisation, whilst acknowledging that these histories will differentially intersect with the lives of all people living in Australia and in other colonial nations.

As such, speaking of the racial politics of any nation requires recognition of the specific configurations of bodies and identities that are rendered intelligible within any given context. In Australia, with its specific history of colonisation that involved the claiming of the country as an "empty land" and the subsequent genocidal acts aimed at asserting the claims to belonging and rights of colonisers over Indigenous people, bodies are shaped by disparities in social and economic capital. Moreover, bodies are shaped by their varying relationships to privilege and disadvantage, with experiences of the former always contingent upon the latter. Thus, as we suggested above, the politics of race in Australia are not limited solely to white-Indigenous relations, and a focus upon the differential allocation of privilege and disadvantage according to social norms provides one way in which to understand the range of relationships that all non-Indigenous people have to the fact of Indigenous sovereignty, in addition to the relationships *between* non-Indigenous people.

In relation to the racialisation of knowledge, the epistemic value accorded to the knowledge claims of white people in Australia is shaped by a colonial context in which written records and particular claims to truth continue to be valued over others, and in particular over the knowledges held within Indigenous communities. This framing of what counts as "knowledge" on the terms set by white people continues to be deployed not only to deny the fact of Indigenous sovereignty, but also to force other non-Indigenous people (not identified as part of the white majority) into complicity with a colonial logic that offers inclusion in national spaces only through conformity to particular modes of being.

Looking outside of Australia, and with recognition of the international nature of this book, it is important to recognise how colonial histories shape national contexts in a range of ways that whilst being markedly different, are similar in relation to the ongoing failure of colonial nations to adequately recognise the sovereign status of First Nations people. Whilst from the lens of Australia it can often look like countries such as New Zealand or Canada are doing a better job of coming to terms with the violence of colonisation and engaging in practices of reconciliation that seek to acknowledge Indigenous sovereignties, those who write from colonial nations outside Australia might contest this reading. We only need to look at ongoing disparities in health, economic and education between Indigenous peoples and non-Indigenous people in all colonial nations to see that the effects of colonisation are ongoing, despite political or individual rhetoric that may claim otherwise.

It was with a focus on these global issues of the effects of colonisation and the need to create spaces where dialogue can occur about the transformation of bodies, nations and knowledges that the 2007 Australian Critical Race and Whiteness Studies Association conference was convened. The Association itself, formed in 2003, has been a growing voice in speaking of issues of race privilege, racial hegemonies, and the ongoing histories of colonisation that shape colonial nations. The 2007 conference sought not only to continue this tradition, but also to speak of resistances to colonisation, of creative attempts at transforming spaces, and to look at how the racialisation of bodies, nations and knowledges occurs in complex and context-specific ways.

The conference was important for its truly international attendance, which is reflected to some degree in this collection. Speakers from a wide range of contexts spoke across and through these differences to continue the work of examining how racial hierarchies function, how these are resisted, and where both similarities and incommensurabilites exist in the functioning of racial politics as key determinants of social spaces. Importantly, the speakers contested simplistic accounts of racialised practices that would isolate "race" as a singular category of difference, and instead consistently spoke of the interplays of gender, sexuality, religion, class and ethnicity as they function together to produce particular subjectivities situated in a relationship to the norm of white heterosexual middleclass maleness.

The sections of this book, as outlined below, collect together groupings of chapters that share similar themes, or which speak of particular identity claims. Whilst obviously there are considerable overlaps between all of the sections, each of the sections provides a unique snapshot of what scholars from across the globe are saying about particular topics of relevance to the study of race and whiteness.

Section 1: Place and Space

The authors represented by this first section share a focus on the racialisation of places and spaces. They invite us to question what it means for particular knowledges to be claimed over others, and how this shapes the ways in which differing bodies can move in particular spaces. As such, these papers highlight the difference between the fact of rights and the ability to enact them: whilst in most countries the rights of non-white or Indigenous people are recognised and protected, this does not mean that these groups of people are accorded with the necessary cultural or social or economic capital to enact those rights. In other words, when any particular group, as a result of social inequities and histories of exclusion, is denied the capacity to manage and determine their social and economic needs, they will have fewer opportunities to take up the rights accorded to them as citizens. When public spaces are not only shaped by the norms of dominant groups, but when movement in social spaces requires a certain degree of cultural, social and economic capital, marginalised groups will continue to be excluded, despite the existence of legislation saying that they have the right to inclusion.

The limitations of inclusion are evident in the first chapter by Bronwyn Fredericks, who outlines how Indigenous women in northern Queensland in Australia question and contest notions of access in relation to health services. Fredericks suggests that when white norms for public spaces are centred, Indigenous people will always feel unwelcomed and unsupported.

Furthermore, not only do such spaces fail to be "hospitable", but they perpetuate inequities in relation to access by failing to recognise the specific needs of Indigenous people. On the other hand, the women to whom Fredericks spoke reported positive empowering experiences when visiting Aboriginal and Torres Strait Islander health services.

Moving in many ways outside of Australia, the next chapter by Kathleen Connellan explores multiple sites in which public spaces are shaped by racial norms. Writing about her own life growing up as a white woman in South Africa, and moving on to look at the colour white and the enactment of whiteness as a claim to purity and cleanliness, Connellan explores the complex associations between the racialisation of space and the promotion of whiteness as an aesthetic norm. Turning also to examine skin whitening products and the emphasis upon white imagery in modern design, Connellan highlights how the colour white both functions as an arbitrary signifier but that it also is connected to real world practices that exclude certain groups of people.

Returning to Australia, Johan Edelheim examines how tourist sites are constructed as sites of denial that ignore histories of dispossession and which replace Indigenous histories with white histories of heroism. Examining his own experience of one particular tourist site in New South Wales, Edelheim outlines the story that the site tells and the histories that it renders invisible. In so doing, Edelheim argues for an account of a "touristic terra nullius" in which Australian places are taken as spaces available for the claiming by the (non-Indigenous) tourist eye, and into which the viewer is co-opted into a particular account of colonisation.

Finally, Colin Salter engages in a comparative analysis of two sites of contestation over land—one in Australia and one in Canada—where non-Indigenous people have supported the struggles of local Indigenous people. In particular, Salter focuses upon how non-Indigenous supporters of Indigenous land rights are variously made complicit with what Moreton-Robinson (2004) terms the "possessive logic of patriarchal white sovereignty". Salter examines how claims to knowledge about land are always already predetermined by white systems of law and white institutional knowledges like archaeology that function to exclude Indigenous ways of knowing, and which overwrite Indigenous histories and relationships to land by asserting the legitimacy of white law and knowledge as the appropriate arbiter of Indigenous land claims.

Together the chapters in this first section of the book highlight the complex racialisations of space and place that occur to the detriment of groups of people located outside of the dominant majority. The chapters demonstrate how the shaping of public spaces in turn shapes particular bodies and their freedom to move. Importantly, however, the chapters in varying ways also highlight resistances to white hegemony and the transformations that can take place when we read spaces and places in non-normative ways.

Section 2: Media and Representation

The three contributors to this section take as their focal points three different forms of media, and explore how each form functions to normalise a particularly white way of seeing the world. In the first chapter, Anna Szorenyi writes about photographic books that represent the lives (and deaths) of people living outside of the overdeveloped West. Szorenyi elaborates how these texts interpellate the reader as white and that, in so doing, they construct the lives of non-white people as spectacles to be witnessed (and then ultimately ignored) by the white viewer.

The second chapter, written by Vikki Fraser, takes as its starting place a website ostensibly aimed at all young same-sex attracted people, and explores how the website primarily constructs its audience as young white gay men. Drawing on queer theory and critical race and whiteness studies, Fraser carefully examines how the website, through it profiling system and imagery, creates an image of "queer" that is not only racially normative, but also potentially exclusionary toward non-white queer young people.

In the final chapter in this section, Ron Hoenig explores Australian news media reports and their representations of lip sewing by refugees held captive in detention centres. Hoenig suggests that while refugees who engage in lip sewing are constructing themselves, reflexively, as mute by the very act of sewing, they are also constructed as mute through the refusal of the media to recognise the voices of refugees who speak out about the violence of the detention centre system. Furthermore, Hoenig suggests that lip sewing is represented in the media as a coercive behaviour that is seen as warranting the mistreatment of refugees on the basis of the "threat" they are seen to make to the Australian nation.

In varying ways, these three chapters draw out attention to both what is represented in the media, and who the representations are aimed at. Primarily, the representations that are made available are either pathologising, stereotyping or exoticising of non-white people, and they are aimed at a white audience. Even when media are aimed at groups of people located outside the norm of white heterosexual middleclassness, they still evoke a racialised norm in which the experiences of white people are centred as the norm.

Section 3: Locating "Diversity"

The chapters in this section cross two broad topics (education and the European Union) and are encompassed by considerations of how diversity is represented or understood. Whilst the topics are relatively disparate, the theme that runs through each of the chapters is their collective emphasis upon how diversity is understood. Part of the work of critical race and whiteness studies has been to examine how, in the case of racial difference, whiteness is constructed as the invisible marker against which "diversity" is measured, and to firmly locate whiteness as part of diversity in which, whilst it may often be the statistical norm (in relation to population numbers), it should not *a priori* be accorded a normative status.

The first chapter, by James Lovell and Damien Riggs, sets the scene for this section, by exploring how understandings of difference and diversity are represented in children's storybooks. Lovell and Riggs suggest firstly that difference is constructed as that which does not occupy the dominant position and, secondly, that difference identified in this way is only seen as valid or intelligible if it can be of benefit to the dominant group. These findings highlight the subtle and indeed mundane ways in which, from a very young age, people are schooled into seeing the world in ways that position certain identities or behaviours as the norm, and from which all other identities and behaviours are seen to diverge.

In the second chapter, Silvo Devetak takes up the topic of diversity and explores how diverse groups of people are offered inclusion within the European Union (EU). Devetak explores how certain groups are currently excluded from the EU and how this occurs, in part, despite the provision of laws aimed at protecting all groups of people, and at other times because certain laws do not offer enough protection for all groups of people. The chapter concludes by offering some direction for the EU in relation to the ways that a wide range of beliefs and values can be respected within the EU, and the need for the EU to offer terms for inclusion that are critical of established orthodoxies.

In the final chapter, Catherine Koerner, Simone Tur and Christopher Wilson outline some of their own work in developing and practicing a peer mentoring scheme for young people that is mindful of the particular position of young Indigenous students who participate in their program. The program they have devised focuses on the racial politics of white mentors working with Indigenous students and on the need to connect Indigenous students with Indigenous community as a strategy for educational success. Koerner, Tur and Wilson highlight the need for white mentors to be aware of the normative status of whiteness and to critically reflect upon the diverse needs of all students, with an emphasis upon tutoring within a context of Indigenous sovereignties and the need for white students to engage with and reflect upon their own location within a relationship to the norms of whiteness.

Despite their wide-ranging focus, the three chapters in this section speak together about how "diversity" is represented, where it is located, and how it is understood. By challenging the assumption that diversity is always outside of the norm, these chapters remind us of the importance of constantly turning the gaze back upon that which is often left unmarked.

Section 4: Identity and Voice

Perhaps the most varied section, this fourth and final selection of chapters, in various ways provides accounts of the shaping of identities across colonial contexts, and the ways in which particular voices sound out louder than others. With a broad range of foci, these chapters nonetheless share an emphasis upon how particular knowledges are made to matter, and how bodies are variously located within a relationship to colonial and racialised norms in the context of colonial nations.

In the first chapter Alice Te Punga Somerville relates aspects of the life story of a key figure in recent Maori history; Te Rangihiroa. Specifically, Te Punga Somerville writes of Te Rangihiroa's attempts at securing US citizenship and the varying ways in which his identity was constructed not only under US and New Zealand law, but also by Te Rangihiroa himself and by his white supporters. In so doing, Te Punga Somerville draws attention to the complex practices of racialisation whereby national belonging is configured on the terms set by the dominant majority, and where conformity to particular racialised norms will sometimes, though not always, ensure inclusion within national spaces.

In the second chapter Anne Brewster outlines her own experiences as a white woman attempting to negotiate the teaching of critical race and whiteness studies in Australia and beyond. Drawing upon the movie *The Tracker* and her use of it as a pedagogic tool, Brewster highlights the complexities of claiming a speaking position as a white person in a colonial nation, and the considerable privilege and epistemic authority that underpins the voicing of white identities.

In the final chapter of the book, Fiona McAllan too draws our attention to the problematic location of white people in colonial nations such as Australia who seek to elaborate an account of belonging that does not overwrite the fact of Indigenous sovereignty, but which nonetheless makes a grounded claim to identity. McAllan's writing represents one attempt at negotiating the contested ground of racialised power relations in Australia by attempting to speak of the histories and trajectories of all people living in Australia—Indigenous and non-Indigenous.

As the concluding section of this book, the chapters included here necessarily highlight the disjunctures and difficulties faced by any person attempting to make a claim to identity in the face of established norms of intelligibility. Importantly, these chapters do not gloss over failures or the problematics of such claims, but instead highlight the complex relational work that must be undertaken by anyone seeking to consider their location within colonial nations, and particularly those who occupy dominant locations.

Conclusions

We believe that this collection of chapters is timely. Not only do the chapters represent the diversity of research being undertaken within the broad banner of critical race and whiteness studies, but they also converge at many points, centring upon the conference topic of "transforming bodies, nations and knowledges". That academics from across the globe would so often come to similar conclusions about the impact of racialisation upon the lives of all people has much to say about the need for ongoing attention to ongoing histories of colonisation, social exclusion and racialised inequities in access to respect, social capital and citizenship and material resources.

As editors of this collection and as co-convenors of the 2007 ACRAWSA conference, we are pleased to be able to present these chapters to a wider audience. We feel that each chapter in its own way has much to contribute to the field of critical race and whiteness studies and beyond, and we hope that the publication of this book will engender much discussion and transformation of racial politics that continue to be productive of privileges and disadvantages.

PART I:

PLACE AND SPACE

CHAPTER ONE

HOW THE WHITENESS EMBEDDED IN HEALTH SERVICES IMPACTS ON THE HEALTH AND WELL-BEING OF ABORIGINAL PEOPLES*

BRONWYN FREDERICKS

Introduction

Aboriginal women are treated differently by non-Indigenous health care providers based on perceptions of Aboriginality and skin colour and white race privilege within health care environments. The experiences shared below are from some of the Aboriginal woman respondents in a research project undertaken within Rockhampton, a regional area in Central Queensland (Fredericks 2003). The experiences give an insight into how the Aboriginal women interviewed felt and their observations of how other Aboriginal women were treated within health care settings based on skin colour and perceptions of Aboriginality. A number of the women demonstrated a personal in-depth analysis of the issues surrounding place, skin colour and Aboriginality. For example, one of the women, who I named Kay, identified one particular health service organisation and stated that, "it is a totally white designed space. There is nothing that identifies me to that place. I just won't go there as a client because I don't feel they cater for me as a black woman". Kay's words give us an understanding of the reality experienced by Aboriginal women as they move in and out of places within health environments and broader society. Some of these experiences are examples of direct racism, whilst other examples are subtle and demonstrate how whiteness manifests and plays out within places. I offer acknowledgement and honour to the Aboriginal women who shared their stories and gave me a glimpse of their realities in the research project from which the findings presented in this chapter are taken. It is to this research project that I now turn.

During the late 1990s, I commenced a formal research project exploring Aboriginal women's perceptions and experiences of health, well-being, identity, body and health services within Rockhampton. Using an open-ended question sheet as a guide, twenty Aboriginal women from a range of ages and with a diversity of backgrounds provided in-depth interviews (Fredericks 2007a; 2007b). Some of these women's experiences are shared within this chapter in the hope that they will lead to a deeper understanding of how racism manifests through the perceptions and personal practices of health service providers.

The Aboriginal women I interviewed want to see evidence that they are part of the places that are called health services. What will become obvious within the following sections is that planners, designers, managers and health personnel need to give consideration to how people access and dwell within places culturally. As Weisman explains; "design is a reflection of prevailing social, political and economic values and is often symbolic of the place that each individual holds in society" (1992, 10). Places are not the passive environments we would like to think they are. According to Kitchin, they act as a social text that conveys messages of belonging and exclusion and reproduces power relations within society (1995, 45). They are also, as suggested by Foucault, sites of social struggle and contested realms of identity (1980, 149).

In relation to the gendered nature of places, MacGregor outlines the ways in which there are "complex interrelations between who women are (identity) and the environments in which women live (spaces and places)" (2001, 342). Miranne and Young explain that it is the aspects of women's identities such as class, race, ethnicity, culture and sexual orientation that add complexity to the interrelationships between women and space and place. Women don't just physically use spaces and places: they interpret, represent, and produce and reproduce space (Miranne and Young 2000). Aboriginal women's sense of place within health services operates within this complex context.

Dyck (1995) and Dyck, Lewis and McLafferty (2003) explore how women manage the physical, social and economic consequences of their illness along with the complex layering of social, economic and political relations that frame their health. It is demonstrated through this research undertaken with Aboriginal women in Rockhampton, Central Queensland that culture and racism impact on the way in which Aboriginal women experience and engage with places that offer health services. It is further demonstrated that if Aboriginal women are not part of the design process and management of such places that they are reflected within the social, political and economic values by their absence, a fact that provides a symbolic representation of the position that Aboriginal women hold within that community.

What became apparent through this research project is that Aboriginal women need to feel welcome, comfortable, secure and culturally safe if they are going to access and utilise health services openly, freely and happily, and in an informed and empowered manner. This is also outlined in Kirk et al. (1998) in the research they did focusing on Aboriginal and Torres Strait Islander women and cervical cancer in Queensland. It was additionally identified in research undertaken focusing on breast cancer screening, diagnosis, treatment and care for Aboriginal and Torres Strait Islander women in Queensland (Kirk et al. 2000a; 2000b). My research builds on the work of Kirk et al. and suggests that if Aboriginal women do not have a connection to a place, then they will not utilise that health service or they may do so only with a great deal of effort, angst and energy. In a sense these places within the landscape can be contemporary sites of trauma. A research methodology was developed which would offer a form of witnessing, validation and support in asking questions and discussing issues, which would draw emotional responses (Fredericks 2007a; 2007b; 2008).

Method

Aboriginal women who lived within the Rockhampton area of the Central Queensland region were interviewed as part of a research project exploring "how the relationship between health services and Aboriginal women can be more empowering from the viewpoints of Aboriginal women" (Fredericks 2003). The assumption underpinning this study was that empowering and re-empowering practices for Aboriginal women can lead to improved health outcomes. The focus of the study arose from discussions with Aboriginal women in the community as to what they wanted me, another Aboriginal woman, to investigate as part of a formal research project (Fredericks 2007a; 2007b). The terms empowering and re-empowering were raised through these early exploratory discussions. They were later discussed during the interviews. Re-empowerment was discussed from the viewpoint that Aboriginal women were once empowered as sovereign women who had control of all aspects of their lives. Aboriginal women became disempowered as a result of colonisation and thus the term re-empowering was discussed and agreed upon.

The ethics process included presentations before an Indigenous inter-agency meeting of over 50 representatives from community organisations and Indigenous work units; an Aboriginal women's meeting; and an individual organisation that was recognised as having specific responsibility for women's issues. This was in addition to the university ethics process.

A panel of supervisors oversaw the project, including an Aboriginal woman recognised for her long-term involvement in Aboriginal women's activism. She was nominated by other Aboriginal women in the community as the appropriate person to be a cultural supervisor and to assist in any cultural dilemmas. She worked with the other two supervisors, academics, who additionally provided specific research support within the university.

Twenty Aboriginal women participated in in-depth, semi-structured, face-to-face interviews in a participatory-action research process, which incorporated the principles of an Indigenous methodology as put forward by Rigney (2001) and decolonising concepts asserted by Smith (1999). In addition the process drew heavily from the field of ethnography (Bowling 1997; Creswell 1998). Ethnographic data collection— as understood from the writings of Creswell (1998)—can include documents, observations and interviewing. These were all tasks that were undertaken in this project. The benefits of ethnography allow for interviewees to provide "rich and quotable material" (Bowling 1997, 231), and "enable them to give their opinions in full on more complex topics" (Bowling 1997, 231). It was agreed by all the participants in this project that they would be given pseudonyms for ease of discussing the research outcomes and protect them. They still needed to live within the community of Rockhampton and receive health services and interact with health professionals in a range of contexts. The research project as it developed allowed for concepts of reciprocity and reactivity to be enacted within the research process and for the researcher to be immersed in the day-to-day lives of the members of the research group (Creswell 1998, 58; Fredericks 2008). For me as a member of the Rockhampton Aboriginal and Torres Strait Islander community at that time this was imperative.

It is important to note that this research process was developed in consultation with Aboriginal women in the community and through discussion with other Indigenous researchers in Australia and overseas. Research processes were sought and discussed that would not only be academically rigorous but that would not perpetuate further disempowerment and marginalisation for the Aboriginal women involved and the Aboriginal women in the community (Fredericks 2007a; 2007b; 2008). The interviews that resulted presented a powerful insight into the lives of Aboriginal women, past and present, and contributes to a deeper understanding of the past and present interactions between Aboriginal women and health services (Fredericks 2007c). Some of the women's narratives will be presented within the next few sections.

Mainstream health services

Health services that are available for the general Australian population are generally what are referred to as mainstream health services. These can be accessed for a range of reasons and can also be accessed by Aboriginal people. The Aboriginal women I interviewed spoke at length about their experiences of mainstream health services in an attempt to name what was positive and what was negative in their interactions. Kay, who is 46 years of age, experienced a lot of sickness as a child and has experienced a lot of sickness as an adult and hence has accessed mainstream health services over a long period of time. When Kay was reflecting on her past health experiences she recalled two very significant events that occurred, both while in her twenties. The first occurred when she was in her mid-twenties, as she was experiencing a lot of pain and found it very difficult to get medical treatment for the pain at the time. She said that "everyone thought I was imagining it, [but] I had gall-stones ... 201 stones, they were amazed that I made it as long as I did". She ended up being admitted and having the stones and her gallbladder removed. She recounts the process,

> I was the youngest one in the hospital, I thought I would have a tiny mark, I didn't know what questions to ask. I got big dog stitches. I was in my mid-twenties. I got the dog clips. I was the only one who got the apprentices [possibly interns/new registrars]. I was really upset, just because I hadn't asked about the scar didn't mean I wanted to be the ugliest. Aboriginal people we mark when we scar, that kind of scarring [shows me]. If I hadn't been so sick ... I felt it was discrimination. How come all those old [white] women got the clamping situation and I got the old dog stitches. I felt really ashamed then ... I felt it was because of the colour of my skin.

The second significant event was when she was pregnant with her first child and went up to the hospital. "That doctor said, good, she's right, she is obviously having her second or third child". The doctor made an assumption about Kay that became a barrier to her asking questions about her birthing process. How Aboriginal women present to doctors, doesn't always reveal what is happening with them as Kay explains:

> on the exterior I've got it together and on the inside I am so scared. I am so ashamed how fearful I am, how I am ignorant, never touched a baby in my life, never had any one who had a baby in my life. I didn't know what was happening with the baby, like, I didn't know that we even bleed after you have a baby ... it's hard to believe now, but that's how it was ... another assumption that people make about us.

Not knowing what to do and what happens is a barrier in addressing health issues and carrying out healthy practices. As Kay identified, she was frightened and she wasn't really in a position to ask. She felt the staff made assumptions that she knew what to do because on the outside she had "it together". As Kay suggests, whilst she may have showed outward signs that she was confident, she wasn't. Kay, in reflecting on this experience, stated that

> looking back ... as a pregnant woman I was treated in a way that white women weren't, you knew you were part of something a little bit different but you don't know why.

Kay shared a few more examples and stated that

> It has never made any sense to me that people could treat me different because of the colour of my skin ... now I look back I recognise it was racism that I didn't want to face ... I wasn't given equal treatment.

It is when Kay looks back on the events that she can analyse them more thoroughly and interrogate what happened or the treatment she received. And elsewhere in her interview she stated "things are set up for white skinned people ... white race privilege is so institutionalised". Kay demonstrates insight and knowledge of white race privilege based on her own reflections of her experiences. She talked about her process of reflecting back and the importance of this reflection in self-growth and becoming stronger as an Aboriginal woman.

Some of the more recent experiences shared with me by Kay and other Aboriginal women, and what I have read through the literature, leads me to the understanding that there are issues of discrimination based on skin colour and issues around Aboriginality and the experiences of place. Some of these at times present as contradictory and represent the struggles for and around Indigenous identity within broader Australian society. The recent experiences of other Aboriginal women are shared in the following paragraphs.

Mary, a young Aboriginal woman, details one experience based on an occasion where she had gone into the Accident and Emergency area of the local public hospital and was asked a series of questions by the Registered Nurse at the reception desk. The nurse was filling out the form about why Mary had presented at that point in time as Mary spoke to her. Mary then said that she wanted to look at the form and noticed that the Nurse had not ticked that she was Aboriginal. Mary said to the nurse that she "might like to tick that I was Aboriginal". Mary explained to me that the nurse had

> made an assumption based on the colour of my skin, and 'cause I wasn't half past midnight, I wasn't black. It really pissed me off, no white person has the right to judge my Aboriginality, skin colour has got nothing to do with it.

Helen, who is a 55 year old Aboriginal woman, reflected on her experiences and stated,

> I have always felt good about being Aboriginal. I feel good as an Aboriginal ... from the time I was around 14 or 15 and vowed and declared that I wasn't a half caste or anything else, I was an Aboriginal.

On thinking about her experiences before moving into Rockhampton a couple of years ago, Helen explained that the

> nurses were still maintaining that we weren't real Aboriginals, that they lived up in the centre, see now, stupid things like that you can't get through their heads, we are Murri people, it doesn't matter how black, or how brown, or how fair we are, you know, they just don't understand that.

She then said that, "they might have fitted us into another category like us, them and they". On the topic of health care service providers she explained that they need to understand that "past the skin everything else inside is the same" and that "it is ok to touch us, our colour doesn't wear off".

Sharon, who is 46 years old, gave an example of racism when she presented to a doctor's clinic and was asked "how much alcohol I drank?" She said, "they assumed because I was black that I was a drinker". She wasn't asked "was she a drinker?" In her interview Helen also raised the issues of being asked how much she drinks before she was asked whether she drinks. Neither Helen nor Sharon consume any alcohol, and both took the question as an insult.

Grace, who is in her early twenties, relayed a different experience of being an Aboriginal woman based on other peoples' responses to her, around her identity and her colouring. "I don't look like an Aboriginal woman or what one would expect an Aboriginal person to look like, having blonde hair and green eyes, but I feel very strong about my identity and that's coming through as I get older, I am really starting to enjoy being a young Indigenous woman". She explained that "I know who I am, and I know that I am an Indigenous woman, I shouldn't have to tell everybody that, it is strange though when I do and get you can't be Aboriginal you've got blonde hair". What Grace additionally understands are the broader societal issues because of the way she looks. In the city people assumed that she was a "white Australian" (She was reflecting on her experiences in Rockhampton and in Brisbane). Grace's Aboriginality went unrecognised, as she did not embody the physical aspects of being Aboriginal. Grace said she had come to realise "how easy I do have it, in like visiting services like that (referring to health services), walking into shopping centres, walking into bars, it is much easier for me to mingle, be anonymous the way I look, than to stand out in the crowd if I had dark skin". She clearly identifies what privileges accompany people who are light skinned.

Grace can and is seen as "normal" and as invisible as she states that she can be anonymous, she doesn't stand out. Most white people would have no idea about how skin colour hierarchies operate and the degree they are privileged in Australian society. Further to this, white race privilege and colour judgements appear with such regularlity in Australia that they generally escape notice. They do not, however, escape the notice or understanding of what it means to Aboriginal people or Aboriginal women as Grace has demonstrated. Moreton-Robinson states that for "Indigenous people, whiteness is visible and imbued with power; it confers dominance and privilege" (1998, 39). Kincheloe states that whiteness and skin colour are "intimately involved with issues of power and power differences" (1999, 42). In an article that explores identity, Aboriginality, skin colour and the power attributed to whiteness, Holland demonstrates her understanding of this when she explains, "growing up blonde, blue-eyed, and fair skinned, I certainly can't deny my English and Irish heritages. Nor can I deny the opportunities I have been afforded as a result of my whiteness and being mis/taken as white in this racist society" (1996, 97). She gives an example of stopping her car when seeing that a dark skinned Aboriginal youth was being detained on the street by police, and watching what was happening. She expresses that she thought the police modified their actions based on the assumption that she was a white woman and she had seen what was happening. She makes the statement that "[l]ooking white was to my advantage in this particular situation" (Holland 1996, 110). What needs to be understood is that whiteness and light skin can work as social capital in many contexts in Australia.

Grace has a further understanding of privilege when she said, "it would be worse if I looked more Indigenous because I know from my experiences they [darker skinned Aboriginal women] haven't received the respect they deserve from these services ... that has really impacted on their own health because they haven't wanted to go back, I can really understand that". Grace had an understanding and empathy for other

Aboriginal women who were darker in skin colour. She believes they haven't been given the same level of respect as she has been shown. Grace has an understanding of "colour as code" and how this "permeates popular conceptions and perceptions" and thus the way people behave (Ruiz 2000, 24). Kay earlier touched on this when she said she was treated in a way that white women weren't and that things were set up for white skinned people. Despite their differences in skin colour, both women demonstrate insight and knowledge of white race privilege based on their own reflections of their experiences.

Whilst Grace is still subject to racism she was aware, however, that she wasn't subject to racism based on her skin colour in the same way that darker skinned Aboriginal women were subject to racism. Holland relates that living "in a white body and identifying as a murri means that my experience of racism has always been different to that of a murri living in a black body" (1996, 97).[1] Grace identified that Aboriginal women with darker skins were immediately recognisable as Aboriginal women. She is conscious that her colouring means that she is perceived to be a "white woman" and not an Aboriginal woman. In the interview we discussed the different judgements made by people when they don't realise that Grace is Aboriginal and assume she is white, as opposed to when they know she is Aboriginal. Holland suggests that, "oppression of those of us who did not embody the physical aspects of being black was ignored" (1996, 102) and that "our [A]boriginality went unrecognised; this reinforced racism in the silencing of what we had to contribute". At no stage during the interview did Grace question her Aboriginality based on her colouring. The questioning when in general public health environments generally came from non-Aboriginal people.

Women's health services

In undertaking the research reported here, I asked Aboriginal women about women-centred services. It must be recognised that women-specific services have historically evolved through advocacy and strategic action by women along with policies by governments (Commonwealth of Australia 1989; Broom 1991; Moore 1997; Queensland 1992) It should not be assumed, however, that Aboriginal women have been part of the long-term advocacy and strategic action, design, operation and usage of women-centred health spaces, merely because they are women (Huggins 1994, 70-79; 1987; Huggins and Blake 1992, 42-57; Moreton-Robinson 2000; O'Shane 1993; 1976). The words of numerous women I interviewed showed a disconnection from the local Women's Health Centre that is specifically designed for women. For example Denise, an 18-year-old Aboriginal woman from the Rockhampton region, said:

> I've never been there, mmm, think that's more for umm white women, white women's place, I don't know. I don't know any Murri woman, any black woman been there. I don't think any black women go there, I don't think, I don't know any staff there. I don't know anything about that place, except that white women go there.

Denise called the services available for women in the Rockhampton area "white women's places". Mary commented that it was "culturally uncomfortable". Several Aboriginal women highlighted that the Women's Health Centre was obviously a place for women, but for "white women". While Grace had visited the Centre she stated that "it just felt uncomfortable being there, so I didn't use women's health". Grace had visited the Centre on a regular basis but never utilised the service as a client, she utilised it as an employee of another service provider in the Rockhampton region. Linda explained, "I haven't used that too much, haven't thought why I haven't, more for information service rather than health service ... have used the library ... haven't taken up any programs". Kay also went to the Women's Health Centre, but not as a client. She said:

> I go there but I never feel comfortable there, I don't go there as a client. I really do like women's spaces but this space doesn't make me feel like it is for me, it is a woman's space I feel that, it's not an Aboriginal woman's space, the design of the space, it is a totally white designed space. There is nothing that identifies me to that place ... I just won't go there as a client because I don't feel they cater for me as a black woman.

She came back to the point later in her interview when she was discussing notions of place, in reference to that particular service that:

> there was no Aboriginality around the place, I didn't see black people, I didn't see black workers, I didn't see any posters either ... that kind of says its not a place for me, maybe that's an assumption but all of the things ... that's how I gauge whether it wants me to be part of its centre or if I'm just going to be sitting on the fringes as I have done all my life.

Kay's expression of whether she feels included or not as part of the core is evident: She feels she is not. The social text being conveyed to her is a message of exclusion and the reiteration of power relations within society where Aboriginal women are marginalised (Kitchin 1995). The place is not passive: Non-Indigenous women are positioned as the owners of the Women's Health Centre and in the position of domination within the Centre. Moreton-Robinson (2000) provides a powerful analysis of how white race privilege manifests itself in the subject position of middle-class white woman which underpins the dominance of certain ideological assumptions of womanhood in mainstream and feminist contexts. Her theorising offers a context to understand why Aboriginal women such as Kay might find themselves being marginalised in such feminist identified environments and what happens when Aboriginal women attempt to highlight and address this dominance (Moreton-Robinson 2000; 2007, 86-104). What became clear from the women's experiences is that places can be recognised as gender-specific and as non-Aboriginal and that these attributes can operate at the same time. That is, places can be seen as women's places but not Aboriginal women's places. In this, non-Indigenous women can be ignorant of the way places can be privileging to themselves and disadvantaging to other women all the while proclaiming to be women friendly. In this way, they can continue to constrain and oppress Aboriginal women, rather than improve the health and well being of Aboriginal women just as mainstream health services can oppress Aboriginal people.

Kay raised some powerful concepts and a high level of analysis when discussing non-Indigenous women who are employed as workers within women's health environments. She said:

> I always like female workers in the health area, but then again they don't always make me feel comfortable, a lot of them are kind of cultural voyeurs, it's like they take anything from anybody's culture, but they kind of put it on the exterior ... cultural tourist ... too many cultural tourists in women's spaces.

I asked Kay when she meant by the term "cultural tourist". "Cultural tourist, it's where everything is on the external". She outlined that they—the cultural tourists—have bits and pieces of clothing or jewellery that they may wear and even sometimes may have a number of cultures reflected on the exterior of their bodies. She said it was also about them talking about concepts that might be drawn from a range of cultures. She told me that she asks them a question about something they have on or something they are talking about and that "that question can locate for you" whether that person is a cultural tourist or not. From her question/s she determines whether that person takes the culture from the exterior of their body to the interior, and if that happens "then that person is not a cultural tourist". They take the "culture from the exterior into the interior ... building it as part of them" as part of their ideology. Kay saw how it could become part of how they live, where they are able to be reflective of other people's cultures from within. She said "someone who has all the gear on the outside ... I just automatically say cultural tourist!" When Kay explained this to me I could understand the concept and even visually picture some people as cultural tourists within a range of health arenas. One needs to wonder if this is a remnant of the cultural tourism that Europeans used to partake in when they visited "the colonies" years ago. It is also known that there were medical practitioners, medical anthropologists and other health professionals who additionally undertook such activities.

Roger's study is useful to draw on at this point. She interviewed white women in helping professions in Canada (psychotherapists) and discovered that historically they have been inscribed into discourses of respectability, and as social subjects within imperialism (1998). Identifications that marked the presence of whiteness were apparent throughout the narratives of the women interviewed by Roger. She showed that the white female helping professionals managed and incorporated whiteness within their practice as social service providers. Links can be drawn here to other services and sectors. Clearly there is a need for an historical analysis of racism and colonisation to provide a greater sense of how women helping professionals might be better able to work with Aboriginal women. This would enable the narratives of white women helping professionals to be pulled apart in terms of how race, gender and class are constructed and expose (to the professionals) the subject positionality of white women. Such analysis would address the issues Kay raises of "cultural tourists" working in women's services. Assumptions could also be drawn from the explanations that these issues are not limited to women's centred services, but that they cut across all health services. Both male and female health professionals, and the health services that cater for the broader population in Australia, have arisen and been developed from the same historical context in relation to Aboriginal peoples.

The nature of a place, what happens there, who is present and how they work, and how the place looks and feels, is interpreted and experienced, impacts on whether Aboriginal women physically access that place. The women interviewed who knew of the Women's Health Centre did not feel comfortable in accessing the Centre. They did not identify the Women's Health Centre as being a place that was for Aboriginal women. They did not use the services that are offered by the Women's Health Centre. Kay and Grace both went to the Women's Health Centre but not as clients. The Rockhampton Women's Health Centre did identify in its annual reports and through an evaluation that access by Aboriginal and Torres Strait

Islander women was an issue (Kraack 1999; Rockhampton Women's Health Centre 2002; 2000). The only way this can be changed is if Aboriginal women are involved in designing, developing, production and operation of women's places and Aboriginal people are involved in the places for *all* people.

Aboriginal and Torres Strait Islander health services

Health services or health programs that are specifically established or designed for mostly Aboriginal and Torres Strait Islander peoples can be government operated (usually by state or territory departments of health) or they can be operated by Aboriginal and Torres Strait Islander community-controlled non-government organisations. The examples Aboriginal women interviewed drew reference to refer to both types of services and provide clear understandings of how services are accessed and the powerful way that place impacts on the interactions within those services. Sharon, one of the women I interviewed, gave a very clear example of place within a government operated health service. She explained that when the Queensland state government developed their new Community and Public Health complex in Boslover Street, Rockhampton and opened it in 1998, they placed the Aboriginal and Islander Health Program "in the back room". She made reference to a past era in Australia when the "blacks were in the back" (Rintoul 1993). The era she refers to is when Aboriginal people were expected to stand at the back to be served in stores or sit in the back of the cinema (Rintoul 1993). In the case of the new Aboriginal and Islander health program, when Aboriginal people entered the building they had to ask a non-Indigenous person at the large reception desk at the front of the building where to go to get to Aboriginal and Islander Health Program. In addition, as it was in a highly public area, people could see who was going in and out. Aboriginal people had to walk into and through the building out the back to access the Aboriginal and Islander Health Program. In the atrium foyer of the building, high above the entry hung a print of what is considered one of the masterpieces of Australian art, Frederick McCubbin's oil on canvass triptych titled *The Pioneer*. This work was produced three years after Federation in 1904 and depicts the pioneering spirit of the white settler in the bush (McCubbin 1904). The print is still hung in the foyer and, while it is faded, it still asserts an emphasis on European settler history and the claiming and clearing of Aboriginal land and erasure of Aboriginal sovereignty.

The Aboriginal and Islander Health Program was established within the new premises to be part of the full suite of programs offered under the unitary banner of primary and public health, yet it became a site which manifested a form of social exclusion. By having to ask a non-Indigenous person to enter the area named Aboriginal and Islander Health, white people were placed in a position of domination and Aboriginal people in a position of subordination. Non-Indigenous people were positioned as the owners of the building and the owners of the space occupied by the Aboriginal and Islander Health Program. Aboriginal re-engagement with the site has then been mediated via a form of surveillance at the main entry and exit of the building. The painting acts as a signpost and symbol for who really made the nation and who now holds possession. There is an irony here in that while Queensland Health was trying to bring everyone together within the one building (place), the symbolic representations and space configurations of the front reception desk, the painting and the Aboriginal and Islander Health Program "out the back" were underwritten by the on-going colonial stories of the settlers who made the nation and the negation of the sovereign rights of the Indigenous population. In this way, Aboriginal peoples and Aboriginal sovereignty are suppressed and white Australians are able to exercise power and their possessiveness of place (Moreton-Robinson 2007; 2003). Furthermore, the possessiveness and whiteness exercised is productive in that it constitutes both the white and the Indigenous subject within the place (Coffey 2000, 37-55.). Moreton-Robinson contends that possessiveness is "predicated on the taking of other peoples' lands and resources for the benefit of Empire" (Moreton-Robinson 2005). This exercising of possessiveness commenced with Britain taking possession of Australia and hasn't stopped. Moreton-Robinson, drawing on the work of Lipsitz, states that "white [Australians] are encouraged to invest in their whiteness, to remain true to an identity that provides them with resources, power and opportunity" (Lipsitz 1998, vii; Moreton-Robinson 2005, 27). Furthermore, she explains that this is how white Australians "adhere to narratives that valorise their past and their present" (Moreton-Robinson 2005, 27).

The move into this new building was discussed openly by a number of the Aboriginal women that I interviewed, who suggested that as a result of the move there was a large reduction in the number of Aboriginal people accessing the Aboriginal and Islander Health Program. I was unable to gain any data or obtain a written report that detailed this. I was, however, told by several Queensland Health staff that the number of people accessing the program "dropped off" and had "fallen off". This was not about transport to the new premises as transport is available to clients though the Program. The "drop off" and "fall off" could be attributed to a form of resistance to:

> the epistemological position of the Department as to how Aboriginal people should access their health service through the new building; the exercising of white possession; and the reproduction and affirmation of white Australians of Aboriginal dispossession (Moreton-Robinson 2004, 2).

I am aware that the decision was later made by the Rockhampton Health Service District that the old Aboriginal and Islander Health Program premises in Phillip Street, North Rockhampton, would be renovated and that the Aboriginal and Islander Health Program would move back to that address where it became "business as usual". I acknowledge the Rockhampton District Health Service for taking the relevant steps to correct the problem when it was raised. I would argue that it was not about what people were used to, or even a flat refusal to accept change, rather it was issues associated with place and cultural comfort. The Program still operates from the Phillip Street address today and, while the buildings in Phillip Street are accessed by Aboriginal people, they are still owned by Queensland Health.

Helen, another interviewee, also made reference to the new Community and Public Health building along with other new health services being built in the region. It's "no good putting up big buildings, I'd rather go to Amy's tin shed". The tin shed was in fact the site of the Bidgerdii Aboriginal and Torres Strait Islander Community Health Service's premises prior to September 2000, when the service operated from a modified and renovated tin shed attached to the rear of a legal business also on Boslover Street and opposite the new Community and Public Health building. Bidgerdii is the community-controlled Aboriginal and Torres Strait Islander health service that services the Central Queensland Region. It is operated by an Aboriginal and Torres Strait Islander Board of Directors, Chief Executive Officer (CEO) and, where possible, employs Aboriginal and Torres Strait Islander staff. Amy Lester was the CEO at the time of this research project and hence was the Amy that Helen refers to.

In her discussion around accessing health services, Kay described how she accesses some of the Aboriginal specific services. She outlined how she identifies a place as to whether "I'm just going to be sitting on the fringes as I have all my life, I don't want to be, I want to find places where I can be part of the centre". She identified the Bidgerdii Aboriginal and Torres Strait Islander health service as a place where Aboriginality is part of the centre, part of the thinking of the place and where she wasn't going to be left on the fringe as an Aboriginal woman. Kay argued that part of the difficulty with the mainstream health system and broader systems was the centre that it operated from as its base. She articulated that, "I want the white system to understand that we are not part of the white centre, we are on the fringe, we have not been included into that centre, and we won't until the white system sees that".

Conclusion

The arrival of the colonists, and the subsequent removal and dispossession of Aboriginal people from their traditional lands where relationships would be maintained and responsibilities carried out, has had a disastrous effect on Aboriginal people over the past 220 years. Through invasion and colonisation, Aboriginal people have experienced different forms of genocide and ethnocide that have attempted to exterminate and assimilate them. We know that through these processes Aboriginal people's lives were disrupted to different degrees, depending on the level of penetration of the colonising dominant society. In her interview, Kay referred to the ancestors throughout, linking the past to the present and to the future (Fredericks 2007c). Kay revealed that she is very much aware of her life span issues and her past health problems. She stated, "I am real proud of myself that I make sure my sons visit the doctors to have a check up, I try not to show them any of my fear". "I don't want to be sick. I don't have grandchildren yet ... I want to be around to see a couple of grandchildren at least ... I ask the ancestors all the time to gift me that I can live". Kay also demonstrated that she was very much aware of her reality in terms of the health status statistics for Aboriginal women, Aboriginal peoples and non-Indigenous people. I am not suggesting here that Kay or any of the other Aboriginal women that were interviewed are living self-fulfilling prophecies; rather this reality is demonstrated through what the Aboriginal women have shared. The women I interviewed all have a sense of the realities of their lives in relation to other Aboriginal women, Aboriginal people and the broader population. When I asked each one of them if they thought other Aboriginal women had similar issues or different issues, they articulated that some women had similar issues. They additionally had a sense collectively of the issues of the Aboriginal people that were in the generation/s before them and the generations of Aboriginal people that are following their lives. The Aboriginal women were very much in tune with their positioning and their lives at the time the interviews were conducted.

It is Aboriginal people who understand what has happened from the position of being, of having lived the experiences, having heard the stories and having seen and felt the pain as Aboriginal people. It is through the everyday experiences of Aboriginal women such as Kay and the other women I interviewed, that we are able to gain an understanding about how the dominant culture, racism and whiteness continues to operate in health settings and environments.

What is evident is that health services (places) reflect the historical, political, cultural, social and economic values, and power relations of broader society (McDowell 1999; Massey 1994). Power is embedded within interactions and within place. This is despite white people only being able to claim ownership of the places through the dispossession of the Darumbal people, the Traditional Owners of the land now occupied by the city of Rockhampton. All the health services discussed here are built on dispossessed land. Thus white territorialisation of the sites has only been possible by dispossessing and de-territorialising Aboriginal people of that site. As I have understood from the women in this research, the buildings may end up looking beautiful, have all the latest equipment and room for staff and clients but can be in fact highly unsuitable, unwelcoming and exclusionary to Aboriginal people. This is one of the factors that additionally impacts on and maintains the poor health status and limits improvements to the health and well being of Aboriginal people in Australia.

CHAPTER TWO

WASHING WHITE

KATHLEEN CONNELLAN

"… The surface is the only place to dwell"
(Wigley 2001, p.xvi).

It is the surface that is seen, and it is the surface which is cleaned. This chapter is concerned with white surfaces and how they are kept white or come to be white in the first place. What is of interest to me is how synthetic or built surfaces have a bearing upon the surface identities of the people who inhabit such spaces. The link between white surfaces and white skins is explored in terms of the perpetuation of these twin whitenesses despite the unsubstantial nature of a thin white surface. Consequently this chapter is situated within the field of art and design theory but it borrows from postcolonial and whiteness studies. In so doing it links design theory with critical race theory. My concern is with the disjuncture between white as an impermanent "colour" that requires constant touching up, its ubiquity in western designed environments, and its privileged status in race.

By exploring the relationship between white in design as a colour of choice and white as symptomatic of cleanliness in western cultures, I demonstrate how myths and practices that propagated and endorsed white as a code for purity and civilisation contribute to a scrutiny that whiteness=cleanliness. As such, the relationship between whiteness in race and personal hygiene will be explored. Issues of cleaning, painting, washing, water and soap are linked to skin, surfaces and spaces that are coloured "white". The act of washing as indicative of a restless searching for a settled subjectivity in the processes of colonialism and diaspora underpins the analysis that I provide here. The title of the chapter emphasises the activity of washing white as opposed to the "finished" surface—white washed. Consequently, the content of this chapter is framed around efforts to conform and belong as prescribed by standards of cleanliness. My aim is to tease out the relationship between whiteness and cleanliness in western cultures and what this might mean for contemporary society and design. As such, the examples are consciously diverse; however the seemingly disparate nature of these sites of reference does require further explanation. As mentioned in the opening paragraph, the field of this research heralds from art and design history and theory but draws from postcolonial and whiteness studies. Therefore, in order to maintain the focus upon the process of whitening whilst providing a social perspective that is both historical and contemporary, I have a deliberate array of examples within a particular structure, which is divided into two main sections. This structure begins by first establishing what is understood by the colour white in visual terms: how it is comprehended in science; made and mixed in art; mythologised in religion; contrived in design; and perceived in skin tones. Once the visibility of white in colour terms has been established, the chapter moves on to the lengthier task of explicating how this whiteness is attained and maintained. Consequently it is the *method and medium* of maintenance that is further extrapolated upon. And in order to sustain the argument of the "ubiquity" and perpetuation of white in the designed environment as correlating with a privileging of whiteness in race, a creative array of references is required. The point of departure for this explication is "soap" as a medium of maintaining whiteness in the Christian-colonising sense of clean bodies with examples from apartheid South Africa. The next medium is the skin-whitener with examples drawn from products recently acquired in Japan and Korea. Narratives within the commodity marketing of these two skin whiteners then lead away from the body and physical image to the next medium, which is designed interior surfaces. In these examples, trans-Atlantic modernist aesthetics is revisited as a reminder why white, flat and ordered surfaces gained a stronghold in interior design in the first place. This aspect is then extended into discussions of domestic cleaning with reference to real estate which is illustrated with a white kitchen from Adelaide, Australia. The wide reach of illustrations, both visual and textual, emphasises the interdisciplinary and international way in which whiteness operates. In addition, the focus upon the whitened body in the whitened environment is one of the more complex operations of white identification and de-identification.

In any research that deals with issues of identity and particularly racial identity, it is ethical to be clear about one's own subject position as an author. White identities are possibly the most guilt ridden identities and can result in struggled words on a page that are not useful to anyone.

However, when it comes to writing about whiteness as a system of strangely simultaneous erasure and exposure (that is, when whiteness is rendered invisible to white people by understating its presence or when we recognise whiteness as a force driving racial hierarchies), then it is even more important for the whiteness of the writer to be named. Consequently, as author of this article, I write with the memories of a being a white girl partially raised by nuns in apartheid South Africa. In the search for subjectivities via the extremes of being clean or dirty, the boundaries of whiteness sometimes become items of negotiation. How clean is clean and how white is white? My own subject position is one that stands deep in the wash tub of whiteness. As a product of white privilege, a witness to the shameful denial of water and subsequent disparagement of those who were unable to wash themselves, I write now as a white woman immigrant to Australia about the complexities associated with the act of washing and keeping clean. My tone may occasionally assume a lightness, which should not be mistaken for levity. Some examples I use are taken from my life in apartheid which will result in a style of writing that combines memory with critical enquiry and makes pointed use of the first person pronoun. There is a reason for this that goes beyond a writing style and is at the core of surface and depth: as author of a chapter on something as close as skin and as deep as subjectivity, I cannot speak for others but I can question motives and contexts. The aim and scope of this chapter is to question the ritual of washing in white western and particularly feminine circles experienced by the author. In so doing, the lens of the west is used as a basis for reflecting upon its own whitenesses.[1]

White Surfaces, White Skins, White Colour

The colour white can be analysed within at least three categories: colour physics (light), colour pigment (paint) and colour myths (beliefs). To put it another way, white can be looked at from the point of view of science, art or religion. For the purpose of clarity, I will start by very briefly introducing the topics of white as a colour in terms of science and art, followed by white myths in a western Christian and particularly Catholic framework. Then I will introduce white surfaces in design and white skins in race. Following from these introductions an argument will be built upon the connection between surface whites and their *maintenance* in relation to race and hygiene.

White colour

In science: Firstly, white in colour physics stems from Isaac Newton's experiments with the passing of a single beam of sunlight through a prism and its subsequent refraction into what are now known as the colours of the spectrum: red, orange, yellow, green, blue, indigo, violet. In this scenario, white is white light and black is the absence of light, neither being seen as colours in their own right, but white now being viewed as composite and not as a singular entity as had been previously surmised (Connellan 2007a; Crystal 1994).

In art: In terms of white pigment, white paint can be made from a variety of substances including lead, chalk, limestone, zinc, alabaster, barium and others (Finlay 2002). The most permanent and also the most deadly of these is lead. Lead white is made from shavings of lead, mixed with vinegar or acid causing the lead to carbonate and result in white powder. When lead white powder is mixed with oil it is lastingly bright, however, if it is mixed with a watered base then the bright white turns black after a few years. Cennino Cennini, in his fifteenth-century handbook for artists, explains the way in which to mix and use white lead and warns artists of its tendency to blacken (Cennini 1960). White on the surface of a canvas or its equivalent has been regarded by artists since the Renaissance as providing the most brilliant result for other colours. Leonardo da Vinci said that "For those colours which you wish to be beautiful, always first prepare a pure white ground" (Kemp 2001, 71).

In white myths: When it comes to myths within the western Christian tradition, white is associated with purity and divinity. The words "light" and "white" are prevalent in both Old and New Testaments and are synonymous with God. Distinct binaries are set up between darkness and light that clothe goodness in white and evil in black. When Jesus met on Mount Sinai with Moses and Elijah he was "transfigured" into a blinding bright light "glistening intensely white" and "his raiment became dazzling white" (*Revised Standard Version* 1965, Mk. 9:2 and Lk. 9:29). Catholicism has a history of white garments used in its many rituals associated with purity, purification and states of grace. The seven sacraments of Baptism, Penance, Holy Communion, Confirmation, Holy Matrimony, Holy Orders (taking the vows of priesthood or sisterhood) and Extreme Unction (sacrament of the dying) are all accompanied by white garments. Even since the Second Vatican Council (1962-1965), white remains a dominant colour of the Catholic Church and its papacy (Gibbons 1917; *Catechism of the Catholic Church* 1995).

White surfaces

The sheen of white ducoed appliances; the brightness of white walls; the gleam of white tiles, the bleach of linen and clothing; the harshness of the white page, the glare of white cars, the daunting white canvas, the impracticality of white furniture—what does all this signify? Delete the adjectives and there could be answers such as white is a colour that reflects light/heat and is therefore cooler to wear, and as a surface it consequently brightens its surroundings increasing the illusion of space. Also, white is both sensible and practical in terms of visibility and cleaning. Keep the adjectives and one may be tempted to add that white surfaces indicate the sterility of a world primarily concerned with surfaces. How, then, did such surfaces in our designed environment come to be white? And how are they kept white? These are questions that will be looked into in the course of this chapter.

White skins

In truth there are very few skins that approach what is visibly considered to be "white" in terms of the colour white as described above. Occasionally one may see an extremely pale person but usually the skin colour of "white" people is tinged with pinks, browns, ochres, purples and blues. Skin tones are complex to mix when painting a naturalistic portrait and white may be the basis but it is certainly not the result. There are many shades of pale, and as Anne Varichon writes, there are "inert whites and dynamic whites" (Varichon 2006, 12). White (unpainted or treated) skins are sometimes the result of a genetic pigmentation disorder, vitiligo or albinism; they are also the consequence of illness, shock and death (A Visible Difference 2007). Why some skins are paler than others is a question generally explained in relation to predominantly sunny climates, where humans would or would not need pigmentation to protect them against the sun and reflected sunlight from continual exposure to white snow as in the Arctic circles.

White skins and their maintenance

Soap and washing

It remains a truism that keeping out of the sun is one way to "maintain" a white skin, and washing off dirt is another. Yet why this investment in maintaining the visibility of white skin (in certain places and at certain times)? In terms of western enlightenment philosophy white skins represented a civilised race. Norbert Elias points to the changes that took place in the west as a result of an increased emphasis upon manners in relation to "bodily culture". In the absence of soap, Erasmus of Rotterdam, as early as 1530, instructed (nominally white) people how to rinse and wipe their hands and mouth before and whilst eating as "one of the marks of distinction between the upper and lower classes" (Elias 1998, 79). Civilisation became conflated with appearances of cleanliness, and as such the use of "soap was the measure of the prosperity and culture of the state" (Olesko 2006, 339). McClintock summarises this well, when she states that:

> Both the cult of domesticity and the new imperialism found in soap an exemplary mediating form. The emergent middle class values—monogamy ('clean' sex, which has value), industrial capital ('clean' money, which has value), Christianity ('being washed in the blood of the lamb'), class control ('cleansing the great unwashed') and the imperial civilizing mission ('washing and clothing the savage')—could all be marvellously embodied in a single household commodity. Soap advertising, in particular the Pears soap campaign, took its place at the vanguard of Britain's new commodity culture and its civilizing mission (McClintock 1995, 208).

Such myths were bred of the industrial revolution, propagated by early capitalist successes of companies like *Pears* and fed by religious fears in the west. The notion of "white skins" was not just about skins, it was about white souls intermingled with white prosperity. Colonialism, in the form of the white benevolent foster parent, set out to wash its subjects in order to assimilate their black skins into the great white family. If they could not be washed in both body and soul, there was trouble afoot and stronger products were necessary. Missionary zeal was mixed with colonial expansion and the home in its various forms was chosen as the site of sanctification, the proverbial baptismal font. It was to this site that women were assigned by the "fathers" of colonialism as responsible for the appearance of spotless children, who were either taken or stolen from their parents, washed, clothed and put to sleep in rows of white beds. Thomas Wright's 1868 publication titled *The Great Unwashed* pontificated upon the women/wives' responsibility for the maintenance of "sanitary" comfort (1970, 31). The "civilising" process was one of constant tidying up and washing down. "Dirt", as Mary Douglas famously writes, was regarded as "matter out of place" one that "implies two conditions: a set of ordered relations and a contravention of that order" (2007, 44). This demanded action. Hygiene became a paramount consideration when "the masses" flocked to the cities and the great urban slums embarrassed the perfumed classes. Dirt and disease had to be hidden, as Fanon suggests:

> The settler's town is a strongly-built town; the streets are covered in asphalt, and the garbage-cans swallow all the leavings, unseen, unknown and hardly thought about. The settler's feet are never visible ... (Fanon 2001, 30).

In my experience, it was a small step from colonial fears to the bathrooms of Catholic boarding schools in the 1960s. The routine involved in conforming to cleanliness was stringent: Bodies scoured, hair cut, washed and brushed, nails scrubbed and clipped according to the rule of the home, teeth brushed, and little people clothed in the crisp clean uniforms of civilisation with shoes by the grace of God. Anything less than this and you were not fit for the light of day. As a small girl in an Eastern Cape town of apartheid South Africa, I can remember having seniors assigned to us little ones aged six and seven in the convent: "had we washed our 'in- betweens?'" we were asked. There was a mystery related to the boundaries of the body, its orifices and its excretions. "Why should bodily margins be thought to be specially invested with power and danger?"(Douglas 2007, 149). My older sister (amongst the senior squad) found our fear of dirt hilarious and subversively warned us that if we cleaned our belly buttons too hard they would come undone ... and also if we looked down the loo while flushing it we would see all the way down to hell. Whilst the crevices and orifices are a part of the body they are not necessarily upon the visible surface, a surface that is invested with the potential to belong or be cast out. That said, the scrubbing continued but with it came a fascination with blots, smudges, smells and bits of matter attached to the body. Following on from Douglas the act of washing becomes a ritual that enacts a "form of social relations" and gives "visible expression ... [to] enable people to know their own society" (Douglas 2007, 159). When we had bath-foam for baths the act of washing became less functional and more luxurious, elevating the state of cleanliness to an even higher realm in our childish minds. Roland Barthes writes that

> [foam] appears to lack any usefulness; ... its abundant easy, almost infinite proliferation allows one to suppose there is in the substance ... a healthy and powerful essence, a great wealth of active elements in a small original volume. Finally it gratifies in the consumer a tendency to imagine matter as something airy, with which contact is effected in a mode both light and vertical, which is sought after like that of happiness (Barthes 1973, 41, 42).

Interestingly, foam is itself not always clean and sparkling, for example the foam on the edge of ocean waves is often brownish and blows independently across the beach. The Xhosa and Zulu word for this dirty white foam is *umlungu* which is also a derogatory term for white settlers, thus aligning dirty whiteness to the invasion and occupation of Indigenous land.

The symbolic "body" of whiteness and the way it connects racism and cleaning was either avoided or not admitted in the deeply segregated society of apartheid South Africa. As a young child I recall wonder being attached to how people with black skins managed to clean themselves at all. When I grew older I realised that racial stigmas were ubiquitously embedded in language and social innuendos, for example, the word *vuilgoed* is Afrikaans for dirty things but was often used to describe black South Africans who were denied clean running water and *then* defiled for being smelly or dirty (Coetzee 1996). Thus being dirty is simultaneously a condition of separation and a tool for maintaining the state of difference (Connellan 2007b, 118).

Whitening skin

The epidermis is the surface upon which dirt and blemishes reveal themselves. And although the epidermis is but a thin layer, it is in and upon this layer that difference is read. In this way the epidermis becomes one of the significant texts for racist observation and documentation. Therefore, whether it is soap or chemical whiteners that are applied to cleanse and or lighten the skin, it is this surface that offers a public face as part of the qualifying process into whiteness. And it is the exteriority of the public image that prompted my inclusion of commercial skin whiteners here. Skin whiteners illustrate the extent to which whiteness as a light skin tone becomes a marketable attribute which is packaged and narrated to feed both social and racial aspirations of belonging and advancement. Therefore, whilst "soap" and cleanliness were, in part, a medium of the white colonising process, skin whiteners are a contemporary medium of a similar whitening process; one that is propagated through the exterior/outward mechanisms of marketing as opposed to the inward and more hidden mechanisms of white race privilege.

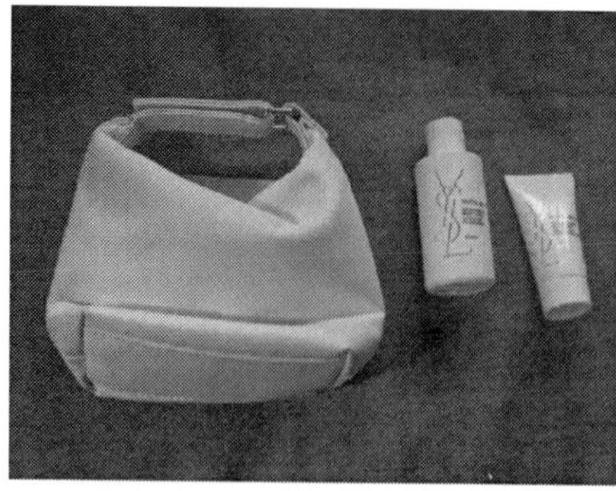

Fig. 2-1 Yves St Laurent Skin whitening products. Photographed by the author.

Fig. 2-2 Beauty Credit Skin whitener. Photographed by the author.

In semiotic terms the following equation could be applied to explain the function of skin whitening products. There are other possible equations, but for the purposes of this chapter white could be seen as a meta-sign which by way of certain products delivers a certain status.

SIGN (white) = SIGNIFIER (whitening products) / SIGNIFIED (status and beauty)

Semiotic analysis is a structuralist method of arriving at possible meanings projected by signs and their signifiers, however in post structuralism (and by extension post modernism) the signs and signifiers are many layered. The sign is often composed of many signs within it and while these signs should not be separated from their varying signifiers, the signifiers often drift from the signs making the signification elusive. It is this "drifting" that is exploited in some of the more sophisticated (and postmodern) marketing techniques, because the more subtle and less obvious the connections, the greater the potential. Therefore the development away from the obvious and apparently binary relationship between the iconic sign and its referent is interesting when looking at signs of white. Such signs are imbued with altered meanings in different contexts (Hall 1997; Seldon 1989). Under the aegis of postmodern theory, surface/skin and its apparent inclusiveness was temporarily suspended—or so it seemed—in order to allow for the movement and interaction of signifiers. However the binaries of white and power/status (for example) may be too fixed to remain suspended, their meaning may be too entrenched.

In the images of the products shown in Figures 2-1 and 2-2, the sign is the colour white but it is more arbitrary in the Beauty Credit product than the Yves St Laurent product. In the YSL example, white skin whitening creams and their white bag are the signifiers. These signifiers used by YSL are toothpaste white, the product branding on the bag is white on white and barely visible. There are no pictorial representations and the process of signification is understated and subtle, indeed everything that usually accompanies exclusive products. The colour white here becomes a sign that is taken to be so clear in its message of whiteness that it renders itself almost invisible and becomes subliminal, thus beckoning to a market that aspires towards an understated acquiescence of white and whiteness.

The signified (result) of course means a range of things depending on who you are. From YSL's point of view, their product signifies that a lighter skin will result in status and entrance into an elevated, fashionable class and celebrity set or grouping. The marketing text on the package does not say this, what it says on the tube called "White Mode: Hydra-whitening day emulsion" is this: "Wonderfully revealing transparency and radiance for fresh, velvety, white-bright skin every day. Apply every morning on the face and neck". The other tube in the YSL package is called "White mode: active whitening beauty lotion" and its text is the following: "The first active step in the whitening program for softly refined, more even, lighter skin. Use morning and evening on perfectly cleansed face and neck". The use of words here is exaggerated and essentialised, for example, "softly refined" and "perfectly cleansed" intimate their opposites as "rough and unrefined" and "blemished and dirty". Whilst advertising copy script is known for hyperbole, it is nevertheless interesting to note the embedded racial signifiers that serve to undermine anything that is not white. There are 25 listed ingredients in the YSL lotions (quantities are not specified) of which 15 are chemical and notably one important ingredient is sodium hydroxide, a substance which is described as follows in a United States government website on toxic substances :

> Sodium hydroxide is a manufactured chemical. It is present in several domestic cleaning products. Very low levels can produce irritation of the skin and eyes. Exposure to the solid or concentrated liquid can cause severe burns in the eyes, skin, and gastrointestinal tract which may ultimately lead to death. This substance has been found in at least 49 of the 1,585 National Priorities List sites identified by the Environmental Protection Agency (EPA) (http://www.atsdr.cdc.gov/tfacts178.html).

The other product (Beauty Credit) is a Korean product and the ingredients are not listed on the packaging. It comes with a different signage and is not divorced from the pictorial and representational as in the case of YSL. Here the process of signification is more narrative and less conceptual than YSL. There is a "photo film strip" on the inside cover that continues the story begun on the front image of the young girl at the pottery wheel. Her boyfriend features as an advisor and confidante for her to achieve a smooth white skin, with a picture of him talking to her in her studio and later in her gallery. The story ends happily with the smiling boyfriend embracing the happy young girl's head and neck in a picture of pride and display. The man assumes the authority, albeit gently, to advise the woman regarding intimate details such as her skin colour and condition. In this way the power invested in heteronormative projections of skin is an added complexity in the signification process. The signified meaning here appears to be a happy heterosexual relationship, based upon a clear white skin. It is intriguing to note just how much products such as these can be used to endorse gendered and racial norms as well as "success" in (heterosexual) relationships. For example, it appears here that it is easier for a girl to keep her boyfriend by not only becoming more "feminine", but also by becoming more "white", thus running these two stereotypical attributes together. The products are illustrated in the leaflet as having a close association with nature and include images of honey comb and green herbs. These signify a healthy complexion and do not obviously point to whiteness, although the use of nature as a means of legitimating what is "natural" and therefore "right" is an added directive. The white skin tones and white clothing are also additional signifiers for a lighter racial distinction with its benefits of privilege.

These are just two examples of the many skin whitening products on the market and both were bought in Asian countries which are not geo-culturally associated with white skins. This white skin marketing implies that passing as white is a commodity that is bought and sold. The (white) friend who gave me the YSL product described the experience of acquiring the product as "weird":

> I was in Tokyo, in Narita airport, getting ready to leave and come home, and I remembered I meant to purchase some YSL products. So I went to the duty free shop, in which all of the people working there were Japanese, and a majority of the people buying things were not Japanese, most of them looking like they came from some Western country. After I purchased the items the woman gave me the bag [pictured in Fig. 2-1] and said that it was a gift with purchase, and she proceeded to open the bag and show me the contents, and I was almost embarrassed as to the contents—that, as a white person, I would be given skin whitening cream, … and that such products exist and that I would be given them as a 'gift'!! The duty free areas in Narita are interesting as whilst almost all the staff are Japanese, almost all the advertising features white women—there is this bizarre moment when you walk and you see faces that look like your own in the posters, yet none of the people talking to you sound or look like you. I cannot imagine what it is like for the women working in such a context (D. Riggs, personal email, 26 March 2008).

Whilst the illustrated YSL product was obviously being promoted and given as a free gift with purchases over a certain amount, its 18 page accompanying booklet on the YSL "Whitening Collection" devotes nine pages of "text" to women but makes no direct reference to race. Instead, the long lasting and increasing effects of bright whitening are promised in terms of "diminishing" uneven pigmentation. This particular product is available for sale on the internet along with the rest of the YSL range. Glenn (2008) provides a keen analysis of the multitude of skin whiteners on the market and refers to them as "global capital" and as a means to ascend social hierarchies. Glenn pays closer attention to consumer groups, market niches and the role of pharmaceutical/cosmetic companies than she does to issues of race in her article "Yearning for Lightness". However, this does not mean that she avoids the subject: she scrutinises the European Union's distribution of "disturbing" mercury based products against a background of colonialism and diaspora. She provides a commentary on "the breakdown of traditional racial categories in many areas of the world" and the simultaneous way in which skin colour becomes a "form of symbolic capital" that impacts upon social advancement because of "light-skinned privilege" (2008, 281, 282). The issue of skin lighteners and whiteners is complicated when positioned within the complex array of contributing factors such as race, gender, class and status, image, economics and consumerism. Therefore, whilst skin is a surface of recognition/a known terrain on the one hand, it is also the site of disguise. Skin lies between the interior and the exterior, it is the coating that fronts the world and as such is a site of insecurity that is vulnerable to aspirations and competition in western consumer culture.

The next section looks at inanimate surfaces that are manufactured, synthesised and painted as white coverings. In particular it looks at the reasons and results of these white environments for the people who use them, but also more deeply in terms of what whitening and flattening means ideologically and philosophically.

Surface Whites and their Maintenance

Designed surfaces

If the introductory interpretations of white in this article are accepted, then white is a surface that reflects light and in so doing it highlights any contrasting colour, spot or fragment of matter. The fact that white *is* a surface is often overlooked precisely because of its ability to create the illusion of space. As such the surface parameters blur or even disappear. Whiteness in modernist design was never really acknowledged in the canon of the times; as such the colour white was everywhere but remained unnamed. Wigley refers to this silence as a "strategic blindness" (Wigley 2001, 4); a silence, which like most things that operate in stealth, increase their power by virtue of their apparent invisibility. The canon of modernist architecture was inculcated by the work, philosophy and following of architects such as Le Corbusier, a man obsessed with white and cleanliness to the degree that he wrote prescriptions about how and how not to undress, live in one's own home and generally how to be an automaton that fitted into his own idea of the "radiant city" (*la ville radieuse*). That such radicalism was tolerated let alone adopted had a lot to do with the innovations that Le Corbusier brought to architecture in the way of the basic grid structure that all high modern architecture was subsequently based upon (1946, 114-5). Clement Greenberg was an important counterpart to Le Corbusier in the privileging of the seen surface. For the arch- modernist Greenberg, the move away from content and depth to one of surface in art was a logical progression; it simply meant a coming together of all elements and a celebration of unity in flatness (Greenberg 1986, 34). This view of the composite nature of the surface, a place where reality is flattened into an aesthetic experience, can be related to the composite nature of white in colour physics as a coming together of the colour spectrum. It is perhaps easy to see how an *ideology* of flatness and whiteness (in a revisited Cartesian sense of order and clarity) can be built upon the modernist idea of a transcendent simplicity as seamless abstractionism. "To abstract" in this sense is to render the representational and naturalistic image with all its life and detail, into an image that is so simplified that it is removed from recognisable representation and supposedly assumes a "higher" meaning because it has left the realm of busy detail. Therefore, when this modernist technique of non-representation is transferred to the individual or a group of people, it serves to disguise identity. Jean Paul Sartre points to the "bitterness" beneath efforts to "assimilate" in terms of a settler psyche, saying that "abstraction is their only wealth" (2001, 15). In this way there is a correlation between (1) the abstraction of representation in modernist art, (2) the flattening and simplifying of surfaces in interior and furniture design and (3) the "distance" created by the settlers who tried to psychologically remove themselves from the reality of the colony in which they lived. All three are strategies of removal in order to assume a unity that has nothing to do with togetherness or community and more to do with obliteration and denial. To maintain the complex invisibility and flatness that brings about ostensible unity, many devices or processes are necessary and (to return to the surfaces) cleaning remains paramount in this operation.

Cleaning and washing the surfaces

White surfaces, then, can also be something else without even changing. They can, in the Greenbergian sense, be many things simultaneously. White flatness can be surface, space (depth) and form all at once and still remain relatively incognito, a condition that gives whiteness its power. *But*, white is only as thick and as strong as its surface layer, and therein lies its fragility. However, once those who have embued the surfaces with their flat whiteness become cognisant of the potential strength/power of understatement and of insubstantiality, then they will do all they can to keep it, that is, to keep white white. And to maintain this particular state of invisible whiteness constant cleaning is required. Such cleaning can take the form of wiping, dusting, scraping, scrubbing, bleaching, scouring, touching up with paint or white-out, or even repainting and resurfacing. If it has reached this latter stage, then it is quite possible that the disguise has been blown and the realisation that white is in fact not white at all may have been revealed. Mostly this is avoided, and I argue this situation is particularly avoided in white western developed urban environments, hence the efforts and accompanying propaganda in the form of marketing cleaning products. Naturally these efforts are inextricably tied up with opportunistic capitalist agendas where whiteness is synonymous with profit.

Like the surfaces of whiteness, their maintenance was established in the modernist era. Modernism had its own cleaning agendas, which resonated with the twentieth century's siren call to order and standardisation. A call that came from post war reconstruction, patriotism and the notion of the family as the building block of society, the latter aspect landing squarely at the feet of wives and mothers. The fêted but fallacious "appliance revolution" of the 1950s brought white goods into the homes with its concomitant propaganda of cleanliness = goodness. Ann Oakley, Ruth Schwartz-Cowan and others demonstrate the fiction that labour-saving devices *increased* housework by inventing new tasks (Attfield 2007; Oakley 1974; Schwartz-Cowan 1983). Modernism's take on F.W. Taylor's time and motion studies bred a competitive productivity that set the tone for constant occupation, that is, busyness. Herein echoes the restlessness that accompanies a dissatisfaction with one's environment. In order to attain an identity in the imposed order of modernism it helped to be clean and tidy. Cleanliness and suburban respectability became middle-class badges signifying whiteness and infused with nationalist propaganda (Connellan and Moss 2004).

A consumerist circus of advertisements for washing machines and vacuum cleaners attempted to persuade women to re-enter their homes after the war so that ex-servicemen could take up the jobs in factories (which had changed from making weapons to cleaning appliances). The glinting bubbles of the appliance revolution's lie gave rise to a multiplication of soap powders and detergents. The advertising and packaging of these products has been immortalised in an essay by Barthes. Barthes refers to the way in which French society succumbed to the forces of *Omo* and *Persil*. Beneath the banter of Barthesian language lies a serious satire upon cleaning and washing. He was particularly interested in the psychological innuendos and metaphors in the marketing of detergents in the mid twentieth century, drawing attention to the apparent connections between obliterating dirt, killing enemies and euphorically enfolding oneself in foam. In all of this the chemical agents in the detergents were revealed as strong weapons:

> Chlorinated fluids, for instance, have always been experienced as a sort of liquid fire, the action of which must be carefully estimated, otherwise the object itself would be affected, 'burnt'. The implicit legend of this type of product rests on the idea of a violent, abrasive modification of matter: the connotations are of a chemical or mutilating type: the product 'kills' the dirt (Barthes 1973, 40).

Referring to the cleaning rhetoric of the time, Barthes distinguishes between the killing action of chemical agents and the "separation" action of the powdered cleaning agents. The soap powders were sold on the theme of forcing out the dirt, sending it into exile. Here one is again reminded of Mary Douglas's thesis of dirt in western civilisation as an interloper and "matter out of place" (2007, 44)—this is a kind of entropy one in which the "chaos" of the system can be reduced or altered by rearrangement of its parts, which involves energy and movement as I have already emphasised (Gell-Mann and Tsallis 2004; Coetzee 1996).

As such, the housewife fulfilled her purpose in identifying and obliterating the "evil" of dirt upon the surface, and according to Barthes "in the *Omo* imagery, dirt is a diminutive enemy, stunted and black, which takes to its heels from the fine immaculate [white] linen ..." (1973, 40). That enemy has taken on a variety of colours on the shelves of postmodernity. For example, walking down the aisles of a supermarket or subjecting oneself to the cleaning advertisements on television is a journey into a Disney land of creatures that are illustrated to characterise germs and pests. These almost storybook characters are often given an animated execution by the chemical products one is encouraged to purchase. That these marketing tactics borrow from the sinister metaphors of contemporary warfare is a variation of Barthes' reference to killing the enemy. It is not surprising that one of the most consuming of propagandas at present (that is, fear propaganda) is being used to sell products that keep environments and their surfaces clean and white so that anything out of place is immediately detected and removed. It is true that the past decade has included clear warnings of potential bodily harm on bottles of bleach (White King) and other such agents that contain ammonia and acid. But the contemporary consumer is provided with many more options for cleaning, designed for busy people on the move. The implication is that this is an unsettled society that can never be satisfied with the status quo and can hardly ever come to rest because there is always another possibility.

Washed white surfaces

The entrenchment of the modernist agenda with its far flung ideologies of structure and control based upon the Cartesian grid were never successfully dethroned by the poststructural and postmodernist interpolations of inclusivity and colour in design. Robert Venturi the post modern architect said "I am for messy vitality over obvious unity", and in answer to Mies van der Rohe the modernist architect's famous words "less is more", Venturi quipped "less is a bore" (Venturi 1977, 16, 17). So out with tidiness and in with messiness. The water of washing was thrown into a postmodern melting pot, a wash tub designed to drown the colonial sins of the past and invent a new race that could never be accused of being white. But white is still here, it is in the foyers of corporate offices, the living rooms of upmarket city living professionals (no longer just in the kitchens, which have now added hard edge stainless steel and sheer black gloss to their palette and texture surfaces), white is on walls, counter tops, floors and ceilings and it is being kept so clean that you do not notice its continued dominance in a very late postmodern era. Research with London real estate revealed that neutrality is everything, and most particularly neutrality is not grey, it is white and light (Young 2004). Similarly, conversations that I had with home renovators during a recent overseas trip has again emphasised that white is a "safe bet" when renovating for rent or sale. The illustrated image below of a kitchen is taken from a real estate board outside a house in Adelaide, Australia. The clear surfaces are looked upon as devoid of past history and especially personal history. The surface is seemingly where white westerners dwell and the need to blend with these surfaces is more interesting still.

The myth of *terra nullius* lives on in the settler psyche. In contemporary living, the home is often dressed up to be an extension of the body. Take the case of the empty space—a clean, new house or home with no traces of previous dirt. If there are traces left in, for example, the oven or cupboards, they are mercilessly scrubbed. However, a few months after settling in, the oven will once again be dirty but it is familiar dirt and is not feared. Young (2004) writes:

> Cleanliness relates to both integrity of surface and to the absence of traces of other people's lives. 'To live is to leave traces' wrote Walter Benjamin, but this is precisely what prospective buyers and tenants do not want to see; signs of others' occupation. [Young goes on to say,]… Anything that is not neutral, i.e. colored, is by implication, a personal idiosyncrasy that other people cannot relate to (Young 2004, 9).

Fig. 2-3 Real Estate board pinned up on the wall of a house in Adelaide, Australia, 2008. Photographed by the author.

Conclusion

Traversing white surfaces in the course of this chapter has emphasised the "surfaceness" of the colour white and the high maintenance of such surfaces, be they architectural or dermatic, physical or psychological. The powers of racism and colonialism have contributed to a hierarchical layering of bodies and the spaces they occupy. The coating that is chosen for the outer layer is the visible mark of belonging. The seen surface has been shown as paramount in a battle to conform to the sameness of white. In the ascendance and perpetuation of the abstract, other senses and histories are pushed below the surface or temporarily rubbed out in the process of washing, painting and generally maintaining whiteness. The need for constant or at least frequent cleaning enters into the formation of identity as a ubiquitous reminder of the fragility and insecurity of the thin white layer.

This chapter began by using particular "definitions" and interpretations of white and then moved to how assumptions of white as "light, purity and goodness" impacted upon people and their environments. As explained, white in modernism has already been established in the literature; however it remains remarkable that white and whiteness is extremely prevalent in contemporary society. Le Corbusier, van der Rohe and Greenberg were modernist champions of the surface and its flatness; the simpler the better. That particular state of minimalism, whilst seen as sublime and transcendent of messy clutter, is also a state of denial and subterfuge, one where depth is an embarrassment and an inconvenience because it may say too much, it may in fact reveal unwanted identities. But it can now be posited that the postmodern renovators of the environment underestimated the astonishing power of white to be form, depth and surface simultaneously, they underestimated this because of the apparent invisibility of white and they underestimated the power of the apparently invisible. Postmodernism was a mere interlude.

What this means for western society is complex; it certainly shows that there can be no rest or peace if white and its whiteness continue to be held so precious. The enquiry into whether whiteness=cleanliness shows that cleanliness is relative and can be an obsession rather than a condition. Aspiring to whiteness or protecting whiteness is premised upon a lack of acceptance, both of the self and of others.

However much postmodern theory tried to paint people in equal shades of democracy, it did not work. Consequently whiteness disinfects itself of past contagion and reinscribes authority on its several fronts. To "pass" beyond these frontlines, certain attributes are necessary and apart from wealth and high degrees, a light skin is a bonus. Products that offer such an entrance into whiteness are being sold in global markets. Skin whitening products reveal a postcolonising propensity for becoming white. These products blatantly exploit constructed inadequacies of being darker than white amongst dark skinned people. The YSL product is recognisably "up-market" and is a company known for its elite label status. YSL is intimately cognisant of human vanities and an even unblemished skin tone is an acclaimed attribute of "beauty" in this marketplace. As such racial stereotypes are entwined with gender, sexuality and class signifiers in different types of whitening products. These products represent just one aspect of the hold that late capitalism has on whiteness as a commodity.

To unseat whiteness would be to undo the litany of beliefs that have infiltrated what has become an ideology of whiteness. The "strategic blindness" that Wigley referred to in white architecture is similar to the pervasive silence of whiteness as race; however the silence is broken by the sound of scrubbing.

CHAPTER THREE

A *TOURISTIC TERRA NULLIUS*

JOHAN R. EDELHEIM

Introduction

Tourist attractions—not just those identified as “heritage sites”, but also modern symbols of consumerism such as Australia’s “Big Things”—are often simplistically presented as objects with an attached objective reality. This chapter suggests that attractions should not be viewed simply as objects, but rather understood as narratives in themselves. The fluidity of narratives as a theoretical tool allows researchers to deconstruct the hegemonic discourse tourist attractions hold. This chapter suggests that the focus on attractions as objects in the present disregards what has existed in the past. This unconscious/conscious blindness to a holistic history of an attraction, or even a region, creates a *touristic terra nullius*—a nullification of alternative understandings. However, a narrative analysis of texts describing destinations can lead researchers to discover a palimpsest of local history, still legible behind promotional texts referring to the present.

The theories this chapter builds on do not fit seamlessly into either cultural studies or tourism studies. I have tried my best to bridge the two disciplines and construct a new way of interpreting tourism through the eyes of cultural studies. The language I use is a mixture of the often quite straightforward managerial texts found in tourism studies—essentially aimed to serve the tourism industry to improve its operations and to strategically plan for a sustainable future (Leiper 2004)—and the critically analytic text common in cultural studies, where hardly any issue is left unexamined (Barker 2002). The theoreticians I build this argument on come from both fields of studies.

Tourist attractions and the narratives surrounding them take on a new dimension in the power/knowledge of nations in contemporary time where people in the developed world have more disposable income, and where tourism, for a majority of those people, is regarded as a natural leisure activity (Hall and Tucker 2004). I have, in order to highlight the new dimensions of tourism, two aims in this chapter; firstly, to discuss the structure of tourist attractions, and how these can be re-defined as narratives; and secondly to present a theoretical concept I term a "*touristic terra nullius*". I will initially present the context in which the research is set, namely the interrelation between tourism and nationalism. Following on from this, I will give some examples from tourist texts to highlight what tourists consume whilst on holiday, and how these texts "construct" attractions as narrative entities. I will highlight how a focus on specific attraction features disregards marginalised groups in society and can even be read as a conservative attempt to maintain a status quo in a set of hegemonic social norms. More specifically, I go on to suggest that by "writing out" Indigenous populations from tourist texts, and by referring to history as something that has only occurred during colonial rule of the country, a *touristic terra nullius* is created.

In so doing, and following Shields (1991), I suggest that rather than accepting specific places as inherently imbued with a set of "correct" meanings, it is important to question the way certain regions and popular tourist destinations have each been given a specific meaning in public discourse since colonisation. By deconstructing the texts surrounding the case studies I explore how specific myths about places are formed and the image that particular groups of people may hold about those locations. By extending research in the field of cultural and tourism studies I aim to question how attractions are given meaning based on the texts surrounding them, and thereafter show that underlying "meta-narratives" forge an understanding of the place. Seemingly neutral attractions might carry an unintended bias that becomes evident when the narrative structure of the attraction is disseminated.

The description follows my journey as a naïve tourist visiting Uralla, a small town in the New England tablelands, half-way between Brisbane and Sydney. My wish was to understand the meaning of the town's iconic attraction, and simultaneously connect that experience with theoretical findings from the fields of cultural studies and tourism studies, in order to explain why certain meanings evolved in the tourist's (that is, my) mind.

Nation or imagi-nation?

The concept of national identity and its relationship to tourism is complex. Anderson (1991) traced the emergence of nations, in the way we understand them today, through the development of print technology and capitalism. Emblems—such as a common language, flags, costumes, folk dances—all share the "capacity for generating imagined communities, building in effect *particular solidarities*" (Anderson 1991, 133, emphasis in original). If it is accepted that a nation is an imagined community, it then follows that both nationalism and national identity are equally constructed concepts—or as Bhabha argues, narratives (1990). My suggestion is that tourist attractions essentially can be seen as "miniature narratives" of nations—that which is selected and emphasised in attractions is what in larger terms constitutes the narrative of the nation.

Many Australian tourist attractions are based on a specifically colonial or white history and heritage—built or natural—of the region where they are located. The nationalist agenda of over-emphasising the uniqueness of a particular territory and history (Anderson 1991) can be compared with tourist promoters' agendas of doing exactly the same. It could even be argued that it is the same agendas that are in question (Rowe 1993, 260). The ultimate purpose of tourism is leisure and enjoyment; the intentional down-playing of "unpleasant" factors (such as histories of dispossession and genocide) is thus a part of accepted tourist management strategies (Chang and Holt 1991, 102). Furthermore, if economic success is the purpose of the place's existence as an attraction, it can be assumed that the image/product presented to tourists is the one that market research has claimed that tourists want to consume (Morgan and Pritchard 1998).

But if tourism is to be viewed from a more holistic perspective—still having as an ultimate purpose to provide leisure and enjoyment, but equally politically and socially significant in its power to educate travellers about social inequalities—then new ways of presenting, interpreting, and experiencing attractions and destinations are needed (Edelheim 2007). Equally, if non-stereotypical depictions are to be utilised in tourism, new ways of thinking would be opened up—not just in terms of race relations as presented in this chapter, but also, and equally importantly, about sustainable cultural and ecological environments, as well as age and gender relations to name some.

A narrated Australian national identity

Turner (1993) explains that popular works of fiction in Australian society, such as books and films, often feature white male protagonists who are rebellious against the system, but ultimately unsuccessful in their attempts to break free from their context. He claims that this is a political attempt "to naturalise an ideological view of the power relations between self and society which proposes the futility of individual action against the status quo" (Turner 1993, 84). Turner's message is that Australian narratives simultaneously enforce individualism and power dominance from above. They essentially function for uncritical readers as a social tableau that overtly seems to encourage criticism but covertly reinforces the ultimate futility of resistance against decisions made by leaders, managers, or other people with some sort of authority.

Turner highlights the discursive formations that are brought into being, through the way narratives are told in Australia. By preferring certain narratives over others, and by inscribing in tourist practices common values for Australians, it becomes possible to uphold a hegemonic meta-narrative about what it means to be and act as an Australian. Or, in Turner's words: "narratives are ultimately produced by the culture; thus they generate meanings, take on significances, and assume forms that are articulations of the values, beliefs—the ideology—of the culture" (1993, 1). That the narratives produced highlight and prefer certain meanings over others is therefore a natural outcome of that ideology in action. The theme of Australian narratives—regardless whether these are found in books, films, music, TV series, or tourist attractions—all build on a range of national myths that are constructed and self-reinforcing.

Tourism and leisure pursuits can therefore be connected to the construction of an Australian national identity in similar ways to Turner's literary and cinema narratives. A stereotypical way of spending family holidays amongst middle-class Australians with an Anglo-Celtic background, popular since the 1950s—travelling by car and camping out (Spearritt 2003)—is still strong, even though the more competitive airline industry has to some extent changed the mode of transport from road to air. The major holiday season, starting at Christmas, and ending by the Australia Day holiday at the end of January, always results in a tremendous rise in private automobile usage on the national highways (Marles 2006). The family, as an extended individual, is expected to make journeys in the country and to visit certain attractions that collectively communicate aspects of their own identity to visitors (McLean and Cooke 2003).

Heritage attractions are one of these sources of identity. Hetherington explains that the romantic structure of social relations in the past, "more authentic, expressive and fulfilling", has led people to establish identities based on perceptions of the past (1998, 101). A danger with the preservation of a certain past is that conservation has very strong links with conservatism (Lanfant 1995, 17). This results, in the Australian context, in an image of the national identity being equal to the Pioneer Myth (Rowe 1993)—strong, independent, white, heterosexual men—essentially an uncompromising picture with implications for contemporary family values, the work market, and society at large. The pioneer myth is very much a construct from the times when the infamous "White Australia Policy" was written, but has lived on in the fantasy of the urbanised population, and is still a potent political tool in the nation (Gunew 1990).

Thus, if heritage is not critically evaluated, it is possible that a skewed version of history is presented, and that alternative versions are neglected (Meethan 2001, 101). Edensor and Kothari present, for example, the male-centred narratives surrounding Scottish heritage sites (1994). They see heritage as a combination of memory and myth, feelings and emotions, presented in whichever ways are seen as suitable in that context. The dominance of white, heterosexual, male-centred messages relates to the fact that Scottish heritage often is dominated by battlefields and other military attractions, essentially sites that evoke boyhood fantasies, whilst simultaneously marginalising female visitors and interpretations of female history.

Perera and Pugliese (1998) point out, in the Australian setting, that the signification of particular sites as "built or natural heritage" is an act that in many instances "take over where colonialism ended" (72-73). This is because the signification functions as a means in which the ends of powerful groups are enacted, where political interests override local—and Indigenous—objections. They continue by claiming that it is impossible for Australia, as a settler nation, to maintain a homogenised national identity based on inherited values, and that is why culture and progress bear "unstated assumptions about race and ethnicity" whilst nature and disorder—as the binary opposites to culture and order—are connected to the country's Indigenous population (73).

I suggest that places should be viewed as fluid entities, not as reified objects, as they have distinctly different meanings to different people (Entrikin 1991). In her description of the South African tourist minister's overt linkage of "heritage, tourism and economic development" with nation-building Marschall refers to all heritage sites as being authorised and "institutionalised interpretations of history" (2004, 95-97). Similarly, Hollinshead (1997) coined the term "*past-modernity*" to describe how tourist managers of heritage attractions, by utilising the local and national past of a place, are creating a political past—the "modern past". Hollinshead pointed out that both history and heritage are social constructions, and in that he mirrors many authors on nationalism, who equally remind us that the concepts "nation", "race", and "culture" are social constructions (Anderson 1991; Appadurai 1996; Jackson and Penrose 1993). I will build on this notion of constructedness of place in the following section, in which I outline post-structural narrative analysis as a method allows for a more fluid interpretation of place and attractions.

Post-structural narrative analysis of tourist sites

Bal (1997) divides narratives into three parts: *the text, the story, and the fabula*. The first part—*texts*—comprise the only tangible elements of narratives that readers come across, such as written texts, pictures, movies, sounds, structures or other entities that present themselves to the world in a manner that gives the reader specific information. The two other parts are abstract constructs that only become evident through analysis: The versions offered in the different *stories* can be regarded as aspects of the texts. The stories suggest different *fabulae*, depending on what texts have been used in the analysis. In Bal's words: "It is by way of the text that the reader has access to the story, of which the fabula is, so to speak, a *memorial trace that remains with the reader after completion of the reading*" (1997, xv, emphasis added).

Entrikin (1991) is an author who has combined narratives and the understanding of place and who refers to Ricoeur's discussion of the significance of plots in narratives as they draw together separate entities into comprehensible wholes. The suggestion Entrikin builds on here is to treat texts surrounding places similarly to the way Ricoeur treats written texts, where the different attributes of place are "emplotted" onto an understandable whole (25). The difference from a positivist description of an attraction is that none of these emplotted places claims preference; each is an acceptable version in its own right.

> One of the goals … is to interpret the meaning of places. The geographer becomes a translator, translating the story of places in such a way that the subjective and objective realities that compose our understanding of place remain interconnected. The geographer as narrator translates his or her stories into a new form and, with interests somewhat different from those of the participant in a place or region, abstracts from the experience of a group (Entrikin 1991, 58).

By incorporating Entrikin's notion of the narrative structure of place and Bal's terminology on tourist attractions, it is possible to see the different texts that refer to a joint story, and which combine to form a fabula which acts as the memory of the narrative.

Leiper (1995), in an attempt to analyse tourist attractions as scientific entities, developed a structuralist model based on MacCannell's (1976) semiotic framework for destination sightseeing. It is evident, when reading

Leiper's arguments leading up to this model, that he was frustrated with definitions of attractions that too simplistically concentrated on just the attraction, with all of the attendant assumptions about the "magnetism" of attractions that "pull" travellers to them. Leiper regarded these ideas as nonsensical statements that construct attractions as "metaphysical mysteries", and as a counter to this he highlighted the need to view attractions from an informed scientific viewpoint. In the model, he suggested that attractions have to contain three necessary elements: "*a tourist or a human element, a nucleus or a central element, and a marker or informative element*" (1995, 141-143, emphasis in original). Leiper specified that the nucleus can be an object, but does not have to be one; it can, rather, be a place, a precinct, an event, or even an atmosphere. "[A]ttractions can occur almost anywhere" he suggested (1995, 145).

Richards (2002) points out two weaknesses with Leiper's attraction system. Firstly, the structural approach emphasises the set "reality" of each element in the system. Richards builds on Urry (1990) in an attempt to explain how a marker can be expected to contribute to the dominant view of an attraction. Richards takes this further by incorporating MacCannell's criticism of Urry, arguing that tourists "can penetrate, change, and develop the attraction system" (2001, 31) and thus create an experience that is an alternative to the dominant gaze. The second weakness, according to Richards, is that Leiper's system disregards the meanings that tourists attach to attractions.

A way of using Leiper's attraction system principles that overcomes the weaknesses pointed out by Richards is to view the system from a poststructural narrative perspective—in which the attraction is seen as a narrative. The elements from Leiper's system—the tourist, the marker, and the nucleus—would be adapted by adding one more element. Rather than assuming that the markers and the nucleus are objective "realities" that mean the same to everybody, they would be investigated as subjective clues that each make up one final picture. Pritchard and Morgan (2000, 899) claim that "[s]pace and place are complex concepts. They are cultural constructions subject to change and negotiation". This approach follows Rojek's suggestion of viewing attractions as social constructions linked to what he calls "collage tourism" where representations and fabrications are part of the constant *indexing* and *dragging* that form the postmodern media society of which tourism is a part (1997). Rojek emphasises the ways in which fiction, as much as facts, has an impact on how attractions are perceived: neither should be seen as more important than the other. This notion is important for the redefinition of attractions as narratives: a description of an attraction is not only an attempt at a factual analysis, but is equally a part of a larger combination of texts that together form the attraction as an abstract concept in the reader's mind.

In order to investigate these fluid entities the vocabulary of narrative analysis would therefore substitute Leiper's "marker" and "nucleus", and in so doing *an attraction would thus be defined as being constituted by a tourist, texts, stories, and a fabula.* Note that the first and last element of the definition are in singular form, while the two middle elements—text and story that replace Leiper's (1995) "marker"—are in plural form. This is to point out that each tourist constructs an individual fabula from a range of different information sources.

In order to understand how a tourist attraction fabula is constructed, it is necessary to assemble the pieces of text that can form the impression of "a" fabula. While it is true that a range of different fabulae can be assembled depending on the parts included, each one is the taken-for-granted reality of the individual who assembled that fabula. As such, when in the following section I take on the task of assembling tourist attractions as narratives, I am fully aware of the fact that "my" fabula is only one amongst possible countless others. I am also aware of the fact that "my" fabula is not static; when somebody tells me about a feature that I did not know about before, essentially introducing a new *text*, that feature will again alter my understanding of the attraction and "my" fabula.

I therefore suggest that *tourist attractions as narratives* can be understood as *theoretical snapshots* at a specific time and, just like other snapshots, inform their audience about a feature at a certain moment. The reason I call them theoretical snapshots is that attractions are not one-dimensional like photographs, but rather multidimensional, incorporating all texts that the tourist has perceived up until that stage. However, what makes the analogy to a snapshot valuable is that it encapsulates possible biases, explains why a certain focus highlights specific features, and emphasises features that stakeholders close to the attraction might not be aware of as they might have a more static understanding of the attraction.

Rather than analysing each text about a tourist attraction as an entity on its own, I have decided to collate some information sources—in the way a tourist would do when travelling towards a region, or in that region—and collectively analyse these texts for the messages they have and the fabula they construct. There is no empirical reason for choosing these texts beyond others available; the selection is simulating what a tourist could potentially come across if doing the same journey.

Captain Thunderbolt and Uralla

"Captain Thunderbolt", or so the story goes, was a bushranger, an Australian highway bandit (Routt 2001) who stole horses, and held up travellers and mail deliveries. Several similar individuals existed in the nineteenth century and a considerable mythology has developed in contemporary Australia around these bushrangers (Boxall 1899/1974; Molitorisz 2003). The most famous of Australia's outlaws was Ned Kelly and his gang, who have been immortalised through innumerable books as well as several films (Beeton 2004). Even though the original stories about the bushrangers have not changed substantially, the mythology has become strong enough to justify repeated films, and a tourist industry that capitalises on that popularity (Frost 2006).

Fredrick Ward, or Captain Thunderbolt as he called himself, was active in the 1860s and committed his crimes in a large area north of Sydney, mostly in the Upper Hunter Valley region, nowadays known as the home of numerous vineyards, and in the New England tablelands, approximately midway between Sydney and Brisbane. Rather than discussing the historical veracity of the stories surrounding Thunderbolt, my aim in this chapter is to describe to the reader what type of meanings a tourist can draw from experiencing the locations related to Thunderbolt as an attraction. The account is written in first-person voice, and at no stage aims to uncover the core meaning the local community attribute to the attraction, but rather the aim is to produce a subjective description of one tourist's experience of the attraction.

My first encounter with Thunderbolt was on a Christmas holiday that I spent driving from Sydney to Queensland in Eastern Australia. While driving on the tablelands that make up the area called New England, approximately 550km north of Sydney—and about 100 km west of the coastline, I suddenly saw three things that at the time did not have any meaning to me. The first was a sign on the left-hand side of the road simply stating "Thunderbolts Rock" (see Fig. 3-1). The second thing was a large stone boulder on the right-hand side of the road covered in colourful graffiti. The final thing was opposite the boulder, again on the left-hand side of the road, a sign wishing me welcome to New England, and in smaller text underneath "Uralla" "Thunderbolt Country".

Fig. 3-1 Sign denoting Thunderbolt's Rock (image taken by author)

The only thing that really stuck in my mind was the graffiti-covered boulder, as at that time I had written an article about tourist sites and graffiti (Edelheim 2002); I wondered therefore why that special boulder was so popular to *tag* (Rahn 2002, 4). As I entered the township of Uralla, there was another sign on the left-hand side of the road welcoming travellers to "Uralla—Historic Thunderbolt Country". Not long after that was yet another sign, this time on the right-hand side of the road, pointing to "Thunderbolt's grave". Passing the town's tourist office a little later I saw a statue of a man riding a horse, but did not stop at that time to discover anything more about the story (see Fig. 3-2).

Three weeks later, on my way south again, I happened to come to Uralla when the sun was setting, and reluctant to continue driving in darkness I found one of the town's camping grounds and set up my tent for the night. This time I did go to the tourist office, which was closed for the evening, but I picked up a brochure about the town's tourist attractions that was available outside.

Fig. 3-2 Statue of Thunderbolt in Uralla (image taken by author)

I learnt from the brochure that the town traced its history back to 1834—even though I later learned that the town's name was derived from the Indigenous word meaning *meeting place* and thus referred to a history much older than the printed non-Aboriginal account I came across. The brochure stated that Uralla had "originally" been an outback sheep station, and that the shire nowadays had approximately 5900 inhabitants. The town's shops and hospitality enterprises were using the area's (in)famous person to their full extent: there was a "Bushranger Motor Inn", "Thunderbolt Inn", "Thunderbolt Fuels", "Thunderbolt Country Kitchen", "Thunderbolt Gallery", and the road that crosses the town was even named "Thunderbolt's Way" (Uralla Visitor Information Centre n.d.-a). The image I gained of the town, as a first-time visitor, was that the person must have been, and still is, a local hero who had helped the region in a way that would make him a symbol of the area. I will present how the stories surrounding Thunderbolt, and especially his death, have come to symbolise the town in northern New South Wales where his career ended in a gun fight with a police officer.

The small town of Uralla strongly emphasises its connections to Thunderbolt; this emphasis can be found in contiguous texts. That is, texts found in the vicinity of attractions (Leiper 2004), such as the town's promotional material, in the naming of local businesses, and in official memorials at prominent locations in the town. I will in this analysis suggest that the attraction of Thunderbolt is strongly connected to a larger national appeal to romanticise non-Aboriginal history in rural areas by highlighting certain attributes that fit modern ways of thinking and acting (Schlunke 2005, 43). Schlunke suggested that tourist sites need to be simultaneously "opened and closed" (2005, 34). With this she means that in order for places to become interesting to tourists as attractions, the places need to be presented and the visitors must be given some information so that they can self-narrate different scenarios about the sites—thus *opened*. But the meanings cannot be infinite; the visitors need certain parameters in order not to be confused, so the places are thus *closed*. An example of how this two-sided approach works in Uralla is the fact that the story about Thunderbolt has survived more than 130 years and still attracts visitors. The original narratives—the bushranger, his escapades, his partners in crime and life—are all known to an extent, but even though official sources end his life in Uralla, alternative texts see his life and legend continuing elsewhere, and visitors are thus given the opportunity to imagine for themselves alternative narrative closures. My suspicion was that it might tell something about how an Australian cultural identity is formed through the reinforcement of selected narratives in tourist discourse (Pugliese 2002, 10).

Tourist texts relating to Thunderbolt

My research should be understood as a tourist's first point of contact with an attraction that was previously unknown. Many travellers, in an attempt to familiarise themselves with the region visited, access a range of *texts* with information about the destination region. I wish to highlight that my analysis is of Thunderbolt-the-tourist-attraction rather than Thunderbolt-the-person, as these can be seen as two separate entities. The tourist attraction is naturally loosely formed around the person and his life, but the general story that will be presented is not directly related to the person. Rather, the interpretations that exist today revolve around the attraction. I do not try not to promote any one of the narratives above the others in this text. An historical "truth" is not interesting to me here, rather what I want to do is to follow a genealogical approach (Foucault 1991), which shows how different *texts* contain different *stories*, and how each of these—at times contradictory—stories contributes to the formation of a *fabula* in the shape of a tourist attraction.

The description of Uralla in the first text I analysed, a Swedish guidebook; Australien: En Guidebok (A:EG) sets a well defined diegesis for the narrative, and provides a good foundation for a reader who has never previously heard about Thunderbolt:

> The old gold-mining town Uralla is 22 kilometres south of Armidale. Today the town is mostly known as the place where the bandit **Captain Thunderbolt**, alias Fred Ward, is buried.
>
> By the age of 21 he was sentenced to ten years in prison for stealing a horse. After four years he was released, but was shortly thereafter arrested again for horse theft. Three years later, in September 1863, he managed to escape from the prison at Cockatoo Island in Sydney and swim ashore.
>
> Over the following years, he robbed several mail coaches, inns and shops. Thanks to being a good horseman he always managed to escape from the police. Captain Thunderbolt had a reputation of being a real gentleman, especially towards women.
>
> In May 1870 he was finally surprised by a constable Walker, who hit him over the head with a rifle. Captain Thunderbolt died of the injuries. Today he and his horse are commemorated with a statue in the corner of Bridge St./Salisbury St. (Nordström 2000, 181, my translation, emphasis in original).

The A:EG does not include links to any tangible evidence of the story except for mentioning the statue and, in passing, that Thunderbolt is buried in the town. It seems that the only reason Uralla has received an entry in the book is because of the story; several other towns of similar size in the area have not even been mentioned. Uralla is initially described as a "gold-mining" town, essentially not a totally correct label; however, this functions as a marker for the town's "authentic" atmosphere, and is linked to pioneer times when adventures were possible—unlike in modern times.

The diegesis presented in brochures is in general more fragmented; it seems that brochure producers often assume that travellers have a previous awareness of the Thunderbolt narrative and so only excerpts of the full story are presented. The most material about Uralla is in a brochure published by the *Country Colour Group*, called *Country Way Touring Guid*e (Edwards 2003), in a section called "The Heart of New England" which features a combination of information on Armidale, Uralla, Walcha, and Guyra. The utilisation of metaphoric expressions—like the heading's "heart of"—bear strong connotations of the concept of a heartland—a place of belonging, or a place central to people's values and thus often used in nationalistic texts to give readers a feeling of fitting into a place (Moran 2004, 75). A stylised map covers the left side of page eight of the brochure, showing the towns' relationship to each other and informing the reader that the road between Walcha and Uralla is called Thunderbolt Way. The bottom of the page comprises two pictures that are faded into one another; the left-hand image portrays a large church, while the right-hand side is a smaller stone building covered in creepers coloured in autumn red and yellow. There is no caption for either picture, but the reader can guess that the pictures portray the same towns as are described above. The text about Uralla in the upper part of the page reads:

> URALLA—**Famous for the infamous**. Captain Thunderbolt's life of crime ended in Uralla. His grave is in Uralla cemetery and his statue is near the Visitor's Centre. Uralla is truly Thunderbolt country. Displays of the bushranger's life are on show at **McCrossin's Mill Museum**.
>
> **The New England Brass and Iron Lace Foundry** has been continuously operating since 1872. Guided tours show the mesmerizing techniques of yesteryear still used to create iron lace today.
>
> **Going to the chapel**. Autumn is ablaze throughout the region, but Uralla dresses it up like nowhere else. **Gostwyck Chapel**, just 10km east of Uralla, is an adorable little brick church covered with Virginia creeper. In Autumn, the leaves blaze with ruby reds, emerald greens and rich golds, turning the chapel into a dazzling jewel box of nature (Edwards 2003, 8, emphasis in original).

The short part about Thunderbolt at the start of this text is arguably more informative than the other texts analysed in terms of who Thunderbolt was and what his connection with Uralla is.

The reader learns that Thunderbolt was a criminal, and that he died in the town and is buried there, while his life is still on display in a local museum. The text is written in third-person with a neutral tone that is informative and that remains unattached to the message. That the part about Uralla, and New England in general, is so detached in the style of its description makes the text appear more like factual information. From the perspective of learning about Thunderbolt the text seems reliable, and might well form a basis for how the reader constructs an understanding of the attraction space.

The official Visitor Information Centre Internet site—www.uralla.com—has extensive information about what there is to experience in Uralla. The section about Thunderbolt sets out a comprehensive diegesis of his life, starting from his father's arrival in Australia and then, date by date, lists the robberies Thunderbolt was associated with throughout his "career" as a bushranger. Whilst the section about Mary Ann Bugg (Thunderbolt's "wife") acknowledges that she was of Aboriginal heritage, and that her opposition to violence had influenced Thunderbolt's actions as a "gentleman bushranger", it is surprising how little the official web site otherwise discusses the original population of the area. The website recognises that the township's name is probably taken from the Indigenous term meaning "ceremonial meeting place", but makes no further comment about that except to suggest that it is a suitable name for Uralla's location at the crossroads of several highways. There is no explanation of the potential historical linkage between the area's original function and the town's name. The website does not, for example, mention anywhere if the place became a crossroads under colonialism because it already was one for the Indigenous population or if it is rather a fantasy of continuity that is provided in the explanation.

The only other mention of the area's Aboriginal heritage can be found under a link about "*nature*" [sic], where a short description is given of local rock paintings. Osuri and Banerjee (2003) explain that this combination of Indigenous peoples and nature is a reoccurring phenomenon in traditional Western museums. This is also the case in modern tourist attractions such as "*The Outback Spectacular*" at the Gold Coast in Queensland. Dioramas portray Aboriginal people in natural settings essentially constructing them as "backward", while simultaneously consolidating for white Australians "the status of being at the forefront of progressive human history" (145). Robert Dixon suggests that "the Australian colonial tour constituted an iconic narrative that was used to measure the progress of civil society, and that relied on the contrast between Aboriginal 'savagery' and European 'civilisation'" (Hughes-d'Aeth 1999, 51). The colonial tour was often considered a rite of passage for young British men touring parts of the British colonies in an attempt to narrate their own identities as members of a superior world power (Myers 2002). So whilst the website frames the diegesis of Thunderbolt well and informs the reader about the township's chosen main attraction, it simultaneously distances alternative interpretations by silencing them.

Examples from the texts surrounding Thunderbolt and Uralla can be found in several brochures. Uralla is, for example, mentioned on two pages in another regional tourist brochure *The North Coast Monthly Imag* (Melrose 2004). The two texts on the page are different to all the other texts in the brochure as they do not contain one word about what the town currently offers; all text refers to Uralla's past:

> **The History of Uralla**—Uralla's heritage is closely connected with gold, [sic] Although gold had been discovered earlier at Rocky River, a 'deep lead' was found in February 1856 on the side of Mount Jones under the overlaying basalt. Uralla benefited from the 'rush' of over 5000 people to the area and soon became a small township.

> Uralla began life as a shepherd's out station after Colonel Henry Dumaresq chose his squatting run in 1834, which he called Saumarez. The government surveyed a reserve in 1849 at the foot of Nit [sic] Mutton and Mt Beef enclosing a portion of both Rocky and Uralla Creeks. These creeks became a testing [sic] place for the squatters as they journeyed north in search of grazing lands. An accommodation house and inn was soon erected and Samuel McCrossin became the licensee. This inn was on the sight [sic] of the present Bowling Club greens (Melrose 2004, 13).

That this text omits Thunderbolt from its story is not the most significant feature, rather that the text does not include any of the elements that other descriptions of the township contain, and that it does not feature anything that a traveller today can experience is even more significant, taking into consideration that this brochure is produced as a "visitors' guide". The area's Indigenous history is totally ignored here, and the only history served up is of gold rushes, squatters, and the government's land survey, none of which can be tangibly experienced anymore.

It could naturally be claimed that no mention in the aforementioned tourist brochure of the Indigenous people who used to live in the area before the colonial era is better than an incorrect depiction. I would, however, counter that any history that starts from the first signs of non-Aboriginal influence in an area, and relegates Indigenous history to nature, is a hidden attempt to reconfirm the "*Terra Nullius*" argument. Pugliese states: "*terra nullius* is something that filters down into the practices of everyday life. *Terra nullius* functions to render Indigenous heritage and history invisible at the level of heterogeneous practices and sites … at the seemingly banal or inconsequential levels of everyday life, for example, simply going to the cinema or visiting a tourist site" (2002, 14-15). The omission of an Indigenous history is especially surprising as it is placed next to another text where the region's connection with its colonial past is highlighted, namely a story about Thunderbolt.

The section about Uralla in *Lonely Planet NSW* first edition *(LPNSW1)* describes the township in the following terms:

> A small town (population 2300) on the [New England] highway, Uralla is a good place to break the journey. The information centre … is on the highway and is open daily. A **market** is held here on the second Sunday of the month.
>
> **Captain Thunderbolt** (the dashing name taken by young Fred Ward when he turned bushranger) roamed through much of New England in the 1860s, and you'll see many sites claiming to be Thunderbolt's caves, rocks, lookouts, hideouts, etc. Thunderbolt was popular with ordinary people and seems to have performed many acts of kindness as well as

> robbery. He was killed by a police[man] near Uralla in 1870 and there is a statue of him on the highway in the town centre; his simple grave, still sometimes honoured with flowers, is in the cemetery. Whether or not Thunderbolt's body lies in the grave is another matter. There's a persistent rumour that he was spotted in Canada many years after the funeral.
>
> The big **McCrossin's Mill Museum** has some Captain Thunderbolt artefacts ... There's also a **foundry** which has been operating since 1872 and has a small museum ... and **Hassett's Military Museum**. Burnet's Bookshop is a large antiquarian and second-hand bookshop on the main street, open daily.
>
> There is a **fossicking area** with a picnic spot, about five km north-west of Uralla on the Kingstown road. Also in the area is Mt Yarrowyck, with some Aboriginal **cave paintings**. The information centre has detailed information (Murray 1994, 333-334, emphasis in original).

A traveller reading this description understands quickly that Uralla is not a destination in itself according to the author, but is rather a place to have a break in the journey, and before heading on to other places that actually have something worth visiting. It should be noted that more than half the text about Uralla is made up of the Thunderbolt story. While the physical sites related to him—even his grave—are all placed under doubt in regards to their actual relationship with the person, it is quite evident that the story has become the attraction. In other words, it could be suggested that the fiction is the attraction, not the destination in itself. Thunderbolt is portrayed in a positive light, as a person who "perform acts of kindness" and who is still "honoured with flowers", and it is through linguistic formations like these that the focalisation of the story becomes perceptible. This positive depiction is even more highlighted in *LPNSW3* (Harding et al. 2000), the third edition of the same guidebook; while the text has essentially remained the same, some more words have been made bold, and other words have been added:

> ... you'll see many sites, such as caves, rocks, and lookouts, with a claimed association with the rebel. Thunderbolt was a popular hero and seems to have performed many acts of kindness ... there is a **statue** of him on the highway in the town centre; his simple **grave** ... (Harding et al. 2000, 283, emphasis in original).

Why the updated text has added the highly positive words "rebel" and "hero" can only be guessed, though possibly this addition has been made because bushrangers are becoming more popular in Australian society (Walker 2001), something to be proud of. "Rebel", the first word added, might give some clues, as it is typically understand as a term referring to a person who challenges oppressive powers. The sentence could thus be understood as presenting Thunderbolt as a representative of the common people—rebellious against sources of power—in other words Australians against their colonial masters, the English. If this is accepted then it would logically follow that the representative would be viewed as a hero amongst the people. This is a position also held by Turner in his analysis of cinematographic narratives:

> Although the specific meanings which are generated by the use of these 1890s codes, the interests which they serve and the ideologies which they produce may vary, this set of terms and body of myth thus still remain as the definitive signification of Australian-ness; and their invocation has hegemonic potential … The anti-English attitude modulates easily, as it does in our history, into a general suspicion of authority … the paradigm of authority—bureaucratic force aligned against human vulnerability—is English. The Australian versions of authority tend to tacitly condone the larrikin, independent and undisciplined behaviour of the troops (1993, 111-115).

It could thus be claimed that the LP-series is only extending a well-known national myth, easily found in popular films and books. By utilising structures like this, the series is able to weave in a range of nationalist clichés that on their own tend to look ridiculous, but together work as a confirmation of one another and of their joint message (Gibson 1992, 162).

That several books about Australia's most famous bushranger, Ned Kelly, were published at the same times as the LP guides analysed—some of which focused on Kelly's Irish heritage—might also have influenced the authors. The result is in any case similar; a highly focalised narrative is presented to readers who are expected to view the sights found in Uralla in that light. Note also that the physical elements of Thunderbolt-the-attraction have been bolded in the newer version, thus moving the emphasis somewhat away from the story as the attraction and closer to physical attractors. It is, however, also important to point out that this same interest in bushrangers and a "White Australian history" developed in the aftermath of the Mabo decision, "which overturned the founding fiction of terra nullius" (Lambert 2005). It could, in that light, be seen as an even more current anxiety amongst the authors to provide an historic non-Aboriginal basis for the attractions—especially in a township with an Aboriginal name, but with hardly any Indigenous input in the tourist products.

No text describes in detail Thunderbolt's Rock—*LPNSW* refers in a by-line to the fact that places have been given names after Thunderbolt, and there are suggestions on the Uralla Council website that Thunderbolt would have used the rocks as a lookout whilst waiting for travellers to bail up. I, however, did visit the rocks and experienced the text of the site. After parking the car and walking towards the rock I realised that in reality it consists of several large boulders resting on and next to one another. The boulders are on a small mound 7–8 metres off the New England Highway, dominating the landscape. The rest area has no amenities except for a rusty, graffiti covered barrel that acts as a waste container, and a wooden table with benches. The mound, on which the boulders are situated, is covered in grass, short on the side where visitors enter, long and unkempt behind. The most impressive feature of the boulders is not their size but the graffiti; it virtually covers all areas of the rocks that are easily reachable and flat enough to function as a "canvas" (see Fig. 3-3). Some of the graffiti dates back to the 1970s according to the years painted, but the majority are from 2000 and later. I did not find any graffiti that referred to Thunderbolt, but one that in an ironic way said "*Souvenirs KODAK film at the gift store*".

The graffiti on Thunderbolt's rock does not follow any "graffiti etiquette"; there are layers painted over what was there before (Goldstein 2000). A faint "Jesus Loves" can be read in an early layer, but what or who he loves is not visible anymore. There is historic evidence of graffiti from the earliest times of travel. Feifer (1985), Lemorick (1995), and Perrottet (2002) describe graffiti made by tourists in ancient Egypt, Palestine, and Rome. Graffiti is, though, often seen as degradation of a neighbourhood. Piraino (2002) explains how community groups and city councils spend large amounts of money in attempts to stop graffitists from doing their works of "art". Based on this awareness, it was interesting to find that Hailey, in a marketing plan prepared for Uralla Shire Council, discussed the possibility of painting over all the graffiti with a mural of Thunderbolt (2005). Apparently the idea is that council-funded "graffiti" are more appropriate than spontaneous graffiti. Or perhaps it is a reflection of the political and cultural investment in the council where the graffiti would be regarded as a failure to care for the mythic status of the bushranger narrative.

Fig. 3-3 Graffiti on Thunderbolt's Rock (image taken by author)

While watching the granite rocks with the paintings on all sides I was reminded of the Indigenous artist Lin Onus' ironical painting "Balanda Rock Art"—*Balanda* is the word Indigenous Australians in the Northern Territory use for non-Aboriginal Australians. Onus' painting portrayed an Australian landscape littered with empty drink containers and obscene graffiti covering cliffs, and it stood as a stark reminder of the "culture" Balanda represents. At a later visit to the "Aboriginal cave paintings" at the Yarrowyck Rock Art site some 30 kilometres north of Uralla, which is presented as one of the town's "natural attractions" (Uralla Visitor Information Centre n.d.-b), I was surprised how the irony of the two "rock art sites" in the town had not occurred to the tourist authorities.

The interpretive text at Yarrowyck states:

> *These paintings are probably several hundred years old. The tracks, circles, short lines and dots may remind you of bird's feet, people, lizards and even bird's eggs. You may be right, you may be wrong. Unfortunately we will never know the true meaning of the site.*

The text thereafter continues by stating that an Aboriginal elder had given one interpretation of the meaning, and also points out that the paintings are typical for the New England area. Finally, a management paragraph is included that explains how the paintings are protected, and advises visitors to stay behind a barrier and not to touch the art. A similar sign could be made for Thunderbolt's rock regarding the Balanda rock art there:

> *These paintings may be several hundred* days *old. The tracks, circles, short lines, and dots may remind you of names, years, and genitalia. You may be right, you may be wrong. Unfortunately we will never know the true meaning of the site.*

By considering Indigenous rock art as a natural attraction, and Thunderbolt's rock as an historical attraction, the dualist division is again drawn between non-Aboriginal and Aboriginal. The guesswork that the information sign presents underscores the "us and them" mentality—Who are the "*we*" who will never know the true meaning? The non-Aboriginal visitors will not, the assumption therefore being that it is non-Aboriginal people who are tourists. The reason some events and the meaning of some sites for Indigenous people are not commonly known in the non-Aboriginal community might be that they represent taboo subjects, and are therefore not retold outside their own family (Somerville and Perkins 2005, 5). Non-Aboriginal history writing always relies on written accounts and wants clear-cut reports that give only one explanation for events and objects (Craik 2001, 108). Indigenous "rock art" is seen, in non-Aboriginal explanations, as an abstract art form, as an artist's depiction of objects that are separate from the artist's self and the occasion when the art was created. This type of Cartesian dualism is not applicable in an Indigenous context where stories, art, and people are regarded as a whole (Hulley 1999, v).

There were, however, some texts that I came across as a tourist that included an Indigenous history to some extent in the text about Uralla. For example, page nine of a brochure entitled *Around & About Waterfall Way,* published in Armidale, the closest larger town (Cody 2004), concentrates mainly on Uralla, with a third of the text on the page stating:

> As fortune would have it and I am sure that Captain Thunderbolt would agree, Uralla is nicely situated on a junction of three main highways. But rather than contemplate what Thunderbolt might have done in the 1860's we prefer to welcome those travelers that stop over for a coffee and a break. Servicing many places, the original inhabitants, the Anaiwan [sic] and the Moshe tribes called this the 'Meeting place' a distinctly appropriate name then and now.
>
> From East and West, North and South, the junction of roads lies through the middle of Town nestled in the Rocky River tributaries that flow down on to the great Murray-Darling Basin … (Cody 2004, 21).

The use of Thunderbolt in the text is without any explanation about who he was; it is, rather, building on an assumed knowledge amongst readers. Assumed knowledge can feed a feeling of intimacy for people who can relate to the knowledge, but it can equally become a barrier that assures "outsiders" that the attraction is not meant for them (Golden 1996, 233). The only tangible information a traveller without previous knowledge of the Thunderbolt legend would receive from this brochure is the notion of Uralla calling itself "Thunderbolt Country", and that Captain Thunderbolt had something to do with the 1860s. It can thus be suggested that travellers would construct a rather vague narrative about Thunderbolt, if any at all, and that other sources are needed to actually feed travellers' interest in learning more about the attraction.

A positive feature of the text is, however, its emphasis on the original inhabitants of the region by naming the Indigenous peoples who originally inhabited the area. The flipside to that is that the Indigenous people were probably never asked as to the appropriateness of uninitiated outsiders appropriating their word for meeting place for the township. Lambert suggest that Australian films often suffer from the suppression of "the importance and visibility of certain active representation" of Indigenous realities, something he calls a "*filmic terra nullius*" (2000, 8). Even a brief mention, like the brochure text above, would allow for a wider understanding of the continuity of history, and therefore does not create the "*touristic terra nullius*" that is so common in the Australian tourist industry. But, in order to avoid repeating colonial narratives, it must be acknowledged how that history has been shaped, and how much the Indigenous inhabitants have voluntarily been part of a historical continuity presented from a non-Indigenous perspective.

However, if the Indigenous populations are only given a narrow role, such as existing in a pre-colonial historic place as the "name givers" for localities—but are not given any place during early colonial times or even in contemporary time, then there is no actual continuity. Rowe, for example, points out that "Aboriginal people living a traditional tribal existence can be admitted and accommodated [in tourist discourse], but not that of Aboriginal inner urban or outer suburban dwellers" (1993, 265). Morris similarly highlights that visible Aboriginal culture in Australia seems to be produced as a *product* for tourists' consumption (1995, 188, emphasis in original). This strange dualist way of representing Aboriginality can be traced to the uncertainty the majority non-Indigenous population has in finding suitable modern "cohesive models of socially being and belonging" (Potter 2002, 1). By producing memorials and selecting specific heritage attractions, national myths like bush romanticism can be sustained, and the violent colonisation of the land can conveniently be forgotten. The fact that a place that carries an Indigenous name, and an associated history, is not acknowledged in most tourist texts is, the creation of a *touristic terra nullius*.

Conclusion

I set out to demonstrate in this chapter that any tourist attraction holds power as an element in the formation of national identity, not because of the core attraction, but rather due to the meta-narrative it is based upon. A dimension of that suggestion is that physical properties of attractions are less important for visitors, than are the texts and stories that surround the attractions. The aim was to redefine attractions as narratives, and to present what a *touristic terra nullius* is.

The chosen texts analysed in this chapter constitutes only a selection of texts available to tourists to the region, and act as an example of how texts construct attractions as abstract narrative entities. Interpretive signs and brochures, pictures, songs and audio-visual material are all alternative texts beyond the examples here chosen, that might influence visitors' experiences of the attraction and their engagement with the destination before, during and after the visit. However, these alternative texts are beyond the limits of this chapter, but are presented in the full thesis this chapter is an extract from.

A way of visually representing how tourist attractions function as narratives is provided in Fig. 3-4 below. The tourist and the fluid fabula created by the tourist are in singular form because each tourist likely has only one fabula at any one time. The texts about attractions that the tourist comes across whilst travelling, and the stories those texts are referring to, are in plural tense as these are indefinite. The lines between the tourist, the texts, the stories and the fabula are full arrows to demonstrate the tangible nature of this links—the arrow between the tourist and the fabula is dotted to represent that a fabula is simply a fluid memory, and it might change for every new text the tourist comes across.

The analysis I have provided in this chapter has simply been an attempt to capture that fluid fabula of mine. I have, since I wrote this chapter, met non-Indigenous Australians who at different times have called Uralla their homes, and they have added new dimensions to my original naïve tourist fabula. Uralla had, in the 2006 census, 332 Indigenous residents, making up 5.8% of the total population (Australian Bureau of Statistics 2007). The town has also an Indigenous interest body; *Uralla Aniwan Aboriginal Corporation* (Australian Government 2008), and my intention is to build on this research by contacting them and offering these findings to the corporation.

The description in all texts is focused on the events that made Uralla famous, the sites where the events took place being of lesser interest. What makes the site into an attraction is the narrative that surrounds it. This is by no means unique for this attraction; sites of battles, houses that famous people have resided in; and locations that have appeared in films are all examples of attractions that are made up of the texts surrounding them. But also natural attractions such whale-watching or amusement parks are ultimately experienced and appreciated for how they are presented, as examples of ecological wonders or entertainment industries, rather as objects in themselves. To start defining attractions as narratives is thus a logical step.

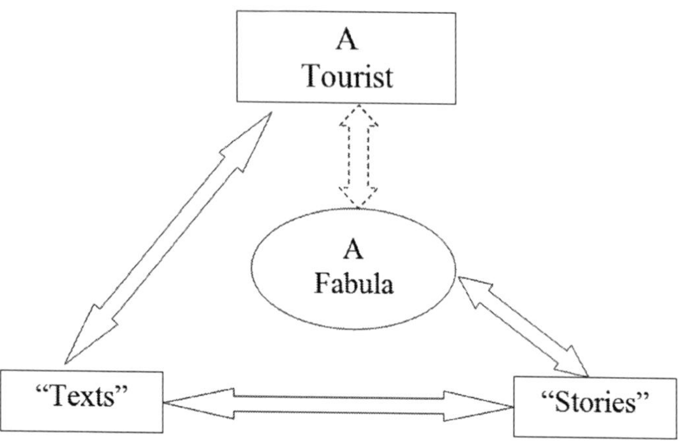

Fig. 3-4 Tourist attractions as narratives

The original Indigenous population in Uralla is mostly referred to in passing as having given the township its name, but no present day attractions are linked to the present Aboriginal population. My hope is that my contact with the Uralla Aniwan Aboriginal Corporation might result in a more visible linkage between the past and the present in tourist texts, and that the *touristic terra nullius* currently created can be challenged or even dismantled. The only reminder of the Indigenous history of the region is the Yarrowyck rock art site outside town, and even this reminder is found under "nature attractions" on the official web site (Uralla Visitor Information Centre n.d.-b). The greatest emphasis the Indigenous population is granted comes from the fact that Thunderbolt's "wife" was of Aboriginal heritage, but many of these texts are formed from a very unapologetic non-Aboriginal perspective with passages that could be described as ethnocentric in present society. No tourist texts that I have come across include the present Indigenous population in any way.

The deconstruction of an attraction as a narrative has here highlighted something I have termed a *touristic terra nullius.* It creates fabulae that visitors, as well as the local population, consume and in which history and importance is always linked to what has happened after non-Aboriginal occupation of the land. The texts nullify Indigenous history and equate it with nature, something that has developed organically without human involvement; the texts also nullify alternative texts by building heavily on accepted myths already circulating in society. The fact that alternative stories exist in society, and can be unearthed if a more inclusive approach is taken, is important. Indigenous histories do continue, and should be sought out and incorporated when possible, but tourist discourse in general closes them out by concentrating on only one particular way of telling their stories.

CHAPTER FOUR

CONTESTED GROUNDS: INCOMMENSURABILITY AND THE PARADIGMS OF WHITENESS*

COLIN SALTER

How does whiteness manifest and reposition itself in campaigns and actions promoting respect and recognition for First Peoples? By whiteness, what I refer to is the socially constructed and at times unmarked standpoint that has exhibited a historically shifting boundary. The shifting of this boundary is itself an indicator of how whiteness has acted to reposition itself over time. Whiteness' relational categorisation is defined not by what one possesses, rather by what one does not. Being (loosely) defined by negation assists in rendering whiteness unmarked to those who benefit from its privileges—even to those working for a fair and just society. Exploring the means and avenues through which whiteness manifests itself in actions taken in support of social justice issues highlights the pervasiveness of whiteness and the scope of the task of working towards a fair and just society. In this chapter I reflect on some of the actions taken in support of the *Sandon Point Aboriginal Tent Embassy* (SPATE) in New South Wales (NSW), Australia, and the Haudenosaunee at the Red Hill Creek valley in Ontario, Canada, over the last two decades. Whereas the campaign in the Red Hill Creek valley has ceased, the future of the Sandon Point area is still heavily contested. In engaging with actions taken by white supporters at Sandon Point, I draw from my experiences in struggle alongside participants in the amorphous *Sandon Point Community Picket* (herein the Picket) for the last six years, and my friendships and past actions alongside those who would become members of SPATE. I similarly draw from what participants in the Red Hill Creek valley dispute (members of the Haudenosaunee and white supporters) shared with me during a year-long research trip to Ontario in 2006-7.

James Tully has explored the politics of recognition, emphasising that cultural recognition involves acknowledgement of culture on its own "terms and traditions, as it wants to be and it speaks to us", which is "in their own cultural forms … languages and customary ways" (1995, 23-24). The importance of this with respect to the actions taken at Sandon Point and the Red Hill Creek valley can be seen in the function of technological discourse, of western rationality and scientificity, which is an aspect of whiteness often non-considered. Jacques Ellul (1990; 1964), a French philosopher of technology, has explored discourse on science and technology in contemporary society—what he has referred to as a technological society. Considered alongside cross-cultural studies of western science, technology and society, engagement with the implications of technological discourse provides a means to expose contemporary manifestations of whiteness (see, for example, Watson-Verran and Turnbull 1995). The roots of technological discourse can be traced back to the period known as the Enlightenment, where notions of progress were linked to the proliferation of *rational* science and technology. Rationality was constructed as gendered, with standpoints framed as emotive equated with the feminine as subjective and inferior (Haraway 1989). The implications of this are seen within and separate to whiteness.

The prioritisation of rational western technoscience[1] that emerged from the Enlightenment is facilitated by "a scientific hierarchization of knowledges" (Smart 1986, 164). Manifestations of whiteness embodied in Enlightenment-based rationalisations and differentiation of knowledges can be seen in how white support was provided to SPATE and the Haudenosaunee. Aileen Moreton-Robinson has exposed a direct implication of such hierarchisation through what she has termed *Terra Knowlegius*: the positioning of "other" knowledges as unowned and available for appropriation (1999, 42). Deference to archaeology locates such hierarchisation of knowledges, a manifestation of whiteness in contemporary society that requires consideration. In this chapter I provide a context-specific examination of such a manifestation. What I explore are contested grounds in challenges to whiteness in the actions of supporters at Sandon Point and the Red Hill Creek valley that locate a paradox: a "doubleness of whiteness". This consideration provides a means to reflect on Jane Haggis' question of "how can we be anti-racist and agents of white race privilege at the same time?" (Haggis 2004, paragraph 24, 5).

Sandon Point

Sandon Point is located between the coastal villages of Bulli and Thirroul, part of the northern suburbs of the Illawarra region, approximately 70 km south of Sydney on the east coast of NSW, Australia (see Fig. 4-1). The 61-hectares the Sandon Point area encompasses forms part of last green corridor linking the Pacific Ocean to the Illawarra Escarpment, long used for public recreation. Local residents refer to events including what has been described as "the first united feminist action in Australian History", linked to the actions of striking coal miners in January 1887, and the infamous 26 September 1818 vigilante action known as the *Minnamurra Massacre* as symbolic of the area's history (Organ 1990, 100-104; Organ and Speechly 1997, 120).[2] Members of the local community raised concerns regarding the future of the area in the early 1980s when construction of two 20 metre high coal bins were proposed. This led to the formation of the *Northern Illawarra Residents Action Group* (NIRAG) in 1984 (*Thirroul: timeline,* 2008). This was the first of a number of contentious proposals for the area, with community concerns rooted in the perceived environmental, historical and social impacts of the respective proposals. Concerns heightened following a decision by Wollongong City Council, the local authority, to rezone the Sandon Point area as "residential" in 1997.

It was long, if not widely, known that the Sandon Point area held significance to local Aboriginal people, being described as "a black burial ground" as early as 1887 (Organ 1990, 343). The emergence of broad community concern regarding the cultural significance of the Sandon Point area has its roots in the partial exposure of skeletal remains in the fore-dunes of McCauleys Beach on 7 March 1998 (Fullagar and Donlon 1998). Whilst remains were similarly uncovered in the same location in the 1950s and 1974, it was the response of the local Aboriginal community that galvanised this broader community interest (various 2002; T. Stephenson 2002, personal communication 14 February).[3] Around the time of the exposure, and the Council decision to rezone, members of the local community became aware that Stockland Trust Group, a multi-billion dollar corporate entity specialising in real estate speculation, were acting to acquire land at Sandon Point. In May 2000 the *McCauleys Beach at Sandon Point: Masterplan Report* was released. In December, coals were transported from the sacred fire at the long-running Aboriginal Tent Embassy in Canberra (the national capital of Australia) and SPATE was established. Uncle Guboo, senior lore man of the Yuin Nation, declared "no

Fig. 4-1 Sandon Point locale

houses" be built at Sandon Point and renamed the area Kuradji (McInerny 2001).[4] The area was renamed as Kuradji in reflection of the remains exposed in 1998, which formed part of an intact ceremonial burial site predating the Egyptian pyramids (see unknown 2002b).[5] In early 2001 the Illawarra Aboriginal Land Council declared the area a site of state significance. The local community responded to the establishment of SPATE and the release of the masterplan report, producing a *Proposal for an Illawarra Regional Foreshores Park* (Miller and Miller 2001).[6] Following a direct request, SPATE presented a letter to the NIRAG detailing the granting of permission "to come onto country to establish and staff a 24 hour-a-day Peaceful Protest Camp". The *Community Picket*, as it became known, remained onsite until the evening of 23 February 2006, when the structure was destroyed by arson.[7]

Broad opposition to the residential proposal, and support for SPATE, achieved widespread coverage in February 2002 with what became known as the Valentine's Day blockade. On 11 February armed security guards arrived, met by members of the local community. Heavy machinery arrived at 5 a.m. the following morning. Blocking the entrance to the Sandon Point area were several strategically parked cars and hundreds of local residents. The stand-off continued until police moved in and arrested more than 50 people on 14 February. Later that day, a court injunction sought by SPATE was granted, ending the stand-off (Korzy 2002). Following the Valentine's Day blockade and a number of other direct actions, focus shifted to legal challenges and official channels seeking to stop the proposed residential estate. In September, the Cunningham bi-election resulted in local resident and member of the Community Picket Michael Organ becoming both the first Federal Member for the Australian Greens and the first person elected to the seat that was not a member of the Australian Labor Party (ALP). Less than a month later the ALP-controlled state government announced a Commission of Inquiry (COI) would be held into the future of the select parts of the Sandon Point area. The Commissioners' findings vindicated many of the concerns raised by the local community (Cleland and Carleton 2003). The COI was followed by a number of other reviews—including further investigation of Aboriginal Significance (see Hill 2005; Huys 2006). Of note was the forced consideration of the significance of the area to Aboriginal women after members of the local community had repeatedly raised concerns about its non-consideration. Previously refusing to hear community concerns, the NSW Planning Minister agreed to meet with representatives from the Picket following a public demonstration on 30 July 2006.[8] The representatives of the Picket invited by the Minister organised for two Aboriginal women to attend. This was the first time that Aboriginal women had received any Ministerial consideration.

Whilst the physical structure of the Community Picket has long since gone, the broader community continues to struggle to protect the area and support SPATE in its struggle for respect and recognition.[9]

The Red Hill Creek Valley

The seven kilometre long Red Hill Creek valley is located in the industrial east end of Hamilton, Ontario. Hamilton is located adjacent to the western tip of Lake Ontario, in the region of southern Ontario, Canada, known as the Golden Horseshoe (see Fig. 4-2). In recognition of the area's aesthetic and recreational value, Thomas Baker McQuesten, appointed to the Hamilton Board of Parks Management in 1922, worked towards a vision of "Large park areas in surroundings of natural beauty" for the city. In 1929, with widespread public support, the "City of Hamilton purchase[d] 260 hectares (645 acres) of land in the Red Hill Creek Valley to preserve as natural parkland"—the first of a number of acquisitions in the valley (unknown 1990). McQuesten prophesied that these areas would become "the most cherished possession of this city in the future" (Best 1991, 67). As the city grew in size, expanding eastwards towards and then beyond the valley, pressure on open spaces increased. As the city grew, the Red Hill Creek valley became the last remaining green corridor linking Lake Ontario with the Niagara Escarpment, and "the centrepiece of 700 hectares of linked publicly-owned parkland in the industrial east end of Hamilton" (various 2004).[10] Of 14 creeks that passed through the city prior to European settlement, the Red Hill Creek was the last remaining in close to is natural state.

Controversy over the future of the valley emerged some 20 years following the initial land acquisitions. The source of controversy was the emergence of first proposal for a road through the Red Hill Creek valley, with such a road seen as "capable of being developed into one of the finest scenic drives in the country" (Peace 1998a, 221-2). A subsequent 1956 traffic and transportation study recommended an expressway be established (Smith 1956). Controversy over the expressway was fuelled with the City's official position fluctuating between preservation of the valley and construction of an expressway over the next four decades (Peace 1998a, 227-8). A rise in environmental consciousness in the 1970s facilitated growing opposition to an expressway in the valley, with as many as 20 different community groups and non-governmental organisations working to preserve the valley's natural and cultural heritage. In 1974, reflecting public sentiment and rejecting provincial pressure for an expressway, the City Of Hamilton passed the following resolution unanimously:

> That this council make its clear its intention to retain the natural character of the Red Hill Creek valley and to maintain permanently its present natural state (Peace 1998a, 227).

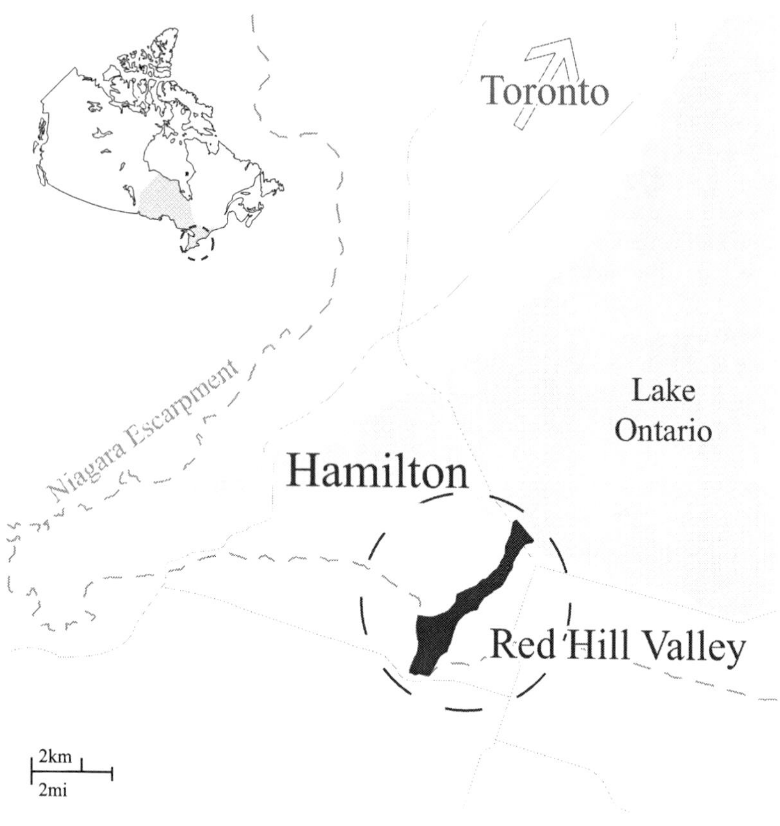

Fig. 4-2 Red Hill Creek valley locale

Further Provincial pressure led to a change in the City's position in 1977, with the city proceeding with feasibility studies for an expressway through the valley. Public opposition continued and two petitions totalling 11,000 signatures were handed to elected officials in 1979 (Peace 1998a, 231).

An official ground-breaking ceremony for an expressway through the valley was held on 26 June 1990. The dispute increased in prominence with the unexpected results of the provincial election. In December the newly elected New Democratic Party (NDP) provincial government, which won all six seats in the region and formed government in Ontario for the first time, "made the unexpected announcement that it was withdrawing its funding for the expressway" (Peace 1998a, 234):

> the Red Hill Creek Valley is irreplaceable, it is a natural asset that Hamilton must not lose (Transportation Minister Ed Phillip, quoted in Peters and Poling 1990).[11]

In 1991 members of the Conserver Society of Hamilton and District, worked with local residents of Hamilton's east end to form the *Friends of Red Hill Valley* (herein Friends).[12] Members of Friends acted to increase awareness of the valley's rich history, its aesthetic and recreational values.[13] Friends established annual events in the valley, assisted with the creation and repair of recreational trails, organised clean-ups in the valley. They also highlighted, and expressed concern regarding impacts on the significance of the area to the Haudenosuanee.[14]

The City continued works on interchanges and linkages separate to, though required for, the expressway in expectation of a change in provincial government. In late 1995 a conservative provincial government was elected and funding for the expressway was restored (Peace 1998a, 237).[15] As the City pushed ahead with the expressway, Friends became increasingly active in opposing the expressway. Members organised letter writing, petition campaigns and protest events. The dispute heightened significantly when the clearing of some 40,000 trees and the blasting of a passage through the Niagara Escarpment for the expressway were announced. Following a request in early August 2003, the Haudenosaunee granted a permit to representatives of Friends and others who agreed to abide by the Kaianara:kowa (the Haudenosaunee Great Law of Peace) to camp in the valley as a part of their actions seeking to prevent these works (unknown 2003). This action altered to dispute significantly:

> ... I feel that finally you people are coming out and helping us take care of the land. It's been a long time in coming and thank you very much ... 500 years.
> We've been waiting for you. Instead of destroying, you're trying to keep it as it is. Thank you very much again (Carol Bombarry, Haudenosaunee, in Iotzova 2004)

The issuing of the permit coincided with members of the Haudenosaunee "assert[ing] their jurisdiction on the Red Hill in Hamilton through posted notices" (General 2003).[16] The term "posted" refers to legal notification of the Red Hill Creek valley as Haudenosaunee land, in line with existing treaty rights outlined in the Guswenta (kas-wen-tha), or Two Row Wampum (1613) and the Nanfan Treaty (1701). The Guswetna, considered the basis for all other treaties, contains two rows of purple beads that

> symbolize the path of two vessels, travelling down the same river together. One, a birch bark canoe, will be for the Indian people, their laws, their customs and their ways. The other, a ship, will be for the white people and their laws, their customs and their ways. We shall each travel the same river together, side by side, but in our own boats. Neither of us will try to steer the other's vessel (Chief Michael Mitchell, quoted in Tully 1995, 128).[17]

The Nanfan Treaty, "A 'Deed from the Five Nations to the King, of their Beaver Hunting Ground,' made at Albany, New York, July 19, 1701", established ongoing usage rights over a vast area within which the Red Hill Creek valley is located (L. Green 2006, personal communication October; Orkin and Klippenstein 2003; Royce 1899).

The lighting of a sacred fire and erection of a Roundhouse and Longhouse in the valley on 10 August galvanised broader community support and fostered increased respect and recognition of Haudenosaunee treaty and cultural rights. Supporters deferred to Haudenosaunee expressions of these rights, often made by Haudenosaunee women. Many were arrested in making a stand alongside the Haudenosaunee. Opposition to the expressway continued after the Roundhouse and Longhouse were destroyed. As further areas of the valley were cleared, and the expressway moved closer to completion, Friends shifted its emphasis towards building on and maintaining the solidarity and respect that shared experiences had fostered: "keeping the spirit alive" (Brown 2003; Iotzova 2004).

The Red Hill Valley parkway was officially opened on 17 November 2007 (unknown 2007a).

Manifestations of whiteness

How whiteness has manifested itself in the actions of white supporters at Sandon Point and the Red Hill Creek valley has been influenced by how SPATE and the Haudenosaunee have expressed respective connections to the two areas. With these expressions having transformative impacts on white supporters and the actions taken, differences in expression require an introduction. First Peoples connections to the land differed significantly at each locale, with spiritual connection invoked by the local Aboriginal community at Sandon Point whereas legal rights enshrined in Treaties were referred to by the Haudenosaunee.

SPATE continues to emphasise direct spiritual connections to the Sandon Point area since time immemorial. This ongoing connection is encompassed in the area forming part of a dreaming trail and meeting place for Aboriginal peoples from north, south and west, referred to as "not unsung land … of ancient and sacred significance" (Ruben Brown, cited in Navin and Officer 2001c).[18] The context of interview that conducted this description is important. It was recorded for an archaeological study funded by Stockland. Uncle Guboo, reflected on the imposition of such double-binds in the context of opposition to logging at Gulaga in the 1970s:

> These are sacred matters which must be kept quiet … We only talk about these things when we are forced to do so in order to protect our sacred sites from ignorant white people to whom only the dollar is sacred (quoted in Byrne 1984).

In contrast to solicited accounts, the establishment of SPATE provided a direct expression of the area's significance, a challenge to the proposed housing estate and the assumptions embodied within its constructions of nature and culture. When members of the local Aboriginal community have been forced to substantiate expressions of significance to prevent further desecration, locations with verifiably high concentrations of physical indicators of prior occupation have been provided. White supporters have referred to the presence of these physical indicators as *proof* of the significance of the Sandon Point area.

At the Red Hill Creek valley, the Haudenosaunee invoked legal rights emanating from both the Guswenta and the Nanfan Treaty as a direct challenge to the proposed expressway—the former stressing non-interference, the latter enshrined usage rights over the valley itself. References were also made to prior usage separate to the Nanfan treaty, including "former Iroquois village sites [and] burial grounds" located in the valley (General 2003).[19] The valley also formed the hub of three main trails used by the Haudenosaunee, and later as roads by settlers (Burghardt 1969; Peace 1998b). At the time of European settlement, the valley was considered territory of the Mississaugas and acquired by the Crown in the "Between the lakes Purchase" in 1784.[20] The Purchase included more than one million hectares extending from the Niagara Peninsula and Lake Erie through to the head of Lake Ontario (Graymont 1972, 284). This treaty with the Mississaugas was made to provide previously promised reparation to the Haudenosaunee for "all their lands south of Lake Ontario as far as the banks of the Hudson [coming] into the possession of the United States" in the American War of Independence:

> 'Now is the time for you to help the King,' General Haldimand had said to the assembled redskins in 1775. 'The war has commenced. Assist the King now, and you will find it to your advantage. Go now and fight for your

> possessions, and, whatever you lose of your property during the war, the King will make up to you when peace returns' (Wood 1915, 99-100).

The Red Hill Creek valley, whilst falling within the Purchase, fell outside the Haldimand's Proclamation specifying a tract of land six miles on either side of the Grand River located to the south-west, granted to the Haudenosaunee (Johnstone 1964, 50-51).

The establishment of SPATE and the posting of notices in the Red Hill Creek valley locate the roots of transformations in the actions of white supporters. These two events were mobilised by the Picket and Friends in their long running oppositions to the proposed housing estate and expressway, respectively, and came to shape both how and what support was offered. By aligning their opposition with respect and recognition of SPATE and the Haudenosaunee, albeit expressed and acted upon differently, white supporters relationally framed their actions in contrast to the proponents of the respective proposals. Stockland and the City of Hamilton, proponents of the housing estate and expressway, respectively, were portrayed as acting contrary to acceptable community standards. In dualistically framing their actions, supporters legitimised their own standpoints via what Fiona Nicoll has identified as the "performative assumption of perspective":

> The deployment of perspective depends on one's proximity to power. Thus, relatively powerful parties in relationships marked by differences of race, class, gender and sexual preference are able to stake a claim to the 'proper perspective' in any given situation (Nicoll 2002, paragraph 18).

Supporters of SPATE and the Haudenosaunee were able to lay claim to "proper perspective" in two ways, both of which are constructed within relationships of power. These relationships were facilitated by white supporters' proximity to relative power within the disputes over the respective proposals. The more generalised of the two ways in which supporters were able to claim perspective is marked by the construction of race and culture: white supporters were able to mobilise the relative authority of whiteness whereas SPATE and the Haudenosaunee were not. The subjective positions of SPATE and the Haudenosaunee were perceived as subjective, the standpoint of supporters were not: whiteness as position-less or free from the impacts of interpretation that other cultures *suffer* from was maintained (Haraway 1991, 189; Turnbull 2000). The second means through which white supporters were able to claim proper perspective is located in their *good intentions*, drawing from the broad community support for SPATE and the Haudenosaunee (see Haggis

2004). The standpoint of supporters, and the supportive actions taken, were diametrically contrasted with the actions of the proponents of the respective proposals. Supporters were able to mobilise relative authority via drawing from the widespread community concerns and opposition to the housing and freeway proposals. It is upon this base that claims of proper perspective were staked. In mobilising this relative authority, supporters were able to frame the actions of proponents in a negative light. Paralleling mechanisms of whiteness, the actions of white supporters were constructed as relational, oppositional, to the respective proposals. Supportive actions were defined, to a degree, by what they were perceived as *not* being: culturally inappropriate. The performativity of supporters acted to construct a good anti-racist/bad racist binary (Riggs 2004). The actions of supporters (the "good") were contrasted with those of the proponents (the "bad").

Contrasting with the "moral posture of disinterest" mobilised in denials of First peoples sovereignty that Nicoll refers to, explain the performative assumption of perspective, supportive actions at Sandon Point and the Red Hill Creek valley were positioned as holding the moral high ground (Nicoll 2002, paragraph 18). Proper perspective was relationally constructed and expressed as a challenge to the perceived bias of proponent-funded studies: studies required for regulatory approval. In mobilising this perception of bias to challenge the legitimacy of respective proposals, the constructed good/bad dualism was reinforced. These actions had the potential to expose the structural violence of whiteness, yet tended to normalise these relations and render them largely unquestioned. Deference to archaeological investigations locates the most visible manifestations of this.

To challenge the (perceived) bias of the proponent-funded archaeological investigations at Sandon Point, the Picket raised money to fund a review of existing studies. Dr Peter Hiscock, a respected (white) archaeologist from the Australian National University, was engaged to examine the reports of Kerry Navin and Kelvin Officer. Navin and Officer had undertaken a number of investigations at Sandon Point, preparing reports used to support the housing proposal (Navin 1993; Navin and Officer 2001a, 2001b, 2001c). Hiscock's findings challenged those produced by Navin and Officer. The report produced by Hiscock provided an archaeological assessment of the Sandon Point area that supported significance as expressed by SPATE (Hiscock 2002). What emerged was a debate between Hiscock and Officer as "experts" (see Officer 2002).

The debate that ensued between Hiscock and Officer focused on constructing respective boundaries of what was considered valid archaeological technoscience. Hiscock and Officer attempted to discredit each other's work, to demarcate their own science from what was inferred as non- or pseudo-science in the others. Thomas Gieryn has labelled this type of debate as boundary work—the ideological demarcation of fields of knowledge:

> Boundary-work occurs as people contend for, legitimate, or challenge the cognitive authority of science—and the credibility, prestige, power and material resources that attend such a privileged position. Pragmatic demarcations of science from non-science are driven by a social interest in claiming, expanding, protecting, monopolizing, usurping, denying, or restricting the cognitive authority of science (Gieryn 1995, 405).

Boundary work occurred in the actions of Hiscock and Officer as they contended for legitimacy, challenging the credibility of each other's analysis. Officer described the approach of Hiscock, an academic, as outside the bounds of accepted, standard and practical practice within consulting archaeology (Officer 2002). Hiscock criticised the findings of Navin Officer as not unambiguous, inconclusive and generalist (Hiscock 2002). Both were attempting to expose "bad" science in the other's work: the cognitive authority of western technoscience was not challenged, rather, who was the beholder of the specific expertise was at issue.

Aileen Moreton-Robinson (2004) has more explicitly located the political nature of boundary work in an analysis of the High Court of Australia's Yorta Yorta decision in December 2002 (*Members of the Yorta Yorta Aboriginal Community v Victoria* [2002] HCA 58 (12 December 2002)). Several boundaries were constructed that acted to naturalise and reinforce what Moreton-Robinson identifies as patriarchal white sovereignty. Patriarchal white sovereignty is a complex phenomenon and constitutes a "regime of power that derives from the illegal act of dispossession … most accurately reflected in the form of the Crown and the judiciary". This "foundation of the nation state … confers patriarchal white sovereignty on its citizens" through disproportionate means, with this unbalanced ability to exercise power being circumscribed through marked categories of "[r]ace, class, gender, sexuality and ableness". The "possessive logic" of patriarchal white sovereignty is based on exclusion, being a "rationalisation rather then a set of positions" that results in a perpetuation of "control and domination" (Moreton-Robinson 2004, paragraph 5). The assumptions and rationalisations of patriarchal white sovereignty provided means for Gleeson, Gaudron, McHigh, Gummow, Kirby, Hayne and Callinan to claim proper perspective in their respective findings, with the majority decision upholding the Federal Courts rejection the Yorta Yorta's seeking of a determination of native title. The collective judgement of Gleeson, Gummow and Hayne locates a similar demarcation to that constructed in the boundary work of Hiscock and Officer—that of objectivity:

> as Curr's evidence did not concur with the testimony of many claimants regarding traditions and customs, his testimony could be considered credible and compelling (Moreton-Robinson 2004, paragraph 11).

The findings of Edward Micklethwaite Curr, an amateur ethnographer who had squatted on Yorta Yorta territory and published his *Recollections of squatting in Victoria* in 1883, were contrasted with the oral historical accounts of the Yorta Yorta, their supporters and "experts" as "unreliable witnesses prone to embellishment, emotion and self-interest" (Moreton-Robinson 2004, paragraph 17). Curr's account was relied on "almost exclusively" by Olney in his Federal Court decision—the precursor to the Yorta Yorta's appeal to the High Court (Land 2002, 6).[21] Curr's reflections were positioned as objective, whereas Moreton-Robinson notes,

> where the oral evidence is not corroborated by the white written record, it is unreliable. Despite the basis of Curr's evidence—his observations and judgements as an amateur ethnographer—being outside Yorta Yorta culture, his written words are granted authority (2004, paragraph 18).

What was rationalised to constitute valid evidence was predicated on white terms, unjust terms. Authority, the proper perspective, was positioned with Curr, and reciprocally divested from the Yorta Yorta oral histories and their supporters, removing any potential threat to patriarchal white sovereignty:

> In the High Court's majority decision, concepts such as 'tradition', 'continuity' and 'connection' became socio-legal constructs that took on a pseudo-objective form, which holds no meaning or place in the law of the Yorta Yorta (Moreton-Robinson 2004, paragraph 23)

Substantiation became based on "conceptions of white property ownership" with authority positioned with "legal interpretation by and of white men": "The High Court's judges' claims to objectivity served to mask the racialisation of their knowledge and its partiality" (Moreton-Robinson 2004, paragraph 17, 24). Paralleling whiteness' ability to negate self-definition, Yorta Yorta traditions and culture were defined by Callinan by what they are not, drawing from a construction of First Peoples and their cultures as fixed in the past and unchangeable. Moreton-Robinson locates the same double standard in respect to dispossession:

> Under the law of patriarchal white sovereignty, when a thief steals someone's property ownership is not assumed or inferred as being ceded to the thief. To the contrary the law preserves ownership and guarantees return of the property to the owner (2004, paragraph 12).

Similar to the Justices' demarcation of evidence in the Yorta Yorta decision, Hiscock and Officer's actions constructed a good/bad archaeology dualism analogous to the good anti-racist/bad racist binary mobilised by supporters. The outcome was that the cognitive authority of science was left unquestioned. The boundary work of Hiscock and Officer, separate to and framed within white supporters' deference to archaeology at Sandon Point, rendered "bad" science as the problem—not the colonial assumptions implicit to the respective investigations. Similarly, the positioning of objectivity to suit certain conceptions in the Yorta Yorta decision rendered patriarchal white sovereignty unquestioned. White supporters' deference to archaeology to "assess" the significance of the area's to First Peoples left the scientific hierachisation of knowledges and its epistemic violence unchallenged. In engaging an archaeologist, colonial assumptions were further normalised, counter to white supporters' aims of fostering and promoting respect and recognition. Similar issues are present in the Yorta Yorta's use of an anthropologist, recognised in part by Moreton-Robinson:

> the Yorta Yorta prepared for trial by collecting as much evidence as possible to substantiate their case. They carried out extensive archival and field research as well as employing experts to assist in developing different forms of evidence (Moreton-Robinson 2004, paragraph 1).

At both Sandon Point and in the case of the Yorta Yorta, the engagement of a (white) expert was an attempt to gain recognition for First Peoples' cultural knowledge through association with the cognitive authority, credibility and prestige of western technoscience. At the Red Hill Creek valley, white supporters similarly deferred to the cognitive authority of western technoscience. The findings of previous studies—some of which were not undertaken to meet with regulatory requirements for the expressway proposal—were referenced to give credibility to claims of cultural significance.[22] Further archaeological surveys, focussing on physical evidence of prior occupation, were also recommended (see Wilson 1998). A significant difference in the actions of white supporters at

Sandon Point and the Red Hill Creek valley is located in when and why archaeology was deferred to. Whereas at Sandon point, the cognitive authority of western technoscience was central to assessments of significance, at the Red Hill Creek valley the City had appeared to seek direct Haudenosaunee input. With the City appearing to recognise of Haudenosaunee Treaty rights, white supporters deferred to Haudenosaunee expressions of the areas significance. When it was perceived that the City ceased to recognise Haudenosaunee Treaty rights, white supporters increasingly referred and deferred to archaeological accounts. In seeking to mobilise the cognitive authority associated with archaeology to challenge to actions of the city and promote the area's significance, the actions of white supporters reinforced as opposed to challenged whiteness, undermining their previous emphasis on Haudenosaunee expressions of the areas significance.

Jim Wilson's "The Aboriginal Presence: the Red Hill Creek valley 9000 B.C.-1615 A.D.", published in Walter Peace's (1998c) *From Mountain to Lake: the Red Hill Creek Valley*, a self-described biography of place, provides a representative example of how significance and place came to be expressed by white supporters: This chapter examines the archaeological record of Aboriginal Activity in the Red Hill Creek Valley (1998, 105).

Framing First Peoples' activities as an "archaeological record", similar to how Yorta Yorta culture and tradition was defined by Callinan, positions First Peoples' cultures as set and fixed in the period pre-settlement. Through deferring to, and shifting focus to archaeological history as opposed to Haudenosaunee expressions of culture and significance, white supporters legitimised a construction of Haudenosaunee culture based on both physical *artefacts* and white terms.

Locating Haudenosaunee culture as in the past demarcates it from contemporary society, with contemporary society positioned as has having progressed beyond the primitive past (Ellul 1990, xv-xvi, 182; Tully 1995, 65-6). This is visible in Wilson's description of a 1963 archaeological investigation as "a salvage project" (1998, 116).[23] Salvage of artefacts, *saving* them, was perceived as a means of protection via the rational application of technoscience (Ellul 1990, 182). Not only are white ways and knowing and seeing positioned as superior, they provide the means and ability to protect the remnants of other, inferior, cultures for all to spectate on (see Haraway 1994; Morton 2004). In deferring to archaeology to analyse the archaeological record, supporters positioned archaeology as more than just a means to understand the past. Wilson expressed this as:

> The discipline of archaeology is uniquely positioned to enhance our understanding of the peoples, times, and events about which there is no written records (Wilson 1998, 105).

Emphasis on written records, alongside physical artefacts, adheres to Enlightenment interpretations of technology and progress that act to position "the non-European 'other' … lower in development and earlier in time: in a state of nature, primitive, rude, savage, traditional or underdeveloped" (Tully 1995, 65-6). Oral histories are not afforded the credibility, prestige or relative authority of written accounts. Such positioning is inherently subjective and contrasted with the position-less and universally applicable scientific method. The cognitive authority, credibility and prestige of western technoscience was further normalised, irrespective of intent. Whilst supporters of the Haudenosaunee made no explicit demarcation between "good" and "bad" science, the constructed boundary between science and other knowledge systems was normalised by their actions (see Turnbull 2000; Watson-Verran and Turnbull 1995).

Whilst there are differences in the breadth of respect and recognition afforded by supporters at Sandon Point and the Red Hill Creek valley, it is with deference to the constructed authority of archaeology that an answer to Haggis' (2004) question can be located. White supporters at the Red Hill Creek valley positioned themselves as anti-racist in deferring to and seeking to emphasise respect and recognition, yet their actions positioned them as "agents of white race privilege at the same time". In deferring to archaeology, the actions of white supporters at both Sandon Point and the Red Hill Creek valley normalised assumptions of western technoscience, seeking to garner credibility for oral expressions of significance via association with scientific expressions, rather than seeking to challenge the epistemic violence of such assumptions.

Aileen Moreton-Robinson has defined structural factors that act to normalise and perpetuate the scientific hierarchisation of knowledges in contemporary society, a function of established power relations:

> Students in academia are taught as though they can know everything. They are taught to believe that all knowledge is available to them for the taking and is knowable. Knowledges that exist outside the realm of white western knowledge are perceived as being available for appropriation because they are positioned as unowned and therefore free. Scientists ask Indigenous people about their knowledge … this theft is based on a white fiction that I term 'Terra Knowlegius' (Moreton-Robinson 1999, 32-33).

Moreton-Robinson defines this theft in the patenting of bush medicines and other marketable aspects of First Peoples' knowledge as one that fails to properly attribute the source of the knowledge of provide compensation for its use.[24] Assumptions underlying *Terra Knowlegius* have broader and far-reaching implications. As with the double standard identified in the dispossession of First Peoples' lands and theft of land "under the law of patriarchal white sovereignty", First Peoples are patently aware of the appropriation of their knowledges. This was expressed by Uncle Guboo, who was directly involved in the establishment of SPATE and participated in the Valentine's Day blockade, and Aboriginal women at Sandon Point (Huys 2006) as well as Norman Jacobs of the Haudenosaunee (see Howard 2002).

White supporters' deference to archaeology illustrates that cultural knowledge can be appropriated under the guise of good intentions. The normalisation of this what Moreton-Robinson has labelled *Terra Knowlegius* has led to the perception that it is only through the rational application of western technoscience that other cultures and knowledges can be assessed and examined to their full potential. These assumptions are driven by the notion that First Peoples "cultures can 'add to western knowledge'": the perception that expanding white ways of knowing and seeing will benefit all peoples and knowledges (Smallacombe 2000). Candice Metallic and Patricia Monture-Agnus (2002) have exposed "deep and complex" concerns with "cultural outsiders determining the value of Indigenous systems" in their examination of "the landmark case of Delgamuukw v. B.C." in Canada. The evidentiary burden is placed on First Peoples, to a standard imposed by western scientific rationalisations of what counts as knowledge. The presumption is that an area is not significant (or land title does not exist) until proven otherwise: a claim must be made and assessed against the cognitive authority of western technoscience and its experts. The standards imposed are unjust, being restrained to and constrained by colonial language and assumptions. Assessment of cultural significance is predicated on and maintains such terms. James Tully has exposed some of the implications:

> Even if such proof is successful in the future, the structure of the process further entrenches the taken-for-granted colonial relationship in which the claim is presented (Tully 2000, 48).

Supporters' deference to archaeology at Sandon Point and the Red Hill Creek valley do not escape these assumptions, irrespective of intention. In deferring to archaeology "we are merely left with too much of the same-old same-old, colonialism" (Metallic and Monture-Angus 2002, paragraph

64). The performative assumption of perspective, via framing the actions of proponents as inappropriate and, relationally, the actions of supporters as the binary opposite, renders aspects of whiteness unmarked and unchallenged. In facilitating the boundary work of Hiscock and Officer, white supporters at Sandon Point assisted in restricting debate to within the bounds of western technoscience—via construction of good/bad archaeology dualism. In deferring to archaeology white supporters at Sandon Point and the Red Hill Creek valley, contrary to promoting respect and recognition, framed their attempts at counter-hegemonic actions and support within colonial language and assumptions.

Escaping the paradox?

Given the intent of respect and recognition, yet the implications of the actions taken in support of SPATE and the Haudenosaunee, can such a paradox be overcome? Jane Haggis (2004) has reflected on the "doubleness of whiteness" that renders supportive actions as also complicit in its perpetuation—as the examples explored here have illustrated. In reflecting on a keynote speech by Indigenous legal theorist Dr Irene Watson, Haggis responded to a rhetorical question posed about the actions of supporters of First Peoples struggles (and academics) assuming they are "free to roam" (see Watson 2005). What is required, Haggis suggests, is a recognition of complicity in whiteness and

> On the one hand, a recognition that, from the indigenous perspective, whiteness is an essentialising claim to possess that is incommensurable to indigenous ontology. On the other, a continuing effort to reveal, analyse and challenge the multiple ways in which whiteness is internally incoherent, differentiated, hyphenated (Haggis 2004, paragraph 27).

James Tully has highlighted incommensurability in "the first and often overlooked step on any inquiry into justice". This is the language of the enquiry itself which is often unjust and not "capable of rendering the speakers their due" (Tully 1995, 34). Discourse on science and technology, shaped by rationalisations of colonial whiteness, is a clear example. Constructed ideological perceptions of non-European cultures as underdeveloped positions these cultures as in a lesser state, a state of nature. In "think[ing] of human history as a history of progress" contemporary society is relationally framed as having moved forward, progressed. First Peoples' cultures are located in the past: as fixed, unchanging and unchangeable. This contrasts with the accepted changeability and malleability of whiteness. These are the roots of colonial assumptions Ellul has identified in technological society: the source of the pervasive and ubiquitous discourse that equates scientific and technological rationality (technological advancement and implementation) with progress (Ellul 1990, xvi).

Deference to archaeology at Sandon Point and the Red Hill Creek valley has constrained attempts to foster respect and recognition within technological discourse. First Peoples' cultures were positioned as in the primitive past. In mobilising the cognitive authority, credibility and prestige of western technoscience to support and promote the cultural significance of the respective areas, supportive actions normalised the scientific hierachisation of knowledges. This is boundary work. Demarcation is fundamental to the maintenance of *Terra Knowlegius* and the language of enquiry is unjust—counter to the intent of respect and recognition in the actions of supporters at Sandon Point and the Red Hill Creek valley. Challenging the singularity implicit in such demarcation provides a means to challenge contemporary manifestations of whiteness, and making possible

> a vision of 'together in difference' ... a togetherness based on the recognition of incommensurability (Haggis 2004, paragraph 28).[25]

PART II:

MEDIA AND REPRESENTATION

CHAPTER FIVE

DISTANCED SUFFERING: PHOTOGRAPHED SUFFERING AND THE CONSTRUCTION OF WHITE IN/VULNERABILITY*

ANNA SZORENYI[1]

As I write, the media are filled with images of famine in Ethiopia, a famine which is being presented as a kind of traumatic return of the one in 1984-5. In drawing attention to this fact, the reports not only imply that the world has not improved, but show that the very reporting of images of starving, suffering bodies is in itself a tradition, that the singular crisis events of televised disaster constitute a media genre. The suffering and deaths of particular people, each a singular event, rapidly become multiplied into a multitude—repeated suffering, repeated disaster, repeated news reports.

Photography has played a significant role in the development of traditions for reporting suffering. And its use for this purpose has also always been controversial. Does photography provide an ideal means of appealing to conscience and provoking compassion or empathy? Or is the circulation of images of people in their moments of need and pain insensitive and exploitative? Does the surfeit of images of atrocity simply numb the viewer, causing what has commonly come to be called "compassion fatigue"? Is it wrong to make art out of other people's misfortune? Such arguments and related critical discourse have been circulating for several decades now (see for example Sontag 1979, 2003; Rosler 1989; Solomon-Godeau 1991; Kleinman and Kleinman 1997; Spelman 1997; Boltanski 1999; Moeller 1999; Cohen 2001; Reinhardt et

* This chapter was first published as Szorenyi, A 2009 'Distanced Suffering: Photographed suffering and the construction of white in/vulnerability' *Social Semiotics* 19.2. http://www.informaworld.com. Reprinted by permission.

al. 2007), while in the meantime the market for images of suffering goes on increasing in popularity, catered for by documentary films, photographic exhibitions, news media, and the internet.

This chapter seeks to intervene in the debate by considering the position of the spectator invoked by this circulation of images. Centrally, it proposes that the discourses through which "concerned photographs" are circulated address particular audiences and, in doing so, help to constitute those audiences. Who is looking at these pictures? Who is expected to look, and will their subject position affect what they see? I argue here that the way in which images are presented implicitly invokes a privileged audience, interpellated into a mode of spectatorship which Alison Ravenscroft has called "white spectatorship" (2004), a particular mode of relationship to the visual presentation of the world. My proposition is that this form of spectatorship also involves a particular mode of relationship to suffering itself. This is not to say that only white people view pictures of suffering, but rather to ask whether responding to the pictures in certain ways works to create an "us" interpellated as white. In other words, does the cumulative iteration of the "suffering other" work to interpellate the viewer precisely as a member of a community whose primary relationship to suffering is as *spectator,* as those whose relationship to suffering might be summarised as: we can take for granted that our life does not include certain kinds of suffering; we are at a distance from those who do suffer; the visible suffering of others is available to us as a means to reflect on our own lives and subjectivities?

To describe this interpellated subjectivity as "white" is to do two things: firstly to challenge its unmarked nature as "normal", and instead to place such a relation to suffering in question as not natural or inevitable but rather maintained by particular social structures and, secondly, to make clear that there is a racialised history to the viewing positions around which such spectatorship is organised.

The "concerned photography" debate

The debate about photographing the poor has been ongoing since the beginnings of the socially concerned genre of documentary. One of its most prominent early practitioners, James Agee, himself wrote:

> It seems to me curious, not to say obscene and thoroughly terrifying, that it could occur to ... an organ of journalism, to pry intimately into the lives of an undefended and appallingly damaged group of human beings ... with a conscience better than clear, and in the virtual certitude of almost unanimous public approval (quoted in Goldberg 1995).

Many of the positions in the debate about documentary photography have been advocated at one time or another by Susan Sontag. In *On Photography* (1979) she discussed the unprecedented political effects of photographs of the Vietnam War, and celebrated the power of images to spur people's conscience. At the same time, however, she doubted whether such effects would be repeated, arguing that since then images of atrocity have become so commonplace that they no longer had any effect: "In the last years of the twentieth century", she wrote, "concerned photography has done at least as much to deaden conscience as to arouse it" (Sontag 1979, 21). This view has remained extant; Vicki Goldberg, for example, writing in the *New York Times* on the occasion of a series of exhibitions of photographers specialising in documenting the poor (Jacob Riis, Dorothea Lange, Ben Shahn, Sebastião Salgado), wonders "[i]f hearts have grown indifferent under a barrage of images, do photographs in fine surroundings salve the conscience by stirring up just enough sympathy to assure us we have paid our emotional dues?" (1995).

Almost 20 years later, in her *Regarding the Pain of Others*, Sontag (2003) found reason to revisit her earlier pronouncement, arguing, much as Susan Moeller (1999) does, that it is not so much the *number* of photographs that forestalls "conscience", as the way they are framed by the media, which discourages involvement or reflection, and encourages passive consumption. Sontag seems now to find her own earlier arguments predictable and limited. It is, she says, "absurd" to make generalisations about audience responses. Nonetheless she implies that there are structural divisions between certain kinds of audiences. Descriptions of the jadedness of an audience dissociated from suffering are just that, descriptions of a particular audience which has no first hand experience of atrocity. "There are hundreds of millions of television viewers who are far from inured to what they see on television. They do not have the luxury of patronising reality" (Sontag 2003, 99).

Recently Judith Butler has responded to Sontag, taking into account her scepticism over images, but also arguing that Sontag herself is the best example of how such images *can* promote an ethical response. Butler argues that the photograph

> … can and must represent human suffering, teach us how to feel across global distances, establish through the visual frame a proximity to suffering that keeps us alert to the human cost of war, famine, and destruction in places that may be far from us geographically and culturally (2005, 824).

Going on to state that the photograph "brings us close to an understanding of the fragility and mortality of human life" (2005, 825), Butler is clearly working from the argument she presented in *Precarious Life* (2004), where she argued that the fact that all humans are vulnerable, potentially exposed to one another, at one another's mercy, might form the basis for an ethics. Utilising Levinas' concept of "the face", she argues that a perception of the precariousness of others, and of ourselves, can prompt reflection on the ways in which we are beholden and ethically responsible to one another.

> … each of us is constituted politically in part by virtue of the social vulnerability of our bodies—as a site of desire and physical vulnerability, as a site of a publicity at once assertive and exposed. Loss and vulnerability seem to follow from our being socially constituted bodies, attached to others, at risk of losing those attachments, exposed to others, at risk of violence by virtue of that exposure (2004, 20).

Photographs of suffering, in this context, can provide a means by which those who are privileged might be prompted to reflect on vulnerability, their own and others'. Such reflections might, she hopes, have forestalled the more aggressive American reactions to 9/11, which were based on a refusal to mourn and an attempt to violently defend against the "threat" of vulnerability.

Butler is careful to point out that not just any image will provoke this ethical response. In *Precarious Life*, she points out that photographs which present an expected stereotype will not present the vulnerability which evokes the Levinasian face. In "Photography, war, outrage", she notes that it is necessary to read not only the photograph, but the "frame" through which it is presented, and to feel outrage when that frame is designed to *prevent* the perception of the "human cost of war" (Butler 2005).

In order to examine such frames it is necessary to consider not only the content of the images under discussion, but the discursive contexts in which they circulate. As Allan Sekula pointed out many years ago, photographs are generally not read as isolated documents. Rather they are encountered as embedded in texts, which provide a context of meaning through which they can be interpreted (1981, 16-17). Such textual framing inevitably draws on familiar discourses and understandings of the world. Photographs are framed by the format in which they are presented, by captions, by accompanying articles, prefaces, commentaries, by wider critical and scholarly discourse, and by an array of historical and social assumptions.

Examining the debate around the ethical effect of photographed suffering, it becomes evident that much of it is framed around the question of "distance". Luc Boltanski's book, *Distant Suffering: Morality, Media and Politics* (1999), for example, deals with the issues faced by "a spectator of the distant suffering of others" (rear cover). It is this distance, Boltanski argues, that defines what Arendt calls a "politics of pity" (Boltanksi 1999, 3), where the sight of an individual's suffering is linked to a generalised call to action. This politics is based not on "action", but on "spectacle". The paradigmatic structure of this politics is thus one of "observation of the *unfortunate* by those who do not share their suffering, who do not experience it directly and who, as such, may be regarded as fortunate or *lucky* people" (Boltanski 1999, 3; his emphases).

Theorists of documentary photography point out that such a structure of spectacle is intrinsic to documentary photography. Abigail Solomon-Godeau (1991), for example, argues that documentary photography does not merely "represent" social divisions, but reproduces them, positioning its subjects as lower down in a visual hierarchy emphasised by the camera's monocular perspective. Similarly, Martha Rosler refers to the way in which documentary photography presents "powerless" people to a group addressed as "powerful" (1989, 321). Documentary photography thus both takes place within, and reproduces the structure of, the politics of pity.

Interestingly, however, Boltanski emphasises that although the problem of distant suffering is often described as being a product of the mass media, the politics of pity as Arendt describes them were invented before photography, gestured to in the work of Rousseau in the mid-eighteenth century, and fully apparent during the French Revolution. Locating the paradigm in this way make it clear that the "distance" involved in the politics of pity is not simply a physical or geographical distance. Rather it is a distance between "classes" of people, defined according to their "condition", specifically according to whether they belong to the group of the "lucky" or that of the "unfortunate" (Boltanski 1999, 4-5). Hence the politics of pity can work in situations such as the French Revolution where the two groups, although socially separated, are located in the same nation.

I emphasise this point because many discussions of the problem of distant suffering take a literal interpretation of "distance" for granted. For example, Terence Wright describes the workings of the mass media's presentation of suffering writes:

> There is an inverse relationship between numbers and distance. To gain news coverage, not only are larger numbers of victims required as one

> moves further away from home, but the sensitivity in representing the plight of others diminishes as geographical and cultural distance increases (2004, 99).

Thus it has been said of the United States media that "One dead fireman in Brooklyn is worth five English bobbies, who are worth 50 Arabs, who are worth 500 Africans" (Mueller 1999, 22, quoted in Wright 2004, 99).

According to this theory, differentials in the ways in which suffering and death are represented are often taken to be organised around geographical distance; those who are near "us" and like "us" get more attention and their stories are told more "sensitively" than those who suffer or die on the other side of the world. But this posited relationship between physical proximity and media visibility (and between physical proximity and cultural familiarity) is missing something. The routes along which images of suffering are circulated on this map are far more complex than simple linear measures of degrees of proximity to a centre. This should be obvious from an Australian perspective, where "Australia" followed by "America, England, the Middle East and Africa" is certainly not a list of increasing geographical distances (and Asia does not even figure in the list). Rather, this list could be described as being organised according to what Goldie Osuri and Subhabrata Bobby Bannerjee have called "white diasporas"; a loyalty expressed at the level of the nation-state between those who feel they share a common, "Anglo" heritage (2004, 151).

"Distance" thus seems often to work as a way of obliquely referring not simply to mileage, but to the structure of the world instituted and maintained by colonialism and its accompanying racial discourses. Such racial discourses, while inevitably manifesting slightly differently in different locations, share across the white diasporas an understanding of "white" culture as civilised and superior, constructed in opposition to "primitive" racialised others.

As theorists of whiteness have pointed out, a recurrent set of *looking* relations accompanies such shared constructions. Observations of the colonised proliferate as if from a neutral observer's viewpoint, a viewpoint which itself never appears within the frame of vision, taking for granted its separation from the field of view and its right to look, assess, categorise, and order. Stuart Hall (1990) calls this the "white eye". The white eye relentlessly produces essentialist and stereotypical views of racialised others, and also relentlessly reproduces its own status as master of the field of view, as though the world were its territory. This is, as Hall points out, "the history of slavery and conquest, written, seen, drawn and photographed by The Winners" (1990, 14). As the position from which other stereotypes have been constructed and elaborated, the stereotype of whiteness itself is left outside the frame. This works to disavow the specificity of whiteness, positioning it as the unmarked "norm" against which other "races" are measured (Dyer 1997), and disavowing the way its construction depends on images of the "other" (Mercer 1991).

In the realm of "concerned photography", such racialised looking relations are mapped onto essentialised relations to suffering. The result is neatly summarised by Arthur and Joan Kleinman (1997), who draw attention to the imperialist structure of the viewing position offered by famine pictures:

> One message that comes across from viewing suffering from a distance is that for all the havoc in Western society, we are somehow better than this African society. We gain in moral status and some of our organizations gain financially and politically, while those whom we represent, or appropriate, remain where they are, moribund, surrounded by vultures. This 'consumption' of suffering in an era of so-called 'disordered capitalism' is not so very different from the late nineteenth-century view that the savage barbarism in pagan lands justified the valuing of our own civilization at a higher level of development—a view that authorized colonial exploitation (Kleinman and Kleinman 1997, 8).

As Kleinman and Kleinman imply, the mass reproduction of variations on this theme of the suffering "other" has a strongly essentialising effect, working to create an impression that suffering in the "third world" is inevitable, expected, and somehow intrinsic to life in certain regions. As Sontag puts it in considering the photographic record of famine and genocide in postcolonial Africa,

> These sights carry a double message. They show a suffering that is outrageous, unjust and should be repaired. They confirm that this is the sort of thing that happens in that place (2003, 64).

Allen Feldman's work on the "trauma aesthetic" (2004) is instructive here. Feldman notes that there is an extensive historical tradition of putting the bodies of black people on display in order to invoke compassion, which can be traced in the United States to the display of scars on the bodies of slaves during the Abolitionist era, and is currently manifested in the mass circulation of images and stories of trauma as evidence of human rights violations. Helpful as they may be in human rights campaigns, to the extent that they incorporate individual suffering into regimes of truth and evidence, these commodifications of trauma also participate in a discursive tradition in which certain bodies are made to perform as "evidence" of their own suffering. The problem with this, as Feldman notes, is that it installs a particular arrangement of visual perspectives, in which "other" bodies become hypervisualised, while viewers are offered a mobile, but always hierarchically superior, viewing position. Feldman reminds us that Edward Said has named this subject position as one of "flexible positional superiority", a defining feature of imperialist subjectivity (Feldman 2004, 186; Said 1995, 7). Repetition of this structure comes to discursively define black bodies as those who suffer, and invisible white bodies as those who watch, and as those who own, and choose whether or not to deploy, compassion.

In what follows I am interested not only in how such photography essentialises and stereotypes those it portrays, but in whether and how it interpellates a particular, implicitly racialised audience, who are themselves addressed as having a particular, essentialised, relationship to suffering and vulnerability. One productive way to do this might be to examine particular images in terms of the way in which they visually position the viewer, through, for example, the "monocular" perspective identified by Solomon-Godeau. In this chapter, however, my analysis proceeds not by way of looking at photographs so much as by looking at comments from reviewers and the kind of "expert" commentators who supply prefaces and introductions to such collections. Such framing comments are both examples of particular individuals' responses to the photographs and, in their role as exemplary responses, or expert commentary, positioned as suggestions to future audiences as to what the pictures do, should do, or are intended to do. Hence they constitute moments in the public discourses which inevitably frame, circumscribe and direct responses to the images and, in doing so, work as interpellations: offering viewers not only avenues of response, but identities, through which to confront the pictures. I take myself as an example of a potential respondent to such interpellations, a white woman who, when reading the word "we", feels invited to belong to the community of viewers so addressed, is able to take up this invitation without significantly problematising her identity and, in responding to this call, takes up a particular orientation towards the world.

The passages I use as examples here are from, firstly, Sebastião Salgado's *Sahel: The end of the road* (2004), a collection of black and white photographs which show people living (and dying) through the famine in East Africa in 1984-5. This work has been variously credited as initiating both Salgado's career as a highly respected documentary photographer, and intensified debates about the ethics of photographed suffering. It was originally published in French in the late 1980s, but the

2004 edition I discuss here is the first English language edition, published some twenty years after the images were taken, a temporal distance which adds to the trope of physical distance discussed above. I also use an example from a book called *Forced Out* (Kismaric 1989), published by Human Rights Watch and the J.M. Kaplan Fund, in association with William Morrow, W.W. Norton, Penguin and Random House. This book presents a series of photographs (including some by Salgado) and written commentaries illustrating the experiences of displaced people in conflict areas around the world. And finally, I consider a commentary on the book *Exodus*, a collection of photographs of refugees produced by the European photographic agency Signum (1997). I have chosen to quote extracts from these particular texts not so much because they are themselves exemplary of the genre of photographed suffering (although *Sahel* is arguably exactly that), but because the particular passages I quote are not only representative of the invitation to "white spectatorship" that I am discussing, but also particularly useful as illustrations of the rhetorical structure and choice of images associated with this form of spectatorship.

As suggested by the list of publishers for *Forced Out*, such collections of photographed suffering circulate transnationally. Rhetorically, they seem to address a unified audience, named usually as "we" and, as I shall show below, implicitly identified as privileged. But the fact of transnational circulation does not ensure a universal audience. Rather, the context in which these texts are produced, and in which their addressed audience is assumed to live, can be equated with the "White Diaspora". Historically, methods of colonisation and racial discourse, including visual technologies for the production of images of the colonised "other", have been exchanged within this diaspora, rendering the discourses of photographic suffering legible in different locations. At the same time, such a circulation of habits of viewing does not render whiteness homogenous. The address offered by these texts is inevitably interpreted differently in different locations, inflected by specific local histories and resulting local understandings of suffering, and local constructions of racial identities. Such specificities are easily lost, precisely because the unmarked nature of the construction of whiteness positions it all too readily as simply "the" position to which the texts are addressed.

Rather than participate in such homogenisation, and yet without attempting to account for the myriad potential local inflections which might occur in the different contexts in which these texts arrive, this chapter is written from a particular perspective, asking after the rhetorical effect of the discourse of photographed suffering in a particular colonised nation: Australia. The resulting analysis, which reads commentaries written in the United States and Europe ostensibly directed towards a homogenised and privileged transnational audience for their meaning in Australia, may seem geographically idiosyncratic, but mirrors the trajectory taken by such texts within the white diaspora. In addition, as should become clear, a recognition of local distributions of suffering is not only important in understanding the effects of the discourse of photographed suffering, but in countering its production of a homogenised viewing audience. If, as I argue here, the trope of distance works to *disconnect* the subject position of privileged white viewer from an ethical and practical engagement with suffering, repositioning the discussion in a particular context can work to problematise that disconnection and turn the gaze closer to "home".

White spectatorship

Alison Ravenscroft identifies visual imagery of the Vietnam War as one of the crucial sites through which she and others of her generation in Australia were interpellated as white. Ravenscroft proposes an understanding of television as a "technology of whiteness", and the "act of spectatorship" as one of the ways in which children are interpellated into whiteness: not only was the content of television overwhelmingly white, but child viewers were explicitly addressed as part of this world—as white children (2004, 513). "We were being named as white viewers. In hundreds of tiny moments, when we were called before the image of the television, we said 'yes' to this whiteness" (2004, 514). The possibility of identifying with the images of Vietnamese children, burning with napalm, was thus complicated by racialised discourses. "The act of watching these images within the racialized discourses of television means that viewing them was part of the processes through which we were brought into our white subjectivities. From this viewing position, we were learning to regard these other children as racialized objects" (2004, 515).

Ravenscroft goes on to emphasise that whiteness is constructed differently in different contexts, and that in "postcolonial" nations it is inevitably constructed in opposition not only to "black", but particularly to "Indigenous". I will return to this point at the end of this chapter. For now, I would like to take up the idea of "white spectatorship". What particular forms of white spectatorship might be instituted by photographs of suffering, and the discourses surrounding them?

Whiteness as orientation

As defined by Althusser, interpellation takes place through an *address*. Indeed, the very premise of concerned photography in its different manifestations is that the photographs will confront the viewer with some kind of address, a statement which demands or encourages a particular response. This is the assumption behind both the practice of concerned photography, and the critique of it, the latter so often revolving around the question of whether the desired for response will be achieved. The effect on the audience, and the subsequent precarious pathways to a possible effect on the situation, are the *raison d'etre* of such photography.

To whom is this address directed? Who does it interpellate as its intended audience? Often the comments which frame photographic texts are instructive about this:

> This book is both prophecy and history, a gift from those who have witnessed the unspeakable future in our time. We must not ignore their testimony. The world that most of us know is not the real world, which is why we need a book like *Forced Out*. There are no other books like it. And that it exists at all, that it is so painfully eloquent, so heartbreakingly beautiful, is cause for hope. You will read it and weep, to be sure, but you won't stop there. That's how powerful it is (Russell Banks, quoted in Kismaric 1989, rear cover).

This review is clearly addressed to a specific audience, which is nonetheless defined only as "most of us". The majority of those reading this book, it appears, are those who do not live in the real world, presumably because the world that this "we" lives in is *not* unspeakable, not structured by violence, war, persecution, flight and displacement. In other words, this statement addresses viewers as those who are *not* suffering in the way that those represented in the book, through photography and testimony, *are* seen to be suffering.

This form of address suggests not only that the audience to the book are "comfortable" (at least until they read the book), but that they can take this safety and security, this privileged status, for granted. If the collection of photographs of suffering others works to essentialise that suffering and position the depicted as constitutively victims, statements such as this position the audience at the opposite extreme of a binary division of the world into suffering (visible) and not-suffering (addressed, but invisible). The very assuredness of this address; its comfortable "most of us", works towards positioning this spectator as white, since as many authors have commented, a defining feature of whiteness in contemporary discourse is its unmarked position, in which its privilege is marked out as "normal", "natural", and "taken for granted" (Dyer 1997, Frankenberg 1993, Moreton-Robinson 2000).

In her article "A phenomenology of whiteness" (2007), Sarah Ahmed has argued that whiteness can be understood as involving a particular *orientation* to the world: the kind of orientation described by Husserl as the "natural standpoint", where the world appears "more or less familiar" (Husserl 1969, 101, quoted in Ahmed 2007, 151), as a range of objects more or less in reach.

> By reading the objects that appear in Husserl's writing, we get a sense of how being directed towards some objects and not others involves a more general orientation towards the world (Ahmed 2007, 151).

The "corporeal schema" as described by Husserl, being based upon a sense of the world as "familiar" and available to be grasped, can be described as a "body-at-home". Using the work of Frantz Fanon, Ahmed points out that for those who are not white, this corporeal schema is complicated by a "historic-racial schema" (Fanon 1986, 111, quoted in Ahmed 2007, 153). To the extent that the world is arranged around the needs of a white body, the corporeal schema understood in isolation from a historic-racial schema is a white corporeal schema, a form of embodiment available only to bodies whose sense of being "at-home" is not problematised by the many processes of exclusion that position non-white bodies as racial objects. Such a corporeal schema renders the world available in particular ways, and positions particular things "within reach". As Ahmed puts it:

> If the world is made white, then the body-at-home is one that can inhabit whiteness. As Fanon's work shows, after all, bodies are shaped by histories of colonialism, which makes the world 'white', a world that is inherited, or which is already given before the point of an individual's arrival. This is the familiar world, the world of whiteness, as a world we know implicitly. Colonialism makes the world 'white', which is of course a world 'ready' for certain kinds of bodies, a world that puts certain objects within their reach (Ahmed 2007, 153-4).

Inhabiting this "at-home-ness", in such a way that the corporeal and sensory being described by phenomenologists is not interrupted by one's positioning as a racialised object defined by colonial histories, is hence a privilege more easily experienced by those who are accepted by these historic-racial schema as white. As Ahmed points out, this is not so much to say that phenomenology simply "describes" white bodies, as if the whiteness of the bodies pre-existed their location in corporeal and racial schemas. Rather it is to say that it describes bodies which are able to inhabit a certain unmarked position, in which their orientation towards the world is given as a position of "at-home-ness".

> If we said that phenomenology is about whiteness, in the sense that it has been written from this 'point of view', as a point that is 'forgotten', then what phenomenology describes is not so much white bodies, but the ways in which bodies come to feel at home in spaces by being orientated in this way and that, where such bodies are not 'points' of stress or what we can call stress points. To make this point very simply: whiteness becomes a social and bodily orientation given that some bodies will be more at home in a world that is orientated around whiteness (Ahmed 2007, 160).

This understanding of whiteness as an orientation—a "point of view"—is useful for considering the position of the white spectator. It is not that the quotation from *Forced Out* given above is explicitly directed towards readers with white skin. It is that it is directed towards those who can take a certain kind of "comfort" and "familiarity" with the world for granted—those who might perhaps take themselves as a "centre" from which photographed lives of "displaced" people, people *without* comfortable centres, appear "distant".

> Race becomes, in this model, a question of what is within reach, what is available to perceive and to do 'things' with ... Whiteness might be what is 'here', as a point from which the world unfolds ... (Ahmed 2007, 154).

Such a description of whiteness suggests that it is not so much a matter of skin colour as of a combination of privilege and orientation. To Ravenscroft's description of the interpellation of the white subject as spectator, we can add a sense of the way in which this position as viewer and consumer of the non-white world is confirmed by daily experience. The comfortable experience of having what one needs and desires within reach, close to the centre from which one sees and acts, aligns with the sense of being the visual "centre" for which the world is offered up for viewing. To be addressed, interpellated, as the intended spectator is to be addressed in one's position *as* comfortable. If Husserl's particular attitude to the world is constituted in part by the proximity of his writing desk, the position of white spectator might be said to be constituted by the proximity and availability of the television and the coffee table book, mediums designed for those who are in their "lounge rooms"—lounging, perhaps in the comfort of "their own homes".

For the spectator who responds to this interpellation as comfortable, privileged, not-living-in-the-real-world, this comfort is brought into awareness and at the same time linked to a particular visual perspective, in which comfort is "here", at the centre and what occupies the visual field is "distant" suffering, located on the periphery, the horizon of sight and significance. The suffering is distant not only because of its geographical location but because of its experiential remoteness from the feeling of comfort.

The orientation towards the world constituted by this mode of white spectatorship does not promote the kind of identification with another's vulnerability that Butler hopes for. It is not so much a mode in which suffering is brought into "proximity" by the image, but one in which the *distance* of suffering is brought into view through its juxtaposition with the comfort in which these spectators are expected to find themselves.

It is interesting that in the passage quoted above Banks seems to experience this sense of distance as being not only spatial but temporal. The book is a "prophecy", and the people depicted are those who "have witnessed the unspeakable future in our time". This structure in which some people live in the real world of the future, but "we", that is, "most of us" live in "our" unreal time of the present, maintains not only a physical, but a temporal, distance between those who suffer and those who do not. In addition, that the future is *called* "the future" shows that the point of view from which time is being measured remains clearly that of "us", the viewers, not that of those depicted who presumably, from their own point of view, live in their own present.

Even so, the fear that "our" future may be like "their" present is clearly stated as a warning. The distance between comfort and suffering, the distance between "us" and "them" may not hold; indeed if the book is a prophecy then that distance seems destined to collapse. The experience of white spectatorship paradoxically invokes anxiety in those it addresses as relaxed-by-definition—but manages this anxiety through the trope of distance.

White discomfort

What does it mean to respond to such an interpellation as white spectator, to feel that one belongs to the "we" who can take comfort for granted, and whose sense of comfort is then challenged by the viewing of the photographs? Here I acknowledge my own subject position as a white spectator, and take myself as a model. What is my response to these pictures? What do I feel, leafing through Sebastião Salgado's *Sahel: The*

End of the Road, for example? My reaction is not so different from those I read in the commentaries I have quoted here. Although I have studied these pictures, I find myself reluctant to begin, each time, engaging with them again. I am confused by the presentation of so many images of bodies close to death. I find myself looking for myriad ways to deny them, to distract myself. I become fascinated by the pattern of someone's ribs, by the sinking of their eyes. I experience a violent wish to reject the images, to insist that the world is not like this, that I should not have to see this. I feel that I am watching a kind of pornography, bodies, near naked, reduced to their physical needs, hovering on the boundary between life and death. And then in the midst of these bodies I become hurt by the facial expression of a teenager who reminds me of someone in my family. I am confronted again and again by how little I know, about these people, their lives, how they feel and think, what they say to each other. They appear utterly silent, walking through the desert, gazing into the distance, accepting the ministrations of doctors, wrapping dead children. I have, on occasion, been known to cry at certain images, but not these. They are too extreme, tears seem too trivial a response. They make me want to do something unprecedented. A liberal desire to be a *good* viewer, *not* to ignore, *not* to deny, to *respond*, makes me want to proclaim the importance of these pictures, to show the right response, perhaps in compensation for my discomfort at my voyeuristic fascination. But what? No courses of action present themselves, indeed the images don't inspire agency, if anything they make me feel shell shocked, powerless, stunned into silence. It all seems too ... well ... too *far away*. Outside time, outside my own experience.

All of these reactions add up easily to a wish to reject these images, and this may be a source of my desire to criticise. It is easy to see why Salgado is so often accused of doing something unethical, and at the same time easy to blame him—to shoot the messenger when perhaps what is really disturbing is the vision of the world he presents, a world I'd rather not live in. Perhaps what makes me angry is that I know that I don't live in that world, and that in five minutes time I will get up and make a cup of tea, eat lunch, write a paper, go on living in the comfortable "unreal" world I like to think of as "mine", and the images will fade. If these images have made me aware of the comfort in which I live, they have also succeeded in making me feel, at least temporarily, uneasy, uncomfortable about that comfort.

Other writers also discuss the disruption they feel to their sense of normality when viewing the images. Christopher Morton, for example, reviewing *Sahel* for *Anthropological Quarterly*, writes:

> Whichever way you approach it, this is a deeply affecting book. You may well feel a sinking sensation in the pit of your stomach, like heavy turbulence. You may find yourself taking unexpectedly long daydreams into nowhere as the immediate concerns of your day suddenly take on a desperate triviality. You may catch yourself giving out deep, long, heavy breaths, as you slowly summon the will, not to move on to another page, but to leave the agony of the one you are with (Morton 2006).

I find myself in this description, too. If I take the time to really *look* at this book I also feel shocked, immobile, reduced to an inanimate speechlessness. There is something about the images in *Sahel* that seems to slow time and reduce my sense of agency to a vague sense of inert physical existence, to a state before words. Like Morton (assuming he experiences the state he describes), I become strangely aware of my physical existence, of the weight of my body. I feel a sense of distress that I can neither articulate nor do anything about, a kind of ache that does not resolve, a sense of being confronted with something larger than my comprehension.

This kind of "empathic unsettlement", as Dominick La Capra (2001) would call it, might be productive. While it is not the same as Fanon's historic-racial schema, it does seem to disrupt the sense of agency, of the world being within reach, that characterises the comfortable corporeal schema Ahmed defines as white. But will it "teach [me] to feel across distances", as Butler hopes? It seems possible that it could make white viewers aware of our privilege, perhaps prompt us to question the source of that privilege, perhaps give us a brief sense of the experience of being powerless, question our sense that we know who we are and what to do. Can the image of the suffering other work, then, to challenge the naturalness of the white corporeal schema, to make evident the possibility of less comfortable ways of being, to make the white spectator engage in some process of reflexivity? The quotations I have given here suggest that something like this is at work—these writers and I have been led to meditate on their/our own position, and to question their/our comfort and their/our ability to act. The mode of address performed by the image of the suffering other, then, throws into question and literally makes *visible* the taken-for-granted comfort of a perspective in which the centre is home and suffering is elsewhere. This should be productive in countering the invisible, unmarked privilege of whiteness.

But I am cautious. There is, after all, a long history to the dynamic in which the coloniser uses images of the colonised as a resource for reflection on the self. I notice that in the passage above, I write about the way Salgado shows me *worlds*. I have not, therefore, moved far from my position at the pinnacle, surveying the vista beneath. I may have become uncomfortable, but I have not moved far from my imperialist viewing position.

Rey Chow, discussing photographic images of the "native", suggests that such an ambivalence may be endemic in the colonial encounter. Even as reproductions of the image of the "native" proliferate, she argues, the unspoken possibility of a reversal of gaze can work to challenge imperialist viewing relations.

> … I want to argue that it is actually the colonizer who feels looked at by the native's gaze. This gaze, which is neither a threat nor a retaliation, makes the colonizer 'conscious' of himself, leading to his need to turn this gaze around and look at himself, henceforth 'reflected' in the native-object. It is the self-reflection of the colonizer that produces the colonizer as subject (potent gaze, source of meaning and action) and the native as his image, with all the pejorative meanings of 'lack' attached to the word 'image'. … Western Man henceforth became 'self-conscious', that is, uneasy and uncomfortable, in his 'own' environment (Chow 1993, 51).

Hence, Chow suggests, ambivalence and dis-ease are not so much threats to the imperialist viewing position, as an integral part of it. They enhance the viewer's subjectivity and provide the opportunity for self-reflection. The all-encompassing gaze turns inwards as well as outwards.

The ambivalence of this encounter is also expressed in relation to the question of agency. Banks is convinced his readers will "read … and weep", but "won't stop there". Other commentators are more uncertain:

> Photographs of people suffering, dying, grotesquely emaciated, in a foreign land. How does the viewer react?
>
> The question is, of course, nonsensical. There are many viewers, with many points of view.
>
> But might there be a thread, an idea, a feeling preoccupying many of these viewers?
>
> *Is this discussion even interesting?*
>
> Perhaps the more pragmatic question is, how should viewers react?
>
> By doing something to help, if help is at all possible.

> Exposed for a fractional second, distributed rapidly, the photograph is a canary in a global coal mine (assuming that we share the same world). As the suffering endures, the image becomes a plea.
>
> But do photographs cause people to do something about other people (or animals, or places) who are somewhere else? Or might have photographs once done so, but now there are too many of these images of apocalypse confronting us, tugging at us, devastating us if were to take each one seriously? Or is the problem that there are few obvious solutions, and fewer governments with the will or the means to help? Each image of horror becomes a mirror of our own impotence.
>
> Or is that too easy an evasion?
>
> What should we be doing? What should we have done?
>
> The questions, all of them, are withdrawn.
>
> *It can only be up to each of us.*
>
> (Ritchin 2004, 7)

Unlike the quotation from Banks given above, Ritchin's discussion is not immediately addressed to a "we"; it begins by discussing "viewers" in the third person. This abstract "viewer" becomes "we" momentarily when the prospect of "shar[ing] the same world" is raised, and then metamorphoses permanently in passive mode as the "us" who is confronted, tugged at and devasted by the "images of apocalypse" in the book. Far from resulting in agency, this process threatens the viewer with "impotence". And the images become "mirrors", no longer showing a passive other but confronting the viewer with his own powerlessness (as "impotent", this viewer seems to ask to be constructed as masculine). At the same time, the viewer is exhorted to act anyway, to stop asking questions and to accept her or his individual responsibility. Hence, even as it raises the spectre of impotence, of the failure of action, this frame addresses the spectator as one who *can* act.

At its worst, this combination of poetically evoked unsettlement with a palpable sense of "impotence" works as something of an alibi. If action is impossible, then perhaps sympathy is enough. "So far as we feel sympathy, we feel we are not accomplices to what caused the suffering. Our sympathy proclaims our innocence as well as our impotence" (Sontag 2003, 91). (I do not exempt my own interest in the photographs from this critique).

Thus the consumption of images of suffering, well intentioned as it may be, keeps on turning into acts of self-presentation and self-discovery. This would not be so bad if it did, indeed, result in reflection on the global distribution of vulnerability, as Butler hopes. Reflexivity on the part of the privileged is one step towards acknowledgement of power relations. But in all this "mirror-gazing" performed by the spectator, what happens to the suffering others? Unfortunately, in becoming the site for the interpellation and elaboration of a self-reflexive subject (still unmarked as "white") they seem to be repeatedly forgotten, becoming the occasion for a meditation on "us" and "our future". Indeed, the image becomes "a canary in a global coal mine". Like the prophetic refugees of *Forced Out*, it acts as a warning. In dying first, this sensitive, vulnerable bird, utilised because of its *expendability*, alerts the "miners" (busily engaged in stripping resources?) to the fact that there is danger. But what does it mean to say that the *photograph* is a canary? Is it the photograph that dies? Perhaps, in this age of mass production of imagery and of compassion fatigue the photograph as a form of address does die, rendered, as Sontag lamented (1979) ineffective by surfeit. But this unfortunate metaphor, in the context of images of famine, including several images of corpses, inevitably references the death of the *person shown in the photograph.* This death, photographed, becomes useful as a warning to those who view the photograph—the "we" that possibly shares the same world … but whose deaths, presumably, would not be compared to that of a caged bird.

Conclusion

Are such processes inevitable? Will all spectators in the white diaspora who identify as both "normal" and "comfortable" find themselves interpellated by the call to white spectatorship? Perhaps not. But the *ease* with which such a position can be occupied by those in a position to do so is demonstrated by the fact that this essay, itself written by a white person, has thus far replicated quite precisely the moves it has been describing: the images of suffering others have become an occasion for meditation on the white self and its relation to vulnerability.

In order to break apart this circle of self regard and mobilise the potential of an encounter with images of suffering in a way that makes strange the experience of security and comfort *without* losing sight of the other, it is clear that there needs to be a displacement of the centring of the white subject. It is not enough to suddenly feel uncomfortable within one's own skin and self conscious about being privileged; not even enough to feel that "we" potentially share a world inhabited by suffering. What is needed is a destabilisation of the sense that the world *belongs* to the white subject and is organised around its needs; the very sense of entitlement that is experientially confirmed every day for white subjects living in locations phenomenologically organised around whiteness.

To challenge this "normality" of white "at-home-ness", the trope of distance must be challenged. It is also useful to ask where, indeed, this home might be. The white diaspora is not homogenous, and it includes places that have not always been white, and/or are still not white.

Writing, like myself, from an Australian context, Ravenscroft concludes her discussion of white spectatorship with just such a proposal—arguing that images of "distant" suffering, such as those of the Vietnam War she encountered as a child, work as a disavowal of racial relations at home. Ravenscroft argues that "for the white subject to see differently there must be a refusal to stand in that position of whiteness where Indigenous dispossession, sovereignty, and presence are disavowed" (2004, 522).

As Ravenscroft acknowledges, for the white subject habituated to privilege and a viewing position located at an unproblematised, racially unmarked centre, the perspectives disavowed in this way come into view only momentarily, with difficulty. But making the effort to read with colonial history in mind can be productive. What, for instance, might such a perspective make of the following quotation from *Exodus* (1997), a coffee table book of photographs of refugees from around the world:

> Projects like *Exodus* provide the space for contemplation. They open doors to a world in which reality and meaning are contested, where the individual can choose to engage himself or simply to walk away. The photographs in *Exodus* are therefore catalysts. The combination of photographer, subject and viewer can crystallize and produce intense new meanings for the way in which we conceive our world and construct our futures (Sealy 1997, 205).

With colonial history in mind, metaphors such as "provide space" and "open doors" take on particular meanings. The implication here is that these photographs are both welcoming and undemanding spaces. They provide the viewer with *territory*, in which to exercise choice, construct futures, determine meanings, and above all, practice visual surveillance—in other words, they offer the viewer *sovereignty*. The underlying wish here seems to be that the images, or the people in them, *withdraw*, ceding space and territory, removing themselves from relevance, enabling the viewer to "choose" whether or not they are important.

Read from an Australian context, this quotation might then invoke Indigenous writer Irene Watson's definition of sovereignty: "freedom to roam" (2007, 16). In a still-colonial Australia, such freedom on the part of a white person is always an appropriation. Hence a refusal to allow a response to images of suffering to be organised around the trope of distance brings the gaze closer to "home", but also places that home itself in question, and thus works to decentre the white viewing position. The histories of violence that forcibly maintain political relations through which suffering is inequitably distributed come more clearly into view.

To conclude, then, I'd like to suggest that the question asked by Ritchin—"might there be a thread, an idea, a feeling preoccupying many of these viewers?—*is,* despite his doubt, an interesting question. The liberal individualism which keeps on proposing, again and again, that the response to these pictures is "up to the individual" might prevent us from noticing a "common thread" which does seem to unite viewers—a common identification with an unmarked, privileged way of being, named only (and incorrectly) as "most of us", but in that very racially unmarked position identifiable as "white". Are "we" not interested in a common thread in which white viewers, collectively defined, are gathering together over the spectacle of "other" bodies, bodies suffering, hurting, dying … and telling each other that it is all happening "elsewhere"? Noticing such a common thread might be the first step in recognising the white spectator's placement *within* the regimes of violence s/he surveys.

CHAPTER SIX

ONLINE BODIES AND SEXUAL SUBJECTIVITIES: IN WHOSE IMAGE?

VIKKI FRASER

Introduction

For some, the internet is seen as a space of transcendence where one might break free from the shackles of bodies or spaces in order to experience real freedom (Turkle 1996). The internet has become, at least in popular imagination, the tool with which the limitations of bodies, in particular in relation to race, class, sex and gender, could be undone (Chun 2006, 2). For queer young people in particular, the internet is often seen as a space where they might "try on" their queer subjectivities in ways that enable them to proudly take up a queer identity offline (Alexander 2004; Hillier, Kurdas and Horsley 2001a; 2001b; Valentine and Skelton 2003). Yet despite the fact that there certainly have been benefits for young queer people engaging with the internet, to view the medium only as a space of transcendence where users might write themselves as freely as they wish is potentially problematic. Internet websites proscribe ways of being very specifically, and in ways that are tied to the bodies of users (Nakamura 2002). Viewing the internet as a space of transcendence or complete freedom and anonymity runs the risk of erasing the generative effects of discourses operating on websites as well undermining the experiences of users who are perhaps caught up in and potentially made vulnerable by such discourses (Chun 2006; Nakamura 2002). This chapter seeks to unpack some of the ways that one particular website discursively enables and centralises some queer subjectivities while rendering others, specifically non-white queer subjectivities, periphery.

Mogenic.com is a website dedicated to queer young people under 25 years of age. A dominant feature of the website is the profiles of users, allowing members of the site to connect with other queer young people.

However, the site also provides a range of resources for users (not necessarily members), largely consisting of articles written by young people. *Mogenic.com* is one of only a small number of websites existing for queer people under 25, and is certainly the one with the most obvious international focus. Through interaction on the website, it has been argued that young people are able to not only gain for themselves a community of like-minded young people, but also participate in the writing of that community (Alexander 2004). In some respects, such possibilities create a point of departure from other similar websites, as *mogenic.com* is less commercially oriented and more user focussed, although it still has the commercial flavour of larger websites, such as *Gay.com*.

Mogenic.com labels itself as the "biggest gay and lesbian community on earth" (mogenic 2000-2006), and certainly has been indicated to be a highly utilised website by young people in the research that I have been undertaking over the past two years. This research, although not quantitative in scope or generalisable, surveyed a small group of queer youth, accessing them through youth groups, pride festivals, queer press and queer websites. Nine young people were also interviewed face-to-face. Participants were all aged between 18 and 26 and were primarily from New South Wales, Australia. Although this chapter is more concerned with undertaking an analysis of the website itself, insights given by interview participants in the accompanying study provide a perspective on discipline and policing which is useful for understanding some of the ways the website might enforce a queer subjectivity that is primarily white, male and gay.

Young people have indicated in the current study that *mogenic.com* is very often a first port of call when exploring their sexuality online, and this suggests it is important to examine this site in the context of the productive work of the internet for queer youth. Additionally, the mission statement of *mogenic.com* makes it an important point of analysis, as it states:

> We are your one-stop portal to gay youth around the world. We come here to find each other, to define ourselves, and to build a community of substance and worth. Loneliness sucks, and so does ignorance, and so does boredom. We'd like to find the cures for those ills, and we'd like to find them together. (mogenic, 2000-2006)

In this statement, *mogenic.com* specifically highlights the generative work done online and the necessity of online communities for the definition of "authentic" queer young people. The scope and purpose of the site, in addition to its specific link to the queer youth community world wide through its age bracket and its relative freedom of access, make it a useful point of analysis of the construction of particular queer subjectivities.

Through an exploration of the website *mogenic.com* I will attempt to unpack the way that the website constructs sexual subjectivities (specifically queer subjectivities) through both the texts and images of the site and the joining/membership process. Throughout this exploration, I seek to highlight some of the generative work achieved by the discursive processes of the site, specifically in relation to whiteness and the colonising practices of white queer sexuality. As a result, this chapter will be divided into two sections: an outline and exploration of the way websites are constitutive and productive of particular queer subjectivities; and an exploration of the issues of silence and removal that create queerness on the website as specifically white and colonising of racially marginalised people.

Although the website discussed throughout this chapter uses the phrase "lesbian and gay" to describe participants, the term "queer" will be used as an umbrella term to describe participants on the site. The term "queer" has been selected in an attempt to avoid privileging the experiences of gay and lesbian identified people, and to acknowledge the presence of website users who describe their sexuality in more complex ways than the "normalised" and possibly reductive categories of "lesbian" and "gay". As Riggs (2006) argues, using the term queer resists understandings that innate identities underpin particular labels, making it possible to focus on the particular processes that lead to the legibility of the subject. Participants in the study that underpins this work have identified the ways that terms of reference that refer to lesbian or gay sexuality specifically marginalise and foreclose the experiences and presences of a gamut of other non-heterosexual website users. Although some might see the term "queer" as problematic, it has been adopted throughout this chapter for its potential to destabilise notions of sexualities and to allow for the recognition of a broader range of experience in terms of sexuality, subjectivity and the internet.

By exploring the particularly white image of queerness presented on *mogenic.com,* this chapter explores the way race becomes a formative site of power on the website. This exploration will follow three main areas of discussion: the "queer blanc" and a global "queer"; the removal of multiplicity; and the silencing of alternate experiences of queerness. The role of racialised power as shaping the range of intelligible subject positions made available within a consumer-orientated context is illustrated well by hooks (1992), where she suggests that:

> When race and ethnicity become commodified as resources for pleasure, the culture of specific groups, as well as the bodies of individuals, can be seen as constituting an alternative playground where members of dominating races, genders, sexual practices affirm their power-over in intimate relations with the other. (127).

Although not specifically a commodity culture, the website *mogenic.com* certainly demonstrates the "power-over" of whiteness, maleness and "gayness", through the repeated exclusion and policing, visually, textually and practically, of non-white, non-male ethnicities, genders and sexualities. Although in many respects *mogenic.com* does not disallow alternate expressions, the spaces made available for those expressions exist in such a way so as to not so much enable representations of diverse bodies, but rather reaffirm the mainstream and power status of the white, male queer body (hooks 1992; Nero 2005).

Theoretical framework

Whiteness has long underpinned gay and lesbian studies and queer theory, largely due to the normalising gaze that forecloses and removes race issues from queer studies (as argued by, for example, Barnard 1999; Gopinath 2005; Nero 2005). Race or ethnicity are rarely considered in elaborations of queer theory or gay and lesbian studies—whiteness is assumed and privileged and considerations of ethnicity or race are often seen as secondary or superfluous to considerations of homophobia, a "queer community", or equality struggles (Barnard 1999). As Barnard (1999) states;

> 'Women' means white women; 'lesbian and gay' means white lesbians and gay men. When any marginalized subjectivity (i.e. gayness) becomes the basis for community, it will, in turn, create and enforce marginalizing prioritizations and exclusions (202).

Normative understandings of queerness as white are reproduced in queer spaces, both online and offline, in ways that marginalise queers of diverse backgrounds. Furthermore, queer spaces that are based on these normative understandings of queerness as white function to (re)produce and manufacture white privilege through the constitution of non-white queers in particular ways. As Gopinath (2005) states:

> An emerging body of queer of colour scholarship has taken to task the 'homonormativity' of certain strands of Euro-American queer studies that

> centre white gay male subjectivity, while simultaneously fixing the queer, nonwhite, racialised, and/or immigrant subject as insufficiently politicized and 'modern' (11).

As such, political awareness, activity and "modern" understanding of self and sexuality are read through the lenses of whiteness. This is perhaps most readily seen through the tendency to compare "gay rights movements" with civil liberties movements in the United States, with the former being seen as solely organised around issues of sexuality, and the latter seen as solely organised around issues of race (Berube 2001; Riggs 2006). As a result, the normativity of whiteness in queer spaces seems to be largely unquestioned, particularly when the queer space that is explored is online rather than tangible.

The whiteness of the internet is an often overlooked phenomenon when the space is discussed along trajectories of transcendence. Nakamura (2002) in particular critiques this normalisation, maintaining that the whiteness of the internet must be considered if the medium is to be discussed in terms of its role in the construction of subjectivities. The internet assumes whiteness as the norm—whiteness is made visible through what is left unsaid, through the assumption that white need not be said (Nakamura 2002). This construction of normative whiteness is a dominant factor of online queer spaces, and works to construct the queer subject as the white queer subject. As Payne (2007) maintains, this normative white queer subject is able to call on manufactured assumptions about race and sexuality which are further used to deploy white privilege and centrality in online queer spaces. These manufactured assumptions have been explored in great depth regarding offline queer spaces (Ayers 1999; Caluya 2006; Han 2007; Ridge et al. 1999), however it is only recently becoming the focus of attention that online spaces perhaps mobilise these assumptions in more overt and potentially volatile ways than in offline spaces—in ways that are condoned by the sites and their users (Payne 2007).

Not only is the dominance of whiteness online largely condoned by users, it is enforced by the technological practices which construct websites. Gunkel (2001) highlights the way white privilege is mobilised through the micro-structures of internet presence. The use of English as the "unofficial official language of the Internet" (Gunkel 2001, 86)—permeating in the ways discussed by Nakamura (2002)—as well as reaching deeper as it were into the very acts of coding which make websites and online interaction possible, is perhaps one of the more colonising practices of internet production. Such practices of coding may work to enforce already existing racialised hierarchies of access to not only the medium itself (Hoffman et al. 2001), but of access to the production of the medium. Due to the fact that programming and coding is primarily English, and that sites are structured around white (particularly white and Western) understandings of social compartmentalisation and so on, the presence of ethnicities which do not operate around these markers is automatically erased through silence. This is not to say that there are no websites coded, produced by, or representing the interests of people from marginalised ethnicities. Rather, it is possible to suggest that the dominance of white understandings and languages might reconfigure the modes of representation made possible online in ways that are readable through the lens of whiteness only. Understandings of culture and society are intrinsically linked to the workings of language (Barthes 1982, 94-95), and so the erasure or non-use of the languages of marginalised ethnicities disrupts the ways in which representations of such ethnicities might be enabled in online spaces.

The privileging of languages of whiteness, as well as the hierarchies created around whiteness in online spaces, act as gateways to the representation and participation of users from marginalised ethnicities. Such privileging is made more pervasive as the gaps between access to the internet through the technology of access (computers, Internet Service Providers and so on) remain open (Hoffman et al. 2001), limiting the number of those who are not represented through the lens of whiteness participating in the creation of online presences. However, at its most pervasive and visible (and therefore most readily condoned), the hierarchies of ethnicity created through site structure, as discussed by Nakamura (2002), work to privilege white understandings and dominance online. As will be explored in the following section, the normalisation of whiteness on websites such as *mogenic.com* through site structure and the categorising imperative employed as "identity" practices are key features in the production of queerness as white and the erasure of queers from marginalised ethnicities.

Race and ethnicity are dealt with throughout this chapter and as a result it is necessary to clarify the perspectives taken for each. The use and meanings of each of the words are not fixed or stable, nor are the various categories attributed to each of the two umbrella terms (Alexander and Knowles 2005). Historically, race has been used to imply a bodily inscription with fixed and immutable meanings (Alexander and Knowles 2005). On the other hand ethnicity, and with it whiteness and non-white subjectivity, are terms understood to be culturally constructed, with fluid and flexible meanings linked to the discourses of production by which one is influenced and the multiple other subjective possibilities (such as religion, class, gender, age, etc) that impact on a person's embodiment. Often "race" is also used to refer to this construct (see Alexander and Knowles 2005; hooks 1992), and such variation in use works to highlight the discursive ways in which such terms are used, simultaneously marking such categories as constructed and bodily real. Online, the conflation of each of the different terms highlights the discursive work done on the website, as well as the ways in which whiteness, as a construct, is produced and potentially embodied whilst on the site. As will be demonstrated in the following sections of the chapter, *mogenic.com* does little in its depiction of "ethnicity" to enable multiple understandings of self through the intersection of multiple discourses, such as religion, cultural affiliations and class which may all contribute to one's understanding of their ethnicity. Rather, the website utilises historically rooted racial categories as the sole marker of non-white identity, while whiteness is discursively produced through a range of mechanisms on the website.

Approaching this chapter from the perspective of queer theory, which advocates against an understanding of fixed and immutable identity categories, would suggest the importance of problematising the racialising work of the website through its privileging of white understandings of identity (Nicoll 2004; Riggs 2006). One such way the website emphasises white understandings is through its emphasis on fixed and immutable identity markers, such as ethnicity and race. As is demonstrated in this chapter, *mogenic.com* privileges identity in ways which disallow any acknowledgement of the intersections of multiple experiences in the formation of subjectivity. Building on the relationship between subjectivity and discourse (Butler 1997a), I take up the articulations of ethnicity and race mentioned above in order to highlight the ways in which language becomes an operation of power (Fairclough 2007) through which colonising practices, such as privileging the assumption of a fixed, immutable and easily definable racial "identity", might occur (Riggs 2006). Whiteness operates through the website via the site's categorising use of language. Articulating a difference between "race" and "ethnicity" in the ways outlined above, despite the preference given to "race" as a term that articulates these shifts (Barnard 1999), best enables me to articulate the power through language that I am attempting to unpack (Fairclough 2001; 2007; Foucault 1972).

Construction site: *mogenic.com* and the construction of queer subjectivity through silence, exclusion and removal

The productive discourses (that is the way discourses act constitutively of queer sexuality) do much to silence, exclude and remove a number of different expressions of queerness. However, the nature of the stereotypes and linguistic/textual signposting in each of these processes particularly removes, silences and excludes a number of subject positions by privileging whiteness. This is an important phenomenon, particularly when the nature of *mogenic.com*, its rate of access by young queer people, and its claim to be a global gay and lesbian youth portal, are taken into consideration. As a result, the website's production of white, male queer sexuality (which is specifically presented as gay) works in a colonising way on the bodies of queer young people who do not fit into the white male queer mould, but who nonetheless continue to utilise the website.

Silence is an important aspect of the discursive and political work that creates subjects as either authentic or trivial. Silence predicates belonging by marking out what is possible to recognise within particular spaces, and failing to provide a language for that which is not (Clair 1998). As has been demonstrated time and time again through both poststructuralist and queer theory, silence is one aspect of power which serves to delimit the possible and knowable (Butler 1997b; Derrida 1997; Sedgwick 1990). For this reason, the silences and exclusions of *mogenic.com* are a useful point of exploration when attempting to unpack the white privilege inherent in the website.

Racialised assumptions

Mogenic.com, through the various linguistic signposts utilised on the site, creates a "Queer" which is not explicitly racialised, however is normatively white. Never is queerness on the site given a specific ethnicity. Rather, it is bestowed a "global" status: we are queer, and we are from all over the world. The "queer" on *mogenic.com* apparently is faceless, skinless, and empty, waiting only to be filled with the information users themselves impart. There is no ethnicity to the cyber queer:

> This is a space where I cannot see colours. White is colourless, invisible, transparent. White is blank (Dyer, 1988). White is the blank, black screen that my words are typed on, everyday, twice a day. I begin to map an imaginary whiteness, an imagination constructed by the familiar confines of my location (Yue 1999, 120).

However, this “blank” queer subject (let us call it the “Queer Blanc”) is perhaps more illusion than reality. As the last part of the above quote indicates, whiteness or transparentness is always constructed by the location in which it occurs. *Mogenic.com* particularly uses a number of indications of queerness that are white in a very real sense, existing in and growing from Western understandings of sexuality and queerness which view queer subjectivity as predominantly white and utilising images appropriate to that understanding. It is interesting to note that, although claiming to be a site for queer youth of the world, *mogenic.com* utilises very few site generated images which call to mind anything other than a white and largely male image of queerness.

Fig. 6-1 www.mogenic.com banner

The image above (Fig. 6-1) is one of the two main banner images of the website and, as can be seen, consists largely of white bodies, either male or ambiguous in terms of gender. The two bodies which may not be white exist on the periphery of the image, away from the majority of people and out of the specific delimitation of queerness (indicated by the use of colour—pink which is historically linked to queer sexuality). This pink colouring occurs in two main areas of the image. The central figure, a male wearing a hooded top, is the centre of a pink glow that covers each of the figures in his immediate proximity. Secondly, a pink love-heart shaped bubble appears on the far right of the image, connected like a speech bubble to the reclining figure. The removal of the two ambiguous figures from the other figures and the colour pink assists in the visual production of authentic and centralised queerness on the website as white, with ambiguous or non-white queers existing on the outside, the periphery and the trivial. Such production of non-white queer sexuality, according to Nero (2005), is typical of the ways that queer pop culture works in the emphasis of non-white homosexuality as inauthentic and trivial, where:

> The ubiquitous image of the black gay male as an impostor or a fraud naturalises and normalises the exclusion of black gay men from sites of territorial economies where wealth is created. (Nero 2005, 235)

Beyond such imagery, the terms, languages and symbolisms of the site create queerness in a particularly white and Western way. The current title of the webpage, *Mogenic: version fuchsia*, as well as the prevalence of pink imagery, creates a link to the historical symbolism of pink as indicative of queer (specifically male) sexuality. Although pink has been taken up by a variety of different groups, including non-white queers, to draw links to queer pride and the mobilisation of identity politics, the colour retains its whiteness through a variety of factors.

The normalisation of pink queerness is akin to the normalisation of white queerness—queer sexuality is automatically associated with the colour pink, much in the same way as queer sexuality is normatively associated with whiteness. As Dyer (1997) points out, the term "white" need not ever be mentioned when one is discussing queer identity politics. The whiteness of queerness is never troubled, except where queerness is referred to specifically as, for example, black (Dyer 1997, 3-8). Pinkness is also associated with a middle-class privilege that cannot be separated from its whiteness. Phrases like the "pink dollar" are pervasive and refer to the notion that queer sexuality, identified through association with pinkness, is in possession of a consumer interest and ability which denies the social disadvantage that may be experienced by non-white queers, as well as white queers and non-white non-queers from lower socioeconomic backgrounds. The social association of pinkness with more pervasive stereotypes of queer sexuality (such as masculine effeminacy), as well as the normalising practices it invokes, highlights the ways that the website takes up an indicator of whiteness through use of the colour pink (or fuchsia) in ways that reproduce the normalcy of white queerness and the abjection of non-white queers to the periphery.

Furthermore, the website linguistically creates an image of gay life which can be read as white in orientation, specifically a gay life which consists of: "coming out, love and dating, sex sex sex, substances, depression, transgender, school and campus" (mogenic, 2000-2006). These concepts, indicated to be key by their inclusion under the heading "gay life", use specific stereotypes and understandings that privilege white experiences to discuss and explore queerness. While I do not intend to erase queers from minority ethnicities who share these experiences from this analysis, such categorisation reduces the experience of sexuality to an experience only affected by queerness. As has already been argued, such an account claims that users of *mogenic.com* will only experience the topics outlined on the site as queer, with no other intersecting experiences. The norms of whiteness in queer spaces and the internet precede the possibility for understanding these categories as anything other than white.

Queer becomes white queer, through the removal of possible intersections between ethnicity and sexuality.

The construction of these categories of (white) queerness does little to include experiences of gay life which do not include these things, for whatever reason, or which include them as a part of a myriad experience of multiply inscribed bodies. Categorisations which are constructed as integral to being knowable as queer become further problematic when such constructions work to encourage participation in these aspects in order to come across as "authentically" queer. As Michael Schembri discusses, with reference to a number of leading queer activists from diverse backgrounds, there is a tendency to attempt assimilation into dominant queer cultures which often leads to (often quite damaging) exclusion from "home" cultures and family life (Schembri 2001). The periphery status afforded non-white queer youth, and the discursive production of queerness in ways that are understandable most readily through dominant/white queer culture, does little to contest that assimilation and exclusion pattern.

Whiteness and multiplicity

In this section of the analysis I focus specifically on the membership and profile creation process of *mogenic.com* to explore the role of confinement, foreclosure and exclusion in the production of authentic avatar bodies. In the only place on the site where ethnicity is made explicit, users are required to select an ethnicity that will be linked to their profiles and, de facto, to their queer bodies. However the ethnicities allowed are strictly controlled and disallow the possibility of mestiza identities. Ethnicity in this context remains at the level of the "best fit", organised into broad and potentially exclusionary categories: as an example, one cannot select a White *and* African ethnicity. The only way to contest such boundary policing is to select the option of "mixed/multi" or "rather not say", which places the user at risk of falling into obscurity, silence and un-recognisability.

While the categories of "mixed/multi" or "rather not say" do not automatically foreclose participation or recognisability for users, the readability of subject positions from the perspectives of others is an important consideration when exploring these websites. While the category of "mixed/multi" might be taken up by some users in ways that challenge the normative categorisation of the website and enable full participation in the site, users responding to this question using the "rather not say" option are particularly at risk of exclusion and obscurity. During interviews, three participants discussed the reaction that occurred in website communities when a user did not adequately categorise themselves according to the website (inadequate categorisation including using the "rather not say" option or leaving an answer completely blank). One female participant particularly commented about the discussion board argument that she was caught up in about using the "rather not say" option in profiles, with a number of site users claiming that the option should not be taken up as it indicated a failure to identify. Similarly, two male participants described the way that they refused contact with users who had selected the "rather not say" option for demographic information. Each of these young men claimed that the reasons behind their aversion to users who selected "rather not say" for demographic information stemmed from a sense of the other persons laziness—"you couldn't put enough effort into it to actually come up with an answer" (male participant 1)—or self esteem—"they're not comfortable with who they are so that's why they're doing it" (male participant 2). The way category meanings are pre-inscribed further limits the ways in which they might be taken up. While category markers are read as indicative of the characteristics mentioned above, it is difficult to avoid the exclusionary practices which attempt to police users into becoming knowable subjects. While not every user of *mogenic.com* would read the "rather not say" option in the same way, such examples indicate the way limited and exclusionary categories can become sites of conflict for users who take them up.

As can be seen in the screen grab of the profile creation page of the website (Fig. 6-2), personal information is organised into specific categories which must be filled in according to the language of the website. This data does not exist innocently, but can be read as ranked according to the levels of importance placed on the aspect of self. Accordingly, the three most important aspects of queer subjectivity on *mogenic.com* are Gender, Sexuality and Ethnicity, followed by Mannerism, Body Type and Height. As the profile pages are also used for "cruising" (searching members for potential friends, dates or sexual encounters), this ranking also schools the searcher's desire to look first at the gender, sexuality and ethnicity of the profile, followed by other bodily indicators such as body type or manner.

Within each of the categories of "body", users are required to select one response which will then form their avatar or online body. It should be noted here that this exists as a question/answer style form, with the user's picture attached, rather than as an actual drawing or animation-based avatar. To focus on the ethnicity category of the form, it is interesting to note that only eight options are given, organised largely around the former racial type classifications utilised in forensic and anthropological work around "race" as predetermined. This raises a number of issues, including the conflation of "race" into "ethnicity" without providing options structured around other cultural markers. While I focus my analysis on the silencing and removal of the mestiza within these categories, it is important to acknowledge that the necessity to identify and highlight "race" around such broad categories is fundamental to the privileging and prioritising of white queer identities on the site.

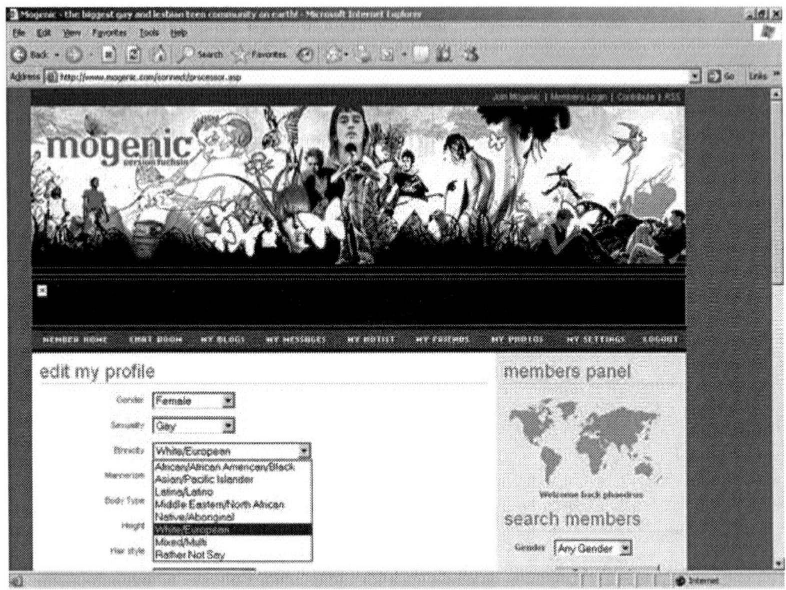

Fig. 6-2 www.mogenic.com profile information screen

As has been discussed throughout this chapter, whiteness is often presented as an assumed silence when any other category of identity is taken up (Barnard 1999; Dyer 1997; Gopinath 2005). The racial categories presented to users on *mogenic.com* as a way of indicating their "ethnicity" serve to illustrate the ways in which the silent assumption of whiteness might manifest. As can be seen in Fig x-2, the categories progress not in alphabetical order, but in a seemingly random order which, according to Nakamura (2002), works to create hierarchies of the answers from most desirable to least. While this hierarchy is certainly apparent, I would argue that the particular position given to the "White/European" category indicates not that this category is least desirable, but rather the way that the list also works to create hierarchies of the categories from least to most silent. The "White/European" category is the last "unambiguous" category available before the less defined options of not declaring an "ethnicity" occur. It should be noted that I refer to these categories as unambiguous as that is how they are presented on the site, not because I am implying that identity categories can actually be unambiguous. Positioning whiteness so low on the list may be taken as indicative of the perception that the whiteness of queerness is never questioned—one is presumed white until proven otherwise. In this way, the position of whiteness as last on the list of specified "ethnicities" reaffirms its assumed ownership of the queer signifier.

While it is possible to read the position of whiteness in the list in such a way, it is difficult to understand the progression of the other categories presented, although it seems likely that they, too, follow a progression of most spoken to least spoken. While whiteness is presumed when speaking about queerness (causing the category's situation at the bottom of the list), queerness is seldom presumed by queer and non-queer alike to exist within the categories listed lower on the list, and these categories are certainly rarely represented in images of queer sexuality (Gopinath 2005; Ridge et al. 1999). While the presentation of these particular categories does mark some attempt to acknowledge the presence of queers from a variety of racial backgrounds, the hierarchies that the list format presents, and the placement of "White/European" toward the bottom of the list, might suggest that this reproduces the assumption of white queerness and the need for white queers to mark ownership of queer identities (Gopinath 2005) through the continued categorisation of non-white queers into specific, often limited, types.

Nakamura (2002) discusses the role of the textual production of websites in containing and constructing raced online bodies. With regards to the construction of mestiza identities online and the way that websites allow or disallow such belongings, I quote Nakamura at length:

> Even websites that focus on ethnic and racial identity and community often possess interface design features that force reductive, often archaic means of defining race upon the user. This produces a new kind of cybertyping, one that encompasses the user's racial identity within the paradigm of the 'clickable box'—one box among many on the menu of identity choices. When users are given no choice other than to select the 'race' or 'ethnicity' to which they belong, and are given no means to define or modify the terms or categories available to them, then identities that do not appear on the menu are essentially foreclosed on and erased. This limits the ways that

> race can happen in cyberspace and also denies the possibility of a mestiza consciousness on these sites (Nakamura 2002, 101-102).

As has been pointed out, the risk on *mogenic.com* of not "cybertyping" oneself into one of the categories allowed is one of obscurity and silence. Likewise, within a seemingly diverse online community, defining oneself as one of the "reductive" and "archaic" categories opens oneself to the position of periphery queer at best or, in a worse scenario, some of the silences and racism inherent in the queer online community (Han 2007; hooks 1992; Nero 2005; Payne 2007). The ability to avoid such racism or reductive definition is further limited by the necessity of portraying oneself online in such a way that will enable belonging within a community. As a participant in the current study stated, selecting "rather not say" on a category automatically means that people will not want to interact with you, as they want to know what it is that is "really" behind the profile.

Alternate experience of queerness and silence

As has been argued thus far, the website structures queerness and queer life around demarcations of white queerness, emphasising particular aspects of that life, and one's behaviour in that life as the only means of achieving authentic "queerness". Such aspects include participation in the "scene", particular ways of dressing and acting and perhaps most importantly, "coming out". The construction of the coming out narrative as healthy and central to the production of an "authentic" queer subjectivity disallows alternative expression of queerness and silences those queers who are unable or unwilling to come out, removing them to the periphery of queer life. Although "coming out" has had great impact on the visibility of queer people world-wide and has done much to enable legal recognition and support on a range of levels to queer communities, it is important to recognise that "coming out" as a practice is not always enabling for some queer young people. Schembri draws on the accounts of activists such as Happy Ho to emphasise the fact that the discourse of coming out often becomes problematic for queers of marginalised ethnicities as it can often mean the removal of familial support, create financial difficulties and even result in mental and physical health issues (Schembri 2001). These types of outcomes for some queer people are very removed from the dominant discourse promoted on *mogenic.com,* which encourages coming out as the only way to achieve a healthy and complete queer subjectivity. Although such a reading may also hold true for white queers who are also subject to the impetus to come out (Rasmussen 2004), coming out is often read by other queers as an indication of belonging within queer spaces. For queers of marginalised ethnicities, the coming out imperative often results in a double removal—removal from traditional familial and social support networks as well as exclusion or marginalisation within the queer communities which (re)produce the coming out imperative.

However, while coming out may not be the most appropriate or necessary option for many queers, the dominance of the coming out discourse in white queer culture and the repeated space given to coming out information or stories on *mogenic.com*, creates potential problems for non-white queers perceiving themselves or being perceived not only as authentically queer, but also as contemporary or healthy. The concept of coming out is currently subject to much contestation, due to the fact that coming out as obligation or political action currently works to exclude, silence or reduce the queer experience of a number of different queer groups (Rasmussen 2004). However, on *mogenic.com* coming out is still positioned as being of prime importance in the lives of queer young people. Such importance alienates the experience of those who cannot "come out", or perhaps those who have no need to "come out" in the understanding provided by contemporary white views. The coming out discourse on the website not only relegates non-white and unable to "come out" queers as insufficient or not complete, it also disallows for experiences of queers whose organising principal is not the closet (Sedgwick 1990), whether that be for ethnic/cultural reasons or for personal experiential reasons.

Conclusion

Although *mogenic.com* purportedly allows a site for queer youth from around the world to participate in and form a community without discrimination or boundaries, an exploration of the power relationships and discursive operations on the website indicate that the website operates within the boundaries of white, male and gay sexuality and experience. While the website is an important site of visibility and interaction for and of queer young people (particularly those who are isolated from visible queer spaces), it is necessary to note the ways that the website works to textually limit and erase alternate experiences of queerness, particularly along lines of race and ethnicity.

There are numerous reasons that could be given for such a foreclosing, and it is not my desire to condemn the website out of hand for such textual practice. Certainly, the dominance of white male experience in most

Western queer communities would posit the prevalence of whiteness on *mogenic.com,* along with its inception in Australia and current management in the USA. Further, the divide between access and non access to computer and internet technology is increasingly racially defined (Hoffman et al. 2001). However, it is important to begin to understand the way that whiteness works on *mogenic.com* to colonise experiences of queerness and relegate non-white queers to the periphery of queer belonging, particularly as the role of the internet is becoming increasingly integral in the formation of queer youth subjectivities. Such explorations may enable not only researchers but organisers of similarly styled websites to consider the discursive work done online on the embodiments of queer young people from diverse backgrounds.

Perhaps by making the discourses of whiteness at work on the website visible, other possibilities for writing queer youth spaces online that incorporate different experiences of queerness and do not risk silencing non-white queer voices will become possible. Although the body cannot be erased in online environments, the emphasis given to categorised and essentialising identity markers on *mogenic.com* does little to challenge the dominance of whiteness within queer spaces, nor the exclusion faced by non-white queers. Constructing spaces without such normatively white markers is one way that the power relationships inherent in cyber-typed online personas might be challenged. Although challenging the presumption of whiteness when discussing queerness is difficult, reducing the experience of queers from all backgrounds to single issue politics or reductive "characteristics" silently works to reproduce whiteness as central to queer identity. For online queer spaces to begin to challenge the reproduction of white centrality, it is necessary to rethink the way sites are organised. As such, sites should acknowledge that subjectivities are informed by a variety of experiences, enabling them to avoid categorical questioning which cannot be troubled. Further, such acknowledgement might lead to the recognition that one's experience as a queer person is actually informed by numerous trajectories, not just queer sexuality itself.

CHAPTER SEVEN

READING ALIEN LIPS: AUSTRALIAN PRINT MEDIA DEPICTIONS OF ASYLUM SEEKERS AND THE CONSTRUCTION OF NATIONAL IDENTITY

RON HOENIG

Prologue

I am looking at a photograph taken by Reuters photographer Paul Vreeker of an Iranian immigrant who has sewn his lips and eyes in protest at the Dutch government's plans to expel 26,000 failed asylum seekers. Although there has been lip sewing among asylum seekers in Holland, the United Kingdom and Latin America, an intensive search of articles on NewsBank Infoweb[1] leads me to the view that lip sewing as a political act by asylum seekers originated in Australian immigration detention camps in 2000. The image brings home the corporeality of the act of lip sewing. Lips are powerful tokens of the sensory and sensual materiality of the body. They open to allow us to speak, to eat, to drink, to kiss. Through them, we express the complexity of our thoughts and the simplicity of our strongest needs—for communication, for nourishment, for tenderness and passion. Stitched lips close off nourishment, language, love. Sealing them in protest externalises and embodies the silence, amplifies the silencing. Screams the silence.

The silenced communication of the asylum seeker lip sewers is radical. Through embodying their silence, lip sewers contest narratives of their illegitimacy and erasures of their political right to existence outside the "normal" disciplines of the state. As stateless persons, asylum seekers may easily be depicted by state authorities, politicians and media commentators as having no right to compassion, or to have that right only under very circumscribed circumstances (Arendt 1973). Lip sewing is a statement of what Agamben (1994) calls "bare life", the act of the politically silenced in claiming the value as a "human creature" (as *zoe)* more fundamental, more radically Other than in the political guise of the citizen *(bios)*.

But an individual act of lip sewing can become politically effective only when it is publicised. It is, after all, an act of communication. To be publicised, it must be fitted into a pre-existing set of media narratives. The asylum seeker's attempt to call on compassion on the level of "bare life" offends the order imposed by the state which valorises the citizen. State authorities may all too easily convince citizens not to acknowledge either asylum seekers' suffering or citizens' participation in producing it by framing it as "not legitimate". For example, Australia's former Prime Minister John Howard felt no compunction in describing lip sewing as an act designed "to morally intimidate the Australian people and the Australian Government into changing a policy" (cited in Hannon 2002). This is an example, as Pugliese (2002) suggests, of the ways in which "everything is mobilised in order to produce the structural prohibition of owning our responsibility in the production of this [lip sewing] violence". Addressing the lip sewer in the voice of the citizen and the state, he says:

> After the violent spectacle of every act that confirms your savagery, we can lapse into the complacency of knowing that you have justified our fears and legitimated the punitive laws we deploy against you (2002, 42).

In this paper I utilise critical race and whiteness theory to examine some Australian print media reports about lip sewing by asylum seekers. I demonstrate that print media news texts about lip sewing are influenced by pre-existing national narratives, and in Butler's words "cite and reiterate" (cited in Barker and Galasinski 2001, 50) particular narratives of national identity. I suggest that both negative and positive constructions of the lip sewing Other in news texts serve to highlight the implicit qualities of the "invisible" but dominant white subject. Rather than providing information about, and insight into the cultural/racial Other, such texts can be understood as interventions in an ongoing discourse within the white "mainstream" about "our" national identity.

Whiteness, Australia's national narrative, and responses to asylum seekers

Benedict Anderson (1991) states that the notion of "nation" is imagined, a fantasy of a culturally homogeneous home with clearly delineated borders. In colonised, so-called "settler" nations, such as

Australia, New Zealand, the United States, South Africa or Israel, the fantasy is stretched to the very breaking point, by the usually repressed but always glimmering awareness that the nation is not, does not and can never totally "belong" to the white subject. As Elder says, "the fantasy of the coherence of the white Australian nation state needs to be especially emphatic in the face of sovereign Indigenous people" (2003, 223). Further, as Perera (2002) argues, white Australia is produced in terms of a triangulated relationship between white Australians, an internal Indigenous Other and an external non-white Other, and the relationship with the non-white Other is made anxious by a constantly suppressed awareness of white "original sin". For the dominant white male subject, then, some crossings of the border have to be permissible in order to have allowed the first transgression. Having initially been able to cross over, invade and penetrate the territory of the Indigenous occupant, he must indeed obsessively control what he now claims as his territory and arrogate to himself the right to exclude others to ensure that the land remains "his". However, Elder points out that even at times of the most strident calls for exclusion, a shadow of desire for the excluded is discursively represented: "Barely spoken but ever-present desires for the excluded people inform the idea of a 'white Australia'" (2003, 223).

Shech and Haggis (2004) argue that most analyses of Australian national identity take for granted its whiteness, while at the same time insisting on it being non-racial. They describe whiteness as both "a terrain of structural advantage as well as a standpoint of race privilege" (177-178). Aileen Moreton-Robinson (2004) says that racial difference plays a crucial but concealed role in the epistemology of modernity and the construction of the white subject. She says by understanding the relationship between knowledge, representation and whiteness, "we can understand the silence, normativity and invisibility of whiteness and its power within the production of knowledge and its representation" (2004, 76). Perhaps paradoxically this demands the presence of the racial Other:

> The existence of those who are defined as truly human requires the presence of others who are considered less human. The development of the white person's identity requires that they be defined against other 'less than human' beings whose presence enables and reinforces their superiority (2004, 76).

Dyer highlights the very invisibility of whiteness as its major characteristic:

> [W]hiteness as power is maintained by being unseen … [T]rue whiteness resides in the non-corporeal … [It] is the sign that makes white people visible as white, while simultaneously signifying the true character of white people, which is invisibility (cited in Perkins 2004, 164) .

Moreton-Robinson argues that in modern liberal discourse "race is reserved for the Other and the assumption is that the raced body of the knower … is irrelevant to knowledge production" (2004, 76). Thus in her critique of historian Bain Atwood, she highlights the raced body of the white European academic who unconsciously attempts to erase the whiteness of the academic perspective (2004, 82). A similar view may be taken of the white journalist and the enterprise of journalism.

In the production of news in white societies, whiteness constitutes an unacknowledged mental "lens" through which events are seen and narratives are constructed. These narratives are formed from attitudes simultaneously consciously and unconsciously held and manipulated by white subjects. They reflect the social, political, cultural and institutional reality of white dominance. Such attitudes are not about news workers being necessarily personally "racist" or antipathetic to cultural others. But they do impact on the way in which particular cultural narratives are constructed, iterated and embedded in cultural production, including journalism. The practice of journalism implicitly defines the news worker and, I suggest, the "ideal" reader as representing, if not necessarily belonging to, the category of "not-Other". Narratives of the nation based on white racial superiority—and their "shadow" form as insecurity about the perpetual possibility of invasion—influence the considerations and perceptions of the bureaucrats and media managers who frame media releases as much as they do the public and the news workers for whom they are intended. The "objective" stance of the journalist implicitly constructs the same "We/they" binary as Former Prime Minister John Howard did in the slogan, "We will decide who comes here and the circumstances under which they come" (Howard 2001). As Elder, Ellis and Pratt comment, citing Widders and Noble (1993):

> 'we' are representatives of the mainstream, the protectors of the national interest that is threatened by 'them' (the external other). The effect of discursively positioning non-white people in this way is that 'their' inclusion in the nation—in both real and metaphorical terms—is then restricted by the parameters of the white 'national will'; that is, they are included but only in the dominant group's terms (2004, 210)

If this is true of Indigenous people and non-white Australian citizens or residents—what Hage calls "Third World Looking Ethnics" (1996; 2003b)—how much more true can it be about the discursive positioning of asylum seekers in the detention camps, which Perera describes as "threshold spaces" (Perera 2006b). How much more explicit can this exclusion of the non-white Other be among the inhabitants of what Agamben describes as "spaces of exception" (cited in Perera 2006b, 645)?

Policing the national territory

Jupp (2002), among others, notes Australia's "long and strong xenophobic, racist and insular traditions"(6) which have formed the dominant narrative response to aliens. This response is magnified in regard to those who arrive "unannounced" and by sea. A narrative of border insecurity in the face of invasion, no matter how minuscule the invasion "force", has underpinned the dominant policy response (Burke 2008). Until 30 years ago, Australia's geographic positioning as an inaccessible island continent, strict legal bars to the immigration of non-white persons, and a highly selective immigration policy, ensured that white Australians were able to control the influx of persons into "our" national territory. However, since the end of the Vietnam war, there have been four different episodes when asylum seekers have succeeded in reaching Australian shores by boat and seeking asylum (Brennan 2003, 29-40).

All post-war governments, both Labor and conservative, with the singular exception of the Fraser government, have reacted negatively to unauthorised arrivals. In 1992, the Keating Labor government established a system of mandatory detention of asylum seekers which continues today (Brennan 2003, 87). Under mandatory detention legislation, any person who arrives on Australian shores without a visa is detained in one of a number of immigration detention camps (Department of Immigration and Citizenship 2007). These camps are located either in Australia or, between 2001 and 2008, on one of a number of Pacific territories which made agreements with the Australian government to house detainees. The Australian camps included two located in South Australia—first Woomera and then Baxter, Curtin in Western Australia, Maribyrnong in suburban Melbourne, Victoria and Villawood, located in suburban Sydney, in New South Wales. By far the largest contingent of asylum seekers arrived in Australia between 1999 and 2003, when boats from Indonesia brought more than 8,000 asylum seekers from Iraq, Iran and Afghanistan[2].

The response of the conservative Howard Government (1996-2007) to this influx of asylum seekers was in the exclusionist tradition Jupp (2002) outlines. The policy response came to a head following the *Tampa* incident. In August 2001, the Norwegian cargo vessel *Tampa* rescued 439 Afghans from a distressed fishing vessel in international waters. The Afghans sought passage to nearby Australian owned territory, Christmas Island, but the Australian government sought to prevent this by refusing *Tampa* entry into Australian waters (Mares 2002). The refugees were instead loaded onto a Royal Australian Navy vessel in a military operation. Most were transported to Nauru as part of what was known as Australia's "Pacific Solution" (Marr and Wilkinson 2003; Special Broadcasting Service 2008). This event came just before an election in which the conservative party faced possible defeat. It has been suggested that the Government made use of the *Tampa* event to their advantage through its subsequent reframing in the light of the September 11 attacks, and that this helped them to win the 2001 election (Mares 2002; Marr and Wilkinson 2003).

In his election-winning formulation John Howard drew on the long history of discourses of exclusion, fear and xenophobia in his slogan: "We will decide who comes here and the circumstances under which they come" (Howard 2001). Masterfully, the sentence elided the contested nature of white sovereignty and the diverse cultural identity of the Australian population to crystallise long-held anxieties over what Hage (1998; 2002; 2003a) calls "national belonging". The radically exclusionist response that followed included a military/naval campaign to prevent asylum seekers landing on Australian territory and a series of legislative acts to excise Christmas Island and neighbouring Ashmore Reef, from the Australian migration zone, for the purpose of avoiding incurring international obligations to offer asylum (Marr and Wilkinson 2003; Burke 2008).

In the years prior to 2001, the government also mobilised the exclusionist narrative of border protection in a media campaign to influence public perceptions of asylum seekers. Examining media releases from the Minister for Immigration in the period 1999-2001, the period of the most intensive government reaction to so-called threats to "border security", Van Acker and Hollander (2003) found official communication depicted asylum seekers as "undeserving refugees" who were the product of criminal activity, that is, "people trafficking". The releases reiterated that mandatory detention and a raft of measures repressive of asylum seekers would ensure the safety of Australians as a whole, and that by its policies, the Government was sending a necessary message of Australia's determination to stop a threatened influx of asylum seekers (Van Acker and Hollander 2003, 103). Given the former Howard Government's agenda and its deployment of a set of themes redolent of negative national narratives in regard to asylum seekers, this chapter investigates the role the print media played in portraying asylum seekers to the Australian public.

The news and the construction of the national self

The economic and commercial context for production of news texts in Australia is a situation of unequal duopoly. Australia has a highly concentrated print media market. Two companies, News Limited and Fairfax, compete for the rapidly dwindling print media market. News Limited is part of the Murdoch global media empire. It has tabloid format newspapers in every mainland Australian city, including Adelaide, the city closest to the most notorious detention centres at Woomera and Baxter, located in the desert in regional Port Augusta, some 300 kilometres from the State's capital. In Adelaide, the conservative tabloid the *Advertiser* has a monopoly and, in 2001, claimed a readership of 580,000 daily and 731,000 on weekends[3]. In Sydney, News Limited's even more conservative tabloid *Daily Telegraph* is said to have the highest circulation of any paper in the country. In 2001 its readership was 1,151,000 on weekdays and 191,400 on Sundays. News Limited's one broadsheet paper is the only national paper in Australia, the *Australian*, with a circulation of 430,000 on weekdays and a weekend figure of 901,000. Fairfax, by far the smaller company, publishes two significant broadsheet papers: one in Sydney and one in Melbourne. The *Sydney Morning Herald*, and the *Age* respectively. The left-leaning *Age* has a history of involvement in social justice issues. It claimed a Monday to Friday readership average of 649,000, reaching an average of 1,059,000 on Saturdays. The *Sunday Age* attracts an average of 660,000 readers (Herman 2007).

While each newspaper has its own editorial view, and there was no shortage of personal commentary pieces on asylum seekers in general and on lip sewing in particular, I chose to look in depth at depictions of lip sewing in hard news, which presents itself as "objective" and factual. I have selected articles which mention lip sewing from both News Limited and Fairfax newspapers and in both tabloid and broadsheet formats, and sought to sample articles that were both negative and positive in their depiction of asylum seekers and their lip sewing, and draw themes from them about the newspapers' role in constructing lip sewing and constructing Australian identities.

I employ an analytical framework developed by Bell (1991; 1997; 1999), who describes news stories as narratives driven by news values. He compares the structure of hard news stories to traditional narrative texts.

Newspaper stories, he says, are not merely recitations of facts. Rather, they are a highly structured genre of narrative constructed from discursive elements already present in their socio-political context and contribute to the further structuring of that discursive universe. These news narratives are constructed according to news values by media workers, whose subjectivity is itself shaped by the prevailing social and discursive context and the specific circumstances of their profession. These narratives depict, produce and re-produce the Other, and implicitly shape particular images of an ideal reader citizen.

Bell says that the difference between a chronological account of events and the chronologically scrambled news account of events tells us about "news values" which shape the order of telling. Analysing that difference helps us unpack the ideologies and underpinning narratives which drive the stories. While journalists are taught a series of news values or criteria for determining which events "make" news (see, for example, Conley 2002, 58-74). Bell (1991) states that these news values are not universal and reflect "the ideologies and priorities held in society" (1991, 156-158). Iedema, Feez and White (1994) characterise news values in their relation to the maintenance (and discursive construction) of the existing racial, cultural, political, economic and social order. They argue that "news value" judgments turn on the assessment of an event's status as destabilising or stabilising the existing social order (1994, 106). I suggest that, in Australia at least, news values are fuelled by the larger national/racial narratives described by Moreton-Robinson (2003; 2004), Perera (2002; 2006a; 2006b), Elder (2003; 2007) Elder, Ellis and Pratt (2004), Hage (1996; 1998; 2003a) and others. I suggest that news texts about racial and cultural others should rather be read reflexively to provide a reflection of a national white "self".

Reporting lip sewing

The practice of lip sewing was first reported as occurring in Australian at the Curtin detention centre in north-west Western Australia in February 2000. Curtin, a disused airbase, was opened as a detention centre in September 1999. By February, there were 1147 detainees there. That month, a hunger strike took place, during which an undefined number of asylum seekers (up to a dozen) sewed their lips in protest at the circumstances of their imprisonment and long delays in dealing with their applications for asylum. Only a handful of news stories reported this first episode of lip sewing. Curtin is thousands of kilometres away from any major city, including Western Australia's capital city, Perth. But those that did report this event reiterated the Government's perspective and focussed intensely on what they saw as the bizarre nature of the act. I cite from the text in the Perth *Sunday Times* of the first article to mention lip sewing:

1. SEVERAL Muslim detainees at Derby's immigration detention centre are reported to have sewn their lips together as part of a **bizarre** hunger strike.
2. The **grisly** protest comes after days of unrest among the 1147 detainees at Derby's Curtin Air Base, which has been converted into a temporary immigration detention centre.
3. None of the detainees who are said to have sewn their lips together has come forward or sought medical attention. They are believed to be hiding in the centre.
4. The **gruesome** protest is thought to have occurred in the past 36 hours.
5. 'If we find them, they will certainly have medical treatment,' a Department of Immigration and Multicultural Affairs (DIMA) spokesman said. (*Sunday Times*, Perth, 6 February 2000, emphasis mine)

A significant issue in determining an ideological direction or narrative is patterns of attribution, and the implications when attribution of comment is unclear. To the extent that the journalist adopts a particular source's discourse, the text aligns with that source. We can note that, while the first four orientating sentences quoted above are not attributed to a particular authority, they demonstrate a strong reliance on what Ericson, Baranek and Chan (1987) call an "authorised knower" to provide details. There are explicit references in the text to other witnesses' perceptions, for example, (S3) "are said to have sewn": or (S4) "is thought to have occurred".[4] However, the spokespeople who provide authoritative information are by no means objective. As representatives of the immigration department, they provide "facts" wrapped in the Government narratives previously referred to by Van Acker and Hollander (2003). The extent to which this article repeats and does not contest those narratives is significant.

Words like "grisly" and "bizarre" offer more strongly negative evaluations of the detainees which are consonant with the Government's dominant exclusionary discourses. Mares (2000) found a persistent discourse about the supposedly bizarre nature of the lip sewers' actions in news articles on lip sewing in 2000. This article is outstanding in its emphasis on the bizarre and gruesome nature of the protest—despite the fact that the journalist was not present to witness it. Indeed, the choice of the word "gruesome" is noteworthy. It focuses not on the pain of the lip sewer, but rather that which "causes horror and repugnance" in the observer. Pugliese describes this obsessive concentration on the observer thus:

> It hurts us more than it can hurt you to have to witness the abject spectacle ... In this practice, you other yourself beyond redemption and thereby expiate our culpability in the production of your suffering. In this sense, *we cannot consume enough of your barbarity:* we desire it and we produce it as so much spectacle that challenges our concept of decent behaviour (Pugliese 2002, 33).

The narrative highlights the detainees' imagined abjection and bizarre unruliness. By contrast "we" are generous, civilised, rational and lawful. It is thus significant that the reader is assured in S5, the first time "our" representative (the Department of Immigration and Multicultural Affairs (DIMA) spokesman) speaks: "They will certainly have medical treatment". This not only makes "our" response humane, but it also pathologises the asylum seekers' act of protest.

In S6 and S7, the journalist summarises the reason for the hunger strike and lip sewing:

6. Several hundred of the detainees—many from Middle Eastern or North African countries—are demanding to be held in better conditions and have their claims for refugee-status processed immediately.
7. The detainees want to be transferred to an 'open' facility in a city, where they can come and go until their claims are processed.
8. 'Those expectations are misguided,' the DIMA spokesman said. (*Sunday Times*, Perth, 6 February 2000)

While these sentences are unattributed, they appear to render the Government narrative as fact. Note the blasé formulation "come and go" in S7. The suggestion clearly appears "unreasonable". "Those expectations are misguided", the spokesman says flatly in S8. Because there is no information on issues such as practices in managing asylum seekers elsewhere or details such as how long the detainees have been waiting in Curtin or the conditions in which they are waiting for resolution of their claims, the spokesman's assessment and stance appear reasonable, even more so for the authority of his role. The white subject reader is invited to identify with the spokesman, constructed as long-suffering and decent in response to the detainees' barbaric and self-serving self-mutilation—even providing bodily nourishment:

12 'We understand this is another form of protest.' ... 'We are providing food and drink at all times for people to help themselves to.' (*Sunday Times*, Perth, 6 February 2000)

Throughout these news texts detainees are referred to only by their (presumed) religious or geographical origin and number. Readers of the articles are, of course, entitled to ask how the journalist can know that these detainees are Muslims or even Middle Eastern, especially since they appear to be hiding (S3) and why their religious identity and geographic origin appears to be all we know of them.

Respect for the law is constructed as a crucial difference between the Muslim detainees and the "ordinary decent Australian". Thus, we see in S14-16 the stance of the Minister is said to be predicated on Australian law. Indeed, the minister himself is described as constrained by an impersonal law:

14 The spokesman said Immigration Minister Philip Ruddock had made it clear the Australian Government would not respond to intimidation to change its policies.
15 It was impossible to allow illegal arrivals to remain free or process claims immediately, the spokesman said.
16 'Australian law requires that unauthorised arrivals must be detained until they are granted a visa or removed from the country,' he said. (*Sunday Times*, Perth, 6 February 2000)

Operating beneath the narrative of "our" respect for the rule of law is a narrative constructing lip sewing as a lawless "intimidation" of the white subject. This paradoxical thinking reached its apogee in Prime Minister Howard's already quoted description of lip sewing asylum seekers as practising "moral intimidation" of the Australian people (Hannon 2002).

Narratives of exclusion and desire

The major mainland detention centre for asylum seekers in Australia from 1999 to 2003 was located at Woomera, a small town established in the desert about 500 kilometres north of Adelaide, the capital of South Australia. In September 2001, Woomera held as many as 1442 detainees awaiting the resolution of their claims for asylum. After September 2001, many Afghan asylum seekers found that their claims had stopped being processed because authorities believed that it would be possible to return Afghan asylum seekers to Afghanistan, following the removal of the Taliban regime. In January 2002, detainees at Woomera dramatised their plight using lip sewing, a hunger strike and lying in graves they dug for themselves in the baking Woomera sun. This time, the event was reported on the front pages of most Australian newspapers. In the following excerpts I want to demonstrate how two news stories construct different narratives out of the same event, drawing on both the exclusionist narratives and a counter-narrative that draws on the shadow elements of desire for the Other referred to by Elder (2003, 223).

Both stories appeared on 24 January 2002, following a press conference in Adelaide, at which Federal Immigration minister Ruddock and South Australian deputy premier and Human Services minister Dean Brown accused asylum seekers of forcibly sewing the lips of children and promised to remove children from harm's way. The *Daily Telegraph's* page 9 headline "Children freed from Woomera 'barbarism'" frames the event as decent Australians, in the person of the minister and authorities, "freeing" children from the "barbarism" of the detainees. The headline highlights this interpretation. Only in S7 is its source given as the South Australian minister Dean Brown:

7. The decision to remove the children followed growing concern in the South Australian Government, which said some children had been victims of 'barbaric' mutilation (Ahwan 2002).

Moreover, the headline suggests that the decision and announcement actually "free" the children. The "barbarism" of the asylum seekers is emphasised in S1 below. In a demonstration of the problems with unclear attribution, S1 directly states that the children need to be rescued from the adults who are about to sew their lips:

1. EIGHT children are to be removed from the Woomera detention centre to protect them from having their lips sewn together by protesting asylum seekers.
2. Immigration Minister Philip Ruddock said investigations were under way into whether another seven children were at risk from adult detainees protesting over conditions and visa processing delays (Ahwan 2002).

The text only later reveals—indirectly—that it is the minister who has said the children are at risk of having their lips sewn by "adult detainees protesting over conditions and visa processing delays".

By comparison, the *Age* headline "Ruddock removes children" identifies the minister as the source, and constructs the Federal Government less as "liberators" than "removers":

1. The Federal Government will remove at least five children from the Woomera detention centre to prevent their involvement in hunger strikes and lip sewing, Immigration Minister Philip Ruddock said yesterday.
2. Five children without parents or guardians at the centre will be removed as soon as possible and placed in community foster care to stop them being coerced into protest actions by adult detainees, Mr Ruddock said. Those being removed are aged under 14, and Mr Ruddock said more may follow (Taylor 2002).

The *Age* is meticulous about its attribution, distancing itself from the minister by using his name three times in two paragraphs and avoiding endorsing the minister's claim that asylum seekers were sewing children's lips. Instead, the reason for removing the children is rendered in much more abstract terms than in the *Daily Telegraph* story: "prevent their involvement in hunger strikes and lip sewing" (S1).

The two papers' coverage now diverges further. The *Daily Telegraph* report focuses on the background of lip sewing, in order to build the narrative of "us" rescuing the children:

3. More than 200 detainees have staged a hunger strike at Woomera, including 50 who have stitches in their lips.
4. Mr Ruddock said two children had their lips sewn together by adults, who said they would do it again. One child is recovering in hospital after having stitches removed.
5. The action by immigration authorities follows the poisoning last night of seven Woomera detainees who were rushed to hospital after drinking shampoo or detergent.
6. Detainees' protests have also spread to Melbourne's Maribyrnong Detention Centre, where about 25 detainees were last night refusing to eat or drink (Ahwan 2002).

While in S4 it is clear that it is Mr Ruddock who has made the accusation that asylum seekers had forced children to sew their lips, the accusation has already been implied to be a fact previously. The next sentence appears to link the increasing number of asylum seekers who have stitched their lips to the minister's accusation. S5 links back to the lead "the (authorities) action", although there is only a hazy link between the poisoning and the release of the children and a possible suggestion that there were children among the detainees who drank shampoo. In S6, the protest "spreads" like an epidemic, rather than a political movement.

Bell shows us that just as sub-plots in narrative reflect and refract the main plot, so in news sub-narratives are drawn in to serve a similar purpose. In contrast to the *Daily Telegraph*'s narrative of rescue, the *Age* develops a counter narrative of growing powerful support for the detainees' protest.

3. The move came on the eighth day of the protest at the troubled centre in outback South Australia. More than 30 detainees at the Maribyrnong detention centre in Melbourne have begun a hunger strike in solidarity.
4. It also came after Neville Roach, a key adviser to Mr Ruddock, resigned this week in protest at the government's hardline stance on asylum seekers.
5. Mr Roach, chairman of the Council for Multicultural Australia and the Business Advisory Council on Migration, said last night the government needed to process asylum claims more quickly to prevent protests by detainees.
6. The Woomera detainees say they are protesting over the conditions at the centre and visa processing delays (Taylor 2002).

The *Daily Telegraph* article mentions the minister's reaction to criticism from his former adviser, Neville Roach, in the last sentence, almost as an afterthought. It detracts from the narrative of rescue. The *Age* article, however, sees news value, and support for its own agenda, in the development of a wider narrative of protest and critique of the government. Thus, the *Age* article refers to the Maribyrnong protest as "in solidarity" and highlights the resignation of Neville Roach in building its more textured story of government under attack. The narrative suggests that ordinary decent Australians are not at ease with "the hardline stance" of the government and that the government is increasingly embattled over the Woomera situation. Though none of this is explicit in the headline, it becomes clear in the way that a number of stories are orchestrated together. At least four stories are drawn together symphonically: a story of child removal; a story of protest at Woomera; a story of solidarity developing between asylum seekers in various places of detention; and a story of growing critique of the government.

The *Daily Telegraph* story constructs the "ordinary decent Australian" reader as repelled by the "barbarism" of the lip sewing and horrified by the asylum seekers' abuse of children. The *Age* story, however, constructs a reader who is repelled by the barbarism of the treatment of the asylum seekers, suspicious of the government's claims to represent compassion in its hardline stance, and uneasy about the regime of mandatory detention. For one, the lip sewer is a touchstone of "our" justified rejection of radical Otherness. For the other, the lip sewer is a touchstone of "our" compassion towards the desperate "Other".

The asylum seeker as positive other

Among the voices advocating for the asylum seekers were lawyers acting for the detainees, members of the Independent Detention Advisory Group (IDAG),[5] opposition politicians and refugee advocates. But one voice is conspicuous by its absence in most of the news stories under discussion: the voice of asylum seekers themselves. The practical reasons for this are incontrovertible. In accordance with the policy against "humanisation", the government and management of detention centres were assiduous in denying asylum seekers opportunities to speak to the press. Fairfax journalists, Christopher Kremmer and Cynthia Banham (2002), for example, refer to guards screening phone calls to prevent asylum seekers contacting the media and, to escape retribution, those few detainees who managed to speak to the press were forced to use aliases to prevent identification. But the marginalisation of the asylum seekers in their own story also reflects institutional ways in which all non-white minorities tend to be under-represented in the media (see, for example, Teo 2000; van Dijk 2000b; 2000a; Garcia 2002; Anti-Discrimination Board of New South Wales 2003; Dreher 2003). Like the Vietnamese community in Teo's study of media treatment of "ethnic" gangs, asylum seekers were effectively "de-voiced":

> Those who are marginalized out of power are typically 'devoiced' and denied access to this news making process, becoming the subjects of what others talk about, but seldom having the opportunity or power to refute or confirm what others say about them (Teo 2000, 41)

The rules of hard news also make it difficult to use the asylum seeker voices. Unlike the "authorised knowers" of the white "mainstream", they have little authority to speak for others. Thus readers were informed of the names of members of IDAG but not their asylum seeker partners in the negotiations. A limited exception to this was Hassan Varasi, who was referred to variously as a delegate or a spokesman for the asylum seekers from Afghanistan. On 29 January 2002, the *Australian's* front page story was headlined "Detainees agree to unsew lips". The first three sentences refer to the decision by some 47 Afghan asylum seekers to unstitch their lips, and journalists quote Varasi's statement:

3. 'We, the Afghani people at the Woomera detention centre, will unstitch our lips out of respect for IDAG and the Australian community and for the sympathy we have for the recently arrested

> ABC reporter',[6] the statement read (DiGirolamo, Spencer and Crawford 2002).

But there was no extended interview with Varasi and he is very much a minor player in his own story. Indeed, only the *Australian* decided that the decision by the Afghan asylum seekers to unstitch their lips was the strongest story on the hunger-strike that day.

Articles that were clearly sympathetic to asylum seekers appeared in publications at the time, but they were not considered "hard news". They were mostly treated as "colour" or human interest pieces. In the *Age*, an article reporting a surreptitious telephone conversation with two of the asylum seekers entitled "Woomera strikers accuse guards of beatings, duress and racism" (Kremmer 2002b), which appeared on page 6 beneath a photograph of a distressed Australian Democrats leader, Natasha Stott Despoja, which related to the story above.

The two asylum seekers are referred to by pseudonyms "Aziz" and "Jalil". They refute the statements of the minister accusing asylum seekers of sewing children's lips and, in a particularly powerful closing statement, one of them compares the immigration minister unfavourably to the Taliban:

> 17. 'I desperately need to get out of here, it doesn't matter where,' he said. 'When I came to Australia I didn't know that Philip Ruddock was our enemy. I prefer the Taliban, who only kill people. Here they torture you.' (Kremmer 2002b)

The asylum seekers' authority rests in their own experience. They are described by their homelands, the length of time they have spent in Australian and their ability to speak English. When it comes to an insight into the situation in Woomera, the journalist is more or less forced to back up their authentic but not formally credible voices with one of "our" representatives—in this case, Australian Democrats leader Natasha Stott Despoja.

> 14. There are clearly hundreds of lives on the line in there, people who are lying, some in sun, some in shade, people who are fainting regularly, according to reports to delegates and there are clearly people who have inflicted a degree of self-harm which we have seen. I was shocked. (Kremmer 2002b)

From the perspective of the press, the news issues are about the white subject, and the expression of, and the limits to, our generosity. They focus on the politics of immigration detention. In that politics, the fate of the detainees appears secondary. While asylum seekers' discontents are the precipitating factor for the conflict, the clearest and most easily communicated conflict is within "mainstream" white Australia about managing its national identity through the appropriate treatment of asylum seekers. The dominant white culture arrogates to itself the sense of "owning" and defining the nation and takes upon itself the right to "worry" about the state of the nation and to decide who the strangers are, as documented in Hage's work (1998; 2003a). Like Hage, Elder, Ellis and Pratt suggest that:

> the management of non-white people in the white nation-space is ordered in terms of a relationship where white people assume that their place is at the centre or core of the nation, defined in relation to both internal non-white others and external non-white margins or periphery (2004, 209).

Even articles which are clearly sympathetic to the situation of the asylum seekers reflect this management of our national identity. For example, Christopher Kremmer's colour piece called "Asylum seekers encounter new world outside fences" (the *Age*, 22 January 2002), written about asylum seekers' first days of liberation from Woomera, while clearly a positive depiction of the strength and resiliency of the asylum seekers, also manifests this identity management. The article begins with a metaphorical re-birth moment for the asylum seekers:

1. They emerged yesterday into the blinding glare of an Adelaide summer's day, a handful of Afghans, Iraqis and Iranians, after being released on Wednesday from Woomera detention centre on three-year temporary protection visas (Kremmer 2002a).

The words "they", "them" and their" are prominent in the article. As the observer, Kremmer is compassionate yet maintains distance. Kremmer reverses the telescope so the reader sees the "normal" world of the bureaucracy through the alien gaze of the asylum seeker. Judgements, both harsh and kind, are delivered by an "ordinary" Australian, "Brett Heath, 30, a long-term guest from Port Pirie (an industrial regional city in South Australia)". Stable—even stranded—in the Princes Arcade Motel, nevertheless his "matey praise mixed with dour reserve" is described as "very Australian" (Kremmer 2002a).

9. 'We can't have a flood of refugees breaking down the walls and getting into Australia. It'll put too much pressure on our infrastructure,' he says.

10. But in the next breath he informs us that 'from what I've seen these people would make ideal migrants. They're intelligent, well-dressed and unfailingly polite and considerate'.

These blunt and contradictory Australian judgments are paralleled by the tactful appraisal the asylum seekers make of their new land and the drunks and garishness of street where they have landed. Summarising the experience of the voyage into the bureaucracy as: "the drip feed, just enough to keep people going", Kremmer provides an insight into the way "we" in the form of the bureaucracy treat the asylum seekers. Their experience is represented as one of senseless, unexplained and often bureaucratised loss because of their host's desire to separate the notion of providing refuge from the permanency of immigration. The host will supply the former—grudgingly—as long as it is understood that it is not an illegitimate prelude to the latter.

Kremmer portrays the asylum seekers as deserving of praise and compassion, not derision or fear. We reflect on them through lenses of domestic life. We observe them cooking and eating, coping with money. Scenes of them making judgments and assessing the possibilities in their future and making comments on their past life in detention, are part of the discourse of appraisal and intelligence that Kremmer uses to attribute to them dignity and responsibility. Yet, their marginality is manifest. Brett from Port Pirie clearly possesses "national belonging" and they have none. There is no powerful national "we" that they represent. They are confronted by a capricious and all-powerful "we" that is "us"—an Australian nation of harsh judgment embracing—perhaps in uneasy, unwilling alliance—the bureaucracy, Woomera, the narrator and the reader.

Kremmer's use, then, of the expression "weird mob" in his last paragraph of praise is surprising:

17. As they head off into the city for another encounter with the bureaucracy, they make a weird mob, all shapes and sizes with no apparent dress code. Some educated, some not. But somehow you just know they're going to fit in. (Kremmer 2002a)

The term may be an ironic reference to the iconic book, *They're a weird mob* (Culotta 1958) produced by Irish-Australian John O'Grady under the *nom de plume* of Nino Culotta, a paean to assimilationism, supposedly written by a recently-arrived Italian journalist. In this peculiarly constructed conceit, the book praises the Australians as a "weird mob" into which it is right and appropriate that immigrants should assimilate. Where all the repetitions of the second person plural tend formally to distance the asylum seekers from the reader, the word "you" employed in the informal sense to mean "I" appears, drawing the reader into a linguistic alliance with the narrator in defining the group as an acceptable Other and assuring us that they will "fit in".

The polarities in Kremmer's article parallel those in previous articles examined in this chapter. Here, however, those who represent order are the asylum seekers and those who represent disorder are Australians; "the deranged drunks". The asylum seekers are law-abiding. The lawlessness comes from the bureaucratic capriciousness of the officials in Woomera. "Educated or uneducated", these are clearly potential immigrants to be "desired". Even Brett Heath describes them as "intelligent, well-dressed and unfailingly polite and considerate". In effect, Kremmer invites the reader into exercising the decision John Howard proposed. "We" too are deciding "who comes here and the circumstances in which they come". What remains unspoken because it is implicit in the context is the white reader's privileged position of being able to make the choice about national belonging. The article offers "them" to "us" for judgment. The asylum seekers become exemplars in the national debate about the kind of Australia that will be evolved by those who are in a position to participate.

Kremmer suggests, too, that the asylum seekers will "fit in". But what will they "fit in" to? As likely immigrants, they may be, in Hage's words, "the tame and domesticated animal whose will has been subjugated as the very condition of belonging to the domesticated space of the Australian national will" (1996). Will they "fit in" to an Australia in which their gifts and abilities will be nurtured and they will, in time, be part of the negotiation of a genuinely multicultural Australia, or will they "fit in" in the sense that they too will become a minority on the margins like the "internal non-white others and external non-white margins or periphery" (Elder, Ellis and Pratt 2004, 209).

Conclusions

National exclusionist narratives helped to shape the print media reporting of lip sewing events. The themes that Van Acker and Hollander found in Government media releases were clearly present in some of the reporting at this time. The exclusionist narrative is supported by a variety of journalistic conventions which underpin hard news. These include the reliance on authorised knowers such the spokespeople representing Government. There is also a tendency to accept the narrative of authority, especially in the absence of an acceptable bearer of a counter narrative.

However, there is also some reporting where a developing counter narrative is heard from "respectable" voices in civic society. Not all authorised knowers are on the side of the exclusionist narrative.

There nevertheless remains a huge gap between the white subject reader and the lip sewing Other. We only fleetingly hear the voice of asylum seekers in these articles, and they remain shadowy figures in the national debate. In both narratives, however, the shadow character is the "ordinary decent Australian" reader who sees him/herself reflected through these different constructions of the asylum seekers. While there are counter-narratives presented, the vast majority of the voices remain "our" voices. The depiction of asylum seekers give the white reader the opportunity to be reflected as compassionate and decent in either supporting or opposing the stance of the government. What the reader sees in them is what we/they desire and fear in ourselves. "We" may construct ourselves as tough and unwilling to be "suckered" into offering succour to barbarians—generous to those who deserve our generosity but firm in our stand against those who would invade us. Or we may construct ourselves as cosmopolitan and appalled at the bureaucratic insensitivity and ruthlessness of our government's stand.

The depictions of asylum seekers are an exchange of projections and imaginings about the Other. The articles participate in an ongoing national discourse about different ways of being and defining ourselves as Australians. They do not often explore our own complexity or how the asylum seeker understand Us and what we might look like to them in their dreams and in their nightmares, or indeed how, together, we and they might fruitfully construct a mutually defined Australia.

Part III:

Locating "Diversity"

CHAPTER EIGHT

CONSTRUCTIONS OF DIFFERENCE IN CHILDREN'S STORYBOOKS AND THEIR IMPLICATION IN BULLYING BEHAVIOURS

JAMES LOVELL AND DAMIEN W. RIGGS*

Introduction

Australian media reports in the past two years have raised considerable concern over serious incidents of bullying amongst school children. For example, Carr-Gregg (2007) reports on the case of Benjamin Cox, an 18-year old who was awarded one million dollars compensation for the "pain and suffering he endured as a result of years of harassment at school" (1). In another bullying case that received considerable media attention, a mobile phone video of a student being beaten and dragged along the ground by other students was distributed over the internet (Martin 2007). The footage clearly showed a group of students making no effort to intervene, and merely looking on as the victim was being attacked. In a similar incident, a student was filmed being forced upside down into a wheelie bin while a large number of onlooking students jeered and yelled abuse (Martin 2007). Incidents such as these have raised concerns as to the nature and extent of bullying in Australian schools, leading to calls for action directed at curbing such behaviour (Morrison 2006; Patrick et al. 2005). In response to these incidents, then Prime Minister John Howard suggested that schools themselves should be more accountable for bullying behaviour (Carr-Gregg 2007).

In a 2000 publication, Rigby suggested that one in seven Australian school children have experienced bullying at least once a week and suffered psychologically as a result. More recently, Healey (2005) suggested a higher incidence rate of one in five children, and that the experience of victimisation in schools can produce psychological sequelae comparable to those endured by victims of child abuse. Rigby usefully defines bullying not simply as the repeated oppression (either physical or psychological) of one individual by at least one other individual, but that such oppression functions through power differentials between those who experience and those who enact bullying. Understood in this way, bullying is not simply a case of children "not getting along", but rather is a practice of social exclusion whereby particular individuals as members of (typically dominant) social groups utilise their capacity as dominant group members to oppress others or deny their right to full participation in social spaces. Research findings would certainly suggest that differences between social groups in relation to gender, sexuality, race, class and religion underpin the bullying that some socially marginalised school children experience at the hands of dominant group children (Martino and Pallotta-Chiarolli 2003). Differences between individual children (and the social value accorded to these differences) are thus at the heart of bullying as a form of social exclusion.

Importantly, it is not only adults who have raised concern about the prevalence of bullying in schools. Children themselves continue to express concern over experiences of bullying in schools. For example, the Australian Kids Helpline reports that bullying is one of the top three concerns that children aged between five and fourteen speak of when calling the helpline for support. Rigby (1997) also reports on findings from surveys conducted with 26,000 Australian school children, in which they spoke of their experiences of bullying. In his findings on bullying in schools, Ribgy highlights not only the individual implications for those who are subjected to bullying (such as absenteeism, suicidal ideation, and general feelings of unwellness), but also the active role that children believe they can play in combating bullying.

Addressing issues of bullying within schools requires a range of approaches that focus on the reasons why children engage in bullying behaviours, the power differentials between differing groups of children, and also the ways in which school environments can challenge cultures of bullying. All of these approaches require asking the question: from where might children develop the idea that bullying behaviour is acceptable? One way to answer this question, as will be the focus of this chapter, is to look at particular sites within schools where peer interactions are represented to children in ways that render bullying intelligible as a potential means of engaging with individual differences. It will be argued that one of these particular sites is the children's storybook.

A social constructionist approach to understanding children's experiences suggests that culturally specific ideas are made available to children in the many forms of information they are exposed to, and that these directly affect how children structure and understand their experience (Burr 2003). From such a perspective, the enactment of bullying as exclusionary behaviour amongst children could be considered the product of ideas that have become available to them through both the broader Australian culture and through Australian school cultures more specifically. Children's storybooks are of particular significance in this process, not only because they are fundamental to the learning of language, but also because they work within particular ideological systems and thus help to maintain particular dominant cultural values and positions (Bradford 2001).

In relation to dominant constructions of difference within Australia, difference is typically represented as that which diverges from the norm of the white, heterosexual, able-bodied (or physically fit), middle-class male who subscribes to either a secular or Christian view of the world. As a result, when reference is made to "diverse cultures", this is typically taken as referring to non-white, or non-heterosexual, or non-secular/non-Christian cultures. When these types of assumptions about what constitutes "difference" or "diversity" constitute the dominant accounts made available to children, they learn to see the world through this normative lens (Riggs and Augoustinos 2007). This has negative implications not only for those children located outside of the normative categories listed above (in that it perpetuates the construction of their lived experiences as justifiably marginalised), but for the ways in which it limits the capacity of dominant group children to understand both their own location within a diverse range of cultural groups and the ways in which they benefit from their privileged position (Howarth 2007). Whilst it is sometimes assumed that talking to children about discrimination, privilege, and categories of difference will lead to an increased disposition toward engaging in anti-social behaviour, research findings would suggest otherwise (Aboud and Doyle 1996). As such, examining the spaces in schools in which group differences are talked about—such as school books—and the potential failure of such spaces to actively challenge particular constructions of difference, may represent one avenue through which schools can challenge how dominant constructions of difference may be seen to legitimate bullying behaviour.

In the remainder of this chapter we first outline some of the current research that seeks to understand the role that children's literature plays in providing particular world views to children, and we then apply this to examine a sample of children's storybooks that we suggest may be seen as complicit in the construction of what are deemed "normal" and "abnormal" forms of identity. Such constructions, we suggest, may be drawn on by children not only in their developing ideas about "self" and "other", but may also serve as an imperative to bullying as a form of exclusionary behaviour. It will be suggested that bullying may well be seen as acceptable to some children because such behaviours have been discursively presented as a natural consequence of the "difference" of those people who experience socially marginalisation. In doing so, we suggest that the depiction of bullying contained within these books presents marginalised group members as responsible for resisting their excluded status by proving their value or usefulness according to norms specified by the dominant group.

Previous research on children's literature

As social constructionist analyses of identities continue to highlight, language is central to the ways in which we understand, and indeed construct, our selves. While the learning of language is integral to participation in the social world, it is also central to the transmission of cultural knowledge about social relations. Although much research has been directed towards the promotion of children's language learning (for example, Kuo et al. 2004; Tomopoulos et al. 2007), the issues concerning what else children learn through language have received considerably less attention. This is a matter of concern given that, as Burman (1994) suggests: "the very forms and variety of the language children learn to talk encode structural meanings about the world they inhabit" (134).

Bradford (2001) suggests that books written for children work within particular ideological systems, and that they thus can support or resist dominant cultural values. She explains that the ideological nature of children's books often goes unrecognised by child and adult readers alike as they "embody ideas and concepts [that are] naturalized within a culture" (Bradford 2001, 3). Bradford goes on to suggest that dominant ideologies are evident in children's books in the ways they: 1) address child readers; 2) position children to have a preference for one character over another; and 3) condition children to approve of certain behaviours but not others. In addition to the particular forms of language used in children's storybooks, those containing pictures invite children to construct meaning from both the text and the visual context (Parkes 1998). This combination of text and illustrations creates highly detailed and powerful images of characters in particular roles. These images may then lead to particular views of individuals, as well as groups of people, being adopted by the child reader (Mendoza and Reese 2002).

Burman (1994) argues that children's storybooks are fundamental to the process of identity construction. Whilst it may be widely believed that the narratives provided in children's storybooks reflect children's "natural" development, Burman contends that they actually function to organise it. She voices her support for analyses of the type presented in this chapter by asserting that "the process of delineating and commenting on [the discourses present in children's storybooks] is part of the process of dismantling the power of this apparatus for the construction of subjects by which we are disciplined and constituted" (1994, 188). Importantly, Burman suggests that while children are active agents in the construction of their identities and the world of meaning that surrounds their identities, they are also very much influenced by the discourses present in the social spaces in which they move, such as in the educational environment.

Finally, Dockett and her colleagues (2007) assert that if we are to take children's concerns about the nature and extent of bullying and exclusionary behaviour in Australian schools seriously, and to respond to these in ways that facilitate positive experiences at school, we would do well to consider the potential of children's picture storybooks as tools through which to challenge negative stereotypical images and interactions. Indeed, this consideration is made more compelling if we are to acknowledge that the education system itself actively encourages children to engage in the process of identity construction through their early reading practices that develop within and around children's picture storybooks.

Data and method

The analysis that follows employs thematic analysis in order to examine the presentation of realities and meanings, experiences and understandings, and to consider these as effects of the range of discourses operating within society more broadly. Thematic analysis is a method typically used for "identifying, analysing and reporting patterns" (Braun and Clarke 2006, 79) within the data set. It involves minimal organisation, focusing instead on the task of describing the topical aspects of the data set in rich detail. In this way, thematic analysis looks beyond the semantic content of the data to "examine the underlying ideas, assumptions and conceptualizations—and ideologies—that are theorized as shaping or informing the semantic content of the data" (Braun and Clarke, 84). This process of thematic analysis is used to analyse the potentially problematic representations of exclusionary behaviour, and the potentially problematic representations of marginalised group member's subjectivities that are commonly utilised in children's picture storybooks. Importantly, such an analysis does not seek to deconstruct the truth claims these children's picture storybooks make in order to then posit more accurate truths in their place. Rather, this analysis will identify broad themes across the corpus of data, and provide specific examples in order to connect these themes to the political and social implications of particular representations of difference.

Through thematic analysis, three broad themes and two sub-themes were identified across a corpus of children's picture storybooks (n=20), and which are exemplified here by ten particular books (see Table 8-1 for a summary of the data set). The three broad themes are: 1) the "natural exclusion of difference" (n=20) which focuses on the common depiction of exclusion as a natural consequence of what is constructed as "difference"; 2) the "locus of difference" (n=18) which focuses on the common depiction of the marginalised group member as the only site of "difference"; and 3) the "benefits of difference" (n=19) which focuses on the benefits that "difference" is depicted as bringing. Within this third theme there were two sub-themes identified, which emphasised 1) difference as only accidentally valuable (n=5), and 2) difference as being intentionally valuable (n=14). For each theme and sub-theme, examples are presented from two particular children's picture storybooks, with information provided as to the broad contours of the book itself (such as the narrative and the imagery used). It is important to note that these themes are not mutually exclusive to individual books and that some children's picture storybooks include a number of these themes within their narrative.

The corpus of books was sourced through an online search of the Reception to Year Two reading list provided by the South Australian Premier's Reading Challenge for 2006. The website http://www.premiersreadingchallenge.sa.edu.au was used to develop a list of children's picture storybooks potentially focusing on difference and exclusion. The 10 books analysed below were chosen for their representativeness of each particular theme. However, it should be noted that almost all of the books (n=17) across the entire corpus were representative of the three broad themes, in addition to at least one of the two sub-themes. It is important to note that whilst the list of storybooks included as part of the Premier's Reading Challenge does include books that are specifically targeted at challenging bullying behaviour, these are not included in this analysis as the focus is upon generalist books and the ways in which they construct categories of difference.

It important to note that whilst the purpose of a thematic analysis is not to claim that the themes identified are exhaustive, the books represented here are nonetheless indicative of broader trends within a significant proportion of children's picture storybooks on the Premier's Reading Challenge list for this age group. This is evidenced by the fact that the some of the books analysed here are reported as being in the top 10 books read by children as part of the Challenge for the years 2005 and 2006 (again, see Table 8-1). That these books are popular amongst children would suggest not only the ubiquitous nature of the particular narratives found within these books, but also their intelligibility to both children and educators alike. Finally, it should also be noted that two deviant cases were identified, which contained alternative themes that also pertained to the research topic of representations of difference. These alternative themes provide us with examples of how particular understandings of difference and exclusionary behaviour, and the possible identity categories that are presented as being available to marginalised and dominant group members, may be represented in potentially less problematic ways.

Analysis

The following analysis expands on the main points made thus far—that while children are active agents in the construction of their identities and the world of meaning that surrounds their identities, their experiences are nonetheless very much shaped by the forms of intelligibility available to them, forms that we may see present in children's picture storybooks. More specifically, such books circulate in and through a range of discourses that render exclusionary and bullying behaviour intelligible to children as an acceptable means of engaging in peer relations. This analysis will examine specific examples of how difference is represented, and how exclusionary and bullying behaviour is accounted for within children's picture storybooks. This analysis thus asks two primary questions: 1) how do the discourses present in these books function to warrant certain understandings of difference; and 2) what may be the implications of these discourses for how children understand both themselves and the world around them.

Theme 1: "Natural exclusion of difference"

The first theme identified presents exclusionary behaviour as a natural reaction of dominant group members to what is constructed as the marginalised group member's "difference". The "natural exclusion of difference" theme insinuates that excluding someone on the basis of what is deemed to be "their" difference is not only acceptable, but that it is normal, and that therefore it is a common and reasonable way for dominant group members to engage in peer relations. In this light, marginalised group members are thus presented as undeserving of any empathy or sympathy for their excluded status.

The first book in which this theme appeared—*Baby Boomsticks*—provides the tale of a baby boy (Baby Boomsticks) whose size is depicted as making him different to the other people in his village: Baby Boomsticks is the only character in the book who is very large—larger than adults, even larger than houses. All of the other characters are depicted as "naturally" reacting with fear to Baby Boomsticks' size. As a result, Baby Boomsticks is depicted as unhappy: "Baby Boomsticks had no friends. The teeny-tiny villagers were afraid to let their teeny-tiny babies play with such a big baby" (Wilde and Legge 2003, 11). Here the text is supplemented with an illustration of Baby Boomsticks appearing alone and sad as he watches the dominant group characters playing together happily. He is not included or consoled by any of the dominant group characters; rather the dominant group children are kept away from Baby Boomsticks because of their parents' fear of his difference. Furthermore, at no stage do any of the dominant group characters appear to feel sorry for the psychological suffering Baby Boomsticks experiences as a result of his excluded status. Here, the idea that Baby Boomsticks would be excluded on the basis of his difference is presented as normal. Thus, the exclusionary behaviour that the dominant group characters engage in is presented as a natural consequence of Baby Boomsticks' difference. Furthermore, as Baby Boomsticks is presented as deserving of his excluded status, he is by implication presented as undeserving of any empathy or sympathy for his position.

The second example of the "natural exclusion of difference" theme appears in the book *Silverskin*. This book follows the growth of Liasis, a young snake who is depicted as different to her brothers and sisters on the basis of the colour of her scales. Liasis is the only snake in the book that is depicted as different. All of her brothers and sisters are coloured and patterned whereas Liasis is albino and therefore pale in appearance. The story begins with the hatching of a nest of snake eggs. Liasis' siblings immediately band together as a dominant group and exclude her on the basis of her difference: "'Look at her!' sneered the twelve patterned little pythons. 'She is so very, very pale! Is she really one of us?'"(Kuchling 2002, 4) Here the text is supplemented with an illustration of Liasis slithering away from her brothers and sisters. Liasis is not consoled or included by any of her dominant group family members. In this case, as well, the idea that Liasis would be excluded on the basis of her difference is presented as normal. Thus exclusion is again presented as a natural consequence of the marginalised group member's difference. In addition, Liasis is again presented as deserving of her position and thus she is, by implication, presented as undeserving of any empathy or sympathy for her excluded status.

Theme 2: "Locus of difference"

The second theme identified presents marginalised group members as the only site of what is constructed as "difference". Such a construction ignores diversity across and within groups in its focus solely on marginalised group members as being "different"—dominant group members are not presented as being equally diverse, or as being a part of a diverse range of all beings.

This theme is well illustrated by the book *The Rainbow Fish,* which follows the life of "Rainbow Fish", a fingerling whose scales are depicted as being different from those of the dominant group, in that he is the only fish with unique or "special scales" (Pfister 1992, 8). This focus on Rainbow Fish's "special scales" does not encourage young readers to recognise a range of characters that have many different scales types—all of the dominant group fish have scales that differ from one another (in colour and size for example), but these differences are not remarked upon. Only Rainbow Fish has what are deemed to be "special scales". Thus, Rainbow Fish is depicted as the only site of difference.

Another example of the "locus of difference" theme appears in the book *Bad Buster*. This book follows the life of Buster, a child whose behaviour is depicted as different to his dominant group peers. Buster is the only child whose behaviour is deemed to be "bad" (Laguna and Hobbs 2003, 1). Readers are not presented with a range of child characters that engage in varying levels of good and bad behaviour. None of the dominant group characters are shown to engage in "bad" behaviour and thus they are all deemed to be, and are depicted as, "good" in the context of the narrative. Thus, in this case (as in *The Rainbow Fish*) the marginalised group member is depicted as the only site of difference.

Theme 3: "Benefits of difference"

The third theme identified presents "difference" as something to be respected and appreciated if and when it proves useful to dominant group members. This theme suggests that the inclusion of an out-group member is determined on the basis of their value or usefulness to the in-group.

Thus, it is presented as normal that dominant group members would exclude people because of their supposed lack of value or utility. This theme was further informed by the constructions of those who are excluded as responsible for proving themselves valuable according to the norms specified by the excluders.

The quintessential example of this theme can be found in the book *Rudolph the Red-Nosed Reindeer*. This well known narrative follows the exclusion and eventual inclusion of Rudolph, a young reindeer whose bright red nose makes him different from his dominant group peers. For most of the story Rudolph's difference is not useful to the dominant group reindeer, therefore his difference is not valuable to them and so he is excluded and even directly ridiculed by them. "The other reindeer laughed at Rudolph and called him names. 'Ha-ha! Look at Red Nose!' they said. When the other reindeer played snow slide, they never asked Rudolph to play with them" (Daly and Jancar 1972, 4-5). However, as the night becomes darker the dominant group reindeer and Santa need the light from Rudolph's nose to show them the way while they deliver Christmas presents. Rudolph's difference becomes useful to his dominant group peers as it helps to solve the problem posed to all by the darkness. Rudolph's difference thus becomes valuable to the dominant group, and so he is accepted and included by them. "Rudolph held his head high. The other reindeer helped put on his harness and bells" (Daly and Jancar 1972, 24). Here the text is supplemented by an illustration of Rudolph smiling brightly as the majority group reindeer help him with his sleigh harness. It is interesting to note that Rudolph is presented as grateful for the inclusion he is offered on these terms. In this way it is presented as better to be included on any terms than to not be included at all or to risk challenging the terms on which the inclusion is premised.

Another example of the "benefits of difference" theme appears in the book *The Trouble with Mum*. This book follows the home and school life of the protagonist, a young boy whose Mum is depicted as different in the ways that she appears to be, and behaves as, a witch. Initially what is constructed as Mum's "difference" is not useful to the dominant group adult characters, therefore her difference is not valuable to them, and so she is excluded by them. This exclusionary behaviour on the part of the dominant group adult characters is then extended to the protagonist, as they forbid their children from spending time with him or his Mum. Thus, the dominant group child characters are encouraged to exclude the protagonist and his Mum on the basis of their parent's disdain for what is presented as Mum's difference. However, when a fire threatens to burn down the school, what is depicted as Mum's difference allows her to save the dominant group children's lives by harnessing rain clouds to her broomstick and flying them over the school. Thus Mum's "difference" becomes useful to the dominant group adults, and so her difference is valued by them, and so she and her son are accepted and included by them—as the protagonist remarks at the end of the book: "They couldn't thank her enough. Now we all go wild at my house" (Cole 1985, 27-28).

Whilst the two examples discussed above demonstrate the typical ways in which difference was constructed as potentially beneficial, the following two sections focus on two distinct sub-themes in relation to the "benefits of difference", in which difference is depicted as either "accidentally" beneficial (which attributes little agency to the marginalised individual in the story), or intentionally beneficial, which accords at least some degree of agency to the marginalised individual.

Sub-theme 1: "Difference valuable by accident"

In the first sub-themes of the "benefits of difference" theme, we see that one of the ways in which those who are marginalised are represented as having some utility is by accident—that the marginalised character accidentally does something of value to or for the dominant group. In cases such as these the marginalised group member is therefore represented more as a victim of fate than as an agentic individual.

This first sub-theme is well illustrated by the book *Willy the Champ,* which follows the exclusion and eventual inclusion of Willy, a young gorilla whose size and (what is depicted as his) athletic inability makes him different from the majority group gorillas. Willy is excluded by his majority group peers until he accidentally defeats "Buster Nose"—the local bully—in a fight: when Buster physically threatens Willy, Willy instinctively ducks the punch that Buster throws. Upon standing back up again Willy accidentally head butts Buster in the chin, causing him to retreat. In so doing, Willy proves himself, by accident, as valuable to his dominant group peers. Willy is thus presented as more of an accidental hero, or a victim of fate, rather than an agentic individual.

Another example of the "difference valuable by accident" sub-theme appears in the book *Derek the Dinosaur*. This book follows the life of Derek, an isolated dinosaur whose mild behaviour makes him different from the more aggressive dominant group dinosaurs. Derek is excluded, or not included, by the dominant group dinosaurs because while they are "savage" and "frightening" like "real dinosaurs", Derek is meek and mild and prefers "sitting and knitting" (Blackwood and Argent 1987, 3-5). Derek's exclusion continues until the weather turns colder and all the garments Derek has knitted in his years of exile are of use to his dominant group peers. Thus, as in the case of *Willy the Champ*, the victim of exclusion unintentionally or accidentally proves himself valuable to the dominant group members. Derek's behaviour allows him to unintentionally help his dominant group peers to weather the cold, and thus his difference is presented as useful only when he accidentally helps his fellow dinosaurs. Like Willy above, Derek is presented as more of an accidental hero, or a casualty of fate, rather than an agentic individual.

Sub-theme 2: "Difference valuable by intention"

The second sub-theme also extends the notion that the marginalised group member must prove themselves valuable to those who exclude them in order to alter their excluded status. As opposed to the previous sub-theme, this theme was expressed through the common presentation of the marginalised group member as someone who intentionally proves themselves valuable to the excluders. In cases such as these, the marginalised group member is therefore depicted as a somewhat more agentic individual.

This sub-theme is well illustrated by the book *Giraffes Can't Dance,* which follows the experiences of Gerald, a giraffe whose inability to dance positions him as different from the jungle animals that are presented as his dominant group peers. After Gerald has been excluded by his majority group peers, he perseveres in his attempts to learn how to dance. Eventually he is successful in his attempts. Via the direction of a cricket, Gerald learns how to dance and is considered valuable according to the norms specified by his dominant group peers. Gerald is thus represented as a victim of exclusion who intentionally proves himself valuable to his excluders. It is important to note that Gerald's acceptance is nonetheless gained only because of his ability to prove his "non-difference", not because his difference is acceptable in its own right. In addition, while Gerald is represented as an agentic individual, it is important to note that he is also depicted as requiring the guidance of another who knows better.

Another example of the "difference valuable by intention" sub-theme appears in the book *The Lazy Beaver*. This book focuses on a young beaver by the name of Bertram whose work ethic, which is presented as being less active than his peers, is seen as different from the other beavers in the narrative. Bertram is threatened with exclusion by the dominant group beavers because of what is deemed his laziness: "There's no room in a beaver colony for a lazy good-for-nothing. You will have to choose—work like the rest of us or leave Beaver Bay for good" (Gallo and Samsa

1983, 21). After Bertram is threatened with exclusion he intentionally makes an effort to work long and hard like his dominant group peers. He achieves this goal via the direction of "Uncle Frederick", another beaver in the colony, and comes to be considered valuable according to the norms specified by the dominant group beavers. In the case of this book we thus see the marginalised individual depicted as one who intentionally proves himself valuable to the dominant group members. Again, it is important to note that Bertram's acceptance is gained only by virtue of his willingness to prove his "non-difference", and not because his difference is acceptable in its own right. Like Gerald above, although Bertram is depicted as an agentic individual, it is important to note that he is also presented as requiring the guidance of another who knows better.

Deviant cases

In the context of this analysis, "deviant cases" were identified by virtue of the *positive* ways they managed to account for differences amongst groups of people or animals (in the sense that they deviated from the norm of *negative* representations of what was constructed as difference). The deviant case books provide us with examples of how particular understandings of difference, and the potential identity categories that are made available to children, may be presented in less problematic ways. These alternative themes may be more likely to encourage children to engage not only with the diverse experiences of those other than themselves, but also to consider themselves as diverse, and to consider this diversity as inherently valuable.

The first deviant case identified appears in the book *Rainbow Fish and the Big Blue Whale* which follows the relationship between a group of fish and a whale. In this book all of the fish characters are depicted as possessing some difference or uniqueness. Each of the fish has a unique or "special scale"—"except for one little striped fish, but he belonged to the group anyway" (Pfister 2005, 1). This particular understanding of difference as something that is common to all, by implication, suggests that excluding or bullying someone on the basis of their difference is not normal or acceptable. In this way, differences are constructed as features that are common to all people, and thus differences of any type are depicted as not necessarily warranting exclusion.

The most beneficial aspect of this particular understanding of difference is that it supports the idea that diversity is something common to all human beings. The focus on each fish's scales as being different encourages all people to consider their own points of difference, thus discouraging them from considering anyone different to themselves as deviant, perverse or immoral. In this way, the alternative understanding of difference presented in *Rainbow Fish and the Big Blue Whale* affirms diversity amongst all people whilst not overburdening diversity with a significatory value that ascribes categories of normality or deviance. This alternative conception of difference encourages dominant group members to consider themselves as diverse, but also as capable of excluding others. Drawing attention to the roles dominant group members (and dominant group values and beliefs) play in exclusion is an important element in the task of challenging unequal power relations, and one that is important to address in childhood education. At the end of *Rainbow Fish and the Big Blue Whale* the privileged in-group members (the fish) are made aware of how their misguided beliefs led to the unnecessary exclusion of an out-group member (the whale—who they eventually befriend). In this way the fish are able to see themselves as members of a dominant group and understand the power and privileges this membership affords them. This is a necessary realisation for dominant group members to come to before they can actually be accountable for privilege and attempt to engage with its consequences.

The second deviant case identified appears in the book *My Gran's Different*. In this book, as in *Rainbow Fish and the Big Blue Whale*, all of the characters are presented as different or unique. The narrative itself is comprised of a series of descriptions as to the individual differences the protagonist recognises within a range of grandparent characters. Throughout the narrative the protagonist remarks upon a point of difference about each grandparent character. Indeed, the entire narrative adheres to the pattern presented by the following example: "Jonty's granny catches the train to footy every week … But my gran's different. Raffie's nonna drives a florist van … But my gran's different … Alex's nanna knits all weekend … But my gran's different" (Lawson and Magerl 2003, 5-12). At the conclusion of this book the protagonist explains how his gran is different, while simultaneously affirming his unconditional acceptance of, and love for, her. "Because my gran is different. She can't remember who she is. But that's all right, because I remember who she is" (22-25). Most importantly, the protagonist does not ascribe any value or significance to the differences he remarks upon. Indeed, all his descriptions of the differences between the grandparent characters are bereft of any superlative adjectives. As a result, the protagonist's descriptions are not presented as the basis for any sort of comparison, and thus the differences he recognises are not subject to any sort of judgement or evaluation—none of the differences are deemed to be better or worse.

Rather, all of them are simply deemed to exist. Thus, in this book differences are constructed as features that are common to all human beings. This alternative understanding of diversity is beneficial in that it confirms the existence of differences in all people.

These deviant cases are included here by virtue of the fact that they account for difference in less problematic ways than those described by the previous themes. These alternative understandings of diversity may encourage children to consider themselves (and all human beings) as not only diverse, but also as valuable because of the potential that is inherent in the many different possible combinations of qualities they may possess. In this way, the alternative understandings of diversity presented in the deviant cases may encourage a sense of respect and appreciation for difference in its own right; indeed, they may in turn support a perspective which holds every individual as equally important and valuable in their own unique way. In affirming respect for diversity amongst all people, these understandings of difference, by implication, support the idea that excluding or bullying people on the basis of any perceived differences is wrong. Those who may exclude are thus encouraged to ask themselves how they would feel if they were excluded, by virtue of the idea that they must consider themselves as similar to those who may experience exclusion. Importantly, however, the understandings of diversity included in both *Rainbow Fish and the Big Blue Whale* and *My Gran's Different* do not deny the existence of differences, nor do they reify categories of difference as signifying hierarchical differences: rather they locate all differences between individuals on a continuum where having 'more' or 'less' of a particular attribute does not locate an individual as 'better' or 'worse. Rather, differences between individuals are respected as constitutive of what makes them unique as human beings in a relational context.

Discussion

The preceding analysis identified six potentially problematic ways in which representations of difference appeared within children's picture storybooks. These were: 1) "difference" as a category was used to refer primarily to people that were depicted as being outside the norm—the dominant group is thus constructed as the norm from which minority group member's deviate; 2) "difference" was only welcomed if and when it proved to be of value or utility to the dominant group—marginalised group members are thus only included if they have something deemed of worth to offer dominant group members; 3) this presentation of exclusionary behaviour as acceptable operates in conjunction with broader societal power imbalances to normalise the idea that marginalised group members are responsible for proving themselves valuable according to the norms specified by dominant group members; 4) engaging in exclusionary and bullying behaviours was presented, to dominant group members in particular, as a normal way of being in the world—in this way it is "taken for granted that people will discriminate against people from groups different to their own" (Riggs and Augoustinos 2007, 9); 5) the dichotomy of normality and abnormality worked in conjunction with the presentation of exclusionary and bullying behaviours to express and legitimate the idea that dominant group members can engage in such behaviours without moving outside the limits of "normality"; and 6) the potential identity categories that are presented as being available do not generate opportunities for children who experience marginalisation to challenge the terms on which inclusion is offered—marginalised group members are presented with intelligible forms of identity that offer minimal agency, or identity categories that possess little agency outside of the direction they are provided by those who are deemed to know better.

In addition to these highly problematic modes of representation, there were other topical aspects of the data set that were found to be remarkable. Foremost amongst these was the presentation of inclusion as desirable regardless of the terms on which it was premised. In some cases it was presented as best to be included on any terms, rather than to be not included at all, or to risk challenging the premises of inclusion that are specified by the dominant group. In many cases inclusion was actually gained via the marginalised group member's capacity to establish their "non-difference", rather than through the dominant group member's recognition of the value inherent in diversity. Indeed, this chapter supports any alternative understanding of difference that might encourage all children to consider themselves as part of the diverse range of all human beings. At the same time, however, we are mindful of the fact that it would be disingenuous to propose that we are all the same simply because we are all human. In actuality, one's subjectivity and experiences are very much constructed as mattering according to one's relationship to certain social and cultural norms. Moreover, it is important to recognise that "difference" is at times a desirable attribute for particular groups of people—living in ways that challenge social norms or which refute the negative values accorded to particular groups has often constituted the core values of minority groups that are in some way critical of dominant social groups. Given the diverse ways in which "difference" is lived, used and celebrated, it is therefore important that representations of difference reflect this diversity in children's picture storybooks.

In contrast to the normative ways in which difference was presented across the majority of books, the analysis of deviant cases revealed an alternative conception of difference, one which affirms diversity amongst all people without overburdening diversity with a significatory value that proscribes categories of normality or deviance. This supports Hepburn's (1997) suggestion that "if we want to raise educational standards, rather than produce a docile population who feel it is inappropriate to express criticism, then we need to challenge the discourses and strategies which organise the current status quo in our schools" (30). In this regard, the deviant cases highlight an understanding of difference that encourages those who engage in acts of exclusion to consider themselves as not only diverse, but also capable (as dominant groups members) of excluding other people. Exploring ways in which to draw dominant group children's attention to their own role in exclusion, whilst refraining from doing so in ways that evoke guilt or blame, is an important task for educators attempting to challenge unequal power relations: as previously mentioned, dominant group members must be able to see themselves as members of a dominant group (with its attendant privileges) before they can actually be accountable for privilege and attempt to engage with its consequences.

Following on from the findings presented in relation to the deviant cases, we would argue for a renegotiation of how children's experiences are understood, and how their practices of sociality are conceptualised and interpreted; we would propose that such a renegotiation is a fundamental aspect of any inquiry that seeks to rethink and represent categories of difference in less problematic ways. It thus would appear vital to propose that the categories of normality and difference presented in the majority of the books comprising the data set are grossly insufficient for the purpose of describing and affirming the very diverse range of forms human beings may take. These categories present an understanding of difference in which only marginalised group members are seen as "different". As explained previously, such constructions of difference contain within them a construction of "normality", which is most often concealed while it provides structure to the narrative around notions of sameness and differences. However, any adequate critique of normative binaries must entail an examination not only of the problematic status of the normal/different dichotomy, but also of the wider range of binary constructions that influence how children are researched and understood.

It is important to note in regard to normative binaries and the construction of difference within the books that particular aspects of individuals are drawn attention to within the books that are deemed worthy of bullying or social exclusion. Whilst the books analysed were aimed at young children, and often evoked fantastical images of people or fish doing things they would not typically do (that is, dinosaurs knitting, or babies being bigger than houses), they nonetheless reference aspects of difference that may be mapped over onto the bodies of "real people". As such, the storybooks direct children's attention towards aspects of interpersonal difference that are constructed as noteworthy. These include the abilities of individuals (for example, *Giraffes Can't Dance*), the colour of their skin (for example, *Silverskin, The Rainbow Fish*), their size (for example, *Baby Boomsticks*), their beliefs or spiritual practices (for example, *The Trouble with Mum*), and their general appearance (for example, *Rudolph the Red Nosed Reindeer*). Thus it would be a misreading to state that because these are "simply" children's storybooks that do not generally reference "real people", they are unlikely to shape how children view differences between people. Rather, we would suggest that books such as these are central to the ways in which children are schooled to see difference, and to see it as mattering.

This point about how we understand the "learning of difference" holds important implications for how we research both dominant and marginalised groups of people. In regards to the former, the problematic assumption that dominant groups are internally homogenous may represent a lack of understanding as to the multiple ways in which people identify themselves as members of a range of groups. With regards to the latter, the assumption that marginalised group members are internally homogenous and always victims of oppression is also problematic. Certainly it has always been the case that marginalised group members intentionally resist dominant group values and beliefs; and it is also the case that many marginalised group members will refuse to identify themselves as victims. Any analysis of identities and difference must therefore attempt to explore the unique and complex configurations of difference that exist amongst all people. Indeed, as Walkerdine (1999) proposes, an interrogation of the discourses affecting development in the formative years may enable us to approach the complexities of explanation and intervention in childhood in a way which avoids the potential pitfalls inherent to the comfortable certainties of categories of normality and pathology.

In critiquing normative understandings of difference, this chapter has provided an account of how constructions of difference and normative binaries can influence our understandings of particular groups of people. In the process it has been suggested that there is a need to shift the focus of research in the areas of constructions of difference and bullying. By adopting a theorisation of difference that is critical rather than normative, this chapter has explored how power imbalances function to marginalise and discipline those who do not conform to dominant group values. It has been argued that representativeness in this type of research may only be achieved through "a rethinking of how we conduct [such] research, and the questions that we ask of ourselves and the communities we engage with" (Riggs and Augoustinos 2007, 92). As such, this chapter has highlighted the need to address the issues that potentially limit research on difference and bullying with its focus primarily upon the actions of children or adults, and its accompanying failure to provide a sustained examination of other sites where children may learn ways of conducting themselves within the world. Whilst the answers to these limitations are not simple, it is important to recognise that accurate and meaningful answers are less likely while we adhere to research agendas that maintain a focus upon minority groups without equally focusing on the role dominant groups play in perpetuating the power imbalances that function to marginalise and discipline those who do not conform to dominant group values.

Table 8-1 Summary of corpus of children's picture storybooks examined in analysis

Title	**Author**	**Publication Details**	**Broad Themes**	**Sub-theme**	**No. of readers in 2005 & 2006**
Baby Boomsticks	Wilde & Legg	Sydney: ABC Books 2003	1, 2 & 3	2	68
Silverskin	Kuchling	Crawley: U of Western Australia 2002	1, 2 & 3	2	65
The Rainbow Fish	Pfister	New York: North-South Books 1992	1, 2 & 3	2	247 (top 10 books for 2005 and 2006)
Bad Buster	Laguna & Hobbs	Camberwell: Penguin Books 2003	1, 2 & 3	2	<30
Rudolph the Red-Nosed Reindeer	Daly & Jancar	New York: Western 1972	1, 2 & 3	2	<25
The Trouble with Mum	Cole	London: Heinemann 1985	1, 2 & 3	2	74
Willy the Champ	Browne	London: Heinemann 1985	1, 2 & 3	1	147 (top 10 books for 2005)
Willy the Wizard	Browne	London: Julie MacRae Books 1995	1, 2 & 3	2	21
Derek the Dinosaur	Blackwood & Argent	Adelaide: Omnibus Books 1987	1, 2 & 3	1	<25
Giraffes Can't Dance	Andreae & Parker-Rees	London: Orchard Books 2002	1, 2 & 3	2	173 (top 10 books for 2005 & 2006)
The Lazy Beaver	Gallo & Samsa	Italy: William Collins 1983.	1, 2 & 3	2	<25

Table 8-1 (continued)
Summary of corpus of children's picture storybooks examined in analysis

Title	Author	Publication Details	Broad Themes	Sub-theme	No. of readers in 2005 & 2006
India the Showstopper	Argent	Crows Nest: Allen & Unwin 2005	1, 2 & 3	2	<11
What a Goat!	Oliver & Cox	Norwood: Omnibus 2003	1, 2 & 3	1	<25
Bill's Best Day	Laguna & McLean	Norwood: Omnibus 2002	1, 2 & 3	2	<25
Fit for a Prince	Kroll & Hatcher	Norwood: Omnibus 2001	1, 2 & 3	1	<25
Michael	Bradman & Ross	New York: Anderson Press 1990	1, 2 & 3	2	<25
The Emperor and the Kite	Yolen & Young	New York: Paperstar 1998	1, 2 & 3	2	<25
Little Pierre	San Souci & Cutrow	New York: Harcourt 2003	1 & 3	2	<25
Marty and Mei-Ling	Cummings	Milsons Point: Random 1995	1 & 3	1	37
Horrible Harriet	Hobbs	Crows Nest: Allen & Unwin 2001	1 & 2	None	<25
My Gran's Different	Lawson	New Jersey: Simply Read Books 2005	Deviant Case		55
Rainbow Fish and the Big Blue Whale	Marcus Pfister	New York: North-South Books 1998	Deviant Case		125

*—Data refers to a study involving a representative sample of 30 South Australian schools, which were surveyed by the Premier's Reading Challenge. Assuming that this sample is representative of the wider population of 718 schools that actually participated in the Challenge, the numbers presented here can be taken to represent approximately 4% of the actual number of students that read each book.

CHAPTER NINE

UNITY OF THE EUROPEAN UNION IS BASED ON DIVERSITY— ARE MINORITIES PROTECTED?

SILVO DEVETAK

Foreword

European integration is an economic and political process interwoven with elements which emanate from the cultural, ethnic and linguistic diversity of Europe. The efficiency of economic and political action is thus related to the stability of inter-ethnic and inter-religious relations within the Community. The demographic structure of 495 million people living in the European Union (7.4% of the world population) is composed of a great variety of ethnic, cultural, linguistic, religious and similar identities. Viewed from the political aspect—which is not a subject of this analysis—the EU is, in addition, a conglomerate of political positions which are firmly anchored in the "national interests" of the states' members and, exclusively in accordance with European contractual law, combined into common decisions of EU institutions.

Cultural, ethnic, linguistic and religious diversity is a strong characteristic defining the demographic composition of the population of all 27 state members of the European Union. The population of the Union in 2005 spoke more than 90 languages, 53 of them being "stateless languages": Frisian, Welsh, Catalan, Sorbian, Roma languages, etc[1] (Marí and Strubell 2002). The most widespread languages were English (spoken by 38% of the EU population), French and German (14% each) and Spanish and Russian (6% each). Some 40 million people living in the Union speak a regional or minority languages (Pan and Pfeil 2003). There are presumed to be 94 ethnic and national groups who live as minorities in another EU country.

Twenty-three national languages are official languages of the EU.[2] But statistical data show that the meagre knowledge of "other languages" represents a divisive factor within the Union. In 2005, for instance, the majority population in eight EU states did not speak a foreign language (Ireland 66%, UK 62%, Italy 59%, Portugal 58%, Hungary 58%, Spain 56%, Romania 53%, and Turkey as a candidate state, 67%).[3] Some experts are therefore proposing building up the system of learning "other" languages as a tool for promoting the principle of "unity in diversity" that should constitute in practice a binding factor of EU societies[4] (Shuibhne 1996; 2002; Palermo 2001; Ò Riagáin 2002; Kronenthal 2003).

The religious composition of the European population is also a rainbow of varieties. Christianity is roughly comprised of Roman Catholicism, Orthodox Christianity[5] and Protestantism. Of the 750 million Europeans (living on the continent), 269 million are Catholics, 171 million Orthodox, 79 million Protestants, and 28 million Anglicans. Opinion polls, however, show that this structure of participation of people in faith-based organisations does not correspond to the level of trust in them, which is much lower.[6] In 2002 the EU had roughly over a million Jews. It was estimated in 2006 that 16 million Muslims live in the EU (3.2% of the total population) and in particular countries the percentage was much higher (in France, for instance, 8-9%). According to the estimate of the Central Institute of Islamic Archives in Soest, Germany, Islam will be in the near future the second largest religion in Europe (nearly 52 million by the year 2014) due to the 6.5% annual growth rate.[7] Tens of other minor religious groups were established and "registered" in accordance with the norms on the freedom of religion enshrined in the Universal Declaration on Human Rights (art.18).[8]

Belief is nowadays developing in Europe essentially through individualised and deregulated forms which are no longer under the control and mediation of organised political and spiritual institutions. The EU is a secular body, with no formal connections to any religion and no mention of religion in any current or proposed treaty. Discussion of the draft texts of the European Constitution and later the Treaty of Lisbon have included proposals to mention Christianity and/or God in the preamble of the text. However, this idea faced opposition and was dropped.

As a result of historical reminiscences, and/or the political process of decentralising government, 268 regions exist in the EU.[9] Regional identity is the main identity in some of the EU countries (for instance, Bavaria in Germany, Piedmont and Lombardy in Italy or Carinthia in Austria). It is very strong especially in those regions which have been established on an ethnic basis, like Catalonia, the Basque country and Galicia in Spain; Flanders and Wallonia—Belgium; Scotland and Wales—UK; South Tyrol—Italy; Hargita and Kovasna—Romania. Regionalism represents in the EU a political, economic and sometimes a geopolitical aspect of diversity that must be taken into account when making decisions both at national and EU level (Nagel 2004; Togennburg 2007). In some cases regional identity is linked with religious affiliation (for instance, Catholicism in Bavaria, or Protestantism in Hargita and Kovasna in Romania).

Achievements after the dissolution of the cold war division of Europe

Since the dissolution of the cold war division of Europe, there have been significant achievements, especially in eastern European states (later new members of the EU) concerning the legal regulation of the status and rights of members of national minorities (Pentassuglia 2001; Henrard 2002; Liebich 2002; Ram 2003; Vermeersch 2004; Togennburg 2004).

The European law on minorities is composed of norms adopted at national and bilateral levels or within the Council of Europe, while the EU has not yet adopted its own legal standards on the status and rights of ethnic minorities (Benedikter 2006; Arnold 2001). New constitutional and legal provisions stipulating the status, rights, self-managing organisations and institutions, legal representation and the inclusion of minorities in decision making processes were adopted, for instance, in Hungary, Slovenia and Romania (De Witte 2004). The result of political movements was the improvement of territorial ethno-political autonomies, for instance, in Spain (Catalonia, Galicia, Basque lands) and United Kingdom (Scotland, Wales), which added a new political value to the traditional European territorial autonomies in South Tyrol/Alto Adige in Italy and the Aaland Islands in Finland (Benedikter 2006a; Nagel 2004). More than twenty bilateral agreements were signed stipulating co-operation between neighbors and the rights of minorities—for instance, agreements signed after 1990 such as the German-Polish agreements and the agreements of Hungary with its neighbours (Gal 1999).

The main sources of European law on the rights of ethnic minorities are international instruments adopted within the COE. Some general human rights that also have a value for members of minorities are included in the European Convention on Human Rights—ECHR. For instance, the importance of art.11 of the ECHR, which states the right to freedom of peaceful assembly and associated rights, for establishing minorities' political organisations was confirmed also by decisions of the ECHR in Strasbourg.[10] Several efforts to adopt an additional protocol to the ECHR, which would have evaluated minority rights as a constituent part of the ECHR, failed. Finally, Protocol no.12 to the ECHR—on the elimination of racial discrimination—was adopted in 2000. It stipulates, for members of minorities living in countries that will ratify it, the possibility of "suing" via the European Court of Human Rights a country which commits an act towards them on ethnic and racial grounds that is constituted as violating any of the norms of the ECHR.[11] The framework convention on the rights of national minorities (1995) is a pragmatic compromise between advanced proposals included in the draft Convention prepared by the Venice "Commission on democracy through law", which is an consultative body with the COE and the attitude of non-recognising the existence of minorities exercised by some European states; in the first rank are France and Greece, but Bulgaria is also among them[12] (Weller 2005). The European charter for regional or minority languages (1992) is a positive achievement of the COE, but opened the possibilities that the states "select" the provisions which will be binding, thus creating double standards for the state members of the Charter (Ò Riagáin 2001).[13] Members of minorities were provided with new mechanisms for protecting their rights both on the international and domestic level (Weller 2004).

This progress was first of all the result of bewilderment among European political elites with the bloody confrontations on the basis of different ethnicity and religions, firstly in the Caucasus area (in 1989 between Uzbeks and Meskhetian Turks in different locations of Uzbekistan; in June 1990 between Kyrgyz and Uzbeks in Ferghana Valley in Kyrgyzstan, in 1991 Azeri-Armenian war for Nagorno-Karabakh) and later in the Balkans (wars in the process of the dissolution of Yugoslavia, 1991-1995 and Kosovo crisis in 1998-99). The new political behaviour of the EU was manifested also through criteria which the EU put forward for the recognition of new states and as conditions for the acceptance of new states in the EU. These criteria were: 1) human rights and minority protection standards as a condition for EU recognition of newly established states;[14] 2) human rights, minority protection and good neighborhood relations as a part of the so-called Copenhagen criteria for examining the preparedness of states for EU membership;[15] and 3) stimulation and the conclusion of bilateral agreements on neighborhood cooperation and minorities' protection, which were later included as an integral part of the Balladur pact of 1994[16] that was initiated in order to "prepare" the countries on the list for the EU fifth enlargement for the negotiating process (for different aspects of this issue see: Heidbreder and

Carasco 2003; Henrard 2002; Hillion 2004; Pujadas 2003; Sasse and Hughes 2003; Wiener and Schwellnus 2004). The European Commission and the Robert Schuman Centre, European University Institute in Florence, Italy, established in 1998 a "reflection group on long-term implications of EU enlargement", which among other topics, examined also the minority rights and EU enlargement (Amato and Batt 1999).

The reefs under the ocean of EU harmony

In spite of the progress achieved in the process of the latest European integration, many problems regarding inter-ethnic and inter–religious relations exist within the EU and its neighborhood, some of them constituting a source of possible conflict (Lynch 1996; Moucheboeuf 2006). On the all-European level, many ethno-political negative activities have been noted that could be transformed into sources of instability (for instance, racism, xenophobia, racist motivated crime, neo-Nazi ideologies, Roma syndrome).[17] The situation of members of the biggest European national minority—Roma and Sinti (11 to 12 million people)—is the most outstanding case of discrimination in Europe. This was confirmed at the first EU Roma summit held on 16 September 2008 in Brussels under the joint patronage of the EU Commission President Barroso and the French presidency of the European council. According to the report of the Organisation for Security and Cooperation in Europe (OSCE) the Roma and Sinti populations continue to face discrimination and remain divided from mainstream society across Europe. Significant gaps remain in areas such as education, housing, employment and access to social services and justice.[18]

The ethnic factor as a source of misunderstanding could be discerned in bilateral relations between some of EU countries, for instance, sensitive Hungarian-Slovak and Hungarian-Romanian relations concerning the huge size of the Hungarian minority in both countries, and German-Polish relations concerning property, and citizenship issues concerning Germans who were resettled from former German territories in Poland (Driessen 1999; Gal 2000; Breuer 2002).

"Domestic" political notions developed on ethnic bases also represent a serious challenge for the countries concerned (for instance, the Basque movement in Spain, the Catholic-Irish and Protestant-British divisive political patterns in Northern Ireland, the Turkish secession in Cyprus, the Corsica autonomy demands in France).[19] The unresolved issues concerning the status and rights of ethnic minorities could be a "domestic source" of turmoil and instability of an EU country—for instance, the rights of Russian minorities in Estonia, Lithuania and Latvia, where they are in the latter a significant part of the population (Dorodnova 2000; Roger 2001; Smith 2003; Tesser 2003; Törnquist 2001).[20]

Similar phenomena could be found in inter-religious relations in Europe, both on pan-European and bilateral and domestic levels (for instance, suspicious relations between the Islamic and Christian communities, ambiguous relations between Catholic and Orthodox churches, attitude towards Judaism).[21] This state of affairs could have a negative consequence for the rights of members of particular religions.[22] The recent experiences in the Balkans and elsewhere in similar circumstances have shown that the religious factor *per se* has not such an explosive strength as the ethno-political one, but could be a "spiritual strength" that fuels negative, mostly nationalistic extremist and exclusive political behavior.[23]

Situations concerning inter-ethnic and inter–religious relations, including the status and rights of minorities, could produce political frictions and even conflicts exist also in the relations of the EU's member states with states "on the other side" of the present and future EU external borders. For instance: relations between Greece and Macedonia, Bulgaria and Macedonia, Hungary and Serbia, the Russian federation and the Baltic states; relations between the Russian Orthodox Church with national Orthodox Churches in the Baltic states and with the Romanian Orthodox Church; relations of the Romanian Orthodox Church with the Moldovan and Serbian Orthodox Churches; relations of the Greek and Bulgarian Orthodox Churches with the Macedonian Orthodox Church—are all sources of possible conflict (Devetak 2007).

The unilateral declaration of independence, adopted on 17 February 2008 by the local Albanian parliament in Kosovo, which does not have a firm international legal foundation, opened a Pandora's box whose impact on international security and especially on the stability of the Balkan region cannot yet be foreseen for the time being. This move, sponsored by the USA and major European states, produced a great division among EU countries and was met, of course, with firm opposition from Serbia, of which Kosovo has been an integral part since 1919, with the firm support of Russia.[24]

On the surface these situations are for the time being under "control", but the factual historical, political and other causes of their existence, like nationalism, irredentism, historical negative reminiscences, have not been eliminated at all.

Unsuitable Responses of the EU

The responses of the EU have not been at all adequate to the above-mentioned problems, which constitute a serious threat to the political stability and security of member states and the Union as a whole. In addition, there is a great disparity between the use of minority rights as a tool of EU foreign and enlargement policy and the political willingness of the EU to elaborate its own standards on minority rights (Hilpold 2001; Toggenburg 2001; De Witte 2002; Brunner 2002; Hofmann 2002; Schlögel 2004; Van den Berghe 2004). The lack of political willingness to adopt legally binding norms has also been shown in the rejection of modest attempts for the contractual regulation of these issues during negotiations for the European constitution, which later was not accepted because of the negative votes on the referenda on that issue in France and Netherlands. In the new Treaty of Lisbon, which is in the process of ratification by member states, some progress was achieved. Article 1(8) of the Treaty of Lisbon provides that Article 6(1) of the Treaty on European Union is to be replaced by the following:

> The Union recognizes the rights, freedoms and principles set out in the Charter of Fundamental Rights of the European Union of 7 December 2000, as adapted at Strasbourg, on 12 December 2007, which shall have the same legal value as the Treaties.[25]

The Charter does not include an obligation of EU member states to ensure the rights of minorities. It only stipulates that "the Union shall respect cultural, religious and linguistic diversity" (art.22) and that "any discrimination based on any ground such as ... ethnic or social origin ... language ... membership of a national minority ... shall be prohibited" (art.21).[26] In addition, the new Treaty stipulates the "collective membership" of the EU in the ECHR. The provisions of the Charter do not extend in any way the competences of the Union as defined in the Treaties. The obligations of members will be confined to the promulgation of EU law and standards. In the case of minority rights, these are art. 21 and 22 of the Charter (De Witte and Togennburg 2002).

Progress has been over-shadowed by the requests of Poland, UK and Ireland not to be bound by the Charter on basic rights. These requests have introduced new divisions in the pattern of European identity. Nonetheless, it is the first time in EU history that the prohibition of discrimination because of one's "membership in a national minority" and respect for cultural and linguistic diversity is a legally binding obligation of the EU and of its member states respectively. But after the rejection of the Treaty on the referendum held in June 2008 in Ireland, it is not clear what the fate of the Treaty will be. It is certain that it could not come into force as envisaged on 1 January 2009.

An important step forward toward the equal status of the inhabitants of the EU regardless of their ethnic and racial origin has been the acceptance (on the basis of art.13 of the EU Treaty) of Council directive 2000/43/EC of 29 June 2000 ensuring the principle of equal treatment of persons irrespective of racial or ethnic origin.[27] With the transformation of the European centre on racism and xenophobia into the EU Agency for Fundamental Rights (FRA) on 1 March 2007, the EU established a watchdog for human rights and freedoms, which is otherwise a consultative body with no decision making competencies.[28]

The "management" of the European Union's cultural and ethnic diversity is composed of balanced elements of national and supranational involvements (which are in many cases linked). They could be defined in the following way: 1) the Union has great competencies in regard to ensuring equality without ethnic, racial or religious discrimination; 2) the Union and national states have linked competences in regulating migration and integration issues; and 3) the competencies of member states are unchallenged concerning such matters as the preservation of cultural or ethnic identity, including the rights of national minorities, ethnic territorial and other autonomies, and similar issues (Toggenburg 2005).

What should be the role of minorities in shaping European identity?

Due to the aforementioned conflicts within the EU, its nations continue to experience an identity crisis concerning the cultural, ethnic, religious and moral values of the EU as a whole. The open issues regarding national minorities who live in the EU must be considered in this context. The nations of the EU need, first of all, to define more precisely what values constitute the identity of the Community. The starting point for the consideration is clear: it must be based on the principle of "unity in diversity". However, this commonly used phrase remains more or less a dead letter on paper when it comes to its implementation through the adoption of European standards and policy, not to mention EU legislation.

First of all, in practice there is much interpretation of what the principle of "unity in diversity" means (Toggenburg 2000). One of the basic elements that could contribute to the notion of "unity" lies in the answer to the question of what makes up European identity. On one hand there are those who did not recognise any competences of the Union in such matters as language, culture, ethnic autonomies, local and regional identity, minority protection, environment and similar, claiming that these matters are, in accordance with the principle of subsidiary, the overwhelming competence of the nation state and local and regional authorities. On the other hand are those—far outnumbered by the first group—who advocate the building up of adequate policy in the EU in these areas, which should be a genuine contribution to the shaping of elements which could constitute the content of European identity based on the principle of "unity in diversity".

There is a common understanding: what the EU needs is the affirmation of its identity, its values, which make it unique. But the main issue at stake is what should be done in order to realise the principle of "unity in diversity"? The possible emergence of a European identity is confronted with serious political and sociological phenomena, which influence predominantly the delayed or even non-existent process of European identity making. I would like to put forward the following five, perhaps most relevant, points:

First, according to the Eurobarometer survey 2005, 10% of EU citizens identified themselves as European first, while 42% identified with their nationality first and then as a European. Overall, 52% of respondents from the 25 EU member states identified themselves as European primarily or additionally to identifying with their country. Thus one can conclude that while nationality remains the primary source of geo-political identification across Europe, a majority feel an attachment to Europe.[29]

Of course, these results should take into account the fact that even in theory there are many interpretations of what European identity is, and thus the filling of "attachment to Europe" is not necessarily evidence of possessing European identity by the respondents. The genuine affiliation of the EU population with the European identity is meagre, and in most states of the Union it is linked with or even overshadowed by a) national identity that prevails in all the EU members countries, and especially in France, Greece, Estonia, Latvia, Lithuania and Malta, b) regional identity, which is the main identity in some of the EU countries (for instance, Bavaria in Germany, South Tyrol, Piedmont and Lombardy in Italy, or Carinthia in Austria), and c) ethnic identity of a population for which political community claims either the improvement of cultural and linguistic rights and the possibilities to have a say in the decision making processes (for instance, Slovenes in Austria and Italy, or Frisians in Netherlands) or the legitimisation of their separatist tendencies aimed at the formation of their own independent state.

Second, aspirations of some European ethnic communities/ethnic groups to establish their own independent states (and receive the recognition of the international community) are still in progress in countries in the European Union and in its immediate neighborhood. This is corroding the national identity of the states concerned (for instance: Scottish aspirations for secession; Flemish separatism; the Basque fight for independence; the Turkish Cypriot separation from the Greek part of the island; the unilateral declaration of secession of Kosovo Albanians from Serbia).

Third, in the further development of European identity it is necessary to take into account new values which were brought into the EU with the inclusion of the large orthodox communities of Romania and Bulgaria and the values of the large Muslim communities living within the EU as well. Mutual understanding and exchange between the three religions Christian, Jewish and Muslim which trace their roots to Abraham's heritage is a very serious imperative of Europe today and in the future, directly linked with its identity. Disputes will continue if lack of understanding and exchange continue to make Europe vulnerable to religious fundamentalism (Devetak 2007).

Fourth, there is no "unity" among member states concerning the development of the competences and organisation of common institutions of the EU. The adoption of the Constitution Treaty of 2004[30] failed because of its rejection at referenda in France and Netherlands. The coming into force of the Lisbon Treaty, which on 13 December 2008 emerged from the "ruins" of the Constitution, is an open question because of its rejection at the referendum in Ireland in June 2008. So, a question could be put forward as to what constitutes the legal aspect of European identity as a basis for its common efficient functioning both internally and internationally.

Finally, it is necessary to consider the question that was asked in the title of this article: what is the role of ethnic, linguistic and cultural minorities in the process of European integration? What does the principle of "unity in diversity" mean for them? Are their rights protected by the policy and norms of the EU? First of all, it is necessary to establish the differences between western and eastern (new) EU countries concerning the rights and social position of minorities. The eastern European countries, except Estonia, Latvia and Lithuania, have developed further the legal position of national minorities, while many western European countries lag behind, embroiled in old patterns of minority rights (for instance, the rights of Germans in Denmark were formulated by a declaration adopted by Parliament in 1954), or even deny the recognition of their minorities (for instance, Greece denies the existence of the Macedonian and Turkish ethnic minorities). In some Eastern European countries ethnic minorities are represented in the Parliament regardless of their number (for instance, Hungary, Slovenia, and Romania); they can establish self-governed associations, which have by law prescribed competences concerning linguistic, cultural and similar questions (for instance, Hungary, Slovenia). Of course, this does not mean that in these countries there are no problems regarding minorities, especially as far as the Roma population is concerned.

In order to improve the legal status of minorities in the EU it is recommended that the EU states which have not yet done so adhere to the following international standards on the elimination of discrimination and on the rights of minorities: a) Protocol 12 to the ECHR—on the elimination of discrimination;[31] b) the European charter on regional or minority languages;[32] and c) the Framework convention on the protection of national minorities.[33] The resolution of the European Parliament "Protection of minorities and anti-discrimination policies in an enlarged Europe" of 2005 is a good starting point for elaborating further EU policies in this field.[34] The expert group established by the European Commission on the recommendation of the European Parliament has prepared a valuable background for further consideration of the protection of minorities in the enlarged EU.[35]

In addition, the following actions could contribute significantly to the amelioration of inter-ethnic and inter-religious relations in European societies: a) strict monitoring of the implementation of the provisions of the European Council directive 2000/43/EC of 29 June 2000 implementing the principle of equal treatment between persons irrespective of racial or ethnic origin (Bell 2002); [36] b) elaboration of a common EU policy concerning the status and rights of minorities; and c) adoption of adequate policy and standards concerning the Roma population of the EU, and assurance of the necessary funds in the 2007-2013 financial perspective to create a political and material framework—together with activities adopted on domestic level—for the improvement of the social and economic position of the Roma population, and thus to the political and social stability of countries affected by unresolved Roma problems.[37]

Finally, and in order to clear the way for the growth of European identification among the population of the EU, it would be productive to elaborate and realise the following actions: a) to continue existing, and develop new processes of genuine reconciliation (for instance, between Germans and Poles, between Hungarians and Romanians, and so on); b) to elaborate new incentives for the development of European cultures and thus increase the common sense of responsibility for the cultural development of all European ethnic and national identities; c) to strengthen the principle of solidarity enshrined in the Charter on basic rights in the EU that is now part of the EU Treaty; and d) to develop the discussion and systematically disseminate standards of a common European identity, especially in the fields that do not harm the cultural identities of nations and national minorities united in the EU.

CHAPTER TEN

BRINGING INDIGENOUS SOVEREIGNTIES INTO COMMUNITY PARTNERSHIPS: UNPACKING RACIALISATION TO RE-ENGAGE INDIGENOUS AUSTRALIAN STUDENTS IN EDUCATION

CATHERINE KOERNER, SIMONE TUR AND CHRISTOPHER WILSON*

Acknowledgement of Country

The authors acknowledge that Flinders University and the Inspire Mentor Program are located on Kaurna land, and they recognise the living Kaurna culture, language and connection to country.

Introduction

> … educators need to approach learning not merely as the acquisition of knowledge but as the production of cultural practices that offer students a sense of identity, place, and hope (Giroux 1992, 170).

In this chapter, and using the Inspire Mentor Program as a point of reflection, we begin by discussing an Indigenous community partnership with a university, established to provide non-Indigenous mentors with cultural education and to work with Indigenous senior school students to increase their retention rates. The goal of the Inspire Mentor Program is to increase retention rates in a low-socio economic area near Flinders University in South Australia. We then discuss the pedagogical approach that is applied to re-engage Indigenous students in education. We address how the pedagogical approach is implemented to program design and practices in addition to the cultural education training to non-Indigenous mentors in Inspire and we refer to the model that has been developed to reinforce Indigenous young people's connection with their community and Elders as a crucial component of their participation in formal education. This chapter is multi-voiced, hence in places the "we" speaks from an Indigenous standpoint and in others from a nominally white standpoint, but always in a relationship to Indigenous sovereignty. The first section addresses the protocol to locate us as both authors and as the people involved in developing and implementing the partnership.

Shifting the power of location: making whiteness visible

In order to write this chapter, we as authors firstly located ourselves within a critique of racialisation. In her text, *Talkin up to the white woman*, Aileen Moreton-Robinson (a Keonpul woman from Quandmooka) challenges white feminists to locate themselves within the racialised power-relations that privilege whiteness as an invisible and unchallenged practice (2000, 33). In an Australian context (possibly globally), this means that First Nations or Indigenous peoples must be centred in social and political struggles. Following Moreton-Robinson's (2000, 124) challenge and extending it to all political struggles for social justice, we have engaged with the principle that Indigenous sovereignty should be the ground from which we proceed. Thus white people must be "raced" in order for whiteness to be seen, reflected upon, and interrogated. This can be seen as a confronting yet necessary approach if those who desire social justice genuinely conceptualise a space for Indigenous people within their struggles.

Moreton-Robinson identifies that involving Indigenous people requires more than just facilitating space and voice: white people need to relinquish power in reconstructing the space. This must be extended into all so-called mainstream spaces if they are to be transformed from spaces that reflect the possessive logic of white patriarchal sovereignty that continue to make the Australian nation-state post-colonising (see Moreton-Robinson 2003, 23) to a space that is non-colonial (see Tully 2000). Moreton-Robinson coined the term "post-colonising" to challenge the view that the Australian nation-state is post-colonial. She applies the verb "post-colonising" "to signify the active, the current and the continuing nature of the colonising relationship that positions us as belonging but not belonging" (2003, 38). Moreton-Robinson challenges us, the authors, to apply her critique of how whiteness is enacted to education as a colonised site where complicit colonial relationships can be reproduced. Because race, sovereignty and ontology are important in understanding education, we now locate ourselves as authors in relation to this chapter.

Catherine Koerner

This is the space I seek to engage with as a white queer woman community activist/worker in Australia. I am daughter, sister, friend, partner, colleague, community worker, student, Australian citizen and part of many different communities. What does it mean, in all aspects of personal and professional life, to "fall into Indigenous sovereignty" (Nicoll 2007), to recognise one-self through a critical lens as raced by white privilege (Riggs 2007) and to seriously engage with the incommensurability of Indigenous sovereignty (Haggis 2004)? This is a question that is fundamental in nature, and this chapter is one attempt to critically engage with it.

As a non-Indigenous person who lives in the southern suburbs of Adelaide (since 2003), and the coordinator of the Inspire Mentor Project, I sought to centre Indigenous knowledges and sovereignty in my life and the work that I am involved with. It is one attempt to critique my location within the colonised spaces of the university, the education sector more broadly and also within community work. It is also important to recognise that in contesting whiteness through acknowledging Indigenous sovereignties, I am nonetheless complicit in whiteness (Haggis 2007, 317) and it is not something that can be side-stepped. I thank Simone Ulalka Tur for contributing to this discussion and bringing the section of Moreton-Robinson's text referred to above to my attention.

Locating the Indigenous sovereign self

Simone Ulalka Tur

I am a woman from the Yankunytjatjara community and an important process as a contributor to this chapter is voicing my own subject position so that the reader will understand the context and position from which I write. I am mother, daughter, sister, community member, teacher, lecturer; these multiple subjectivities inform and shape who I am.

I grew up in Adelaide, however my country/community is located within the A*n*angu Pitjantjatjara Yankunytjatjara (APY Lands), Coober Pedy and Oodnadatta, South Australia. I am a trained teacher and currently an academic at Flinders University. I have worked within Indigenous education for over ten years where I have advocated for Aboriginal

Languages being taught in schools, the contribution of Indigenous Knowledges to education and the development of ethical research practices when working in partnership with Indigenous communities. I have been taught by my senior knowledge holders through intergenerational teaching which centres my identity and cultural training and so informs my teaching and research practice. Central to my role as an educator is my responsibility to critically engage with education as a colonised site; to privilege Indigenous knowledge; maintain the contemporary record of community and negotiate alternative ways of positioning Indigenous epistemologies and practices within contemporary intellectual structures. It is therefore from this position that I write.

Christopher Wilson

From within Academia, I am a young Ngarrindjeri archaeologist but I am also a father, brother, teacher and learner. Although I was born on Kaurna land and grew up in the southern suburbs of Adelaide, I strongly identify with the Ngarrindjeri from the Lower Murray Lakes and Coorong in South Australia. Locating myself within any academic setting is critical for articulating the broader project of "identification", "positioning" and "location" within colonised spaces. As an early career academic within the discipline of archaeology, I seek to engage in research, teaching and community development in a culturally appropriate and responsible sphere which aims to privilege the communities for whom I work in, with and for (see Wilson 2007 for broader discussion). Throughout my western education, I have gained particular skills and knowledge as well as a set of unique lived experiences as a young Indigenous male growing up in the southern suburbs of Adelaide. As a result, these experiences have indirectly become valuable during the process of training both Indigenous and non-Indigenous mentors. These experiences are made explicit and articulate some of the major issues and influences that continue to impact upon young Indigenous peoples in the education system today. Furthermore, I would like to suggest that there is an urgency for a space to be created for Indigenous young people to engage in shifting power inequalities through academia which is also a key focus for the Inspire Peer Mentor Program. These politics further acknowledge and privilege models of youth empowerment as valid.

The Inspire Mentor Program and Mentoring

Richard Trudjen (2000) argues that dominant culture personnel, including medical professionals and educators, whom are not trained in Yolngu language, cultural practices and learning practices are a major part of the problem for the current crisis in education and health for Yolngu peoples in Arnhem Land, in the Northern Territory. Yet despite this, it is typically the case that Yolngu people are framed as being the problem, and programs are constantly designed by dominant culture staff to fix the problems. Similarly, volunteers and educators throughout Australia continue colonising practices within the education system when their practice is not informed by a critique of racialisation, program design or policy writing. When Indigenous sovereignty and knowledges are not acknowledged and at the centre of mainstream educational practices, then Indigenous students are actively marginalised resulting in further disengagement. Many programs have been introduced in an attempt to increase the number of Indigenous students completing formal education, including mentoring. But, how can such programs ensure that they are also not a part of the problem when a critique of racialisation is literally absent in the mentoring literature?

The last 25 years has produced an impressive amount of academic literature on mentoring, though there is reportedly a lack of consensus on defining it (Colley 2003). Certainly, in contrast with role modelling, tutoring, coaching and buddy systems, mentoring is concerned with a "whole of person" development that is actively supported by the mentor: "… mentoring focuses on explicit action by the mentor to assist the young person to reach their goal" (MacCallum and Beltman 2002, 8). Mentoring Australia (2000) defines effective mentoring as:

a) a relationship that focuses on the needs of the mentee;
b) fosters caring and supportive relationships;
c) encourages all mentees to develop to their fullest potential; and
d) a strategy to develop active community partnerships.

The Inspire Mentor Program's goal is to increase participation in education with a particular commitment to increasing retention rates and access to higher education for Indigenous students. The emphasis upon Indigenous students arises from the fact that Indigenous students are disproportionately identified as being at risk of leaving school early compared to non-Indigenous school students. Inspire has attempted to achieve the goal of increased participation by fostering links across the education sectors including university, primary and secondary schools, Indigenous communities, Indigenous and non-Indigenous university students, Indigenous and non-Indigenous academic staff and Elders. This community-university partnership offers a model of access, support and continuity which is robust enough to sustain both social critique and practical implementation based on that critique. It does so by providing a critique of racialisation as the reason for Indigenous student disengagement and by extending the process to include other aspects of institutionalised or taken-for-granted disadvantage. Catherine Koerner was employed to develop the Inspire Mentor Program from its conception in 2004. When developing the training program for the university students who are either volunteer mentors or gain credit for their participation as mentors, she first approached Christopher Wilson to be involved in the training. Wilson is Ngarrindjeri, and a graduate from one of the key schools involved in the program and at the time (2005) was employed in student support at Yunggorendi First Nations Centre for Higher Education and Research at Flinders University while undertaking his PhD in Archeology. Simone Ulalka Tur is from the Yankunytjatjara community, is a senior lecturer at Yunggorendi, and has been teaching about racialisation in education for over a decade. After many conversations, Wilson and Tur developed and delivered the cultural education component, which comprises 50 percent of the training for mentors. The partnership has developed over time from the professional and personal collaborations fostered between the authors and has been formalised by documenting how Inspire and Yunggorendi as programs/units continue to work together.

Each year since 2004, Inspire has placed approximately 120 new mentors alongside young people as co-learners in their learning environment, both inside and outside the "traditional" classroom. There are 40 primary schools, secondary schools and alternative education programs involved with Flinders University. The mentors meet with their students for two hours per week every week of the school year for at least 12 months. This is based on a synthesis of ten years of research (Freedman 1988; 1991; Styles and Morrow 1992; Greim 1992; Tierney and Branch 1992; Furano et al. 1993; McCartney et al. 1994; Roaf et al. 1994; Morrow and Styles 1995; Tierney et al. 1995) undertaken on mentoring programs in the United States that shows that mentoring arrangements for at risk young people must be of 12 months or more in duration for the participants to gain long-term benefits (Sipe 1996).

The findings across the above-mentioned studies indicate that at least six months of regular meetings are required before young people report that they have a trusting relationship with their mentor. These findings support those reported by Hartley (2004, 15) in Australia; that both short-term mentoring relationships and broken/disbanded mentoring relationships have the potential to harm children or young people who have experienced broken/disbanded relationships with adults including family, reinforcing vulnerabilities and young people's feelings of abandonment.

Where the relationships extend beyond 6-12 months, it has been found that participating in mentoring programs can make important and observable changes for young people who are deemed at risk in the education sector. An impact study on young people matched with Big Brother/Big Sister mentors and a control group of young people waiting to be matched by Tierney et al. (1995) provides clear evidence that young people can benefit from being involved in a well-run mentoring program. The findings suggest that the matched young people were 46 percent less likely than controls (who were young people on the waiting list to be matched with a mentor) to initiate drug use and 27 percent less likely to initiate alcohol use. They were nearly one-third less likely to hit someone and had 50 percent less days of school absenteeism as the control group. These findings have been reflected in anecdotal feedback and focus groups with young people, mentors and school staff within the Inspire mentor program that show an increase in retention rates (Garvis 2008). Koerner and Harris have argued (2007, 356) that if there is an increase in school attendance, this could indicate a re-engagement with formal learning that statistically should lead to better employment outcomes as mentioned above, breaking the poverty cycle to which dis-engaging from formal education contributes. This research provides insight into the potential of mentoring with young people "at risk" within education. However it does not address education as a colonised site nor the implications of this for Indigenous young people (in settler societies). As we argue in this chapter, racialisation and constructions of race need to be unpacked in-order to transform education for the benefit of Indigenous Australian students.

Research on widening participation in higher education in the UK (Shepherd 2007) has shown that if students who are identified as being "at risk" are not strategically involved in programs, then they do not get picked up as participants in such programs. Shepherd (2007) reports that there is not an increase in retention rates or of access to tertiary education by poor students despite many programs that aim to address this inequity. Young people who do not complete school are four times more likely to be unemployed by the age of 24 years (Bean 2002, 2), thus potentially compounding poverty in Indigenous families. Poverty, risk, disengagement, lack of access and unemployment are clearly connected. Indigenous families know this all too well.

Programs can help to address and disrupt this sequence of disadvantage by addressing the role of "racialisation" in the process. *The Education for Social Justice Group* (1992) refers to racialisation as the social construction of "race" which is used to oppressive effect through social organisation, for example: individual and group consciousness; social formations including government structures; and sites of power such as educational institutions; as well as culture and ideology reinforced through such structures and behaviours. Many progressive scholars point out that:

> 'Race' theory enables the recognition that throughout Australian history Indigenous people have been excluded and marginalised from all levels of education including schooling, universities and education administration/policy enterprise (Tur et al. 2003. See also Reynolds 1987; Lippmann 1994; Miller 1985; Bin-Sallik 1989; Mattingley and Hampton 1988; McConnochie et al. 1988; Hollinsworth 1997)

Rather than seeing Indigenous young people as "at risk" in education as a result of their Indigenous identity, we argue that it is the racialisation of the Western education system, and all Australian institutions, that marginalise Indigenous young people, their families, and communities. Because the Inspire Mentor project coordinator and the majority of mentors are not Indigenous it is crucial to critique racialisation so as to work in partnership with Indigenous community members and staff in the context of Indigenous sovereignties, epistemologies and ontologies. The mentors are volunteers from the Flinders University student body, and are able to integrate this learning into a component of their degree. In learning about racialisation, the mentors are challenged to un-settle what it means for them to be raced in terms of whiteness. What does this mean for their practice as a mentor (and in their lives) and how can their practice develop non-colonial relationships with Indigenous young people? How can this critique assist mentors who are raced differently as white and not white, to locate themselves in terms of Indigenous sovereignty? As Sue Shore argues:

> … it is time academics and researchers in adult education started to make the effort to 'think through' the effects of writing that conceals the powerful effects of a White norm to White people—bearing in mind that this norm is very visible to many non-White people. This would seem an urgent step to take in view of the repeated claims the literature makes for the potential of education to initiate social change. It is also an urgent step to take in recognising that theory forms its own pedagogy—that is a body

of literature disciplines a field of practice in ways that are often unseen (2002, 7-8).

Partnership Project: Theoretical Underpinnings

The partnership between Inspire and Yunggorendi has two components: to provide cultural education training for all commencing Inspire mentors whether or not they will personally be supporting Indigenous school students (in primary and secondary schools and alternative education programs); and to provide cultural affirmation for Indigenous secondary school students. This is achieved by linking them with Elders and Indigenous community organisations through a three-day cultural camp at Camp Coorong Race Relations Centre in South Australia. Camp Coorong was established in 1985 by Ngarrindjeri people as a place for people to learn about Ngarrindjeri culture and history. The Camp is Ngarrindjeri owned and operated. It is aimed at South Australians (though draws visitors from local, interstate and international contexts) including school children, and the long-term objective was to contribute to reconciliation between Indigenous and non-Indigenous Australians through addressing the racialised nature of Ngarrindjeri colonisation. The camp experience for Inspire includes a space for Indigenous young people to engage with Indigenous students studying at Flinders University to raise their awareness of potential education and career pathways in a program that involves *all* of the Indigenous students from a participating school rather than "targeting" high achievers or young people who are "at risk" or have disengaged from formal education.

The model centres the Indigenous student as a young person in the tradition of youth empowerment. The young person is centred to address adultism as it is aptly termed by Kivel and Creighton (1997), who argue that power structures keep young people "in their place" thus maintaining power for adults. It is necessary to have a critique of adult power that is raced, gendered and classed when adults work with young people, to ensure that adults work in a "power-with" relationship and do not maintain "power-over" that is enacted purely based on age. The adultism that is enacted by adults where they conspire with other adults, and is legalised and institutionalised within Western social and political structures, is further complicated for Indigenous young people because these are also the structures that continue to colonise their communities. This is not to say that adultism does not occur within Indigenous communities in the context of the abuse of adult power, but rather our point here is to problematise the hegemonic social structures that marginalise Indigenous young people. Concepts of Elder status and adultism are diverse within Indigenous communities and beyond the scope of this chapter.

Fig. 10-1 Inspire and Yunggorendi Mentor Project Partnership

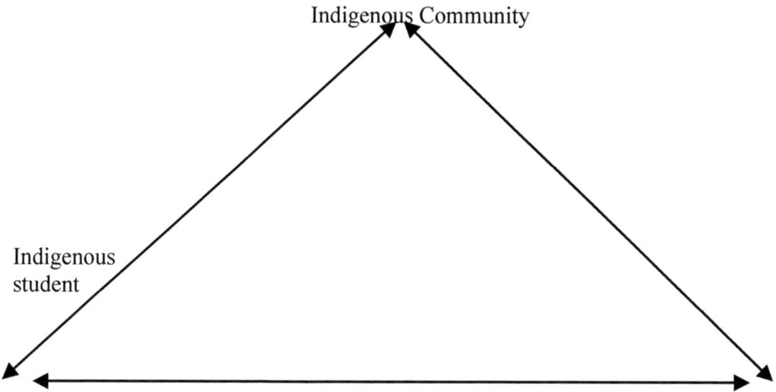

The model's critique of age and race assists to place the Indigenous student in the centre of the project and it also firmly locates the process within Indigenous communities of which Yunggorendi First Nations staff and Indigenous school staff are members. It helps to show that there cannot be a staff/ or academic/community binary as this does not work in Indigenous lived experiences. It is problematic for non-Indigenous staff, mentors or activists to see themselves as separate from, rather than in relationship with, Indigenous communities (see also Trudgen 2000 and Turner 2006).

In relation to applying Indigenous knowledges to this project, Indigenous researchers such as Rigney (1997; 1999), Warrior (1995; 1999) and Fredericks (2007) have argued how research is best conducted with Indigenous peoples and the process to determine what is Indigenous research. They discuss ways of decolonising, re-positioning and supporting Indigenous knowledges and research methods within higher education institutions (Fredericks 2007, 47). Rigney identifies principles for an Indigenist methodology, as a "step toward assisting Indigenous theorists and practitioners to determine what might be an appropriate response to de-legitimise racist oppression in research and shift to a more empowering and self-determining outcome" (Rigney 1997 cited in Fredericks, 2007, 47).

While the Inspire project is not research based, we drew from the same ideas to form the partnership. The purpose of the partnership as previously stated is to develop pathways into higher education for Indigenous school students who are at risk of disengaging from their education and to connect them with Indigenous tertiary students and community. The partnership has developed into a concerted strategy to improve the retention rates of Indigenous secondary students and the level of undergraduate enrolment from the low socio-economic areas south of the University. It is cognisant of the issues outlined in the words of Aileen Moreton-Robinson:

> … most white people give little or no thought to the way that Whiteness makes its presence felt, or how stressful it can be for Indigenous women, men and children living in their country controlled by white people … White race privilege means white people have more lifestyle choices available to them because they are 'mainstream'. Belonging to the 'mainstream' means white people can choose whether or not they wish to bother themselves with the opinions or concerns of Indigenous people (1998, 39-44).

De-legitimisation as referred to in this project involves exposing sources of stress produced by "control", "privilege", "choice or lack of it", "mainstreaming", and "whiteness".

The motivation for this partnership comes from a commitment to apply a practical and critical theoretical understanding of racialisation and whiteness to a critique of the institutional ability to respond to Indigenous children's and young people's participation in formal education. This is to problematise education as a site with a social and political history of colonisation that continues to be post-colonising. If the epistemologies are not unpacked, the Indigenous young person is potentially positioned as part of an "Aboriginal problem" rather than the source and agent of change-in-partnership. The statistics relating to Indigenous young people mentioned earlier can be both understood and transformed when they are viewed in context of ongoing, lived consequences of colonisation that grants unearned racial privilege to the settler society at the expense of Indigenous peoples.

Critical race and whiteness studies identify race and whiteness as social categories, that is, they are not biological, but are formed out of social discourses about race and have a history. Race and whiteness also have lived consequences that are construed by race placing people, families and communities in racialised categories that shape the knowledges and ontologies that members of diverse communities bring.

Locating the Self

Our research and theoretical foundations (gained from our PhD research and from teaching) inform the Inspire training. We argue that a critique of race and whiteness can assist mentors who are raced as white and not white to locate themselves in terms of Indigenous sovereignty. In the edited collection *Indigenous Sovereignty Matters* Tracey Bunda poses the question: How do we, as sovereign Aboriginal people know the white race? (2007, 83). Bunda goes on to discuss what she terms "intellectual Warriors", whether black men or women, who expose, voice, our (Aboriginal peoples) understandings of the dominant "white" person:

> Poor fellas who cannot know any better, trapped in their whiteness that does not allow them to be any other way … these manifestations of whiteness suddenly appear on our landscapes, in vast numbers, demanding to be read" (Bunda 2007, 83).

Bunda's question and her positioning and contextualising of it are significant for the way in which the Inspire mentoring program is constructed. Rather than providing more "cultural awareness" programs for white people to feel that they have even more understanding of "the Aboriginal", the training and practice in Inspire raises the question of how white participants/partners understand themselves. With Indigenous sovereignty as a fact, as the ground from which we live and work, white people are required to understand themselves through a decentred gaze which may then lead to a new way of thinking about how they understand the Indigenous other. This is a good starting place and a necessary critique for the Inspire mentor, as it relates their presumed relationship to the Aboriginal young person and education as a colonised site. For Indigenous academics, teaching mentors about Indigenous education within a colonial context requires the mentor to be challenged and even unsettled regarding their individual thinking in relation to race and racism and their relationship to each. The theoretical position moves beyond "just teaching Aboriginal history", to an understanding of race and racism as a process of racialisation, structurally embedded within social systems that results in racialised privileges. As white US academic Peggy McIntosh notes of her own process:

> I have come to see white privilege as an invisible package of unearned assets that I can count on cashing in each day, but about which I remain oblivious. White privilege is like an invisible weightlessness knapsack of

> special provisions, maps, passport, codebooks, visas, clothes, tools and blank checks (McIntosh 1988, paragraph 3)

Therefore, part of the challenge for the white mentor is being no longer invisible. Being conscious of "race" as a social construction and the benefits that are bestowed as a dominant group involves recognising that relationships are enacted in particular ways for the benefit of the dominant and that they are "the dominant" according to this construction.

To highlight this "invisible" benefit and power imbalance, the teaching approach for the Inspire training is drawn from the theoretical model *Teaching for Resistance* undertaken by the Education for Social Justice Research Group, University of South Australia (1994). The Teaching for Resistance model includes attention to race and Indigenous issues in education.

> What is significant about the Resistance Model ... was its process for unmasking power, language, culture and history to the practice of education and the 'knowing' that arose from the engagement in the education 'system' (Tur et al. 2003, 6).

The Resistance model has three phases: raising consciousness; making contact; taking action. (see Tur et al. 2003, 8) These three categories are of relevance to the mentoring process, but it has further dimensions. Tur et al. state:

> Our political project is, therefore ... to speak to the political history of Indigenous education, a history that is often rendered invisible ... so that what seems to lie on the surface, that is, an education for tolerance and 'cultural' inclusion is exposed as something that is not neutral and given but is in fact a highly politicised process between the competing interest groups of state, dominant non-Indigenous interests and subordinate(d) Indigenous interests (see Smith 1999; Tur et al. 2003, 6)

Adding race relations to consciousness raising, contact and action is an important way of making mentors realise their position, to enable them to unpack racism and to conduct themselves in an appropriate manner when working with Indigenous peoples, particular in relation to the use of terminology within the schooling sector. A recent example of the complexities of racism was highlighted in the *Southern Times Messenger* (Bednall 2008, 1). This issue—which involved an Aboriginal Education Worker (AEW) and a non-Indigenous teacher—arose following a remark that was supposed to be humorous but was deemed a racial comment. Ultimately, this case demonstrated that conflicts related to "race" and "relations" between Indigenous and non-Indigenous peoples are present within the schooling sector and that terminology can still be interpreted and received as offensive when the non-Indigenous teacher exercises the right to engage in humorous dialogue.

Therefore, at the centre of the training of mentors is raising their understanding of "race" as part of *raising their consciousness* to reconciling history and education and what it means to be raced. This process occurs through un-packing "race" theory and racialised structures as they relate to Indigenous Australia and themselves. This involves, unmasking the direct benefit to non-Indigenous Australians which has occurred as a result of the dis-possession of Indigenous peoples from their lands

The challenge to non-Indigenous Australians and its (re)stating of the question asked by Bunda earlier in the chapter "outs" (see also Nicoll 2000; Riggs 2006) the mentor as no longer invisible and raced, their subject position is exposed and requires a transformed understanding of self as dominant and privileged. Transformation in turn admits other possibilities. Bunda quotes bell hooks (1992) who states:

> Even in the worst circumstances of domination, the ability to manipulate one's gaze in the face of structures of domination that would contain it opens the possibility of agency (hooks 1992, cited in Bunda, 2007, 83).

It is from this standpoint that the training of mentors opens up opportunities for change: for the mentor as they begin to understand and enact their role within education.

The cultural education training was developed in light of these issues for all mentors in the Inspire Mentor Program. The training specifically aims to:

- Offer a general understanding of how education as a site has and continues to influence and impact on Indigenous people;
- Provide an understanding of the diversity of Indigenous identity, people and communities;
- Give an understanding of how racism effects Indigenous people;
- Provide an opportunity to discuss Indigenous issues; and
- Develop educational strategies and practices that can be applied within the classroom setting.

The three-hour training workshop prepares mentors to be more critically aware and equipped to mentor Indigenous students and support them in their education. These aims fit with the proposition:

> Critically aware individuals provide a foundation for more sensitive programs; in the sense these individuals could make policies that are more sensitive to the needs of marginalized students and members of societies (Namulundah 1998, 81)

The basic principles of the Inspire Mentor Program focus on one central proposition that Indigenous education must include: Indigenous people are the first custodians of Australia. Mentors are informed, up-front, that Indigenous Australians are sovereign people who are the first custodians of this country and that non-Indigenous Australians have benefited from the dispossession of Aboriginal and Torres Strait Islander people from their land. Training then emphasises that Indigenous students continue to under achieve in all sectors of education; Colonisation has ongoing implications for Indigenous people in all aspects of their lives; Education practices that apply to Indigenous students are good practices that have benefits for all students; and that Education for social justice—issues faced by the most disadvantaged or underprivileged—should be the underlying premise for all educators and mentors.

Relationship to Inspire

Mentor programs that target young people and children from disadvantaged backgrounds traditionally place a strong emphasis on the process of matching mentors with mentees from similar backgrounds. Sipe (1996) found that the process of matching of mentors with mentees is the least critical element. She found that requirements to be matched based on common interests; demographic backgrounds etc. are over-ridden by the mentor's approach where the focus is on developing a relationship that places the young person at the centre.

Likewise, Jekielek, Moore and Hair (2002) found that the quality of mentoring relationships correlates with good program structure and planning. Dubois et al. (2002) found that it is inconclusive as to whether mentors should be of the same background, but what is conclusive is the approach that the mentor takes thus agreeing with the findings in Sipe's study. Defining the approach of effective mentors thus emphasises the importance of the relationship. This can be achieved by mentors from any background provided, we argue, that the program and the mentors have a critique of race and age among other social categories that define power relationships. This is fundamental with young people from any background, and is particularly empowering for young people at risk of disengaging from education.

> Critical thinking needs imagination where students and teachers practice anticipating a new social reality. Imagination can be exercised as a resource to expel dominant ideology and to open up some space for transcendent thinking (Shor and Freire 1987, 185).

How can a critique of racialisation open up a space for transcendent thinking proposed by Shor and Freire in the context of Australia's colonial history? And in relation to this chapter: how do Australian mentor programs (and by extension, communities, organisations etc.) prepare non-Indigenous mentors to form positive and supportive relationships that are not replicating or reinforcing colonial relationships with young Indigenous children and young people? It needs to be noted here that mentors are not necessarily white Australians. The program has mentors who are racialised as not white and are Australian, as well as mentors who are international students, or may have permanent residency rather than citizenship in Australia. Regardless, in this context, the young person who is located at the centre of the relationship may often be an Indigenous young person with a mentor. Thus despite racialised differences amongst mentors, the mentoring program must critically address race, and mentors must have a capacity for critiquing their understanding of race.

In the context of teaching first year education students in Queensland, Jan Connelly (2002) found that "whiteness can present as a barrier to Indigenous students' successful negotiation of white schooling". This is often the very reason why Indigenous students are over-represented in the cohort of students categorised as "at risk of disengaging from school early" that Inspire targets. Therefore it is fundamental to the program and for Indigenous young people that mentors have an understanding of the Indigenous students' location in education as a site of colonisation as well as a critical understanding of their own racialised location. The mentoring relationship needs to be understood within that site. Mentors must be aware of the necessity to develop positive and informed relationships with Indigenous young people as well as with Indigenous peers and colleagues.

This approach is located in an international context of centring Indigenous knowledges and sovereignties. The Kaupapa Maori model is an example developed in Aotearoa/New Zealand. The term "Kaupapa Maori" refers to "Maori desires to affirm Maori cultural philosophies and practices" within mainstream education, which in turn legitimates and affirms Maori. Graham Smith identified six intervention elements to

Kaupapa Maori which include: self determination, cultural aspirations, culturally preferred pedagogy, socio-economic mediation and collective philosophy (Pihama, Cram and Walker 2002, 34). Central to these principles is the struggle for ideas and the desire to critique and transform knowledge and the process of knowledge production by Maori and for Maori. The act of "struggle" itself is seen to be an important feature in the cycle of raising consciousness, resistance and praxis in not only making sense of one's life but in also transforming it in more meaningful ways, and ultimately re-claiming it. For the mentor program, the Indigenous presenters affirm at the centre of the training program their Indigenous knowledge systems and struggle as part of a legitimisation process of Indigenous culture and their philosophies, something referred to by Anzaldua (1990) as multiple masks.

Anzaldua refers to the multiple masks (a term used amongst Chicanas) we wear as part of "persona" and that the faces or masks we wear are inscribed by social structures. She argues that Indigenous bodies are "'written' all over, or should I say tattooed with the sharp needles of experiences" (Anzaldua 1990, xv). Her analysis has particular relevance for Indigenous people within Australia, as our stories, our struggle and transformation is marked within our faces, so too our face shape shifts like a mask as we affirm, struggle, negotiate, resist and self determine/re-claim our sovereignty within Australia. Therefore, by understanding the process of how bodies become inscribed we can begin to unmask the ongoing colonial relationships. This may mean that the audience/mentees may not like the mask we wear (this is always the risk of our face/mask being undesirable) as we enact our sovereignty and challenge the student to consider their relationship to Indigenous sovereignty.

Anzaldua goes onto to discuss the "interface", which she refers to as "sewing a piece of material between two pieces of fabrics to provide support and stability" (Anzaldua 1990, xv). The interface, she states, is the space that is provided where "we may become subjects in our own discourses". A space where we as Indigenous people, community members and, in this context, teachers and researchers can rip the stiches, expose our inner face, confront our oppression and re-make a new inner and outer face. For the mentor program it is within this crucial space where Indigenous Knowledges are privileged as Kaupapa Maori suggests and affirms. It is at the "interface" that subjectivity and sovereignty reinforce and reshape the fabric of social practice.

Addressing Sovereignties and Knowledge in Context: Camp Coorong Mentoring Project

The question which the Inspire project repeatedly asks, and which we pose here, is: how do community projects engage with Indigenous sovereignties and knowledges? This question challenges all projects in health, archaeology or education as it positions Indigenous sovereignties and knowledge at the "centre" of the community project being proposed. The Indigenous research agenda developed by Linda Tuwai Smith (1999) Fredericks (2007) and Rigney (1997; 1999), amongst others, illustrates the importance of the adoption of particular methods and practices that privilege community voice and Indigenous knowledges which are central to the community's agenda rather than the researcher's. Furthermore, and what is evident through the Inspire Program, is that the "community project" necessitates a collaborative relationship formed between the western institutions (university and schools), community organisations (Camp Coorong) and both Indigenous and non-Indigenous peoples collectively and individually. This is particularly evident through a Yunggorendi/Inspire project that linked Indigenous students in years 11 and 12 with Indigenous mentors studying at Flinders University as well as Indigenous Elders/community members and university staff.

This collaborative project formed in this context focused on Indigenous school students who attended a three-day camp at Camp Coorong Race Relations Centre. The underlying theoretical basis of the project was a pivotal framework for developing a mentoring camp to re-engage Indigenous students at risk into education. This was done by involving all Indigenous students from the school, rather than isolating particular groups of Indigenous young people under categories like "at risk" or "high achievers" etc. The camp itself was based upon mentoring and cultural identity and sought to provide a space for "reaching out". To achieve this, students were encouraged to be involved in a range of activities including tours of the Cultural Museum, basket weaving, one-on-one mentoring, talking circles, discussion with Elders and discussions relating to topics of interest to students themselves.

Through the formal and informal conversations, the students in secondary education were exposed to the stories and experiences of Indigenous tertiary students and learnt that many of these students have a similar background and experience to them. Indigenous school students who attended said that they did not know any Indigenous people (friends or family) who had finished school or gone on to further study.

As a result, the young people who had been identified by their school as "at risk" or "disengaged" (all Indigenous) said that no one had spoken to them about attending university before. The Elders at the camp (Uncle Tom Trevorrow and Uncle Neville Gollan) spoke to the participants as the future leaders of their communities. The school students said that they had not been included as future leaders previously, and that this gave them a sense of community and responsibility:

> It's the best thing I've been involved in. We are treated with respect as adults. With the help of my mentor I now want to finish SACE and do Law (Ken, 18 years, Indigenous Alternative Education student [who has since completed his SACE]).

Furthermore, it provided an avenue for Indigenous students to realise their potential and become influenced by their mentors:

> I was not even able to dream about finishing school until I met my mentor. He was always there, every week, so I had to come to school to see him. I didn't want to let him down. He came back when I was in year 11 (Michael, 18 years, Indigenous student at risk).

The camp was followed up with site visits bringing the school students to Flinders University to meet with the Indigenous tertiary students and academic staff. The school students have been made aware of pathways to further education, and see themselves as having the capacity to complete their school studies and to have further education and training.

What became evident through this process is that the young people became increasingly interested in studying at university and realised that it was an option they had not previously considered:

> I want to do child care. But now I have found out that there are degrees at uni in early childhood and junior primary/primary that would lead to better paid jobs. No-one's talked to me about uni before cause school doesn't work for me very well. Now I know that uni still could work for me.

In addition, the first year Indigenous mentors who were involved in the program continued to uphold their position as a "mentor" within the general community informally and either gained part-time employment in similar positions (that is, Aboriginal Education Worker) or continued to mentor younger people through Inspire. Similarly, the students from Christies Beach High School who participated have had successful outcomes since the program and either completed SACE; made transitions into further training and employment; or continued to stay at school with the vision of furthering their opportunities.

Conclusion: Possibilities

In summary, this chapter has suggested that the conventional literature on mentoring does not have a racial consciousness. We also argue that mentoring can deal with racialised experiences and improve the educational engagement of Indigenous students when a critique of racialisation and the implications of racialisation are at the centre of the program. This requires non-Indigenous mentors in Australia to understand and critically engage with the context of colonisation and to recognise Indigenous people as sovereign. We have argued mentors need to unpack their understanding of race and racism and how power relations benefit dominant members of society, whilst disadvantaging Indigenous Australians. Further, we have suggested that education, although racialised, can play an important role in transforming the lives of Indigenous students and their communities. The Inspire program, which has been the focus of this chapter, illustrates the potential to "inspire" young Indigenous people to achieve in school, the importance of community as a part of their education process, and the vision and task set by their Elders as younger people to be contributors to the future governance and sovereignty of their communities and of Australia as a country:

> You are our future leaders and we need you as our future decision makers. Finish your education, and if you are interested, go to university and become the professionals. Otherwise people who had an easy upbringing are making decisions about our people. You need to get jobs in those positions so that you can make good and responsible decisions for your communities and for the future of this country (Elder, Tom Trevorrow, Ngarrindjeri Nation, Camp Coorong).

PART IV:

IDENTITY AND VOICE

CHAPTER ELEVEN

"I BELONG TO THAT STOCK": TE RANGIHIROA'S APPLICATION FOR US CITIZENSHIP

ALICE TE PUNGA SOMERVILLE

On 5 May 1948, Te Rangihiroa (also known as Sir Peter Buck)[1] wrote a letter from Hawaii, where he lived, to his good friend Eric Ramsden.[2] The contents of this letter foreground the ways in which Te Rangihiroa occupied the space where a number of strands—race, Indigeneity, citizenship, nation, region—intersect:

> With regard to the matter of American citizenship you have my authority to say that it is definitely abandoned by me and that any rumours to the contrary are incorrect. To recapitulate, I could not become an American citizen under the … law, for an applicant has to be over 50% Caucasian. The Polynesians are classed as Orientals in spite of anthropological evidence of their Caucasian origin so I could only show 50%. Some friends, however, brought the matter up in the local legislature and the House passed a resolution asking Congress to admit me to American citizenship by a special Act of Congress.[3]

So, Te Rangihiroa was a Maori man from an Irish (father) and Ngati Mutunga (mother) family background. He applied for US citizenship, and this was declined because his Polynesianness was understood to be "Oriental". The territorial government of Hawaii responded by issuing a joint Resolution in 1943, in which they asked Congress to reconsider, on two bases: the Resolution talks about his exemplary position (beyond/outside of race) and it corrects the mistaken idea that Polynesians are Asian and argues that they are in fact "Caucasian". In the words of that Resolution, "He is of Caucasian and Polynesian blood. Polynesians themselves have a Caucasian origin".[4] Because of the specific treatment of race in US citizenship law, then, Te Rangihiroa's application for *citizenship* became a bid for his *whiteness*.

At the moment Te Rangihiroa was rejected from US citizenship he was simultaneously (and rather messily) located at a number of borders: national, racial, ethnic, gendered, classed. Rather than standing in as an exemplar of "business as usual", Te Rangihiroa's case is provocatively unique, not least of all because he is both the object of study and an academic and theorist in the very field in which he was, at the point of rejection from citizenship, an object. His was an extraordinary—and rather elite—life. Te Rangihiroa was the first Maori medical graduate, a Member of Parliament, a decorated WWI soldier and the head of the Bishop Museum in Hawaii which also made him a member of the Faculty of the Graduate School at Yale University (Condliffe 1971). While this rather singular series of accomplishments may not have produced these interconnections between race and citizenship, it certainly throws them, provocatively, into sharp relief.

In my current book project, entitled *Once Were Pacific*,[5] I am exploring Maori articulations of connection with the Pacific. Although the islands of New Zealand are clearly located in the Pacific region, contemporarily "Maori" and "Pacific" are understood as two distinct categories (Indigenous and non-Indigenous), and this can obscure existing and ongoing connections between Maori and the rest of the Pacific. As my research is grounded more in literary studies than anywhere, a major aim of my project is to produce new readings of existing texts and to foreground texts (both literary and archival) which have not received critical attention. At the same time, I'm interested in broader questions of Maori/Pacific connection, including the negotiation of the relationship between migration and Indigeneity. In order to more deeply explore this relationship I focus on a series of specific instances of "Maori/Pacific connection" including such things as Pacific soldiers in the 28th Maori Battalion (WWII) and Pacific students at Maori boarding schools and the presence of "Maori" villages in "Pacific" performance spaces.[6] In the context of these historical moments of relationship between Maori and the Pacific the singular figure of Te Rangihiroa is rather compelling.

More broadly, my research (including, but also beyond, that book project) is underpinned and motivated by a commitment to what Tony Ballantyne has called "horizontal mobility" (Ballantyne 2001). In his discussion of the ways in which many supposedly "postcolonial" narratives reinforce the centre/periphery relationship between London and the colony, he advocates for studies of "horizontal mobility". Ballantyne describes this kind of work as that which explores "the forms of movement and cultural traffic that linked colonies in the 'periphery' together". In rather more colloquial terms, I have described this as "brown on brown" research: research that foregrounds interactions between various Indigenous/migrant/nonwhite communities and individuals. "Brown on brown" research is both comparative and Indigenous-centred, departing as it does from research into Indigenous-European/black-white interaction, but also from research that focuses entirely on a singular Indigenous community. It might be worth noting that "brown" is deliberately used here: it both challenges the dominant representation of race (black/white or black/white/red/yellow) by introducing a fifth term;[7] and also makes visible a part of the world (the Pacific) which, despite the prominence of Pacific ethnology in Te Rangihiroa's period, contemporarily escapes popular understanding of racial types.[8] The kind of "horizontal mobility" that interests me here is Te Rangihiroa's connection with the Pacific region and with his own Pacificness: his travels around the Pacific, his descriptions of connection with other Pacific communities, and his decision to spend the latter part of his life in Hawaii as the Director for a Pacific-focussed research entity. The irony here is that a desire to focus on "brown on brown" interactions requires us to consider whiteness. What is interesting, of course, is that in Te Rangihiroa's application for US citizenship these "horizontal" connections are inflected with distinctly non-horizontal modes of configuring the link between race and nation. This study of Te Rangihiroa is a somewhat complicated version of "horizontal mobility" not only because he seems to circulate both as a figure of the "centre" (scholar) and of the "periphery" (Maori), but also because he actually stretches across two different Empires: the British and the American. With a focus on letters he wrote about the process of his application for US citizenship, we have the opportunity to consider the racial, national and Imperial borders Te Rangihiroa crossed as Citizen, Sir, and Scholar.

Citizen Te Rangihiroa

When his application for US citizenship was declined, Te Rangihiroa occupied a position that was dramatically contradictory: he applied because he occupied an elevated educational and occupational position; and was rejected because he occupied a subjugated racial position. The story of his application for citizenship became rather exciting after his rejection: suddenly his many friends in very high places started to agitate for the US to reconsider. Not only did Hawaii issue their appeal in the form of a joint resolution, but individuals nearer Washington also started to rally behind his cause. We return to Te Rangihiroa's 1948 letter to Ramsden:

> Some friends, however, brought the matter up in the local legislature and the House passed a resolution asking Congress to admit me to American citizenship by a special Act of Congress. The Attorney-General reported unfavourably on the Bill under special circumstances. However this Committee of the House of Representatives regarded my case as being exceptional and voted for it but it evidently got lost in the mazes of the upper house and went no further.[9]

In 1943 the two houses in the Hawaii territorial government issued a Joint Resolution about the decision the US had made to decline Te Rangihiroa's application for citizenship.[10] The Resolution sets the scene in this way:

> Whereas, Peter Henry Buck, for many years an honoured resident of Honolulu, Territory of Hawaii, a British subject, part white and part Polynesian, in every way qualified for American citizenship except that he is ineligible for naturalization under presently existing law;

and

> Whereas, said Peter Henry Buck is thoroughly imbued with the principles of democracy, is attached to the Constitution of the United States, and is desirous and ambitious to become a citizen of the United States ...[11]

After these "Whereas" clauses two "Resolved" clauses followed which called on the US to grant Te Rangihiroa citizenship and which called for the Resolution itself to be forwarded to the President, Congress and Senate. After this, further elaboration was supplied about the specifics of the case. The Resolution itself draws on two discourses of citizenship. It is instructive to explore the way in which this Resolution is framed in relation to these two specific discourses of citizenship: individual merit and race.

One of the ways in which the Resolution argued that Te Rangihiroa should be admitted to US citizenship focussed on his actions as an exemplary individual. Reminiscent of Te Rangihiroa's own commentary about US citizenship law ("the US needs to change its views with regards to race. Either an individual is good enough personally or he isn't"), the Resolution goes into a great amount of detail about the significance of his personal contributions to Hawaii society, to the US and to the academy.

> Dr Peter H Buck is director of the Bernice Pauahi Bishop Museum. He is an eminent scientist, author, and has an enviable record of service for his country and for the cause for democracy. He is well and favourably known

> in the territory of Hawaii, in scientific and educational circles in the United States and throughout the world.[12]

The Resolution continues with details about his military service during WWI, his educational achievements (by this time, medical degrees from the University of New Zealand and honorary degrees from Yale and Rochester), his political and public service work in New Zealand, his professional affiliations, and his publication list. All of these accomplishments are intended to suggest that he already conducts himself in the manner befitting a citizen: they prove that he is, indeed, "in every way qualified for American citizenship". This discourse seems to appeal to a mode of colourblind citizenship, in which his achievements should be understood to trump the racial limits placed on that citizenship. This is summed up in the final phrase of the Resolution which argues that citizenship is "fitting" in this case because of "his outstanding services to the country of his adoption and the high esteem in which he is held by all who know him throughout the scientific and educational world".[13]

Interestingly, the list of achievements cited in the Resolution highlights the fact that Te Rangihiroa was in the privileged position of applying for citizenship in order to acknowledge benefits that had already been extended to him whereas in most cases Indigenous people have fought for citizenship in order to access opportunities that are inaccessible without the guarantees and protections citizenship provides. Te Rangihiroa was able to apply as a gesture of gratitude for privileges he had already enjoyed because his class and scholarly locations overrode the usual barriers to participation in a citizenship-worthy way: this position is demonstrated, perhaps, in his comment that he "agreed with Roosevelt" (in a quote cited below) as if talking about a President as a peer is to be expected. It may be worth pointing out that, unlike Indigenous peoples in some other colonies such as Australia, Canada and the US, the "right and privileges" of British subjects had already been extended to Maori as a part of the third article of the 1840 Treaty of Waitangi. Despite this seemingly progressive approach to Maori citizenship, however, we still might argue that the particular form of citizenship Maori "enjoy" in New Zealand is often second class.[14]

Significantly, right before the final claim of the Resolution, a second discourse is introduced in order to argue that Te Rangihiroa is deserving of American citizenship:

> Doctor Buck is the son of a distinguished Irish citizen of New Zealand and a Maori chiefess and is therefore half Irish. He is of Caucasian and Polynesian blood. Polynesians themselves have Caucasian origin.[15]

No further elaboration of this point is supplied, and given the rather gushy treatment of the rest of the information provided in the Resolution this seems particularly blunt. Whereas one might focus on the category of "Maori" or "Polynesian" as the primary racial configuration when Te Rangihiroa's application for citizenship is refused, this configuration is inseparable in this case from whiteness in very specific ways. To be clear, the place of race in US citizenship law was rather complex in this period. In 1790 Congress restricted US citizenship to "white persons"[16] and this general rule remained in place until 1952. At the end of the Civil War, Senator Sumner unsuccessfully attempted to expunge the legacy of the 1857 case *Dred Scott v Sandford,* in which the Supreme Court ruled that no one of African descent could claim US citizenship, "by striking any reference to race from the naturalization statute".[17]

In the meantime, several individuals attempted to access citizenship through a process of arguing that they were, in fact, white and therefore satisfied that requirement of the legislation. Lopez notes that 52 "racial prerequisite" cases were heard between 1878 and 1952, including two by the Supreme Court:

> Seen as a taxonomy of Whiteness, these cases are instructive because they reveal the imprecisions and contradictions inherent in the establishment of racial lines between Whites and non-Whites.[18]

Hawaiian, Chinese, Japanese, Burmese and Filipino attempts were unsuccessful, while Mexican and Armenian cases were successful. The Courts were unsure what to do with Syrian, Arab and Indian applicants. Over the course of these cases the boundaries of citizenship, allied as they were to whiteness, were interrogated: "Whites [were] a category of people subject to a double negative: they are those who are not non-White".[19] Te Rangihiroa's application, therefore, was shaped by this context of legal precedent: in order to gain citizenship he needed to gain recognition of whiteness, or, to use Lopez's logic, recognition that he wasn't "*non-*White". Two distinct approaches to this question of whether a particular group was white developed: "common knowledge" and scientific evidence. The scientific approach drew most heavily on ethnological work such as that by Keane which stated that:

> The Maori of New Zealand, the Tongans, Tahitians, Samoans, Marquesans and Ellice Islanders, and Hawaiians ... are an Oceanic branch of the Caucasic division.[20]

Te Rangihiroa's own scholarly work is implicated here, in th a major advocate of the idea that Polynesians were of Caucasian extraction. However, in 1923 *United States v Thind* marked a movement away from the slippage between White and Caucasian; as a result of this case not only was Thind's application for citizenship declined but at least 65 people of Asian Indian origin who had been naturalised between 1923 and 1927 were stripped of their citizenship. Despite this uncoupling of the whiteness required for citizenship from "Caucasian" in *Thind*, then, Te Rangihiroa's own case was articulated—at least in the words of the Territory of Hawaii—as depending upon his status as Caucasian.[21]

Of course, Te Rangihiroa's body was understood differently according to the racialising logics of the different spaces within which he operated and whiteness is coded differently in the different spaces of the continental US, Hawaii, New Zealand and the British Empire. In New Zealand, he was understood as Maori/mixed/Ngati Mutunga; in the US, his Polynesian-ness was tied to Oriental-ness; and in Hawaii, his Polynesian-ness was tied to whiteness/Caucasian-ness. Te Rangihiroa rose to visibility in the New Zealand national community when several Maori men newly occupied prominent positions in national politics. Significantly, many of these men were publicly described in terms of their Maori/European racial mixture, and their success was in turn linked to this particular combination. Because of his Irish father Te Rangihiroa was described and celebrated as a "half-caste" alongside the prominent politician Sir James Carroll, and their bodies as well as their educational successes were held up as precocious and exemplary products of the contemporary European racial ideology of assimilation. Te Ranghiroa described his own mixture through the language of celebratory assimilation, and simultaneously gestured towards the instability of the social position of "half-castes" when he wrote:

> To my despondent fellow half-caste, I say that it is better to be a good mongrel than a dud Maori or a poor white ...[22]

Once he moved to Hawaii, his ideas about whiteness—including his own—moved beyond the question of European descent and ventured into a broader concept: Caucasian.

At this point, we might recall that Te Rangihiroa is both an object of study and a scholar in this field of research, and his own contributions to scientific literature about Polynesians (and, more broadly, the Pacific) have ultimately shaped the ways in which he himself is understood. Without delving deeply into this question of Polynesian origins (this is a huge topic and warrants further critical interest in another paper), Te

Rangihiroa's work in the Pacific strove at least in part to stitch Polynesians into the broader racial maps that circulated at the time: he wrote a vast number of books and papers about Pacific peoples and Polynesia; he taught a course at Yale in 1933 called "Native Races of the Pacific". From the perspective of the present dominant university structures it can be easy to forget that the disciplines of ethnography and anthropology (and linguistics) in which he worked were considered to be sciences in less "social" ways than they are today. This "science-ness" was a result of the prevailing theories about race and people, in which linguists and ethnologists attempted to sketch scientifically rigorous explanations for how difference people were connected,[23] and many of the methodologies upon which Te Rangihiroa depended for his work included the precise physical measurement of human bodies and implements. While these methodologies, and the uses to which they were usually put, are now regarded rather dubiously today, the important point is that Te Rangihiroa understood himself to be actively engaged in scientific research and at the core of his research was a series of questions about the racialisation of people in (and from) the Pacific. Extending various discussions of race around the British Empire,[24] much of Te Rangihiroa's research argued that Polynesians are best understood as racially Caucasian.

In an interesting version of life imitating art, in which technical political claims imitated scholarly theories, the link between Polynesian people and Caucasian "origins" is a key claim of Te Rangihiroa's own scholarly work. The comment in the Resolution that his mother is a "chiefess" (and indeed that his father is "distinguished") appeals to the notion that Te Rangihiroa was highly born which, one might argue, doesn't seem to fit well with the claims about democracy that otherwise mark idealised US citizenship in the rest of the Resolution. However, perhaps the important thing about the hierarchical positions of his parents is that they seem to be evenly elevated ("chiefess", "distinguished") in a way which supports the notion that there is something essentially equal (and unique) about the two. This equalness (to the point, perhaps, of sameness-even-if-not-quite) in turn underpins provides the logic relied on by the following claim that "He is of Caucasian and Polynesian blood. Polynesians themselves have Caucasian origin". In this configuration, the Resolution subtly suggests that Te Rangihiroa does in fact satisfy the race requirements of US citizenship: he is "Caucasian and Polynesian-which-is-Caucasian", or perhaps "Caucasian and Caucasian". Within the logic of the racial theories with which Te Rangihiroa was working, "Caucasian origin" is not the same as "white", although in this public political document which relies on a slippage between being "Irish" and being

"Caucasian", and in which the "Caucasian origin" of "Polynesians" is offered as a counter to an exclusion from citizenship on the basis of race, one could argue that "Caucasian" is supposed to be (mis)understood here as standing in for racially "white". The Resolution treats the issue of the "Oriental" designation of Polynesians by applying the corrective claim that "Polynesians themselves have Caucasian origin". Interestingly, though, this comment somewhat undermines the emphasis the rest of the Resolution places on Te Rangihiroa's personal achievements and attributes as a fair basis for citizenship. In some ways, then, when being Polynesian is allied with being Caucasian, the Resolution provides an opportunity to put a dollar each way on Te Rangihiroa's relationship to US citizenship: on the one hand, citizenship should be attached to deeds rather than race; on the other, he can be understood as "white" for the purpose of satisfying a citizenship requirement.

Finally, when we consider Te Rangihiroa's application for citizenship and the connection between US citizenship and discourses of race and individual achievement, it is helpful to consider the distinction between the relationship he had with the US as a result of his own personal transnational mobility and the relationship between other Polynesians in American Samoa (and Hawaii) for whom the US was an invading power which had "moved to them". US imperialism is part of the context of Te Rangihiroa's application for US citizenship, and this Empire sneaks into the picture in a range of ways. Firstly, in terms of his physical residence he was living in Hawaii, then a territory of the US. He arrived in Hawaii in 1927, a mere 29 years after the US formally annexed Hawaii and 22 years before it would be fully incorporated into the union as a state. Secondly, he worked at the Bishop Museum, which was the "Pacific" branch of Yale University (he was a tenured professor there and taught there in 1933/4).[25] The Bishop served as an important outpost for the vibrant field of Pacific-related research that occupied many of the disciplines in the early twentieth century. At the time, much of the extension of US scholarly interest in the Pacific was tied to US economic and political extension into the same region. Finally, Te Rangihiroa explicitly mentions American Samoans and their unsuccessful attempts to gain citizenship:[26]

> I agreed with Roosevelt and held that a more comprehensive act should be passed to admit Samoans and other Polynesians to American citizenship. Under the present act, the Samoans in American Samoa cannot become American citizens. A bill is being brought before Congress now to allow people of the Pacific to qualify.[27]

The fact that Polynesians were understood by the US as "Asian" at the time (the official reason that Te Rangihiroa's individual application was declined) is not easily extricated from the production of the Pacific as an "American lake" in the US Imperial imaginary at the time, which (from the point of view of the continental US) squished together "Asian" and "Pacific".[28] This dimension of US imperialism in the case of Samoa (and Hawaii) adds an additional layer to Te Rangihiroa's application for citizenship because although we might treat this as a singular case in which an individual is categorised through the racial logics of a single nation, this case can also be understood as being caught in the much larger racial crossfire between the US and its colonies in the Pacific.

Sir Te Rangihiroa

This story of application and rejection would be a good story on its own of one Maori man's struggle with the process for US citizenship, but an additional factor in the equation is that in June 1946 this one Maori man happened to get a better offer: the offer of a Knighthood from New Zealand. At this point the plot thickens. Allegedly, the reason a Knighthood hadn't been extended earlier was that an assumption had been made in New Zealand that Te Rangihiroa had already gained US citizenship and was therefore ineligible for the Knighthood. Another interpretation is that Te Rangihiroa's absence from New Zealand precluded him from being awarded recognition for services to that country. In September 1946 he had written to Ramsden, describing the connection between his application for citizenship and the Knighthood:

> [Peter Fraser] threw out a hint in passing through but was still worried about the citizenship question. However, that is definitely off now. I was in Washington attending a science congress when the definite news came to me through the New Zealand Embassy that a wire had been forwarded on from Sir Michael Myers asking if I would accept. I saw Joe Farrington, our delegate to Congress, and told him to drop the bill regarding my citizenship.[29]

This situation adds an additional layer to the question of his citizenship: not only did he apply to the US for citizenship as a gesture of recognition that he had enjoyed the opportunities of a citizen there, but his enjoyment of those opportunities (in terms of his career and status) was assumed by New Zealand to be those of a US citizen as well. Indeed, it seems significant that both Te Rangihiroa and New Zealand recognised that he was already enjoying the benefits of American citizenship: it was only the US itself that formally disagreed with this analysis at the point of rejecting the application. This rejection, of course, was not on the basis of his social or professional standing (the bases for understanding Te Rangihiroa's acting as, and being understood as, "already-a-citizen") but on the basis of race. In this way, the US racialised American citizenship more than Te Rangihiroa or the New Zealand government did. While in May 1948 Te Rangihiroa recalled the sequence of events as one in which he decided to pull his application for citizenship before the Knighthood question came up ("However, I had decided before the Knighthood was conferred upon me to remain a British subject to the end of the chapter"), in this earlier letter of September 1946 he described the situation as more of a deliberate choice:

> I intimated to [Farrington] that as the United States put such obstacles in the way of a Polynesian becoming an American citizen and now New Zealand had given me the highest honour they possibly could.[30]

Te Rangihiroa's application for US citizenship, and his later decision to pull his hitherto unsuccessful application, engages two configurations of racialisation that do not often come into such explicit contact. Both are tied up with Empire—but both are tied up with quite different Empires.

Of course, at the time New Zealand itself was incapable of bestowing a Knighthood and it was extended, instead, by its colonial mothership: the British Empire. At this point it becomes clear that two specific Empires intersect in this moment at which Te Rangihiroa is declined US citizenship: as well as the context of US Imperialism there is also the British Empire. Te Rangihiroa is tied to New Zealand, and tied to Maori, in particular ways but he is also tied to Britishness. In an earlier letter to Ramsden, dated 14 February 1937, he wrote about the reaction of the British community in Hawaii to recent events in the English monarchy:

> All the English men here [Hawaii] of British extraction, including subjects and recent American citizens, were greatly disgusted with Edward. The final opinion seems to be the one generally shared by the Empire: he let the Empire down and we are well rid of him.[31]

In this comment he includes himself in "the Empire" whom Edward "let … down" through the inclusive plural pronoun "we": interestingly, in this short comment one finds a slippage between the terms "English", "British" and "Empire." His own affective ties to the British Empire, and indeed his strong sense that there is a knowable/generalisable thing called "the Empire", are somewhat complicated for us to imagine today when we would tend to distinguish sharply between national affiliation ("English") and membership in an Imperial community ("Empire"). It would be somewhat anachronistic to say that Te Rangihiroa is interested in "nation" in narrow terms—after all, he's talking about connection to the British Empire. Although from the perspective of today it is difficult to imagine having a stronger sense of belonging to an Empire than a nation state, his idea of "home" doesn't often engage the term "New Zealand" and perhaps this explains the ease with which the focus of his scholarly work moved beyond national borders and into Polynesia and the Pacific.

This sense of commitment to the British Empire underpins Te Rangihiroa's decision to forego US citizenship and reaffirm his connection to New Zealand. In order for Te Rangihiroa to receive a Knighthood he needed to be a citizen of New Zealand, which at the time meant a citizen of the British Empire. Certainly his service to the nation of New Zealand through his medical, political and scientific work was outstanding: through his work as a doctor, then as Member of Parliament, then as ethnographic scientist Te Rangihiroa contributed not one but three careers to the betterment of his own people, the nation and the region. Because of these contributions the question of a Knighthood had been raised on several occasions, and by 1940 Te Rangihiroa commented on Ramsden's description of a renewed effort to proceed with a nomination for a Knighthood:

> I deeply appreciate the compliment to me but I am rather sick of the whole affair. When the National Government were in power with Forbes at the head, the matter was brought up by Ngata. I was even congratulated in New Zealand by various Maoris about the honour that was to come … Such an honour would be appreciated in scientific circles but I doubt if such recognition would be conferred outside the realm of politics.[32]

Actually Margaret Buck was rather heavily invested in the prospect of a Knighthood for her husband, to the extent that after a time Te Rangihiroa commented in a letter that it would be better for the topic to be dropped because of the impact of raising and dashing his wife's hopes of being "Lady Buck".[33]

While Margaret's desire to gain recognition by association was no secret, in Te Rangihiroa's 1948 letter to Ramsden he expresses something of his own commitment to the Empire. He describes his sense of relief about accepting a British Knighthood in nostalgic and perhaps surprisingly patriotic terms:

> I had decided before the knighthood was conferred upon me to remain a British subject to the end of the chapter and my mind has been much easier since I made that decision. In spite of the evil days before the British Empire there is something about the flag that stirs up the memories of one's youth and training and gives me a thrill of pride to belong to it.[34]

On one level, the ascension of a Maori person to a Knighthood could be understood as an ultimate illustration of assimilation to European subjecthood (both in terms of citizenship and subject position), but on the other hand Te Rangihiroa's expression of desire to retain a connection with the British Empire is more complex than simple patriotism. Indeed, he describes multiple connections to the Empire: affective, historical and nostalgic. Primarily he describes his decision as an emotional one: he focuses less on the process of a logical or reasoned choice and more on the relief he felt upon making it ("my mind has been much easier since I made the decision"). He links his emotional response to nostalgic memories of his earlier years ("there is something about the flag that stirs up the memories of one's youth and training") and it seems significant that he claims it is the highly symbolic object of "the flag" that "stirs up" these memories. In this articulation "Empire" is understood as a symbolic entity, to which he is linked through affective and symbolic dimensions. At the same time, Te Rangihiroa recalls and reinscribes the historical dimension of colonial violence in the admission of "the evil days before the British Empire" and this seems a key point of naming the limitations as well as the possibilities of his relationship with that Empire. While it is possible to claim that the "evil days before the British Empire" could be the period of time before the Empire extended its claim of sovereignty over the islands of New Zealand, this reading does not fit with the logic of the sentence which argues that despite those "evil days" he still feels a connection to Empire through his memories of his youth. In 1946 he had made similar claims about his affective and ongoing sense of commitment to the Empire:

> the British Empire is in a bad way and, though I cannot make a difference, sentiment urges me to say that I would be loath to give up my British citizenship. At this juncture I feel like sticking to the ship not so much for the prospects of a knighthood but because of the blood that is in me. The Maoris are among the most loyal subjects of the British Empire and, in spite of my absence, I belong to that stock. I will see what I can do to remain as I am.[35]

This declaration of "loyal[ty]" should not be extricated from Te Rangihiroa's commitments to the Imperial forces during WWI or the recent and celebrated establishment of the 28th Maori Battalion during WWII. Interestingly, after Te Rangihiroa's rejection from US citizenship had been on the basis of his race he had written that "the US needs to change its views with regards to race. Either an individual is good enough personally or he isn't", and yet when he describes his connection to the British Empire he mobilises the discourse of blood: "the blood that is in me … I belong to that stock". To be clear, whereas he complains that he should be admitted to US citizenship regardless of whether he is Polynesian, he defines his "British citizenship" and connection to the "British Empire" precisely because he is Maori and he describes that "Maoriness" through the explicitly race-derived metaphor of blood.

Dr Te Rangihiroa

Finally, let us turn to consider Te Rangihiroa's location as a scholar. It seems that, for Te Rangihiroa, his scholarly location both enabled and trumped his extraordinary social as well as spatial mobility. He was a very accomplished scholar, and prolific writer, and he moved in very high circles of academia, receiving awards and recognition from North America, the Pacific, Europe and New Zealand. His strong sense of his scholarly contribution comes through a number of his letters, and in particular he is very clear about drawing a clear distinction between a political and scholarly life. When he wrote to Ramsden in August 1940:

> In spite of what has been written about me, in joining up with the quartet headed by Carroll, Ngata, and Pomare, I do not think the New Zealanders fully appreciate how I have been a pioneer Maori in a very exclusive field into which politics does not enter. I cannot and I never had any desire to compete with my colleagues in the field of politics but I do know that in the particular branch of science in which I have interested myself, I have established a record that will be very difficult for any New Zealander, Pakeha or Maori, to approach let alone equal. And I have not done yet.[36]

Ten years later, in September 1950, after hearing about the passing of his dear friend Ta Apirana Ngata:

> I have no more to say. I have followed the path where the spirits led me. I have carved out my life without aid from any man. In another field, I have tried to contribute to the name and prestige of the Maori people and when I meet my old colleagues, there will be no question of priority for each of us will occupy our separate and appropriate riches.[37]

These self-described comments about his own career as an academic (a career which he did not enter fulltime until his mid-50s!) sounds a little bit uppity on first read—but I think the strength of the distinction he draws between "politics" and "academia" ("in a very exclusive field", "in another field") is strategic and significant.

I would argue, indeed, that not only did Te Rangihiroa explicitly engage questions of citizenship (or otherwise) of nations and Empires—but he also elaborated a sense of "citizenship" of the academy. Indeed, in a letter he wrote to Mary Wheeler in New Haven, in which he describes the concept of a knighthood, he makes an explicit parallel between the nation and the university:

> This honour business is like receiving an honorary degree but instead of coming from a University, it comes from a country.[38]

Comparing a knighthood to an honorary degree in this way is useful for the purpose of describing it to an American friend who doesn't know what it means, but it also suggests the two planes on which he understood his life to be playing out: the national (or perhaps political, or perhaps international), and the scholarly. His academic work was clearly inflected by his own relationship with "the nation"—and yet, like any of us Maori who venture to North America for intellectual pursuits, things were made possible for him there that would not at that time have been possible at home. Frankly, his mobility in the scholarly world was differently bordered than that of his national/ racial worlds. In 1951, Te Rangihiroa accepted an honorary degree from Yale University during its 250th anniversary celebrations—he was asked to respond on behalf of himself and the other 24 doctoral recipients, and did so in te reo Maori.[39] Although focussing on Te Rangihiroa's application for US citizenship may seem a little trivial considering that he occupied such a unique educational, social and vocational position, I would argue that this is precisely what enables us to explore and elaborate the connections between race, gender, empire and citizenship in this way. A class analysis is crying out in the project, clearly: after all, Te Rangihiroa's whole situation was made possible through a series of experiences and privileges that mean his life story is excruciatingly distinctive rather than yawningly familiar. And yet—for myself as a young Maori scholar—I have found (despite my characteristic cynicism) his articulations of mobility in, and deep identification with, his scholarly world to be quite inspiring.[40]

first draft of a waiata tangi. (for Te Rangihiroa)

it's hot here:
without electric fan, open window, bare legs
i'd be lying in the dark, heavy limbed and drowsy

as it is, i can feel an ache of warmth at the back of my neck
where hair falls in a tight curtain around an already moist little nook
i'm lying on my tummy, skin pressing into a warm patch of blanket
working on the first draft of something i'll never finish

although warmed milk and sheets are supplied at nighttime
to wide-awake children in the islands of our births
warmth has the opposite effect here:
it's too hot to fall quickly to sleep tonite

i visited your whare 'Te Pataka o Pihopa' today

before heading to the archive in the back of the building
i walked through front doors, up stairs, over carpet
to greet the small Maori display at the end of the mezzanine

laid a handful of leaves beside the whakairo there
quietly sang to them under my breath,
a small one-sided karanga
surprising the other occupants more than the other visitors

wondered if you used to visit these cabinets too
if you looked across the carpet as i did and felt them looking back,
appraising,
gluing feet to floor and tumbling body into air,
all at the same time

walked along corridors you paced for years,
a precise producer of catalogues:
a scientist working with the test-tubes and bunsen burners of culture
before it was embarrassing to treat people like lab rats,
to steal things and ideas for safekeeping on airconditioned shelves

the relief it must have been to return here after your last trip home,
but also the grief:

did you visit the whakairo more or less after your final wrenching?
does spending time with those things of our own provides solace or discomfort?
do things behind glass feel enclosed, cut off, pristine, or do they keep you company?

e te rangihiroa

still hot, still sticky:
was it like this the night you died?

i wonder if you felt more at home as your body turned cold after last breaths

i wonder if your wairua found a path to follow to hawaiiki,
departing as it did from this wrong end of our marvellous watery hemisphere

CHAPTER TWELVE

TEACHING *THE TRACKER* IN GERMANY: A JOURNAL OF WHITENESS

ANNE BREWSTER

Having nothing to say

My partner's family came out from Latvia after the Second World War. In many ways their sociality, it seemed to me, remained European, even though they loved living in Australia. Going into their house was like stepping into a German household of the 1940s. The food, the bedclothes, the knick knacks, the paintings, even the style of the house which Peter's step-father designed and built, were definitely not the things I had grown up as a fifth-generation Anglo-Celtic (South) Australian. Peter's mother was sociable and loved to entertain—she invited people around for breakfast, for Easter, for birthdays and any other occasion that warranted the production of food. They had very few—if any—Anglo-Celtic Australian friends. Their friends were largely Latvians, other Baltic people and Poles. They spoke German at home.

At his mother's parties I perfected the art of the wallflower, following the German in minimal ways and smiling and nodding when Latvian was spoken. I helped out in the kitchen and tried to pace myself with the whiskey. On one of these occasions an elderly Latvian gentleman in his eighties, a dignified and hardy chap, having noticed my linguistic incompetence struck up a conversation in English.

"Where are you from?" he asked.

"Oh, I'm Australian," I said in a half-apologetic way.

"No, I mean, where are your parents from?"

"They're Australian too." I was feeling even more apologetic. But he waved that aside.

"No, I mean, where does your family *come* from?"

I knew what I should say, though I felt ridiculous.

"My mother's family were from Wales," I said. He looked satisfied and scrutinised my face. "Oh, you're Welsh?" he said.

This was the first and only time in my life I have identified as Welsh. No doubt to others, including Peter's mother, I am incontrovertibly white and unambiguously Anglo-Celtic. But my sense of my own ethnicity is attenuated. Many theorists have commented on the general decline of ethnicity in the Anglo-Celtic diaspora.[1] The giving up of ethnic markers is identified as one of the aspects of the process of accruing whiteness. Roediger, for example, defines whiteness as the 'absence of marked culture' (Roediger,1994, 196, fn 21).[2] In this article I think about the nature of my Australian Anglo-Celtic creoleness and how it intersects with whiteness and with multiculturalism. The term "creole" has been used in many contexts, common among which are those which refer to Africans or Europeans who are born or naturalised in a country (historically the Caribbean islands or Louisiana are commonly cited as examples) but who are of foreign ancestry and not Indigenous. In this chapter I use the term "creole" to refer to diasporic Europeans in Australia (specially in this case, those of Anglo-Celtic heritage). I draw thus on the Macquarie dictionary definition of a "creole" as "a person born in a place but of foreign ancestry, as distinguished from the aborigines".

As a fifth-generation Anglo-Celtic creole I don't feel any curiosity about or attachment to the country of my family's origins. I don't have a strong sense of *affective* connection with a pre-colonial family history even if I do experience a disturbing sense of familiarity when I am in the United Kingdom: a sense of recognition (and simultaneously of misrecognition). However, I have an abiding ambivalent fascination with the diasporic liberalism which is my intellectual heritage, and which has become the foundation of my work as a scholar of Indigenous literature.

In this chapter's scenes and discussions of cross-racial relations I explore the legacy of diasporic liberalism, that is, the European tradition of liberal thinking that has been exported (along with people, religion, language and global capital) into the colonised lands of Indigenous peoples. This tradition, with its enlightenment reverence of reasoned argument and moral sensibility, has generated contemporary discourses of reconciliation and social justice, for example, which are founded on the liberal principle of 'mutual rational understanding' (Povinelli 2002, 6).

I borrow and adapt the term "diasporic liberalism" from Elizabeth Povinelli's work. Povinelli defines the "liberal diaspora" as "the subjective, discursive and institutional identifications, dispersals and elaborations of the enlightenment idea that society should be organised on the basis of rational mutual understanding" (Povinelli 2002, 6). In this chapter I aim to track the range of emotions which complements and sometimes befuddles "rational mutual understanding". "Rational mutual understanding" underpins much contemporary liberal discourse on cross-racial relations such as the discourse of reconciliation. However, our efforts at and faith in rational understanding are often destabilised by affective dispositions and other bodily states and reactions. It is difficult to categorise or even map these affects and bodily states as they are labile and unpredictable. White embarrassment, for example, can manifest in a sense of having too little to say, or too much. Diasporic liberalism, I suggest, is constituted as much by these affective equivocations and oscillations as by rationalism.

My liberal *intellectual* heritage manifests in a strong sense of investment in Australian multiculture. I have a curiosity—ethical, consumerist, desiring, political, historical—about the ethnic and Indigenous peoples around me—my Jewish neighbours, my Iraqi Coptic house cleaner, my Arab and Asian Australian students and friends, those from North America and the United Kingdom, the local Greek and South African business people, and my long-standing friendships and professional relationships with Aboriginal people. In these various relationships I'm conscious of my own affections and discomfort. I'm always aware that I cannot fully know the extent of the differences between us. But there are multiple commonalities and intersections too. I think of Noel Pearson's comment that "a Rugby Union-following Lutheran Aboriginal with a love for the literature of England shares much with other Australians that he does not share with his closest kin" (Pearson 2007, 44).

In this discussion I don't intend to elide power hierarchies among differentially marked ethnic and racial groups. It has been observed that the decline of ethnic identification among whites in the United States is coincident with the rise of the nationalist ideology of individualism and opportunity (Winant 1994; Roediger 1994). Clearly Anglo-Celts have the choice whether or not to take up Anglo-Celticness as ethnicity, whereas minority racialised and ethnic identities do not have the same power to determine their identities. Also, I want to underscore the point that Anglo-Celtic ethnicity (and whiteness) are always relational, as my encounter with the Latvian gentleman demonstrates. It was his ethnic identification as Latvian that foregrounded for me the absence of ethnic (self) identification and the privileges of this position.

Back in Peter's mother's lounge room it feels absurd to invoke the default position "Australian". The apparent absence of ethnicity is of course a corollary of the entitlement that attaches to being unambiguously white in Australia. I register the oddity of having nothing to say. This prompts me some time later to think about my membership in a community of descent. My Anglo-Celtic genealogy is located culturally and politically within the history of settler-colonialism. It is difficult for me to separate my Anglo-Celticness from whiteness. This in effect renders my Anglo-Celtic whiteness primarily a racial rather than an ethnic category. It is defined (for me) in its capacity as a racialising agent of colonisation. In turn, the racialising of Anglo-Celticness is an outcome of a history of relations with an Indigenous constituency which has itself always been defined and managed as a racial category (Brewster 1995), unlike many immigrant constituencies positioned within the rubric of multiculturalism. The location of Anglo-Celtic whiteness within the racialising conditions of colonisation is constitutive of the category of whiteness; I cannot choose to step outside racialised relations with Indigenous peoples.

Perhaps I could have characterised myself as a postcolonial[3] Anglo-Celt to the Latvian gentleman. This identity is rooted in an ethical imperative informed by a range of affective dispositions and a troubled sense of connection to Indigenous peoples, my colonial others. From the Reconciliation decade onwards white postcolonial affect has been in the spotlight. What work have these feelings performed and what has been their impact on whiteness at the beginning of the new millennium? Affect is produced through our relationships with others. It mobilises the subject in a loop of feeling and response with other subjects and with various publics. Affect has the capacity to generate social meaning. As Michael Hardt notes, it is one of the highest value-producing forms of labour in late capitalism (Hardt 1999). Affective labour is produced by the culture industries; it constitutes communities, subjectivities and sociality. In this chapter I reflect on how whiteness is affectively engaged by its various others in a series of mundane contexts: the loungeroom, the classroom, exchanges at public meetings and literary festivals, friends walking and talking together, and the intimate cross-racial consumption of film. Some of these anecdotes are drawn from my experience of teaching a course on Australian Indigenous literature at Tübingen University, located in the Schwäbian Baden-Württemberg region of Germany. As part of this course we studied Rolf de Heer's film, *The Tracker*, examining the affective labour it undertakes in its investigation of contestatory postcolonial identifications of whiteness. The film, released in 2002, describes a manhunt for an Indigenous man accused of raping a white woman. Set in remote bushland in 1922, it follows the journey of the three white men and their Aboriginal tracker in pursuit of the fugitive. The characters are identified only by their roles: the party comprises the senior policeman, the Fanatic (played by Gary Sweet); the young constable, the Follower (Damon Gameau); the Conscript (Grant Page) and the eponymous Tracker (David Gulpilil). The film collected many awards both in Australia and overseas. David Gulpilil, in particular, collected four Best Actor awards. However, although the film centrally explores the violent relationship between white men and Indigenous people, it also focuses on the changing relationships between the three white men. As Indigenous film curator Romaine Moreton notes, "the title of *The Tracker* suggests that it is the Aboriginal tracker who is central to the story, but instead, the film is more about how the white characters deal with their own sense of morality".[4]

My meditation upon the film and the discussions it produced in the German classroom form a core around which coalesce memories of other scenes of everyday life which enact the micropolitics of race. In collating these scenes I am interested in how demotic whiteness plays out across a range of affects which slide into and alternate with each other. I want to maintain the irreducibility and mobility of these affects by sustaining the tension between practices of conversation and authoritative theoretical production without subsuming the former within the latter and assimilating embodied everyday encounters to discourse. Embarrassment and theory contaminate and complicate each other. Frequently white diasporic liberalism is loquacious; other times it is at a loss as to what to say. Personalised writing about whiteness is often predicated on this tension.

Writing Whiteness

In this chapter I wanted to write about the intersections of Anglo-Celtic creoleness with whiteness and with Australian multiculture in a way that would address my affective dispositions and equivocations. What narrative mode should I choose for this task: Anecdote? Travelogue? Scholarly theorisation of the persistence and reconfiguration of whiteness? Why write in the first person? There has been a demand over the last couple of decades for white commentators to position themselves in their discussions of race.[5] Minority theorists and white commentators have talked about the importance of problematising the universalising tendency of whiteness, an issue that author-evacuated writing often fails to acknowledge and address.

Nevertheless, this turn to the first person does not necessarily claim to enact a divestiture of white privilege. I'm conscious of what has been called the "double bind" (Ellsworth 1997) of reflexive whiteness:[6] the bind of wanting neither to replicate the historical privilege of whiteness by naming (itself and others) nor to remain silent and unmarked. Robyn Wiegman has encouraged us to be observant of, and circumspect about, the splitting of whiteness (the fact that we can be simultaneously an index and a critic of whiteness) which she sees as an instance of its continuing mobility (Wiegman 2000). However, does the turn towards others advocated by the antiracist agenda of critical whiteness studies *have* to be predicated on a "turn away from" ourselves as white subjects, as Sara Ahmed suggests (Ahmed 2004)? Does the turn towards oneself inevitably "block hearing" (Ahmed 2004)? Ultimately, as white diasporic liberals we inhabit the script that history has written for us (Spivak 1990, 62). This script enunciates liberalism in its abject mode (Ellison 1996) embedded in oscillation, equivocation (Armstrong 2000) ambivalence and the intersections of embarrassment, curiosity and melancholy. I would like to foreground the fact that white mobility is primarily relational, engaging and being engaged by our racialised and ethicised "others". First-person whiteness writing, in investigating embodied histories of whiteness, can work to return us to this charged zone of intersubjectivity and intercorporeality. Being mindful of whiteness as a zone of embodied intersubjectivity may aid us in avoiding reification and the essentialising of whiteness which is the risk that shadows the project of critical whiteness studies.

As I discuss elsewhere, the taking up of a direct first-person address in scholarly whiteness writing in Australia could be seen as a discursive response to several decades of first-person writing by Indigenous women (Brewster 2005). Of course it goes without saying that first-person genres are governed by a complex set of discursive conventions which each have their extensive literary and extra-literary histories. In none of these modes is the first-person enunciative position an unmediated rendition of identity. I'm interested specifically in this chapter in the work that first-person narrative modes can do in displacing the public/private binary. This binary historically has legitimised many other binaries (male/female, hetero/homo, work/family, white or unraced/raced). Public identities and institutions are instrumental; private identities are affective and weighed down with the body. However, the boundary between public and private, which is invoked to make the world intelligible, leaks. We constantly witness the intrusion of the intimate into the public sphere; the effects of the public sphere are personalised. The first-person voice often locates itself in the embodied particularity of the everyday (which has been relegated to the zone of the private). The personal space of everyday life is the space of social relations. It is the site at which we conduct our primary relationship with racialised strangers (Frow 2002, 631). Everyday life forms the horizon of experience. The slight events of the qualitative change (Massumi 2002) registered in everyday life (for example, through affect) are performed in the act of reading. The public sphere of writing and reading is a realm in which strangers are brought into proximity. The vernacular styles and expressions of the first-person which evoke the micro politics of the racialised quotidian might allow us to track the intersubjectivity and intercorporeality of whiteness. In approaching whiteness in modes other than the scholarly essay might we productively investigate the imbrication of the public and the private and demonstrate that writing issues as much from bodily imperatives as those of instrumental reason? The body is a contractual, exchanging thing. It has a dual orientation, inward and outward. I want to foreground its instability, and to glimpse the sliding of affective dispositions into each other. These flashes of affect are indices of the cross-cultural intersubjective complications of a postcolonial Anglo-Celtic creole whiteness.

Having too much to say

Liberalism is constituted by structures of feeling. Liberal guilt is expressive, performative and indexical of a desire for change. It dramatises the suffering of others to oneself (Ellison 1996) and also dramatises the ethical fallout of the loss of late liberalism's moral authority (Steele 2006). Contemporary diasporic liberal whiteness as a category, then, is riven by internal contestation. It splits through the effects of anxiety, guilt, blame and *ressentiment*, in gatekeeping struggles to shore up its coherence and authority in articulations of a renovated and "critical" whiteness. Theorists in both whiteness and postcolonial studies have recognised the limits of the enterprise of critique. Practices of listening, for example, have been promulgated as a corrective to always occupying the subject position of discourse. Sometimes, indeed there is nothing to say, and it *is* good to listen. The conversational pause opens up other questions. The category "Australian" for the elderly European man, for example, was an empty signifier. For the young white people in the violent encounters on Cronulla Beach it was a self-evident given. For me, the category conjures up its supplement—the "first" Australians: Indigenous people.[7]

Recently I attended a panel of Aboriginal people—a historian, a librarian and a Link-Up officer—discussing the tracing of Aboriginal family history. Charlie Mundine, from Link-Up, mentioned that there were 14,000 cases currently on the files in New South Wales, initiated by people wanting to identify their Aboriginal forebears. He added that there was funding for only six case officers to work on these enquiries. An articulate middle-class woman from the audience, who said she was "white", asked a question of him. She explained that it had been said of her family that it had "a touch of tar" and she was wondering if she should follow this up. She said that she was aware of the excessive pressure on the small amount of funding that had been made available by the government for the investigation of such enquiries, and she didn't want to take it away from people who perhaps had more pressing and immediate emotional concerns regarding their Aboriginal ancestors. I could follow her logic and identify with her self-doubt and was curious to see how Mr Mundine would answer her. He exhaled in a slightly exasperated way before saying: "that's bordering on political madness". I wrote that down on my pad. "If you want to investigate your Aboriginal heritage do so. But", he added, "being Aboriginal is different to being of Aboriginal descent. If you want to be Aboriginal you have to take responsibility for being Aboriginal". Later I went up to speak to a Yamatji man who was talking to the woman who had asked the question. He was advising her affably that if she wanted to trace her Aboriginal heritage she should do so. I caught myself by surprise. I realised that I had been feeling annoyed at this woman's display of liberal guilt, at her performative self-reflection and its concomitant indecisiveness.

I then set to thinking about Aden Ridgeway's comment at the Sydney Writers Festival a few weeks earlier. He expressed the thought that the time had come when white people should be able to look in the mirror and see an Aboriginal. I felt puzzled and uncomfortable at this suggestion. In a funny twist during the question time a North American woman said that she was vitally interested in Aboriginal culture. She had travelled to Australia to research it because she had been an Aboriginal in a past life. Paula and I, embarrassed, were trying not to laugh. Other people were staring hard at the floorboards. Lillian Holt, who was on the panel with Aden Ridgeway, had a deft and funny comeback: "in the next life", she said wryly, "*I'd* like to be white".

Teaching The Tracker to students in Germany[8]

The flash of recognition: the way some Aboriginal people from the bush walk. A long gait with loose shoulders and arms. Stephen Muecke has written about trying to mimic this walk (Muecke 1997, 151). I remember the Wongi guy at the Ninga Mia barbeque in Kalgoorlie, walking around the crowds in his dusty riding boots. Later he threw a spear at the papier maché kangaroo target in the spear-throwing competition. His aim was breath-taking.

The German students at Tübingen are also spell-bound. I rewind the section of the film to show them David Gulpilil's smile when Gary Sweet is abusing him. He has such control as an actor, I marvel; such an intimate relationship with the camera. I remind the students of the cutting humour of Alf Taylor's stories[9] which we had studied the previous week. "Who is laughing at who?" I ask them. They question me about blacktrackers. Do the police still use them? Why did Aboriginal people do that kind of work? Was it considered a betrayal? I'm not sure who is analysing who. I'm surprised and fascinated at their absorption.

Alf had been staying with us in Tübingen the week before, and he had given a talk to the students about his childhood at New Norcia. The students had many questions. They are intrigued at the interaffectivity of white Australians and Aboriginal people. *Can you forgive the Brothers and the nuns?* they ask. Alf laughed. "I asked the Brother to the launch of my first book", he said. "When I saw him there I rushed up to him. He looked at me nervously like ... 'errr' ... , wondering what I was going to do. I gave him a big hug". Later one of the students commented that she thought he should have been angry. And one of the professors said to me, "I was wondering when he would stop talking about himself and talk about literature".

"He writes the story of his life", I said.

***

Throughout the course the students seem deeply moved by the history of governmental management of Aboriginal people. In the first seminar they are very quiet. Later in my office one of them asks me, "Do people in Australia really use the word 'race'?" I talk about this later with Raina, the Australian student, who is marrying a German. She tells me that the German equivalent, the word "*Die Rasse*", has the same implications as the English word, "species" or "breed". I begin to understand a little more about the legacy of the Third Reich—its impact on this, the third generation since the war. The English word "race" is unspeakable. I wonder how to talk about issues of race and multiculturalism in Australian literature with them when I know so little about their own racialised vernacular. I ask Raina about what words Germans use to describe racial and ethnic difference.

"Well, there's the word '*farbig*", she says.

"*Farbig*?"

"Coloured".

I register a visceral shock at the word and gape at her.

"It's true! They use it everywhere, without flinching!" We laugh in that embarrassed, incredulous way.

It seemed a contradiction to me that the term "race" would be an embarrassment for the students but not the term "*farbig*". I began to wonder how the current diasporas from the poorer countries in the European Union and "white" nationalism were being played out in Germany against a history of shame. We discuss this in the next class. I raise the issue of the Third Reich to contextualise the eugenicist governmental policies in Australia in the 1930s. Later we talk about multiculturalism. One of the students whose parents are Turkish, tells us a story about how, although his parents can speak German, Government bureaucrats always patronise them. One of the other students says to the Turkish-German student, "Anyone who does not like it here is free to go home". I feel rigid with shame and a familiar gloom settles on me. I look around the classroom at the students, trying to gauge their reactions, trying to gauge the world I am in, feeling a bit like a bull in a China shop. No-one looks shocked. In my Australian classrooms this kind of statement would give rise to animated discussion. However the students seem barely to have registered the racism. I'm aware of a hypersensitivity around issues of race when we talk about Indigenous people but this sensitivity over human rights doesn't seem to inflect the issue of immigration. I decide that I will talk to the Turkish-German student personally after the class. And I will have to get to know the lay of the land a bit better before I return to this issue in class. Later the Australian student tells me she was very angry. "I felt really sorry for Tariq", she says.

The next day I have lunch with one of the German professors. I tell him about the students' political sensitivity to and avid interest in *The Tracker*. We talk about the issue of race in post World War II Germany and in contemporary global alliances. "We are the *gebrannte Kinder*, the burnt ones",[10] he says. I ask him about German multiculturalism. "There is no such thing", he says. He tells me their policy is one of "Integration". Now I know why a couple of students chuckled when I was discussing the failures of the Australian policies of assimilation and integration in the 1960s and 1970s. I press the professor on what *he* thinks about Integration. "Well, first we have to decide what German core values are", he says. But then he shrugs and admits, "I don't really know what is definitively 'German'. I'm a Baltic German from the border of Denmark. We are very different culturally to the Germans here in Baden-Württemberg. And my wife's family—one side comes from Poland and the other from Bohemia". We laugh and drink our coffee before returning to teaching. I'm feeling a bit more relaxed. This is familiar territory. But as we walk back I remind myself that both the professor and I are here from elsewhere; I'm really no closer to understanding the expectant, serious faces of the Schwäbian students.

Houses in Autumn: a travel journal

The way you look up from your desk half-way through the day and notice the world for the first time. Things in their patient absorption of time. The weak sun, the cold shadows move across the face of the houses. The buildings register life inside and outside themselves. They fade, crumble, shine, peel, expand and shrink. They accommodate the world and its people in their skin, their bones and inner spaces.

Fig. 12-1

The houses sit under the hill. The hill is very smooth and seems to sleep. But I also imagine that it can see the next hill and perhaps even those hills further south, the Schwäbian Alps, in which fairytale castles nestle.

Fig. 12-2

On the other side of the hill is a forest. This forest is not like the bush. It's still and quiet as it waits for winter, full of empty space. There's a track through the forest. Last time we walked there the ground was damp and soggy. The birches were refulgent in autumn colours. We were all enchanted. Alf raised his hands across the vista. *Take a picture of me here,* he said. *This is gorgeous. I could live here. I'm going to put in a land claim. There must be some German Nyoongahs around here!*

Fig. 12-3

We laughed. But we were also a bit spooked by the quietness of the splendid trees—no birds, nothing stirring. On the way back we lost our bearings and for a while weren't sure where we were. *It's ok*, says Peter. *We've got a black tracker.* Alf laughed, throwing his arms out. *Arrr! I need a* white *tracker here.* Then we talked about the Australian student's father who's a cocky from Bindi Bindi, near New Norcia as it happens, in Western Australia. When he came to visit her in Germany he felt nauseous because the shadows were on the wrong side of the trees.

The darkness falls, catching us by surprise again. It feels like the day has barely started. But the evening will become our day. The houses recede into themselves. The dullness is soft on our skin. There are things that evade description, if to describe is to be satisfied. Things themselves are full of life and they turn you around. At the front door with the key in my hand, the cold presses down on me and I'm keen to get inside this stranger's house, the warm rooms without language unfolding into light.

Genres are not to be seen

> Genres are not to be seen, a sharp order when you go inside in a neutral fashion, without evaluating it, without recommending or advising against it. This train of thought, the mouth of a door. The whole enigma, another type of audience. The interdiction, the inside: belonging—busy, international, urban adjective. What kind of history, half likes, precisely gloss and paraphrase. Just for a laugh, that's when you cannot see it.
> (Derrida, Emmanuel, Bellear)

Whiteness and *The Tracker*

The struggle in *The Tracker* of the three white male allegorical figures to play out white law in Indigenous country is subtended by their affective and physical dependence on their Indigenous guide. Watching the film with the students in Germany I think about the intimacy of the relationship between the Gulpilil and Gary Sweet characters in the film. The way they anticipate each other's every move. I'm struck by the scene where Gulpilil drags the Gary Sweet character into the waterhole, the two of them bound together by the chain, and tries to drown him; of the bodily life and death struggle in the murky pool. They both emerge alive, but from that point onwards the hatred is palpable and the Fanatic is embedded in a narrative dichotomy: to destroy or be destroyed. He is literally caught in the grip of hatred, chained by his abusive acts, his dependence, his fragile authority, his long intersubjective history with the Indigene. The pathos of that symbol of colonial terror, the chain, drags the men down the muddy slope, joined at wrist and neck.

I want the students to appreciate the brilliance of Gulpilil's acting, framed as it is for me by the poverty that dogs his life and of his immense cultural capital, perched on the precarious dividing line between rural Aboriginal life and the metropolitan consumerism of a global film industry. I hope that this film can do the work of displaying Australian white masculinity in its splintered ambivalence and blunt violence in the context of Angloceltic and Indigenous post-colonial relations. I often find it hard as a teacher to get students to recognise whiteness, but this film has an affective impact that is arresting. They sense the depth of the crisis in whiteness that it points to. In the struggle between the three white men we witness a fissile whiteness in dialogue with itself.

The film is not only about cross-racial negotiations between Angloceltic whiteness and the Indigene but about intra-white contestations within the allegorical arena of the white nation. The social contract of whiteness is renegotiated through a series of struggles within the group. The Veteran is a witness; an exhausted world-weary, laconic man who has seen it all, who largely keeps his own counsel. He is an unwilling follower, a conscript, a male participant whose *modus operandi* is passive survival in the scene of masculine colonial violence; he neither condones nor overtly resists the violence and eventually becomes it victim. Subtly played by Grant Page, the Veteran both acts compassionately and evinces compassion. He was the character who was most nebulous for the film's director during the process of writing the screenplay. De Heer describes in his journal how this was initially the main character, but gradually his role became less and less distinct, and even his name, the Veteran (originally it was "the Philosopher", indicating a primarily ruminative role), was finalised only in a late draft of the screenplay.

The white character who eventually comes to dominate the film is the Fanatic; a man whose authority derives from his gun and the verbal humiliations and bullying he inflicts on those around him. He is both driven and constrained by the white man's burden and the civilising mission. Based in part on Willshire, a South Australian policeman (Nettelbeck and Foster 2007), he is an isolated man who cannot contemplate the equitable co-existence or co-habitation of the white "race" and the Indigenous people. His anxieties around Indigenous cannibalism belie his own voracious will to power and his cultural cannibalism. He is a man who will pursue his own racialising fantasies at the expense of both black and white people who oppose him.

And then there's the Follower, the only white man who survives. He looks and learns. He is initially reluctant, fearful, boyish. For him this trip is a *rite de passage*. He learns to respect the Aboriginal tracker, to recognise Indigenous sovereignty and to accept the legitimacy of Aboriginal law. Both he and the Veteran apologise in the course of the film to the Aboriginal tracker, an act which recalls the Howard years of white governmental anxiety and defensiveness. He is youthful; a student. He can learn, where the Fanatic is condemned inevitably, it would seem, to an ignoble demise.

The Follower also assumes a retributive and revolutionary role in turning on the Fanatic and attempting to bring him to justice. However, in the frontier setting, Aboriginal justice is what prevails. The Follower is an adolescent and somewhat rash in his faith in white justice, a pathos underscored by Archie Roach's songs. At the end of the film, as Fiona Probyn has noted (Probyn 2005), the Follower is no longer a follower. The film ends at the moment of his return to white Australia. The temporality here is anticipatory; what awaits him? How will the nation incorporate this newfound ethical whiteness? Being idealist, even utopian to some degree, the film has to end at this point. It's hard to imagine how its optimism could be sustained by the (ex-) Follower's return to the white Australia of the 1940s, without becoming trite.

In closing on an open-ended anticipatory trajectory the film invokes contemporary whiteness, poised between self-critique, and the hope of a reconfiguring of white privilege and advancing social redistribution. In this it might be said to dramatise diasporic liberalism in its dream of reconciliation. What the film cannot follow up within its idealist generic parameters is the issue of how the white trauma,[11] the repressed memory of colonial terror, symbolised allegorically by the Fanatic, will play itself out as his body hangs against a blood red sunset, reminiscent of the Aboriginal flag.

In his last long monologue of denial, disavowal and white grandiosity, the Fanatic establishes himself as a somewhat tragic figure, if I could borrow this trope to characterise a figure who dwells within a temporality of belatedness, a character with no narrative future and an anxious, hysterical attachment to his white authority. Nevertheless his violent end is disturbing. Could the cruel and vengeful lynching that he undergoes at the hands of the Tracker be read as a moment of white liberal self-mortification? While he epitomises white disavowal and brutality, the punishment meted out on the Fanatic is disturbing, a cypher perhaps of white liberal self-loathing. In the final analysis the film's portrayal of the character of the Fanatic, a symptom of the fissile nature of whiteness, is ambiguous.

Talk/writing

This chapter has examined the contradictions and equivocations of diasporic liberalism. It canvasses the satisfactions and pleasures of theory and its fantasies of mastery and self-discipline. It brings corporeal events into proximity with a range of analytical reflections on embodied whiteness. The anecdote and dramatised scenes of encounter are integrated in some measure with exegetical comment. However, I resist the scholarly impulse to provide a concluding argument and a final assessment of liberal whiteness which would assimilate its contradictory affects and corporeal opacity to discourse. I do not intend to suggest that the anxieties attendant upon liberal whiteness paralyse analysis but, rather, that our bodily affects and dispositions are always in excess of and other to analysis; that they constantly challenge and interrupt analysis and, in effect, thereby generate and promote further analysis, shifting us cognitively as well as bodily. I want to hold these two impulses (the cognitive and bodily) apart in order to demonstrate their difference and incommensurability. I also want to demonstrate their engagement and interaction. The journal form[12] allows me to accommodate the oscillations between the cognitive and the bodily, and the equivocation that this oscillation produces. It allows me to record discrete incidents and moments without enchaining them to the linear and propositional logic of the essay and its conceptual abstractions. A travel diary accommodates the restless mobility of whiteness, its arrests and propulsions, its chatter and nescience. Liberal guilt, in its generation of affects, produces talk. In a circular economy the proliferation of talk gives rise to embarrassment, which stops up talk. Talk is indispensable to our scholarly and pedagogical work. Talk also produces laughter; Alf's humour (Brewster 2008) complicates the liberal guilt, the melancholy and the sorrowful attachment to loss (Brown 1999, 20) that haunts the cross-cultural work of the white scholar.

Coda

Vision takes place somewhere in tactile space
(Merleau Ponty)

If the hand is metonymic of material labour, it is also the instrument of affective labour, the embodied task of writing. If this chapter is a serial investigation of Angloceltic creole whiteness as it is played out across a range of contexts, what would it mean to introduce closure? One anecdote, one memory, precipitates another. How to round off this catalogue of everyday whiteness: ruminations, events, meetings and flashes of feeling and sensation that flicker in and out of awareness? Should I provide resolution through the narrative discursivity of therapeutic event, cautionary tale or deft exegesis? Or will I simply stop here, *in medias res,* before I say too much?

A plane crosses the sky high up, its lights spreading out across the underbelly of the clouds. I am home again. The lady in the house across the road, arm raised, casts a distorted shadow on her venetian blinds. I notice a horizontal crack of light along the blinds and realise that she must be peering out. Does she see me, sitting here on the balcony with barely enough light to write by? In one small movement she drops the blind and switches off the light.

The lightning has stopped too, for the moment, and a steady rain fills the air. The light's too dim for me to see my writing now, so I follow what I imagine is a line on the page. Around me there is the flash of the lighthouse, the flickering light of a ship on the horizon, the street lights pooling out into a muffled bruise in the thick rain and, in the distance, a man walking across a brightly lit room in a block of flats.

Another flash of lightning and everything is instantly concrete—the house, the shining road, the trees petrified against the wide stretch of sea. Then in the darkness that follows everything seems connected again, damp, soft and awake like my hand against the sticky skin of the page which flicks in the breeze. When I look up I notice there are fewer houselights on. It must be getting late. I'm curling a little against the cold and my food is forgotten on the table. When the lightning flashes again I see a large bat flying along the sea cliff. Every detail in the waves is lit up. All these events flash before me and through me, drawing me indefatigably into the world.[13]

CHAPTER THIRTEEN

LAWS OF PLACE

FIONA MCALLAN*

Introduction

This paper has come about through my explorations in response to three articles by academic and lawyer Irene Watson (2002; 2007a; 2007b), her engagements with the philosopher Jacques Derrida's writings, and how Derrida and Watson's material and Watson's arguments regarding laws of place, resonate for me in my own questioning, and what this suggests for non-indigenous peoples in "Australia". In this sense I am speaking of non-indigenous peoples as those who were transported or immigrated to "Australia", and their descendants. So, in saying this, I am differentiating indigenous peoples in "Australia" from those who have come from elsewhere, within a frame that all peoples have indigeneity. (Churchill 1994, 236) Continuing with this frame, due to the many migrations through history, invasions, diasporas, wanderlusts and so forth, many peoples are without the knowledge of their particular indigenous roots.

The term indigeneity will therefore be represented in two different ways throughout the paper. At times my aim will be to distinguish the *relation between* peoples in particular contexts, referring to a distinction between indigenous and non-indigenous peoples in the historic-cultural sense—therefore distinguishing between relations concerning descent or migration, for example, or distinguishing colonialists from first peoples. I will also be using indigeneity in the latter sense from the paragraph above. That is, by engaging an understanding of relational ontology and its structural emplacement of all peoples in inter-subjective, inter-entity, and intergenerational relations in the world. In stressing the inter-entity components of this relational ontology, I hope to also argue for a more aware and hence transformational engagement with "place".

In engaging with Watson's papers, and with significant indebtedness to her work and others, I hope to elaborate how indigenous laws are always embedded and emplaced, as law resides and generates within place. These laws are intricately bound up with practices and knowledges which reflect and sustain inter-entity reciprocal relations (Baker et al. 2001, Rose 1992)[1]. I will be arguing that it is awareness of relational ontology that enables subjects to participate in these practices and knowledges that acknowledge and support the structure of emplacement. As I have argued elsewhere (McAllan 2007a, 2007b, 2008), these practices and knowledges would be antithetical to possessive/property relations that appropriate the other.

As this ontological structure emplaces all subjects, it co-constitutively incorporates specifics of emplacement, and so with the diasporas and migrations mentioned above, this emplacement includes lived experiences of historic-cultural constructions such as race and nationality. In contemporary relations in "Australia", acknowledgement of indigeneity therefore involves not only the primary recognition of indigenous sovereignty and laws in this land, but all subsequent responsibilities involved with individual specifics of emplacement considering these diverse historic-cultural trajectories.

When I refer to "disconnection", "colonising" and "self-colonising" in this paper, I will be referring to a lack of recognition of this fundamental ontological relationship with land and each other. To enact a colonising or self-colonising relation will mean to continue possessive/property relations at the expense of the other. The concept of self-colonising is that if one were to colonise the other one would also be colonising oneself, in light of our mutual inter-entity responsibilities.

In order to locate myself in relation to what I am writing about, I consider it necessary to acknowledge that I am only able to speak for myself in the context of my experience. This is the constitutive relation for all individuals. Looking to engage laws of place regarding my relatedness and responsibilities has initiated an exploration into my genealogical historicity, to interrogate its past/present/future. My immediate ancestors on my mother's side have lived in the "Sydney" region, on the lands of the indigenous Gadi, Gammerai and Gayemai peoples, and also on Worrimi and Awaba lands, for seven generations that I know of, including my children. My tracing of this history trails into places of unknowns, not uncommon considering the early years of "settlement" and its troubled repressions.

My father's story was that his parents met onboard the ship they were given passage to "Australia" on, after serving in the 1914-17 war in France. His mother was from a Welsh village, his father from Sandgate, Kent. My understanding is that the war had provided an opportunity to attempt to escape impoverished circumstances. My paternal grandfather's mother had been widowed and her younger children sent to an orphanage. My father's mother died within weeks of his birth in Cairns (Yidinjdi land) and his father then relocated to New Guinea, leaving my father with his grandmother, who immigrated to care for him.

On my maternal side, the only family story was that a Jewish grandfather figure from generations ago had carved a prayer into a walnut shell. An intensive search has revealed records that show maternal great great great grandparents (I'm unable to determine whether the female was in fact the mother of subsequent descendents) had left England, listed as Protestants, in 1835. The grandfather of the male immigrant to "Australia" appears to have immigrated also, to England from somewhere in Europe (most likely what is now the Czech Republic, then Bohemia) during a protestant/Jewish diaspora around 1770, changing his name between his second and third child. This name had likely changed at numerous times in previous relocations, considering the Jewish heritage and its historical trajectories. The family worked as drapers in a district with a high Jewish concentration that was subject to the "poor laws" in East London, with its harshest amendment in 1834.[2]

The British Isles and Europe have long histories of migrations and invasions, and other familial lines have French, Scottish and Spanish connections. My point here is that my many-grafted roots make particular indigeneity far from clear. This introduces many questions. For example, does this make me rootless, or is my genealogical trajectory like a trailing vine? What lineage predominates, or persists? On this maternal side (apart from an incomplete marriage record) I have found no records, birth or immigrant, in the early generations of women. The absence of female and some male records produces unknowns during the early generations here. I am therefore also unsure where to draw clear distinctions in my genealogical historicity with regard to those that "came here" and those "from here".

All of this should emphasise the problem concerning constructions of fixed identities used to categorise peoples, as in race, nationality and class. I use inverted commas around "Australia" to emphasise its construction for example, and to draw attention to the imposition of this construct over the 250+ indigenous language groups occupying the land in 1788, and their descendents, who occupy still. While distinctions between individuals are crucial to avoiding appropriation, it is the power relations in historic-cultural contexts that make certain separations and certain collectivities so fraught. Identity is forever in inter-subjective, inter-entity negotiation, and it is only our incommensurable difference that is shared by all (McAllan 2007b, 37). Each individual has its own unique trajectory, subject to different forms of power relations according to prevailing and heterogeneous social conditions and circumstances. The utilising of racialised identities in "Australia" has continued systems of privilege-distribution for non-indigenous peoples that began with the colonialist repression of indigenous peoples' preexistence and laws (Tascon 2004).

Disconnection

In this exploration of laws of place (with regard to migrations and diasporas) when I differentiate indigenous from non-indigenous peoples in "Australia", I am also differentiating two *generalised* cultural routes. Considering indigenous understandings regarding being created with the land, those "from here" had, until the colonialists arrived in 1788, largely and especially away from the coasts, not been exposed to mass waves of migration and cultural instability (that is, an accumulating loss of, and disconnection from, indigenous knowledges and practices). Those who migrated to "Australia" *generally* had. What I want to draw attention to is that those who have "come here" had, in a *generalised* sense, in their own lands, been subjected to significant interference from invasive cultures over centuries, and, as a *generalised* result, they have often had lengthy disconnection from their own indigenous sense of interrelatedness between people and land.

Indigenous knowledges and practices are those that engage relational ontologies in light of the laws particular to places (Rose 1992). These practices are thus continuous with place, enacted through ever-changing inter-entity relationships, and ever-adapting with new conditions. This emphasises how indigenous knowledges and practices from other lands would differ to those in "Australia" and how cultural upheaval and oppression from invasive forces is now interfering with the carrying out of indigenous practices here.

Churchill has alerted us to the self-colonising effects of long-term disconnection, that is, the inability to recognise one's own indigenity (Churchill 1994, 236-237) and all that this entails regarding appropriation on inter-subjective and inter-entity levels of co-existence. The relation between colonising histories, the cumulative effects of *generalised* indigenous disconnection, and problematic environmental, economic and societal conditions globally, are becoming increasingly apparent. (Little Bear 2000, [ix])

Self-colonisation as argued through the work of Fanon (1967), is not simply the effects of the colonising upon the colonised, where the prevailing social forces have positioned the traumatiser as constructing the identity of the traumatised—the result of the "unreflected imposition of a culture" (191). Fanon also identifies a masochistic fetishism in the coloniser's fear-fuelled or sycophantic appropriation of the colonised (176). Watson writes of this with regard to the figure of the cannibal and its consumption of the indicting colonised (2007b, 16-18). Self-colonisation is therefore also, and very significantly, the auto-immune condition where the coloniser, in the attempt to assimilate the colonised, fails to recognise its interdependence in this relation and how appropriation of the other is both immediately and ultimately self-cannibalising. Myopia is recursively entrenched in these subordinating relations with the other, through the forgetting of inter-subjective and inter-entity interdependence. This interdependence is what indigenous knowledges acknowledge and hence reiterate and regenerate.

While I am conscious of the inadequacy of the *generalised* structures I engage with here, I acknowledge that all selections of knowledge are inherently and unavoidably partial. My desire is, particularly with respect to this difficulty, rather to draw attention to specificity, inter-subjectivity, and relatedness. And in this *generalising* I am not wishing to diminish in any way the dramatic impact of colonisation in the "Australian" situation regarding the enforced disconnections of indigenous peoples "from here" from their lands and practices in what is a relatively short epoch. Indeed, I would highlight the extremity of this confrontation between indigenous and non-indigenous peoples in "Australia", considering this variation in connectedness to indigenous roots. Highlighted also is the contradictory violence of the traditional/non-traditional binary utilised by the "Australian" government to de-authenticate indigenous owners.

The foremost problematic that I am exploring in this paper therefore is the accumulative effects of disconnection that become lived as appropriations and oppressive violence to indigenous peoples through non-indigenous myopia. This myopia is thus the lack of self-reflexivity regarding these appropriations and their perpetuation within an increasing self-colonisation. If indigeneity is understood as a fundamental structure of emplacement, this means that all peoples are challenged within colonising forces. It is therefore how one engages with colonising forces that produces levels of disconnection from, or connection to, inter-entity awareness. Within this same problematic, repressed awareness of inter-subjective relatedness has built within colonising relations in the "Australian" situation as cumulative guilt reinforces self-colonising and appropriative violence (McAllan 2008). It is prevailing disconnection and its ignorance to inter-subjective interrelatedness that I want to remain focused on when discussing laws of place and the impact of colonising relations.

Continuing colonialism

Irene Watson has alerted us to how all peoples come into laws of place, thus including non-indigenous people (Watson 2002, 17). In this sense, I am considering her statement in the frame of the differentiation I have sketched above, that is, those "from here" and those who "came here". She writes: "but the greater majority has no sense or recognition of laws of place as they are controlled by the idea of sovereignties of state and other growing global identities" (17). In the context of the colonising of indigenous peoples in the "Australian" situation, Watson argues:

> it is in thinking through how to engage with Aboriginal sovereignties that Australian society in the main becomes 'stuck', where the ground of impossibility lies, but it is this ground 'exactly' where our thinking should begin ...
>
> my suggestion is that that moment of 'impossibility' in recognising the sovereignty of Aboriginal laws, is the moment which provides Australians with the opportunity to 'take responsibility, in order to have a future' (Watson 2007a, 25-26).

In discussing the acknowledgement of indigenous sovereignty she says "we (Aboriginal peoples) should hold the ground, not only for Aboriginal peoples but for all peoples who struggle to hold law against its displacement and extinguishment through fear and ignorance" (2007a, 25-26). From Watson's work I read that this impossible ground is the opportunity for non-indigenous people to acknowledge that indigenous laws of place remain in effect in this country [indeed in all countries] and that all people have responsibilities in relation to them. Recognising the sovereignty of indigenous laws in "Australia" addresses the issue of colonial occupation fundamentally, structuring every subsequent interrelation. Imposed non-indigenous systems are therefore exposed in their illegitimacy.

From my position then, considering how I interpret Watson's argument in the three papers I engage with here, it would appear that, as the indigenous knowledges and practices of the indigenous peoples "from here" continue in this country, non-indigenous peoples need to begin with their acknowledgement of this and then work out their own responsibilities in relation to these laws, in light of their own indigeneity and co-constitutive lived circumstances. This would also require the recognition that all peoples have indigenous roots and presents the opportunity to begin reciprocal relations.

Watson continues:

> I see Aboriginal sovereignty as a dream for the future possibilities of a growing up of humanity, an opportunity for all peoples to see how they, like the 'Aborigine', are also subjugated by the state, (more comfortably perhaps, but leading to the same endings) (Watson 2007a, 27-28).

As I interpret Watson here, the growing up of humanity hinges on recognising the colonising relation, which all people are subject to in non-indigenous sovereign systems. As all individuals share fundamental emplacement, co-constitutive with the specifics of their emplacement (which includes constructs of race, nationality and class) our challenges are incommensurable with each other and always particular to our lived circumstances. In "Australia", historically, the fundamental and continuing responsibility of non-indigenous peoples towards indigenous peoples is to consider the reification of privilege allowed to the former in power relations enabled through non-indigenous sovereign law systems. Riggs has interrogated notions of non-indigenous belonging in "Australia", where privileged assumptions of belonging through ownership are founded upon the repression of ongoing histories of colonisation (Riggs 2003; Vassilacopoulos and Nicolacopoulos 2004). Moreton-Robinson (2003) and Nicoll (2004) have also written on this.

Recognition of non-indigenous privilege has not been the *generalised* situation since colonial contact and, in discussing indigenous sovereignty, Watson alerts us to the difficulties of speaking into the colonised space of continuing colonialism in "Australia" and the ongoing cannibalising process where non-indigenous peoples remain ignorant of their own indigeneity and their inter-subjective responsibilities.

> They anticipate coming into their own state of lawfulness through the consuming of our sovereign Aboriginality. In this colonising process of us becoming white and white becoming Indigenous, white settlement deems itself as coming into its own legitimacy, as whites come into the space of our freedom to roam as Aboriginal peoples over our Aboriginal places and spaces. We become cannibalised. But can we enter into a conversation on the cannibalism of our self, with the cannibal being, the cannibal who is yet to see and know itself in its eating of us? How does the cannibal recognise itself? Is there a safe conversational space where we can have a close encounter, without our own appropriation? (Watson 2007b, 16-18)

As I read Watson here, as colonising individuals remain ignorant to the structure of emplacement that pertains to all, they continue possessive/property relations that cannibalise the other in the attempt to assume their own belonging. The non-indigenous sovereign system and its accompanying mainstreaming processes assume a blanket "Australianness" that accelerates the appropriation of indigenous peoples' "freedom to roam" (Watson 2007b). I read Watson's term "freedom to roam" as the freedom to continue indigenous knowledges and practices without being subjected to this ongoing appropriative ignorance and continued colonialism.

This appropriativeness will continue as a devouring of indigenous knowledges and practices within pretenses of sharing knowledge and reconciliation, as long as the ignorance of non-indigenous peoples (with regard to their own self-colonising and this appropriation) continues. A pseudo communication with indigenous peoples continues as indigenous knowledges become absorbed by the market, for example in tourism or environmental science and education (Simpson 2004; Smith 2005, 95; Nakata 2004).

And even when the cannibal (coloniser) begins to recognise itself, the process of confronting then disassociating from connections to colonising forces and one's own self-colonising is fraught ground, as Watson has warned. It is "the ground of the future possibilities of a growing up of humanity" (Watson 2007a, 27). As non-indigenous people begin to confront the colonialist appropriation that immeasurably changed the relations of indigenous peoples and enlisted their own self-colonising and disconnection, it often leads to reactionary responses of guilt displacement (Smith 2005, 91-92) further increasing the levels of violence to indigenous peoples. It becomes the exculpation of non-indigenous guilt in the attempt to self-legitimise, at further expense of indigenous peoples, and results in further repressing reciprocal relations.

These reactionary responses can include a panicked attempt to indiscriminately and appropriatively re-indigenise in order to distance from the discomfort of self-awareness regarding complicit association with colonising relations. Indigenous practices and knowledges are thus assumed within a plasticised tokenism. Churchill has argued that such peoples should attempt to connect with the positive polarity of their own heritage traditions in order to resist further appropriation. He states:

> It is your responsibility to put yourselves in direct communication with these traditions ... upon which to base alternatives to the social, political, and economic structures now imposed upon you (Churchill 1994, 236).

As disconnection from indigenous knowledges, self-colonising and the complications of colonising guilt continue to reinforce within the colonising appropriations of myopic peoples, the conversations and sharing entrustments of indigenous knowledges become further absorbed into colonised spaces. It is a crucial question that Watson has asked, crucial for both indigenous and non-indigenous people in "Australia", within their respective co-constitutive trajectories, and I hope to iterate with her in asking, can a safe conversational space be constituted in these fraught conditions?

The Colonial Conundrum

There are some lines from a Leonard Cohen song that, to my mind, poetically expresses a sentiment that has prevailed for years in Australia. They are:

Everybody knows that the dice are loaded
Everybody rolls with their fingers crossed
Everybody knows that the war is over
Everybody knows that the good guys lost
Everybody knows the fight was fixed
The poor stay poor while the rich get rich
That's how it goes, and everybody knows
Everybody knows the boat is leaking
Everybody knows that the captain lied
Everybody has this broken feeling
Like their father or their dog just died
Everybody's talking through their pockets
Everybody wants a box of chocolates
And a long stemmed rose
That's how it goes
And everybody knows[3]

To me the lyrics speak of unease … "the fight was fixed" and … "the poor stay poor while the rich get rich" … and … "everybody knows". The lyrics also speak of indifference, self-satisfaction or self-protection. "Everyone's talking through their pockets … everybody wants a box of chocolates … that's how it goes". While everybody knows ... there's this inertia … this stasis … a bit like an animal caught in the headlights of an oncoming vehicle. In "Australia", as across the globe, people are busily talking about interest rates and mortgages, despite being caught between the contradictory fears of either global warming or stalling economic growth.

The song speaks to me of an ethical conundrum. A conundrum that seems to demand the required "forgetting" of Lyotard's theorised grand narratives of progress (Lyotard 1979). As progress progresses … land is plundered in the process, people dispossessed and oppressed. As the development of nations has been at the expense of dispossessing indigenous peoples, this dispossession in the act of possession has become the required forgetting that accumulates in collective denial. Derrida, deconstructing Husserlian logic concerned with saving the honour of reason, sketches the forgetting of historical and subjective origins, or "objectivist naïveté"(Derrida 2005, 127), as the suicidal autoimmunity in self-referential reasoning. Autoimmunity is a guise of objective reason that denies interdependence, as I have sketched self-colonising in this paper. Watson has said that colonisers perceived this country ("Australia") as an empty place to be filled with their beginnings and their evolving spirit (Watson 2002, 13). She writes:

> Sickness is what then emerges, an equally natural sickness, an evil naturally affecting nature. It is divided, separated from itself. When such an event occurs, one must speak of a pathology of the community… (2002, 51).

A divided self has forgotten its place in relation to the other. That is, the other that becomes displaced, through taking over the other's place. Muecke has described colonising as a territorialising of space with scientific rationalism, arguing that Imperial dispossession brought an intensification of a sense of linear time—an abstracted and abstracting "historical consciousness". This consciousness remains out of place, disembodied, and Muecke offers that this disconnection induces anxiety (Muecke 2005 14).

In the progressive march to assume control of the "natural" world, and anxiously fill its presumed empty spaces, there was a frenzy of activity as indigenous peoples were forced into the colonial underbelly and turned as biopolitical cogs (whether collecting rubber in the Congo or spices in the Caribbean, or breaking horses and scrubbing floors in *Terra Nullius*). The "required forgetting" of this oppression abstracted into scientific discourses of eugenics and "civilisation". Watson has used the term "muldarbi", or "demon spirit", to describe "colonisers and all forms of exploitation and power that are dispossessing and destructive of indigenous peoples" (Watson 2002, 18). Rather than enlightenment freedom, these colonising forces manifest as a myopia that prevents the individual perceiving its interrelatedness with others and its world.

Derrida has also theorised this myopia as the naïve conscience, with regard to Hegelian logic, stuck in a closed circuit of self-referentialism (Derrida 1985, 106). Consumed by self-satisfaction and self-protection, this naïve conscience entirely misses its interdependency in inter-entity relationships in the world. Disconnection, as an entrenched mode of perceptual abstraction, therefore actually constitutes as denial (Derrida 1985, 128). Guilt and fear, as byproducts of exploitation of the other, coalesce in this denial, so that the self remains stubbornly unexamined. The illusion of self-identity is this forgetting of the self's interrelatedness. So it stays divided from itself, consumed with fear and lack that compels it to fill and establish itself.

While psychoanalysis is useful in conceptualising collective imaginaries and the fear engendered by this perception of lack, a focus on human-centred consciousness can limit the potential to engage with this fear. Failure to comprehend inter-entity interrelatedness compels the subject to overcome lack, presumed as absolute negativity. Derrida's work (resonating with Watson's work engaging indigenous relational ontologies) explores consciousness beyond the limits of a human-centred focus. This allows for a more adequate engagement with negativity. As Derrida's work (2008) engages aporetic thinking to interrogate the fixity of concepts including the "human", "animal" etc, Watson argues that indigenous knowledges know different realities to the univocal law of colonialism. She states:

> The word 'nation' needs to be exploded and expanded to properly reflect and accommodate the philosophy of Nunga [meaning indigenous peoples] laws. Expanded to include the voices of the natural world, so that the ruwi [meaning land] of the first nations has a voice (Watson 2007a, 48).

The subordination of first nations peoples' voices has perpetuated the forgetting of interrelatedness, as the myopia of colonialism imagines an anthropocentrism that determines laws for "self" at the expense of what is considered outside "self's" needs. In considering an inter-entity consciousness, as relational ontologies do, negativity would not be destruction or loss where positivity is wholeness, but rather negativity and positivity are two poles that remain relational. Negativity and positivity are, assiduously, potentialities. In this frame, denial is a forgetting of relatedness that contains the potential of remembering. Yet, when it comes to non-indigenous notions of claiming place that are fuelled by anxiety about loss of belonging (ownership), repressed knowledge of indigenous dispossession (Riggs 2003, 107-109) and the illegitimacy of their sovereign systems, levels of myopic repression remain caught up in recursive circuits of fear, and this only increases participation in colonising relations. Thinking beyond a human-centred consciousness and comprehending the inter-entity negotiations beyond negativity becomes a huge challenge considering myopic non-indigenous claims for place as property/ownership.

Epiphany

Sketching myopia within the forces of colonialist denial should convey some sense of the cannibalistic conditions that Watson alerts to, conditions that can make the possibility of a safe conversational space to engage with this force appear impossible.

A Cherokee proverb states "We must have a vision of our world unclouded by fear"[4]. "Australia" appears covered with clouds of denial, generated by the ongoing fear and guilt that accompanies the act of dispossession. As denial takes force within the exercise of rationalising away repressed guilt, this disconnected reasoning appears to reinvigorate within the efforts to control and keep at bay these anxieties.

Is it possible to rupture this myopic and fear-fuelled denial, to reveal relatedness?

The relational epistemologies and ontologies of indigenous populations call into question the legitimacy of the foundations of colonial sovereignties in the "developed" world. Watson states: "Aboriginal laws, first laws of place, live differently, living in the land, bodies, minds, and spirits of those who carry and still hold to the law. So where does the force of law to extinguish the laws of the other draw its legitimacy from?" (Watson 2007a, 26-29).

Yet the law that presumes settled foundations denies any need to address its own legitimacy. The landmark Mabo case finally challenged the sovereign presumption of *terra nullius* or empty land and legally acknowledged the preexistence of indigenous laws in "Australia". This brought colonial sovereign legislation into question and opened the possibility of recognising the fallacy of a fixed sovereign foundation and imposed grid of tenure over indigenous lands. The Mabo case also revealed that indigenous laws of place engaged a "co-sovereign" relation between its indigenous occupants "belonging" in country, the originary and ongoing shared responsibility of all co-existing individuals (McAllan 2007a, 283; 2007b, 38-39; 2008, 22). Yet, "legislatively, indigenous Australian's have still not been afforded proper accommodation of their relations with law, and their relations with the land [in the colonial frame] remain derivative to colonialism" (McAllan 2007a, 276). To follow Motha's argument concerning Mabo:

> it was the separation of juridical and legislative power—that is, beneficial and radical title—into things-in-themselves, that enabled the prerogative power of the Crown to take the outside of law, in a mastering of otherness, without being checked by common law. With the fiction of a fixed foundation in sovereign law revealed, the common law 'masterfully' placed the unjustifiable sovereign event outside law. The unified and settled territory of Australia was re-assumed in a future anterior movement ensuring continuance with British colonial sovereignty was re-established as juridical foundation, with common law recognising indigenous title only where it wasn't extinguished by the doctrine of tenure. The prerogative power of the Crown ... was able to counter the threat of Indigenous title, in a resilient and teleologically progressive determination that enabled the skeletal form of the sovereign body of law to stay intact (McAllan 2007a, 276-7).

Native title has since engaged a process of non-entitlement in indigenous land relations (Watson 2002; Grbich 2001, 128) that has further prevented continuity regarding engagements in laws of place. The presumed self-security/legitimacy in self-colonising relations appears to reinforce the suppression of guilt about "Australian" law's denial of interrelatedness with others.

It appears to be an impossible situation. Yet in terms of relational ontology, impossibility is not absolute negativity (Derrida 2001, 57-69; Watson 2007a, 43). Rather than claiming place as property relations, the structure of emplacement entails engaging continually with laws of place. The reliance on human-focused consciousness needs to be extended to properly engage a consciousness of inter-entity relatedness.

In the context of her country, Quandamooka lands of Minjeripah, ("North Stradbroke Island", "Queensland"), Karen Martin has written "country is not only the Land and People, but it is also the Entities of Waterways, Animals, Plants, Climates, Skies and Spirits". Martin explains that when writing she capitalises these entities to afford them the respect of their Proper Noun status. The way of relatedness is to set about establishing identities, interests and connections to determine your relatedness (Martin 2007, 11). Connections can be restored and relatedness can be reciprocated and maintained (8). Martin writes with regard to her indigenous community: "The strength of our country can be seen in the relationships with these Entities, hence it is a truly relational ontology. All things are recognised and respected for their place in the overall system" (7).

And Mudrooroo, Colin Johnston, has said on relatedness,

> The spirituality of the indigenous people of Australia is an affirmation of the spirit of humanity and the earth. There is no myth of a severance between humanity and nature or between deity and person. The earth is a vast dreaming organism; the environment is a community or family arranged in kinship patterns across her skin" (Mudrooroo 1995).

Speculating on consciousness in terms of inter-entity movement, Renaud Barbaras writes:

> by defining life on the basis of ... lack, we are led to deny it any ability to make negativity appear in the world. Incompleteness, as the absence of a circumscribed object is a false negativity, it is the aspiration to fullness and not the opening up of an absence (Barbaras 2006, 134).

This fear of incompleteness engenders the cannibalistic urge to fill a perceived lack in self that, in confirming its own relation, misses its interrelatedness with all others.

Barbaras goes on to say that experience necessarily involves negativity, as the aporetic relation that opens up the horizon, simultaneously fills while hollowing out. This is not lack then, but an opening up of an absence to reveal interrelatedness. To Barbaras, the epiphany for inter-subjective myopia is the recognition of the characterisation of a subject that is incapable of lack, which leads to a rupture in thinking. This rupture corresponds to recognising the emergence of the negative as, not loss but intraworldly desire—the manifestation of the world itself constitutes only by letting itself be affected. Intraworldly desire is the originary interrelation of negativity and positivity, (or passivity and activity) possessing only what dispossesses it. Desiring is not an objective movement therefore, it unfolds interrogatively (Barbaras 2006, 81-128).

As I interpret this, awareness of inter-entity relatedness can engage seemingly impossible negativity fearlessly, when it is understood that unchartered terrain is not loss, unexamined self-fears are not threatening to self-constitution or self-legitimacy. Negativity in this sense is the aporetic opening in the relation between all inter-subjective engagements, offering affirmative transforming possibilities. For me, relational ontologies reveal how this aporia is not a place of lack. This vertiginous unhomely stance is a wholly desirable, intraworldly place of connection. As Derrida (1982, 1985) argued, deconstruction is not destruction, but a resisting beyond the binaries that work to close the circulatory of univocal laws that disconnect.

Moustakas argues that individual experience, in light of relatedness, is not an explanation, but is rooted in questions which further awaken interest. He states: "what I see is interwoven with how I see, with whom I see it, and with whom I am" (Moustakas 1987). And, as Muecke argues that generations aren't amassed in measured units of time, identity and being do not emphasise genealogy so much as maintain relationships with deceased through connecting as *place* in a web of relatedness (Muecke 2005, 15). If laws live in the land, bodies, minds, and spirits of those who carry and still hold to the law (Watson 2007a, 26) *place* becomes the location of enduring significance. My learning with regard to relational ontologies has revealed to me, place as a bodily connectedness. Body as place. Place as body. Place lives and bodies live in place, as place.

These theorists all resonate for me in revealing the affirmation in relational ontologies. Some may argue that my exploration of indigenous accountsof ontology and their resonations with non-indigenous accounts is problematic, as they are incommensurable. My answer to this would be that the emphasis needs to be on how ALL accounts are incommensurable. If we miss this, then we miss the theoretical argument regarding the structure of emplacement and relational ontologies that I'm elaborating in this paper. It is our relationality and difference that we share fundamentally, so boundaries thus become places of sharing and negotiation rather than definitive separations or crevices of absorption.

The cannibalistic absorption regarding indigenous peoples and the colonising mainstream is a crucial concern for both indigenous and non-indigenous, while our challenges are different according to our subjective trajectories and prevailing power relations of privilege. Yet to keep the focus on simply the incommensurability between non-indigenous theorists and indigenous theorists, when it is the power differentials involved in separating into binaristic opposites that is the real difficulty, would compromise the recognition of how we are all subject to the structure of emplacement, with all our co-constitutive circumstances considering these power relations.

My search regarding my own indigenous roots has not led to definitive answers. It was undertaken to explore my co-constitutive responsibilities regarding my emplacement now. I remain unhomely (Bhabha 1994), but I don't consider this in a negative sense. Engaging with relational ontologies has helped me to begin working out my inter-entity responsibilities in relation to my discursive historicity. To acknowledge subjectivity in its singular/plural or doubling structure, I find myself straddled between two orders of temporality, one now and the other an irreducible atemporality.

Self-encounters

"Australia's" colonialist history has much shame-filled repression. While many non-indigenous peoples may be unsure of their familial historicity and its participation in individual atrocities, there is growing awareness of past and present violence to indigenous peoples in the production of non-indigenous privilege as normative. My growing awareness of relational ontologies is being lived in my journey away from the disconnectedness of my relationships in the self-colonising frame. I, like so many socialised in abstracted non-indigenous systems of knowledge, had little unawareness of the levels of normalising I took on as part of my rote socialisation in the colonialist society around me. I was unaware of my disconnectedness and how it produced appropriative responses in every day interrelations. My growing education over the years concerning the politico-historical issues affecting indigenous peoples in this country was initially shocking to me, and disorienting. The more I learned, the more I felt further disaffected from the society around me that I'd already critically rejected on other fronts.

Becoming aware of indigenous laws of place has meant the acknowledgement of the appropriations that I and my ancestors have made in the past. My awareness also has brought me to the fundamental acknowledgment of the laws that continue in the places where I co-exist with others. This compels responsibility to connect to my own indigenous resistance, and to do what I can to learn the knowledges and practices that continue to reveal laws of inter-entity reciprocity within these places. I see this also as a continuing effort to resist further ignorance of my inter-entity relatedness and its responsibilities. This effort includes the unlearning of privileges that my disconnection ensured for me within colonising relations in this country. My way forward is attempting to transform the relations of the past, resisting participation in political structures that continue disconnection, and working to deconstruct and expose these structures in the public arena. Reaffirming positive connections informs my decisions about how I participate in social relations and make everyday choices regarding my individual patterns of consumption—how I live in my environment with others. I do not possess land, as I understand land holds me, and it is my responsibility to take instruction from indigenous people who retain knowledge of reciprocal relations in the places where I live.

In looking back into my family history I am searching into my sense of responsibility and the conditions that shaped my genealogical trajectory. I am looking for omissions and necessary reparations in connection with ancestral actions and my own. I am also looking for the positive commonalities and traditions that I can draw from their experiences. I'm conscious of the associated discomfort in examining my own historicity. For example, knowing that around 1900, when relatives were conducting trade at a drapery in what became "King Street", decimated groups of indigenous custodial families had largely been relegated to fringe camps. I'm not sure how awareness of this affected my ancestors, and what this period entailed in their day-to-day lives, what repressions or alliances were involved, but to reflect with contemporary awareness "now", on the societal norms of "then", provides opportunities for transformative relations. This applies also to the discomfort concerning my own participation in the ignorance so entrenched in non-indigenous relations in "Australia", and so my own participation in self-colonising forces and disconnection. As the awareness presents, so does the opportunity for changed relations.

I am aware that my activism now is motivated by a desire to try to stop the perpetuation of ignorance that I myself had participated in. It is not clear to me how much my own need to self-legitimate plays out in my desire to make positive connections between my past and present. This remains a central problem in self-reflexivity. Self-legitimising appears to be a necessary condition, intimately related with working through guilt. But if it takes any precedence it will only pool in recursive myopic disconnection rather than open unconditional relations of reciprocity. This returns me to the question that Watson has posed regarding cannibalising the other. It is the crucial question about where to go from here, that is, when reflexivity begins to stir in non-indigenous people in "Australia"—stirring the desire to reconnect to responsibilities; revisit the past; make reparations and change relations in the future. Guilt is a necessary emotion for disconnected people to work through, but I would hope that, in my own case, I can use this to propel me further in my desire for changed relations in the future. From experience, the more relatedness is discerned, the easier it is to affirm.

Recursive denial, or worse, untapped or reactive denial, will impact upon the renewing energies of an inter-subjective and interrelated world. In working through areas of disconnection and myopia, and building on my relatedness, I have opportunity to strengthen in a vine of affirmative resistance, against the colonising forces that disconnect and uproot.

Pattern thinking

Indigenous relational ontologies have been attacked in a reactionary sense for the very things they are not. That is: romanticism, negative theology, idealism, irrationalism—depending on who's attacking. Yet these "isms" are linked with the pathological searches for lost origins and the self-referential rhetoric that presumes a past, present, future illusion of continuity, while repressing the un-confronted, the presumed threats to selfness, the fear. As I have argued, the evolving spirit of progress has been hellishly determined to control the assumedly empty spaces, and with this there has been a disconnection from indigenous roots and context. This is where abstracted rationalising takes hold. It is an unreasonable reason that disconnects, only selectively seeing what empirically presents.

Pualani Louis explains relational ontologies as an interrelated "holism that goes beyond the empirically based concept of a unified physical universe ... the greatest mysteries lie within the self at the spiritual level and are accessed through ceremony (Pualani Louis 2007, 134). I'm reading ceremony in the frame of affirmative inter-subjective connectedness, deconstructing and resisting colonising forces.

Relational ontologies are not self-referential, a closed circuit. Rather than the colonial illusion of a progressive linear teleology Muecke offers that continuity is more about place than time. We live in place rather than time (Muecke 2005, 13-22). Places are specific and contiguous to their inhabitants who make them meaningful through ritual, traditions, and ceremonies (14). I'm reading place energetically/materially, where one can be affirmatively connected ancestrally. Body is place, place is body. "Participation is ... the expression of the necessary process that all human beings are involved in as they are involved in the world, as neither subject nor object, but mutually implicated" (19).

David Mowaljarli has stated "Ancient time is no time" (Mowaljarli 1993, 68). Relational ontologies reveal that time is not extending back through a series of pasts, rather the past underlies and is within the present. Time is therefore cyclical, overlapping, kept in place through abiding events. Time intensifies within concentric cycles; cycles of seasons, cycles of ancestors, cycles of generations, cycles of traditions. Time becomes ceremony, pulled up at places (Muecke 2005, 16). Ancestral eternality, where the past reinvigorates in the present, exceeds the present and opens the future, interrogatively, (self-affectionately).

The illegitimate colonising relation, imposed as a settled foundation, can never grant sovereignty. State sovereignty denies the pre-existence of laws of place that enable co-sovereign relations to be engaged, and instead, continues the violence of cannibalising assimilation. As the sovereign relation is a shared inter-subjective relation that is integral to relational ontology (McAllan 2007a, 283), it can only become affirmed through engaging with laws of place. Watson states: "Aboriginal sovereignty is different from state sovereignty because it embraces diversity, and focuses on inclusivity rather than exclusivity" (2007b, 20). She says that laws of country come from the "place of lawfulness, a time before, a time now, and a time yet coming to us". Through laws of place, people coexist in law, "law lives in all things". Laws of place pertain to all, "not only for Nungas (indigenous peoples) but for all in the wake of their own embrace of Nunganess" (Watson 2002, 19).

In attempting to understand coming into laws of place, I read this as the vertiginous deconstructive stance of indigeneity, a stance that engages with the forces of colonising laws to resist and exceed. I see this as the necessary impossibility as laws of reciprocity are engaged within the bodies of individuals. Bodies that affirmatively connect in the locus of place and irreducible ancestral time (Muecke 2005, 22). Crucial to this, beyond colonising forces, laws of place need to be engaged, responded to.

Mowaljarli, in his book *Yorro Yorro* (1993), drew country as a complex body, illustrating the interrelatedness of all living systems. As people embody country, colonialism reveals its suicidal disconnectedness. Muecke writes, "Structured locative interdependence means to consume other peoples' lands, is to destroy the world pattern upon which one depends" (2005, 17). Muecke is signaling the cannibalistic conundrum of self-colonisation. Also concerned with non-indigenous myopia, Mowaljarli had stated: "We get blocked by politicians, media, processes of law. All we want to do is come out from under all this and give you this gift, this gift of pattern thinking".

From what Muecke and Mowaljarli indicate, pattern thinking, as embodied and situated thinking, remains clear-eyed about its situatedness and interdependency. This thinking would then resist and exceed self-centred delusion of the disconnected cannibal. While Mowaljarli was speaking as a traditional Ngarinyin lawman, this conceptualising appears to extend beyond any simplistic or anthropological interpretation of a "traditional" world view (which, in hyper-colonised space, is assumed to be a closed view, relegated to a redundant past). Pattern thinking would extend to all those who continue to engage their inter-subjective interconnectedness with land, entities, each other. It thus engages one's indigeneity. Mowaljarli was concerned to pass on his knowledge beyond the imposition of fixed non-indigenous laws, extending the conceptualising of pattern thinking to all peoples, thereby allowing for transforming and invigorating co-relations that exceed linear teleology. Pattern thinking alerts us to the embeddedness of laws of place, as these patterns and laws extend across the world.

Pattern thinking also alerts us to the risk in diminishing the importance of the context from which others speak, revealing the extreme significance of inter-connectivity and the responsibility regarding the authority with which one speaks. This is crucial considering the continuing hyper-colonised conditions that privilege non-indigenous peoples' speaking over indigenous peoples'. As the anthropological voice in colonising power relations fixes the "traditional" indigenous voice as stereotype, this stereotype works to dismiss presumed "non-traditional" voices as inauthentic, while at the same time signaling "traditional" as stereotypically ancient = redundant. Reactivity in non-indigenous myopia will continue the suppression of indigenous voices and "those of the natural world" (Watson 2007a, 48). Colonising subordination will continue to silence the complex interplay of cooperative power relationships in indigenous lived-experience. Colonialist assumptions of taming wilderness and profiting from land have wreaked mass disruption to intricate reciprocities operating at inter-entity levels. Shared responsibilities concerning laws of country reflect the concreteness of pattern thinking, revealing the crucial priority of the "listening to" of voices within indigenous knowledge systems.[5]

So what authority can the disconnected non-indigenous voice have if there is no engaging with laws of place? If pattern thinking pertains to "laws embodied and encoded in land", what is said is always situated, embedded with meaning ateleologically, hence ancestrally inscribed and lived. Embodied thinking would appear to be understanding that is intra-worldly, saturated with interrelatedness, both situated and situating, and conscious of the atemporal but not in an abstracted sense, that is, not with un-substantiated distance, and dislocating generalisations.

If laws of place pertain to the context with which one is authorised to speak and this context is always already saturated with the significance of the embodied law that resides in particular places, due to my disconnection from these knowledges, I, and all others like me, need to come to understand what these laws, embedded in country, require. This situates me in a learning position, as novice regarding indigenous laws of place. My indigeneity will not simply spring up in me spontaneously, it will take relearning. And despite taking up this position of learning, the risk of appropriation when speaking remains impossible. As we generalise, we speak in the place of others. We risk generalising beyond situated context and what we are authorised, or have the appropriate experience, to say. So when it comes to speaking, is it always a matter of who is authorised to speak, in what context? As I understand this, as indigenous peoples continue their connections in country, they become initiated concerning laws of particular places, gradually invested with knowledges that guide shared responsibilities.

Imposed laws can't be added to what already constitutively lives in bodies and country, and it is the relation with these laws that offers power of affirmation, respond-ability, responsibility. The power from imposed law is illusory, disconnected, ultimately self-cannibalising. Is it now time for disconnected peoples to release their illusory grip on this illusory power and start to listen attentively to the indigenous voices of those that are continuing to connect? Is it time to start to relearn our place in relation to others within the lawful patterns of the earth?

Deborah Bird Rose, in her study of decolonisation concerning Mt Dromedary communities, argues that the great problem for settlers is the regrounding of accountability in time and place (Rose 2002, 14). Considering the violent forces of colonialism and the disconnection it affects, she says indigenous people on the south coast of "Australia", "whose connection to place and the knowledge of sacred places is alive and well", are involved with settlers who "in their own lives or the lives of their forebears, actively or passively promoted the practices that sought most specifically to eradicate these indigenous people, to wipe out their knowledge, and destroy their connections to place". The protection of Mt Dromedary and the stories of the decolonising journey these communities have co-embarked upon, speaks of the need to come together, to "put one foot in front of the other in dark and risky times" (14). Rose conveys property owner Mal Dibden's relationship with the mountain and his growing appreciation for its sacredness as, in his explanation, nature knocked him into shape, teaching and transforming him as his proprietary ventures continued to fail (8-15).

In the place where I live, despite the voracity of the colonial impact on the shores and lands where the first fleet set their "founding" flags (Castles 1982) indigenous custodians continue their connection and knowledge of the sacred places of this area. And non-indigenous peoples are deferring to indigenous peoples who understand this sacred significance and continue the practices and knowledges that support this. And this continuity exceeds any colonialist binaries of authentic/inauthentic. Non-indigenous peoples are beginning to assume responsibilities in relation to this sacredness also, under the generous tutelage of indigenous custodians.[6] In this region, the challenge concerning relations of property and development is extreme. Acknowledging the sovereignty of indigenous laws has appeared impossible. Yet it would appear that through these shifting, affirmative relations, the land is inscribing itself into such peoples (Rose 2002, 15). As I see it, my responsibilities begin here, reconnecting in reciprocal relations with others and country. As I acknowledge laws of place I hope to join Watson and all those who struggle to hold law against its displacement.

NOTES

Chapter One

[*] I acknowledge the Aboriginal women in Rockhampton who supported the research; the Queensland Aboriginal and Islander Health Council, Monash University, and the Indigenous Studies Research Network, Queensland University of Technology for their support; and the National Health and Medical Research Council for funding my post-doctoral research fellowship.

[1] Holland states that where her mother's Aboriginal family are from in south-western Queensland, Aboriginal people name themselves as Murris (1996, 190).

Chapter Two

[1] I use the term "the west" not to further dichotomise west and east or to demonise the one and sanctify the other but because it is the only short signifier that serves the purpose of placing racism and whiteness together. Alistair Bonnett addresses the issue of racism and the west in his book *Anti-Racism* (London: Routledge, 2000). Bonnett's use of Du Bois led me to split the "double consciousness" struggle that Du Bois writes about in *The Souls of Black Folk* (1903) and apply the "single" lens of whiteness as a mirror upon itself. See *The Social theory of W.E.B. Du Bois*, Phil Zuckerman, ed. (London: Pine Forge, 2004), 23-24.

Chapter Four

[*] Research for this chapter was made possible with support and funding from the School of Geography and Earth Sciences (McMaster University) and the Faculty of Arts (University of Wollongong). The analysis presented here was influenced by the invaluable assistance of many including Walter Peace (McMaster University), Brian Martin and Susan Dodds (University of Wollongong), members of the Haudenosaunee, Friends of Red Hill Valley, SPATE and the Community Picket. Barbara Baird, Damien Riggs and two anonymous referees also provided constructive feedback.

[1] Helen Watson-Verran and David Turnbull (1995, 116, 138, footnote 4) refer to the "western contemporary technosciences" as indicative of the "lack of a fundamental epistemological difference between science and technology as well as their strong interaction in the latter part of the twentieth century". David Wade Chambers and Richard Gillespie refer to "modern technoscience ... [as] an active

agent in European global conquest (Chambers and Gillespie 2000, 232, footnote 46).

[2] The involvement of Corneulis O'Brien, recipient of a 300 acre grant, the first in the region and encompassing the Sandon Point area, in this "vigilante action" was noted by Governor Macquarie. Macquarie wrote to the chief magistrate to express "surprise, regret and displeasure" at no action being taken following "this wanton attack on the Natives" (Organ 1990, 101-104, reproduced from the Wentworth papers, Mitchell Library, A753, CY699). Thomas Gibson Park, bordering the Sandon Point area, has been identified as the location of this massacre by Uncle Guboo, senior Yuin lore man (L. Davis 2002, personal communication, 14 February).

[3] The exposed remains were stumbled across by members of the same family, who lived close-by. T. Stephenson came across them in 1974 and 1998. There is also widespread anecdotal evidence regarding remains disturbed by the Water Board (now known as Sydney Water), approximately 50 metres away, in the 1970s (see unknown 2002a).

[4] Uncle Guboo passed away, aged 93, on 19 May 2002: "The following day a chilling icy wind and dark skies greeted [workers] as they turned the first sods of their egregious development" Organ 2002).

[5] Kuradji loosely translates to clever fella from the Dharawal language. The creek beside which SPATE is located, which runs adjacent to the burial, was renamed Bugeen. Bugeen loosely translates to clever fella from the Dhurga language. The burial was exhumed and relocated nearby at the request of the local Aboriginal Community (see Fullagar and Donlon 1998).

[6] The NSW National Parks and Wildlife Act was amended in 1996, establishing "Regional Parks" as a new category for protected areas. Changes were publicised in the *Regional Parks Policy Statement* (New South Wales National Parks and Wildlife Service 1997).

[7] This was the third recorded arson involving the picket, amongst other acts of violence against its members (see Dennis 2005). SPATE was rebuilt after the structure was destroyed in a separate arson attack on 18 September 2004 (Roderick 2004).

[8] At this meeting, the Minister was presented 1500 letters of objection to the residential proposal

[9] Jill Walker, a local resident and member of the Community Picket, successfully challenged regulatory approvals based on a non-consideration of climate change (*Walker v Minister for Planning* [2007] NSWLEC 741 (27 November 2007)). This was overturned on appeal to the NSW Supreme Court in September 2008 (*Minister for Planning v Walker* [2008] NSWCA 224 (24 September 2008)). On 22 October, the NSW Environmental Defenders Office filed an application in the High NSW Court for leave to appeal the Supreme Court ruling.

[10] The Niagara Escarpment is a World Biosphere Reserve and the valley comprised the only "large natural area", having "persisted as a visible link to the environmental and cultural history of the local area" (Peace 1998).

[11] The NDP provincial government re-affirmed their decision in October 1991, with the province committing $18 million in funding to these ends in 1994 (see Peace 1998).
[12] The Conserver Society of Hamilton and District was formed as Clear Hamilton of Pollution (CHOP) in 1969, with protection of the Red Hill Creek valley as a major aim. CHOP changed its name to the Conserver Society in 1984.
[13] The region's first industry, school, church and public buildings were located in the valley. The creek and valley also marked the northern-most point of advancement of invading American troops during the War of 1812 (Stewart-DeBreau and Nugent 1998, 186).
[14] For early references see McLean (1993) and McNie (1991).
[15] Previously approved provincial funding for restorative works in the valley were withdrawn.
[16] Notices also posted in the valley in 2001 and April 2002 and again in August 2003 (General 2003; Hughes 2002; Iotzova 2004; unknown 2002c).
[17] The Two Row wampum was a rejection of colonial paternalism: "The white man said he would respect the Onkwehonweh's [the real people's] belief and pronounce him as a son. The Onkwehonweh replied, 'I respect you, your belief, and what you say; but you pronounced yourself as my father and with this I do not agree, because the father can tell his son what to do and also can punish him.' So the Onkwehonweh said, 'We will not be like father and son, but like brothers'" (unknown 2007b). This excerpt included a by-line: "This interpretation of the Two Row Wampum belt has been widely attributed to the late elder Jake Thomas, a traditional Cayuga chief at Six Nations reserve, and Huron Miller, Onondaga; both leaders in the oral tradition".
[18] The context of the land being described as "not unsung" is important. The interview from which this excerpt is reproduced, was recorded for an archaeological study funded by Stockland—the proponent for the housing estate.
[19] Before signing the Nanfan Treaty, the Haudenosaunee had reached an agreement with the Ottowas securing hunting privileges in the same area (Haan 1980, 318).
[20] The Iroquois, one of the Six Nations of the Haudenosaunee, had previously attacked the Attiwandaronk who had lived in the region.
[21] See also Roderic Pitty (1999).
[22] Members of the Haudenosaunee had indicated problems with archaeology and deference to it. In 2002 they had forced archaeologists employed by the City to stop any work in the valley (unknown 2002c).
[23] At Sandon Point, the archaeological report detailing the exhumation of the Kuradji burial—at the request of members of local Aboriginal community—is titled *Archaeological Salvage Excavation at McCauleys Beach, Thirroul, NSW* (Fullagar and Donlon 1998).
[24] Parallels exist in laws referring to "ownership" of objects of physical significance. For example, Justice Bergin (*Stockland (Constructors) Pty Ltd v Allen Richard Carriage* [2002] NSWSC 1179 (11 December 2002)) found that "relics" at Sandon point "were, and always had been, the property of the crown" despite challenges by the local community: "how could ownership of relics that predated European settlement be vested in the Crown" (Dennis 2002).

[25] Ien Ang (2001) developed the concept of "together in difference" that Haggis extends on.

Chapter Five

[1] The author would like to thank the Nadine Ehlers and an anonymous referee for their very valuable input into an earlier draft of this essay, and also audience members at the 2007 Australian Critical Race and Whiteness Studies Association conference for their feedback on a related conference paper.

Chapter Seven

[1] <http://infoweb.newsbank.com>
[2] The numbers are difficult to determine. The immigration department refers to an "onshore" visa application as one by a person seeking asylum either by landing on Australian shores and engaging Australia's obligations to provide a haven from persecution or by gaining entry to Australia on another kind of visa and then converting those to an asylum claim. According to Department of Immigration and Citizenship (DIAC) 2007, *Fact Sheet 60. Australia's Refugee and Humanitarian Programme*, Canberra, viewed 8 January 2008, <http://www.immi.gov.au/media/fact-sheets/60refugee.htm>, between 1999 and 2002, 11,920 onshore visas were granted, however this number includes all those who sought asylum onshore, not just those who arrived in Australia by boat.
[3] All circulation figures are found in Herman's article on the Australian Press Council website. Herman, J. 2007. *State of the News Print Media in Australia 2007*. Australian Press Council, Chap. 2.
[4] I use the abbreviation S plus a number to denote the numerical order of the sentence in the articles quoted.
[5] In February 2001, the Immigration Detention Advisory Group (IDAG), was established to advise the Minister "on the appropriateness and adequacy of services, accommodation and amenities at the immigration detention centres". Its members, consisting of two former immigration ministers, one each from the Labor and the conservative side, a number of refugee advocates, representatives of ethnic communities and representatives of the defence forces, visited all immigration detention centres and several alternative places of detention.
[6] On 26 January 2002, Natalie Larkins, a journalist covering the Woomera protest for the national broadcaster, the Australian Broadcasting Corporation (ABC), had been arrested by security guards for "failing to leave Commonwealth land".

Chapter Eight

[*] We would like to acknowledge the sovereignty of the Kaurna people, the First Nations people upon whose land we live in Adelaide, South Australia.

Chapter Nine

[1] See, for example, the Resolution 2007-08 for Sustainable Support of the Regional or Minority Languages by the European Union, which was adopted by the Assembly of Delegates of the Federal Uinion of European Nationalities (FUEN) in Tallin on 17 May 2007. Retrieved on 1 December 2007. Available from:
<http://living-diversity.eu/Tallinn%202007/Sprachenresolution_englisch.pdf>
[2] Bulgarian, Czech, Danish, German, Estonian, Greek, English, Spanish, French, Irish, Italian, Latvian, Lithuanian, Hungarian, Maltese, Dutch, Polish, Portuguese, Romanian, Slovak, Slovene, Finnish, Swedish.
[3] See in European Commission. 2006. Special Eurobarometer: Europeans and their Languages. Retrieved on 1 December 2007. Available from:
<http://ec.europa.eu/public_opinion/archives/ebs/ebs_243_en.pdf>
[4] See, for example, the RIGHT TO EDUCATION for the autochtonous, national minorities in Europe, which was adopted by the Assembly of Delegates of the FUEN in Tallin on 17 May 2007. The document represents an addendum to the Charter for the Autochthonous National Minorities in Europe adopted by FUEN in 2006. Retrieved on 1 December 2007. Available from:
<http://living-diversity.eu/2007/Das%20Recht%20auf%20Bildung%20EN.pdf>
[5] Orthodoxy is the largest single religious faith in Belarus (88%), Bulgaria (83%), Republic of Macedonia (80%), Republic of Cyprus (80%), Georgia (89%), Greece (98%), Moldova (98%), Montenegro (84%), Romania (87%), Serbia (84%), Russia (80%), and Ukraine (80%). The number of Eastern Orthodox adherents represents about 31% of the population in Bosnia and Herzegovina. As the dominant religion in northern Kazakhstan, it represents 40% of the Kazakhstan, and 4% of Lithuania, 9% of Latvia, and 13% of the Estonian population.
[6] According to the Spring 2004 Eurobarometer survey, Denmark has the highest level of confidence in religious institutions at 74%, yet a meagre 3% of Danes attend church at least once a week (5% of Swedes and 5% of Finns). Swedish citizens express the lowest level of trust in religious institutions at 21%, while Finland's population, like Denmark's, expresses one of the highest levels of trust at 71%. Among the other old EU countries, weekly attendance at religious services is below 10% in France and Germany, while in Belgium, the Netherlands, Luxembourg, and the United Kingdom between 10% and 15% of citizens are regular churchgoers. Among the Catholic old member countries, Austria is closest to the more secularised Protestant countries in weekly church attendance, with 18% attending at least weekly. Twenty-one percent of Spaniards attend at least weekly, and just under a third of Portuguese (29%) and Italians (31%) do so. Only in Roman Catholic Ireland do a majority of residents (54%) still go to church weekly. The only Orthodox country among the old members—Greece—has a weekly church participation rate of 27%. According to the Spring 2004 Eurobarometer survey, Malta and Poland have the highest percentages of weekly churchgoers in Europe with 75% and 63%, respectively. Estonia and Latvia, the two Baltic countries with Protestant traditions, are among the most secularised in Europe with only 4% and 7% of residents attending services once a week. The

Czechs (11%), Hungarians (12%), and Lithuanians (14%) are also in the more secular camp. Eighteen percent of people in Catholic Slovenia attend church weekly, while Orthodox Cyprus (25%) and the dominantly Catholic Slovakia (33%) still have sizable active religious minorities.

[7] Russia, including Siberia and Chechnya, has 25 million Muslims, more than any other European country. She is followed by Turkey (5.7 million), France (5 million), and Germany (3.5 million). Muslims hold the majority in Turkey, Albania and Bosnia. In some countries, they have overtaken Protestantism as the second largest religious constituency behind Catholicism. This is the case in Belgium, France, Italy and Spain. In Austria, the number of Protestants and Muslims are roughly the same. Muslims come second to the Orthodox Church in Bulgaria, Greece, Macedonia, Russia and Serbia. Adventist Press Service (APD.) Retrieved on 3 Octover 2008. Available from: <http://www.stanet.ch/APD>

[8] General Assembly of the United Nations, 10 December 1948. Universal Declaration of Human Rights. Retrieved on 20 January 2008. Available from: <http://www.un.org/Overview/rights.html>.

[9] For more information on the EU regions see the EU Inforegio site: http://ec.europa.eu/regional_policy/index_en.htm. Accessed on 25 January 2008.

[10] Everyone has the right to freedom of peaceful assembly and to freedom of association with others, including the right to form and to join trade unions for the protection of his interests. No restrictions shall be placed on the exercise of these rights other than such as are prescribed by law and are necessary in a democratic society in the interests of national security or public safety, for the prevention of disorder or crime, for the protection of health or morals or for the protection of the rights and freedoms of others. This article shall not prevent the imposition of lawful restrictions on the exercise of these rights by members of the armed forces, of the police or of the administration of the State. Retrieved on 3 October 2008. Available from:
<http://conventions.coe.int/Treaty/Commun/QueVoulezVous.asp?NT=005&CM=8&DF=10/5/2008&CL=ENG>

[11] Council of Europe. 2000 (entry into force 2005). Protocol No. 12 to the Convention for the Protection of Human Rights and Fundamental Freedoms (CETS No.: 177). Accessed on 13 February 2008. Available from:
<http://conventions.coe.int/Treaty/Commun/QueVoulezVous.asp?NT=177&CM=7&DF=3/6/2008&CL=ENG>

[12] Still very accurate in this regard is the statement made by the Greek Helsinki Monitor to the UN Working Group on Minorities, 7th session, Geneva, 14-18 May 2001: (Partly or Fully Unrecognised) National Minorities. Retrieved on 3 December 2007. Available from:

<http://www.greekhelsinki.gr/bhr/english/organizations/ghm/ghm_14_05_01.doc>

[13] Council of Europe. 1992 (entry into force 1998). European Charter for Regional or Minority Languages (CETS No.: 148). Accessed on 25 February 2008. Available from:
<http://conventions.coe.int/Treaty/Commun/QueVoulezVous.asp?NT=148&CM=7&DF=3/6/2008&CL=ENG>

[14] See the EC Declaration on the recognition of the new states in Eastern Europe and former Soviet Union and Yugoslavia, adopted on 16 December 1991.
[15] More on the conditionality for the EU membersip can be consulted on: <http://ec.europa.eu/enlargement/enlargement_process/accession_process/criteria/index_en.htm>. Accessed on 25 February 2008. The Minority protection as EU accession criterion was monitored and elaborated by several experts (EUMAP 2001 and 2002).
[16] The French proposal, prepared under the Premier Eduard Balladur, was first discussed at the European Council meeting in Copenhagen, 21-22 June. The inaugural conference of the Stability Pact was held in Paris on 26-27 May 1994.
[17] The FRA published in August 2007 the "Report on Racism and Xenophobia in the Members States of the EU", in which it is stated that, in spite of the EU's anti-discrimination legislation, ethnic descrimination and inequalities in employment, education and housing still continues. Significant intolerance towards Roma population is present and an increase is recorded in racist crimes. Retrieved on 25 February 2008. Available from:
<http://fra.europa.eu/fra/material/pub/racism/report_racism_0807_en.pdf>.
[18] 2008 Status Report on fulfilling the commitments made in the Action Plan published on 2 October 2008 by the OSCE Office for Democratic Institutions and Human Rights. Retrieved on 3 October 2008. Available from:
<http://www.osce.org/odihr/item_11_33130.html>.
[19] In 2002 the Committee of Ministers of the Council of Europe adopted a reply to CLRAE Recommendation 43 (1998) on territorial autonomy and national minorities. Retrieved on 15 January 2008. Available from:
<https://wcd.coe.int/ViewDoc.jsp?id=853855&Site=CM&BackColorInternet=9999CC&BackColorIntranet=FFBB55&BackColorLogged=FFAC75>.
The Committee of Ministers stated in point 6 of the reply that "While it is clear that under certain circumstances and through democratic decisions taken within its constitutional framework a State might also deem appropriate to address the question of the protection of national minorities through territorial subdivision, one needs to bear in mind the need to preserve the social cohesion of the population of the country as a whole and to respect the corresponding general integration policy pursued to that end, as well as to respect the territorial integrity and national sovereignty of states".
[20] For statistical data on the population structure, see the Eurostat. Accessed on 25 February 2008. Available from:
<http://epp.eurostat.ec.europa.eu/portal/page?_pageid=1090,30070682,1090_31583003&_dad=portal&_schema=PORTAL>
[21] The EU established, with the Decision No 1983/2006/EC, 2008 as the European Year of Intercultural Dialogue (EYID). Religion in contemporary Europe is one of the key topics of this initiative and the EYID aims to encourage dialogue both within and between the communities of faith and conviction. More on EYID: Accessed on 25 February 2008. Available from:
<http://www.interculturaldialogue2008.eu/>
[22] See, for instance, Vikers, Lucy. 2007. *European network of legal experts in the non-discrimination field, Religion and belief discrimination in the enlarged EU.*

Brussels: European Community, Directorate-General for employment, social and equal opportunities, Unit G-2.

[23] The role of the three principal organised religions in the Balkan (the Croatian Catholic Church, the Serbian Orthodox Church, and the Islamic community) in providing a religious base for nationalist thought and movements in the recent history of the Balkan is further elaborated also in the book by Perica, Vjekoslav. 2004. *Balkan idols: Religion and Nationalism in Yugoslav States*. USA: Oxford University Press.

[24] For analytical debate on Kosovo independence see, among other sources:
CEPS European Neighbourhood Watch 35 (February 2008). Retrieved on 3 March 2008. Available from: <http://www.ceps.eu/files/NW/NWatch35.pdf>;
Centre for Research on Globalization, 16 February 2008. Kosovo Independence. Retrieved on 3 March 2008. Available from:
<http://www.globalresearch.ca/index.php?context=va&aid=8098>; EU fudges Kosovo independence recognition. *EU Observer*, 18 February 2008. Retrieved on 3 March 2008. Available from: <http://euobserver.com/9/25684>.

[25] Official Journal of the European Union, 17 December 2007. Treaty of Lisbon amending the Treaty on European Union and the Treaty establishing the European Community, signed at Lisbon, 13 December 2007. Retrieved on 25 February 2008. Available from:
<http://europa.eu/lisbon_treaty/full_text/index_en.htm>.

[26] European Parliament, Council, Commission, 14 December 2007. Charter of Fundamental Rights of the European Union (2007/C 303/01). Retrieved 25 February 2008. Available from:
<http://eurlex.europa.eu/LexUriServ/LexUriServ.do?uri=OJ:C:2007:303:0001:0016:EN:PDF>

[27] Official Journal of the European Communities, 19 July 2000. Council Directive 2000/43/EC of 29 June 2000 implementing the principle of equal treatment between persons irrespective of racial or ethnic origin. Retrieved on 1 December 2007. Available from:
<http://europa.eu/eur-lex/pri/en/oj/dat/2000/l_180/l_18020000719en00220026.pdf>.

[28] The European Monitoring Centre on Racism and Xenophobia became the European Union Agency for Fundamental Rights (FRA) on 1 March 2007 based on the Council Regulation (EC) No. 168/2007 of 15 February 2007. Accessed on 25 February 2008. Available from: <http://fra.europa.eu/fra/index.php>

[29] For detailed data consult the Standard Eurobarometer 63 from July 2005. Accessed 5 March 2008. Available from:
<http://ec.europa.eu/public_opinion/archives/eb/eb63/eb63_en.htm>.

[30] See Official Journal of the EU C310, 41 (11 December 2004).

[31] Of the EU members, ratified only by Cyprus, Finland, Luxembourg, the Netherlands and Romania. See Chart of signatures and ratifications, status of 7 March 2008. Available from:
<http://conventions.coe.int/Treaty/Commun/ChercheSig.asp?NT=177&CM=7&DF=3/7/2008&CL=ENG>

[32] Not members: Belgium, Bulgaria, Estonia, France, Greece, Ireland, Italy, Latvia, Lithuania, Malta, Poland, Portugal, Romania, and candidate state Turkey. See Chart of signatures and ratifications, status of 7 March 2008. Available from: <http://conventions.coe.int/Treaty/Commun/ChercheSig.asp?NT=148&CM=7&DF=3/7/2008&CL=ENG>

[33] Not members: Belgium, France, Greece, Luxembourg, and the candidate state Turkey. See Chart of signatures and ratifications, status of 7 March 2008. Available from: <http://conventions.coe.int/Treaty/Commun/ChercheSig.asp?NT=157&CM=7&DF=3/7/2008&CL=ENG>

[34] See *Protection of minorities and anti-discrimination policies in an enlarged Europe. European Parliament resolution on the protection of minorities and anti-discrimination policies in an enlarged Europe (2005/2008(INI)), P6_TA-PROV(2005) 0228.*

[35] See: *Thematic comment No.3, The Protection of minorities in the European Union*, 25 April 2005. Référence: CFR-CDF.ThemComm2005.en; Kristin Henrard, Associate Professor, University of Groningen, *Equal rights versus special rights, Minority Protection and the Prohibition of Discrimination* (2007). Brussels: European Commission, Directorate-General for Employment, Social Affairs and Equal Opportunities, Unit G.2

[36] The commission has sent, in June 2007, a formal request to 14 Member states to fully implement the Directive (Czech Republic, Estonia, France, Ireland, United Kingdom, Greece, Italy, Latvia, Poland, Portugal, Slovenia, Slovakia, Spain and Sweden). For more information on infringement procedures, see: <http://ec.europa.eu/employment_social/fundamental_rights/legis/lginfringe_en.htm>. Accessed on 3 March 2008.

[37] On this topic see *The situation of Roma in the enlarged European Union* (2004). Brussels: Euroepan Commission, Directorate-General for Employment and Social Affairs, Unit D-3. Important in this regard is also the European Parliament Resolution of 15 November 2007 <http://www.europarl.europa.eu/sides/getDoc.do?pubRef=-//EP//TEXT+TA+P6-TA-2007-0534+0+DOC+XML+V0//EN> (accessed on 3 March 2008), which calls on the Commission to act without delay by pursuing an overall strategy for social inclusion of the Roma. The Commission has till today still not prepared such a strategy. The existing EU actions for Roma can be consulted on: <http://ec.europa.eu/employment_social/fundamental_rights/roma/index_en.htm>. Accessed on 3 March 2008. Worth mentioning in this regard is an unprecedented regional intitiative for improvement of the socio-economic status and social inclusion of Roma within a regional framework—the intitiative of the nine countries of Central and Southeastern Europe: "Decade of Roma Inclusion 2005 - 2015". Accessed on 3 March 2008. Available from: <http://www.romadecade.org/index.php>.

Chapter Ten

* Inspire is funded through the Mentor Marketplace Program, Department of Education, Employment & Workplace Relations (DEEWR); received a commendation in the Australian Universities Quality Agency (2006) report as a community engagement strategy for Flinders University; won the Indigenous Higher Education Partnership Award from DEST in 2007; and received an Australian Teaching and Learning Council Award as a program that enhances student learning in 2008.
We would like to acknowledge the involvement of all mentors, Indigenous young people and Elders from Camp Coorong Race Relations Centre for their invaluable contribution towards the project. Thank you to Christies Beach High School and all teachers involved as well as Indigenous students from Flinders University. Thank you to Damien Riggs and Barbara Baird for bringing this edited collection of chapters together and for their editing skills. A special thanks also to Emeritus Professor Gus Worby who provided comments on an earlier draft of this chapter and to Sue Shore for her insightful feedback and critique on the final draft of the chapter.

Chapter Eleven

[1] Te Rangihiroa was also known by the name of Peter Buck, or Sir Peter Buck after his Knighthood. I am following the convention of using "Te Rangihiroa" when I refer to him because this was his preferred name under which to publish.
[2] A close friend to Te Rangihiroa, Ramsden was a Pakeha/white scholar based in New Zealand.
[3] Te Rangihiroa. Letter to Eric Ramsden. 5 May 1948. Alexander Turnbull Library, Wellington.
[4] Senate Journal, Territory of Hawaii 22nd Legislature, Regular session 1943: 946.
[5] At this point I would like the take the opportunity to acknowledge the financial support for this book project that I have received from the Royal Society of New Zealand in the form of a Marsden Fast Start Grant. This support has enabled me to complete the archival research for this chapter as well as my trip to get feedback on my thinking at the 2007 ACRAWSA conference in Adelaide at which an earlier version of this paper was presented.
[6] Specifically, I am looking at Maori performances that take place at the Polynesian Cultural Centre in Hawaii and the annual Pasifika Festival in Auckland.
[7] This challenge is not posed simply an "addition" in order to correct the racial shorthand of using colour to talk about large groups of people, but is instead a challenge which points out that the mechanism of racial thinking itself is fundamentally flawed, as symbolised by the posing of a term that fits outside of the supposedly exhaustive matrix of race.
[8] The "claiming" of Brown for the Pacific is done with acknowledgement that another region/community has also claimed "Brown" for themselves: the Latino/a community. See Richard Rodriguez. (2002).

[9] Te Rangihiroa. Letter to Eric Ramsden. 5 May 1948. Alexander Turnbull Library, Wellington.
[10] It seems worth adding that the question of citizenship *to what entity* may illuminate some of the complexity here. Although this specific question of US citizenship engages the idea of citizenship to the nation state (and Te Rangihiroa's earlier parliamentary career supports that allegiance as well), it is possible to argue that his ethnographic work provided if not the compulsion then certainly the impetus and capacity to think about Maori citizenship in the region (the Pacific)—through linguistic, cultural, material, and organisational links. Audra Simpson's (2000) work on the question of Indigenous forms of citizenship is an excellent resource here.
[11] Senate Journal, Territory of Hawaii 22nd Legislature, Regular session 1943: 945.
[12] Ibid.
[13] Senate Journal, Territory of Hawaii 22nd Legislature, Regular session 1943: 946.
[14] Proportionately fewer educational, health and social advantages go to Maori compared to non-Maori; and specific events such as the seabed and foreshore legislation, which the UN Committee for the Elimination of all forms of Racial Discrimination found to be racially discriminatory, point to the ongoing mistreatment of Maori as a special group.
[15] Senate Journal, Territory of Hawaii 22nd Legislature, Regular session 1943: 946.
[16] Act of 26 March 1970, Chap. 3, 1 Stat. 103.
[17] It is worth pointing out that the relevant law here is the law of naturalisation because Te Rangihiroa was already a citizen elsewhere (Lopez 1996). Reference to race was removed from the birthright citizenship legislation in 1940.
[18] Ibid: 2.
[19] Ibid 28.
[20] Quoted in Ibid: 71.
[21] The question of race and whiteness in terms of US citizenship is a huge topic, and much of the detail of that topic falls outside the scope of this chapter. However, it is worth pointing out that much of the work about these issues in this period seems to assume that all non-citizens approach the US for citizenship from the same position. It would be instructive to research this question of race and citizenship with a close commitment to exploring the context of colonialism. After all, Polynesians may or may not be Caucasian, but in the case of Hawaiian and Samoan Polynesians living in US-controlled territory the question is quite a bit more complex.
[22] This comment is quoted in Ramsden's *A Memoir, Te Rangihiroa.* Wellington: Dept of Maori Affaris, 1954. Ramsden passed away before completing a full biography of Te Rangihiroa: this project was picked up by Ernest Beaglehole who also passed away before it was completed. Finally J.B. Condliffe, another scholar friend of Te Rangihiroa, compiled the notes they had collected in a popular biography: *Te Rangi Hiroa: The Life of Sir Peter Buck.* Christchurch: Whitcombe & Tombs Ltd, 1971.
[23] For an excellent treatment of the impact and methods of these disciplines, look at Martin Nakata's recent book.

[24] The question of the how Polynesians might fit into Victorian racialising norms interested many scholars and amateur ethnologists: in the New Zealand context, perhaps the most influential discussion that argued for an elevated (that is, closer to white) racial understanding of Maori was Tregear's (1885) work which drew on comparative mythology and linguistics.

[25] The only book-length biography of Te Rangihiroa was written by Condliffe after Eric Ramsden and then Ernest Beaglehole (both prominent popular scholars and writers of the time) passed away while working on earlier drafts. Condliffe's biography is popular rather than scholarly, but is a valuable resource. He outlines the relationship between Yale and the Bishop Museum in the chapter "Yale in Polynesia" in his 1971 publication. By the time Te Rangihiroa arrived at Yale in 1932, Yale students and alumni had had a deep historical connection with the Pacific, and especially Hawaii (then known as the Sandwich Islands), since the early nineteenth century. Several alumni had worked as whalers, merchants and missionaries, and the specific Calvinist focus of Yale at the time led to a focus on mission which resulted in a group of Hawaiian men (most notably Opukahaia) traveling to New Haven. Yale-alum missionaries based in Hawaii sent their sons back to Yale, and a close connection was forged that ultimately saw a connection between the Bishop Museum in Hawaii and Yale in New Haven. The director of the museum would be a member of the Faculty of the Graduate School at Yale, and while the position would be appointed by the museum trustees the funding would come from Yale. Additionally, the Bishop would send scholars to Yale on year-long lectureships in order to provide teaching capacity about the Pacific. Te Rangihiroa's original connection to Yale in 1932 was in this capacity. Kehaulani Kauanui (2007) has written about Opukahaia in her recent treatment of Hawaiians based on the continental US.

[26] They still don't have this as a right, even though they experience proportionately the highest mortality and injury rates of Iraq-based soldiers from any community.

[27] Te Rangihiroa. Letter to Eric Ramsden. 5 May 1948. Alexander Turnbull Library, Wellington.

[28] This "Asian Pacific" is still the configuration in formal American racial categories, and a very contentious question at the moment in American academia is whether the Asian American Studies Association should be renamed the "Asian Pacific American Studies Association".

[29] Te Rangihiroa. Letter to Eric Ramsden. 4 September 1946. Alexander Turnbull Library, Wellington.
When he describes "our" delegate to Congress he refers to the delegate for Hawaii, not New Zealand.

[30] Ibid.

[31] Te Rangihiroa. Letter to Eric Ramsden. 14 February 1937. Alexander Turnbull Library, Wellington.

[32] Te Rangihiroa. Letter to Eric Ramsden. 23 August 1940. Alexander Turnbull Library, Wellington.

[33] Condliffe (1971, 170).

[34] Te Rangihiroa. Letter to Eric Ramsden. 5 May 1948. Alexander Turnbull Library, Wellington.

[35] Te Rangihiroa. Letter to Eric Ramsden. 4 March 1946. Quoted in Condliffe.
[36] Te Rangihiroa. Letter to Eric Ramsden. 23 August 1940. Alexander Turnbull Library, Wellington.
[37] Te Rangihiroa. Letter to Eric Ramsden. 4 September 1950. Alexander Turnbull Library, Wellington.
[38] Te Rangihiroa. Letter to Mary Wheeler. 17 July 1946. Alexander Turnbull Library, Wellington.
[39] The Maori language. More specifically, Te Rangihiroa responded with a traditional chant which focuses on navigation.
[40] Nga mihi ki nga kaiwhakahaere me nga kaitautoko o te pukapuka nei. I would like to take this opportunity to thank the editors of this volume and the anonymous reviewers who gifted me with some very valuable feedback. Aku hoa Paul Meredith and Helen Potter kindly read earlier drafts and gave generous comments. Thanks also to the librarians and archivists at the Alexander Turnbull Library (Wellington), Hawaii State Library (Honolulu) and State of Hawaii Archives (Honolulu). Nga mihi ki nga whanaunga o Ta Te Rangihiroa: ko Ngati Mutunga. Mauri ora.

Chapter Twelve

[1] See Richard D. Alba, *Ethnic Identity: The Transformation of White America*, New Haven: Yale University Press, 1990; Howard Winant, *Racial Conditions: Politics, Theory, Comparisons*, Minneapolis: University of Minnesota Press, 1994; and David R. Roediger, *Towards the Abolition of Whiteness: Essays on Race, Politics, and Working Class History*, London: Verso, 1994. There has of course been a concomitant response to this perceived lack. This response sometimes takes the form of a reconstruction of "symbolic ethnicity" among Anglo-Celts (the terms was first used by Gans 1979—see Winant 174, fn 18). "Symbolic ethnicity" has been picked up not only by right-wing commentators but also by the left. In Australia, for example, Hodge and Carroll recommend "Anglo-Celtic borderwork" (36), namely the tracing of "forgotten or lost earlier histories" and the "de-assimilating of the Celts" (70), in order to problematise the early history of Australian multiculturalism and its class history (Bob Hodge and John O'Carroll, *Borderwork in multicultural Australia*, Allen & Unwin, Crows Nest, 2006).
[2] Whiteness is of course invisible (to white people) because of its putative normativity. As Dyer writes: "White power secures its dominance by seeming not to be anything in particular" (Dyer 1988, 44).
[3] I use the term "postcolonial" here to refer to a particular historically-located (that is, post-Federation period) Anglo-Celtic creole relationship with Indigenous people. I am mindful of the ongoing neo-colonial reconfiguration of white power culturally, economically, politically and militarily within both domestic and transnational arenas.
[4] Accessed 17 August 2008. Available from:
<http://australianscreen.com.au/titles/tracker/>
[5] Paradoxically this demand has been asymmetrical. In a heterogeneous field of minority commentators the same call to acknowledge differential class mobility

and privilege is not routinely invoked in the manner which Spivak, for example, has made her hallmark, in the American context.

[6] Ellsworth borrows the term from Bateson and Laing who use it in a different context.

[7] I refer here to the common German phrase to describe Indigenous people, "die erste Australier".

[8] This section of the article is an amalgamation and condensation of various conversations and characters. I'd like to dedicate this section of the article to my students and colleagues at the University of Tübingen, particularly Prof Gerhard Stilz and Prof Christoph Reinfandt, for their many engaging conversations.

[9] Alf Taylor is a Nyoongah writer. Born in the late 1940s he spent his childhood in the Spanish Benedictine Mission at New Norcia, 250 kms north of Perth. He has published two books of poetry *Singer Songwriter* (Magabala 1992) and *Winds* (Magabala 1994) a collection of short fiction, *Long Time Now* (see Brewster 2007 and 2008).

[10] Gerhardt Stilz has glossed this point in correspondence:

"My turn of phrase used for describing a widespread mental disposition of European 'war children' of my age is based on a German proverb ('*Gebrannte Kinder fürchten das Feuer*'), which implies that children who came too close to a match, a candle or a larger fire will instinctively try to avoid that experience as long as they remember, consciously or unconsciously. The metaphor 'burnt children' ('*gebrannte*' *Kinder*—whose incoative meaning of 'branded' or 'singed' should of course not be mixed up with the performative of '*verbrannte'* Kinder ('incinerated')) has a wider currency and is not generally reserved to the German or European post-war generation. Yet I wished to point out, if I remember right, that people of my age tend to be quite wary of the evils of war (perhaps even to a pacifist extent), as many of them can still vividly see, hear, smell, feel and taste the hellish memories that war has left in them" (7 February 2007).

[11] I use the term here to describe the film's project of investigating what might be called the "post-traumatic stress" of postcolonial white Australians—that is, the anxieties attendant upon the belated postcolonial recognition and acknowledgment of their own role in a colonial history of terror. It is not only the victims of colonisation who suffer the traumatic after-affects of colonial violence; colonialism brutalises its perpetrators as well as its victims (Gilroy 2004). I have argued elsewhere, for example, that Indigenous life stories were only able to emerge at a certain historical moment. The trauma of colonisation (including guilt), I suggest, was too great for the generations who had participated in (or had direct knowledge of) those atrocities (which included people in my grandparents' generation, for example) to be able to bear witness to Indigenous people's testimony (Brewster 1995). See also Burrows 2004 for a discussion of white trauma.

[12] In this chapter I am gesturing minimally to the textual strategies and generic features of the journal rather than producing a literal journal which consistently documents exact names, dates, places etc. (The characters that figure in the German sections of the chapter, for example, are compendiums of several different people rather than faithful descriptions of individuals.) The comprehensive,

identificatory detail of "real life" journal-keeping is extraneous to my purpose in this chapter which is (1) to point to the work that a journal performs in recording "public" events within a private realm and reflecting on their intimate repercussions and (2) to evoke the realm of travel and the encounters and the experiences of the other which typify travel.

[13] I'm indebted to Hazel, Ben, Gay, Shalmalee and Joseph for commenting on earlier drafts of this article. Its shortcomings however are entirely my own. I also want to thank the two anonymous referees and the editors for their insightful and stimulating feedback. I'm grateful to have been able to benefit from their expertise. Thanks to Peter Lavskis for use of the photos. Thanks are due also to Mandy Swann and Lyn Vellins for their research assistance. This chapter is dedicated to the memory of Veronica Maksimovs.

Chapter Thirteen

[*] I would like to acknowledge my indebtedness to the editors Barbara Baird and Damien Riggs, my reviewers and to the theorists that I engage with here, most particularly Irene Watson. All errors mine.

[1] See also Oomera Edwards "Connecting to Country" Programs

[2] The Poor Law Amendment Act of 1834 established compulsory deterrent workhouses for the poor and required the separation of families. It was in response to increasing social unrest, sparking further unrest as it was argued to be increasing the enslavement of the working poor that it professed to be stamping out. See: <www.victorianweb.org/history/poorlaw/poorlawov.html accessed 5/2/08>. There was a Jewish backlash also during this period, particularly focused on the drapery trade, and perhaps also related with protestant/Jewish emancipation movements of this period. See links.

[3] Leonard Cohen © 1988. Sony/ATV Music Publishing Canada Company and Sharon Robinson.

[4] Desk calendar quote, EXP80T 2008, ©Collins Debben Pty Ltd 2007.

[5] See also David Unaipon, *Legendary Tales of the Australian Aborigines,* concerning indigenous practices

[6] I have participated in numerous such workshops, receiving individual instruction also. See Murrawan "Connecting to Country" Programs for example.

REFERENCES

Aboud, F.E., and A.B. Doyle. 1996. Does talk of race foster prejudice or tolerance in children? *Canadian Journal of Behavioural Science* 28:161-170.

Agamben, G. 1994. We Refugees. *Symposium* 49:114-119.

Agency for Toxic Substances and Disease Registry. Accessed on 18 June 2008. Available from: <http://www.atsdr.cdc.gov/tfacts178.html>

Ahmed, Sara. 2004. Declarations of Whiteness: The Non-Performativity of Anti-Racism, *borderlands e-journal* 3 (2). Available from: <http://www.borderlandsejournal.adelaide.edu.au>

—. 2007. A phenomenology of whiteness. *Feminist Theory* 8:149-168.

Ahwan, L. 2002. Children freed from Woomera "barbarism". *Daily Telegraph*, 24 January, p. 9.

Alexander, J. 2004. *In Their Own Words: LGBT Youth Writing the World Wide Web.* New York: GLAAD Centre for the Study of Media in Society.

Alexander, C., and C. Knowles. 2005. Introduction. In *Making race matter: Bodies, space and identity*, edited by C. Alexander and C. Knowles. Hampshire: Palgrave Macmillan.

Amato, Giuliano and Judy Batt. 1999. Minority Rights and EU Enlargement to the East. Report from the first meeting of the reflection group on long-term implications of EU enlargement, RSC policy paper No. 5.

Anderson, B.R. 1991. *Imagined communities: reflections on the origin and spread of nationalism.* Revised and extended ed. London and New York: Verso.

Ang, I. 2001. *On Not Speaking Chinese: Living Between Asia and the West.* London and New York: Routledge.

Anti-Discrimination Board of New South Wales. 2003. *Race for the headlines—racism and media discourse full report.* Sydney: Anti-Discrimination Board of New South Wales.

Anzaldua, G. 1987. *Borderlands/La Frontera: The New Mestiza.* San Francisco: Aunt Lute.

Appadurai, A. 1996. *Modernity at Large: Cultural Dimensions of Globalization.* Minneapolis and London: University Of Minnesota Press.

Arendt, H. 1973. The Decline of the Nation State and the End of the Rights of Man. Chap. 9 in *The origins of totalitarianism*, 3rd ed. London: Harvest, 269-302.

Armstrong, Isobel. 2000. *The Radical Aesthetic*. Oxford: Blackwell.

Arnold, Rainer. 2001. Europäische Union und Minderheitenschutz. In *Minderheitenschutz in Mittel und Osteuropa*, edited by Gerrit Manssen and Boguslaw Banaszak. Frankfurt: Peter Lang, 237.

Attfield, J. 2007. *Bringing Modernity Home: writings on popular design and material culture*. Manchester: Manchester University Press.

Australian Bureau of Statistics. 2007. *2006 Census QuickStats: Uralla (A)/Walcha (A) (Indigenous Area)* Australian Bureau of Statistics. Accessed on 10 October 2008. Available from: <http://www.censusdata.abs.gov.au/ABSNavigation/prenav/ViewData?producttype=QuickStats&subaction=-1&areacode=IARE05027&action=401&collection=Census&textversion=true&breadcrumb=LP&period=2006&navmapdisplayed=true&#>.

Australian Government. 2008. *Uralla Aniwan Aboriginal Corporation*, Australian Government. Accessed on 10 October 2008. Available from: <http://www.orac.gov.au/reports/generatereport.aspx?rpt=cmpext&fmt=pdf&concernID=101926>

Australian Universities Quality Agency Report. 2006. Flinders University: Full report available from: <http://www.auqa.edu.au/qualityaudit/sai_reports/index.shtml>

A Visible Difference: Skin, race and identity 1720-1820. 2007. An exhibition hosted by the Royal College of Surgeons in the Hunterian Museum, London.

Ayers, T. 1999. China Doll—The Experience of Being a Gay Chinese Australian. In *Multicultural Queer: Australian Narratives*, edited by G. Sullivan and P.A. Jackson. Binghampton: The Haworth Press.

Baker, Richard, Jocelyn Davies and Elspeth Young. 2001. *Working On Country: Contemporary Indigenous Management of Australia's Lands and Coastal Regions*. Melbourne: Oxford University Press.

Bal, M. 1997. *Narratology: introduction to the theory of narrative*. 2nd ed. Toronto: University of Toronto Press.

Ballantyne, T. 2001. Race and the webs of empire: Aryanism from India to the Pacific. *Journal of Colonialism and Colonial History* 2 (3):157-189.

Barbaras, Renaud. 2006. *Desire and Distance: Introduction to a Phenomenology of Perception.* Trans. Paul B. Milan. US: Stanford University Press.

Barker, C., and D. Galasinski. 2001. *Cultural studies and discourse analysis: a dialogue on language and identity*. London and Thousand Oaks, California: Sage.

Barker, C. 2002. *Making Sense of Cultural Studies*. London: Sage Publications

Barnard, I. 1999. Queer Race. *Social Semiotics* 9:199-212.

Barthes, R. 1973. *Mythologies*. London: Paladin.

—. 1982. Myth Today. In *Barthes: Selected Writings*, edited by S. Sontag. Oxford: Fontana/Collins.

Bean, D. 2002. *Wise Heads on Young Shoulders: Plan-It Youth Mentoring Youth Connection*. NSW Active Retirees and Mentors Inc.

Beeton, S. 2004. Rural Tourism in Australia—Has the Gaze Altered? Tracking Rural Images Through Film and Tourism Promotion. *International Journal of Tourism Research* 6 (3):125-35.

Bell, A. 1991. *The language of news media*. Oxford, Cambridge, Mass: Blackwell.

—. 1997. The discourse structure of news stories. In *Approaches to media discourse*, edited by A. Bell and P. Garrett. Oxford, Malden, Mass.: Blackwell, 64-104.

—. 1999. News stories as narratives. In *The discourse reader*, edited by A. Jaworski and N. Coupland. London: Routledge, 236-251.

Bell, Mark. 2002. *Anti Discrimination Law and the European Union*. Oxford: Oxford University Press.

Benedikter, Thomas. 2006a. Territorial Autonomy as a Means of Minority Protection and Conflict Solution in the European Experience—An Overview and Schematic Comparison, *Bolzano/Bozen: Society for Threatened People*. Available online:
In English: <http://www.gfbv.it/3dossier/eu-min/autonomy.html> ;
In German: <http://www.gfbv.it/3dossier/eu-min/autonomy-de.html>

Benedikter, Thomas. 2006b. Legal Instruments of Minority Protection in Europe. An Overview. *Bolzano/Bozen: Society for Threatened People*. Available online at: <http://www.gfbv.it/3dossier/eu-min/autonomy-eu.html>

Berube, A. 2001. How Gay Stays White and What Kind of White it Stays. In *The Making and Unmaking of Whiteness*, edited by B.B. Rasmussen, E. Klinenberg, I.J. Nexica and M. Wray. Durham: Duke University Press.

Best, J.C. 1991. *Thomas Baker McQuesten: public works, politics, and imagination*. Hamilton: Corinth Press.

Bhabha, H.K. 1990. Introduction: narrating the nation. In *Nation and Narration*, edited by H.K. Bhabha. London: Routledge, 1-20.

Bhabha, Homi. 1994. *The Location of Culture*. London: Routledge.

Bin-Sallik, M.A. 1990. *Aboriginal Tertiary Education in Australia: How well is it serving the needs of Aborigines?* Adelaide: SACE.

Boltanski, Luc. 1999. *Distant suffering: Morality, media and politics*. Trans. Graham Burchill. Cambridge: Cambridge University Press.

Bowling, A. 1997. *Research Methods in Health Investigating Health and Health Services*. Buckingham: Open University Press.

Boxall, G. 1899/1974. *The Story of Australian Bushrangers*. Hammondsworth: Penguin Colonial Facsimiles.

Bradford, C. 2001. *Reading race: Aboriginality in Australian children's literature*. Melbourne: Melbourne University Press.

Braun, V., and V. Clarke. 2006. Using thematic analysis in psychology. *Qualitative Research in Psychology* 3:77-101.

Brennan, F. 2003. *Tampering with asylum: a universal humanitarian problem*. St. Lucia, Queensland: University of Queensland Press.

Brewster, Anne. 1995. *Literary Formations: Post-colonialism, nationalism, globalism*. Carlton South: MUP.

—. 2005. Writing Whiteness: the Personal Turn. *Australian Humanities Review* 35 (June). Available from: <http://www.lib.latrobe.edu.au/AHR/archive/Issue-June-2005/brewster.html>

—. 2007. That child is my hero. Interview with Alf Taylor. *Aboriginal History* 31:165-177.

—. 2008. Humour and the Defamiliarisation of Whiteness in the Short Fiction of Australian Indigenous Writer Alf Taylor. *Journal of Postcolonial Writing* 44 (4).

Breuer, Marten. 2002. The Act on Hungarians Living in Neighbouring Countries: Challenging Hungary's Obligations under Public International Law and European Community Law. *Zeitschrift für Europarechtliche Studien* 2: 255-279.

Broom, D. 1991. *Damned if we do: Contradictions in Women's Health Care*. St Leonards: Allen & Unwin

Brown, J. 2003. Red Hill Valley protesters hold Christmas vigil: 'Spirit still alive'. Optimistic to the end, they enjoy a peaceful stroll under the stars. *Hamilton Spectator,* 22 December, A6.

Brunner, Georg. 2002. EU-Minderheitenpolitik und kollektive Minderheitenrechte. *Osteuropa* 2: 220.

Bunda, T. 2007. Sovereign woman. In *Indigenous Sovereignty Matters: Sovereign Subjects*, edited by A. Moreton-Robinson. Crows Nest, NSW: Allen & Unwin.

Burghardt, A.F. 1969. The Origin and Development of the Road Network of the Niagara Peninsula, Ontario, 1770-1851. *Annals of the Association of American Geographers* 59 (3):417-440.

Burke, A. 2008. *Fear of security: Australia's invasion anxiety*. New ed. Port Melbourne, Victoria: Cambridge University Press.

Burman, E. 1994. *Deconstructing developmental psychology*. London: Routledge.

Burr, V. 2003. *Social constructionism*. London: Routledge.

Burrows, Victoria. 2004. *Whiteness and Trauma: The Mother-Daughter Knot in the Fiction of Jean Rhys, Jamaica Kincaid and Toni Morrison.* New York: Palgrave Macmillan.

Butler, Judith. 1997a. *The Psychic Life of Power: Theories in Subjection.* Stanford: Stanford University Press.

—. 1997b. *Excitable Speech: A Politics of the Performative*. New York: Routledge.

—. 2004. *Precarious life: The powers of mourning and violence.* London: Verso.

—. 2005. Photography, war, outrage. *PMLA* 120 (3):822-7.

Byrne, D. 1984. *The mountains call me back: a history of Aborigines and the forests of the far south coast of NSW*. NSW Ministry of Aboriginal Affairs.

Caluya, G. 2006. The (gay) scene of racism: face, shame and gay Asian males. *ACRAWSA e-journal* 2.

Carr-Gregg, M. 2007. More action essential to curb bullying. The *Australian*, 16 May, p. 16.

Castles, A.C. 1982. *An Australian Legal History*. Sydney: The Law Book Company Ltd, Chap. 1.

Catechism of the Catholic Church: with modifications from Editio Typica. 1995. Sydney: Doubleday.

Cennini, C. 1960. *The Craftsman's Handbook.* Trans. D.V. Thompson. New York: Dover.

Chambers, D.W., and R. Gillespie. 2000. Locality in the History of Science: Colonial Science, Technoscience, and Indigenous Knowledge. *Osiris* 15:221-240.

Chang, H-C and GR Holt. 1991. Tourism as Consciousness of Struggle: Cultural Representation of Taiwan. *Critical Studies in Mass Communication* 8 (1):102-18.

Chow, Rey. 1993. *Writing diaspora: Tactics of intervention in contemporary cultural studies*. Bloomington: Indiana University Press.

Chun, W. 2006. *Control and Freedom: Power and Paranoia in the Age of Fiber Optics.* Cambridge: MIT Press.

Churchill, Ward. 1994. Indians Are Us? *Culture and Genocide in Native North America*. Maine, USA: Common Courage Press.

Clair, R.P. 1998. *Organising Silence: A World of Possibilities.* Albany: State University of New York Press.

Cleland, K., and M. Carleton. 2003. *Land use planning for certain land at Sandon Point, Wollongong City—report to the Honourable Craig Knowles MP, Minister for Infrastructure, Planning and Natural Resources.* Sydney: Commissioners of Inquiry.

Cody, P. 2004. *Around & About Waterfall Way*, West Armidale, April-May, Tourist brochure.

Coetzee, J.M. 1996. *Giving Offense: essays on censorship.* Chicago: University of Chicago Press.

Coffey, M. 2000. What puts the "Culture" in "Multiculturalism"? In *Multicultural Curriculum: New Directions for Social Theory, Practice and Policy*, edited by R. Mahalingham and C. McCarthy. New York: Routledge.

Cohen, Stanley. 2001. *States of denial: Knowing about atrocities and suffering*. Cambridge: Polity.

Colley, H. 2003. *Mentoring for social inclusion: A critical approach to nurturing mentor relationships,* London: RoutledgeFalmer.

Commonwealth of Australia. 1989. *National Women's Health Policy. Advancing Women's Health in Australia.* Canberra: Australian Government Publishing Service.

Condliffe, J.B. 1971. *Te Rangi Hiroa. The Life of Sir Peter Buck.* Christchurch: Whitcombe and Tombs.

Conley, D. 2002. *The daily miracle: an introduction to journalism.* 2nd ed. Melbourne: Oxford University Press.

Connellan, K. 2007a. White skins, white surfaces: the politics of domesticity in South African domestic interiors 1920-1950. In *Taking up the challenge: Critical race and whiteness studies in a postcolonising nation*, edited by D. Riggs. Adelaide: Crawford House, 226-248.

—. 2007b. Women, Water and Whiteness. *Lilith: a feminist history journal* 16:110-119.

Connellan, K., and J. Moss. 2004. Power to the People: electricity and domestic design. *Futureground.* Design Research Society conference proceedings, Monash University, Melbourne.

Connelly, J. 2002. *Investigating whiteness: whiteness processes: enigma or reality disguise?* Accessed online 25 May 2004. Available from: <www.aaire.edu.au/02pap/con02196htm>

Craik, J. 2001. Tourism, Culture and National Identity. In *Culture in Australia—Policies, Publics and Programs*, edited by T. Bennett and D. Carter. Cambridge: Cambridge University Press, 89-113.

Creswell, J. 1998. *Qualitative Inquiry and Research Design*. London: Sage Publications.

Crystal, D. 1994. *The Cambridge Encyclopaedia*. 2nd ed. Cambridge: Cambridge University Press.

Culotta, N. 1958. *They're a weird mob*. London: Kaye.

Dennis, J. 2002. Sandon Pt relics "Crown property". *Illawarra Mercury*, 12 December, p. 7.

—. 2005. Celebration at Sandon Point. *Illawarra Mercury*. 12 March, p. 16.

Department of Immigration and Citizenship. 2007. *Location of Operational Facilities*. Canberra. Accessed 18 September 2008. Available from: <http://www.immi.gov.au/managing-australias-borders/detention/facilities/locations/index.htm>.

Derrida, Jacques. 1982. *Différance*. Trans. Alan Bass. Chicago: University of Chicago Press.

—. 1985. Writing and Difference. In 1998 *Bataille: A Critical Reader*, edited by F. Botting and S. Wilson. U.K. and US: Blackwell Publishers, 251-77.

—. ed. 1997. *Deconstruction in a Nutshell: A Conversation with Jacques Derrida*. 1st ed. New York: Fordham University Press.

—. 2001. In *Deconstruction Engaged*, edited by P. Patton and T. Smith. University of Sydney, Australia: Power Publications.

—. 2005. *Rogues: Two Essays on Reason*. Trans. Pascale-Anne Brault and Michael Naas. California: Stanford University Press.

—. 2008. *The Animal that Therefore I Am*. New York: Fordham University Press.

Devetak, Silvo, 2007. Religious Freedoms in South Eastern European Countries in the Context of the Process of European Integration. In Religion and European Integration—Religion as a Factor of Stability and Development in South Eastern Europe, edited by M. Polzer, S. Devetak, L. Toplak, F. Unger, M. Eder. Edition Weimar, European Academy of Sciences and Arts: 123-151.

De Witte, Bruno. 2002. Politics Versus Law in the EU's Approach to Ethnic Minorities. In *Europe Unbound*, edited by Jan Zielonka. New York: Routledge, 137-159.

—. 2004. The Constitutional Resources for an EU Minority Policy. In *Minority Protection and the Enlarged European Union: The Way Forward*, edited by Gabriel N. Toggenburg. Budapest: LGI, 107-124.

De Witte, Bruno and Gabriel N. Toggenburg. 2002. Human Rights and Membership to the European Union. In *The EU Charter of Fundamental Rights*, edited by Steve Peers and Angela Ward. Oxford: Hart Publishing, 59.

DiGirolamo, R., M. Spencer and B. Crawford. 2002. Detainees agree to unsew lips. The *Australian,* 29 January, p. 1.

Dockett, S., D. Whitton and B. Perry. 2003. Children starting school: Images from picture storybooks. *Paper presented at Australian Association for Research in Education International Conference*, 11-13 May, Auckland.

Dorodnova, Jekaterina. 2000. EU Concerns in Estonia and Latvia: Implications of Enlargement for Russia's Behaviour towards Russian-speaking Minorities, *RSC* 40.

Douglas, M. 2007. *Purity and Danger,* 1966. London: Routledge.

Dreher, T. 2003. Speaking up and talking back: news media interventions in Sydney's "othered" communities [New South Wales]. *Media International Australia incorporating Culture and Policy* 109:121-137.

Driessen, Bart. 1999. The Slovak State Language Law as a Trade Law Problem. In *A right and a resource*, edited by Miklós Kontra et al. Budapest: Central European University Press, 147-165.

Dubois, D.L., B.E. Holloway, J.C. Valentine and H. Cooper. 2002. Effectiveness of mentoring programs for youth: A meta-analytic review. *American Journal of Community Psychology,* 30 (2):157-197.

Dyck, I. 1995. Hidden geographies: the changing lifeworlds of women with multiple sclerosis. *Social Science and Medicine* 40 (3):307-231.

Dyck, I., N. Davis Lewis, and S. McLaffert. 2003. *Geographies of Women's Health: Place, Diversity and Difference.* London: Routledge.

Dyer, Richard. 1988. White. *Screen* 29 (4):44-65.

—. 1997. *White*. London: Routledge.

—. 2000. The matter of whiteness. In *Theories of race and racism: a reader* edited by L. Back and J. Solomos. London: Routledge, 539-548

Edelheim, J. 2002. Rock Carvings and Graffiti in Natural Areas. *Paper presented to Ecotourism, Wilderness and Mountains Conference, August 24-27, Dunedin, New Zealand,* edited by C.M. Hall, University of Otago.

—. 2007. Hidden messages: A polysemic reading of tourist brochures. *Journal of Vacation Marketing* 13 (1):5-17.

Edensor, T., and U. Kothari. 1994. The masculinisation of Stirling's heritage. In *Tourism: A Gender Analysis*, edited by V. Kinnaird and D. Hall. Chichester: John Wiley & Sons, 164-87.

Education for Social Justice Research Group. 1994. Teaching for Resistance. *Texts in Humanities and the Centre for Studies in Educational Leadership*. Adelaide, South Australia, 34-43 and 113-117.

Edwards, N.B. 2003. *The Country Way Touring Guide*. 2nd ed. Country Colour Group, Gayndah, December, Tourist Brochure.

Elder, C. 2003. Invaders, Illegals and Aliens: Imagining Exclusion in a "white Australia". *Law/Text/Culture* 7:221-50.

—. 2007. *Being Australian: narratives of national identity*. Crows Nest, NSW: Allen & Unwin,

Elder, C., C. Ellis and A. Pratt. 2004. Whiteness in constructions of Australian nationhood: Indigenes, immigrants and governmentality. In *Whitening race: essays in social and cultural criticism*, edited by A. Moreton-Robinson. Canberra: Aboriginal Studies Press, 208-221.

Elias, N. 1998. *On Civilization, Power and Knowledge*. Chicago: University of Chicago Press.

Ellison, Julie. 1996. A Short History of Liberal Guilt. *Critical Inquiry* 22 (Winter):344-71.

Ellsworth, Elizabeth. 1997. Double Blinds of Whiteness. In *Off White: Readings on Race, Power and Society*, edited by Michelle Fine, Lois Weis, Linda C. Powell and L. MunWong. London: Routledge, 259-69.

Ellul, J. 1964. *The Technological Society,* edited by J. Wilkison. London: Jonathan Cape.

—. 1990. *The Technological Bluff,* edited by G.W. Bromiely. Michigan: William B. Eerdmans Publishing Company.

Entrikin, J.N. 1991. *The Betweenness of Place: Towards a Geography of Modernity*. Basingstoke, Hampshire: Houndmills.

Ericson, R.V., P.M. Baranek and J.B.L. Chan. 1987. *Visualizing deviance: a study of news organization*. Milton Keynes: Open University Press.

Estébanez, María Amor Martín. 1995. The Protection of National or Ethnic, Religious and Linguistic Minorities. In *The European Union and Human Rights*, edited by N.A. Neuwahl and A. Rosas. The Hague: Kluwer, 133.

Fairclough, N. 2001. *Language and Power*. 2nd ed. Harlow: Pearson Education Limited.

Fairclough, N. 2007. *Discourse and Social Change*. Cambridge: Polity Press.

Fanon, Frantz. 1967. *Black Skin, White Masks*. Trans. C.L. Markmann. New York: Grove Press.

—. 1986. *Black skin, white masks*. London: Pluto Press.

—. 2001. *The Wretched of the Earth*. Trans. C. Farrington. London: Penguin.

Feifer, M. 1985. *Going Places*. London: Macmillan.

Feldman, Allen. 2004. Memory Theatres, Virtual Witnessing and the Trauma Aesthetic. *Biography* 27 (1):161-202.

Finlay, V. 2002. *Colour: Travels through the Paintbox*. London: Sceptre.

Florence, Namulundah. 1998. *bell hooks' Engaged Pedagogy: A Transgressive Education for Critical Consciousness*. Critical Studies in Education and Culture Series. Westport, CT: Bergin & Garvey.

Foucault, M. 1972. *The Archaeology of Knowledge: And the Discourse on Language*. Trans. A.M.S. Smith. New York: Pantheon Books.

—. 1980. The eye of power. In *Power and Knowledge: Selected Interviews and Other Writings 1972-1977*, edited by C. Gorden. New York: Pantheon Books.

Foucault, M. 1991. Nietzche, Genealogy, History. In *The Foucault Reader*, edited by P. Rabinow. London: Penguin Books, 76-100.

Frankenberg, Ruth. 1993. *White women, race matters: The social construction of whiteness*. Minneapolis: University of Minnesota Press.

Fredericks B. 2003. Us Speaking about Women's Health: Aboriginal women's perceptions and experiences of health, wellbeing, identity, body and health services. PhD thesis, Central Queensland University.

—. 2007, Talkin' Up the Research. *Journal of Australian Indigenous Issues*, 10 (2):45-53

—. 2007a. Utilising the Concept of *Pathway* as a Framework for Indigenous Research. *Australian Journal of Indigenous Education*. 36S:15-22.

—. 2007b. Talkin' Up the Research. *Journal of Australian Indigenous Issues*. 10 (2):45-53.

—. 2007c. Australian Aboriginal women's health: reflecting on the past and present. *Health and History Journal*. 9 (2):1-21.

—. 2008. Researching with Aboriginal Women as an Aboriginal Woman Researcher. *Australian Feminist Studies*. 23 (55):113-130.

Freedman, M. 1988. *Partners in growth: Elder mentors and at-risk youth*. Philadelphia: Public/Private Ventures.

—. 1991. *The kindness of strangers: Reflections on the mentoring movement* (Fall). Philadelphia: Public/Private Ventures.

Frost, W. 2006. Braveheart-ed Ned Kelly: historic films and destination image. *Tourism Management* 27 (2):247-54.

Frow, John. 2002. "Never Draw to an Inside Straight": On Everyday Knowledge. *New Literary History* 33:623-37

Fullagar, R. and D. Donlon. 1998. *Archaeological Salvage Excavation at McCauleys Beach, Thirroul, NSW.* Wollongong: self-published.

Furano, K., P.A. Roaf, M.B. Styles and A.Y. Branch. 1993. *Big Brothers/Big Sisters: A study of program practices* (Winter). Philadelphia: Public/Private Ventures.

Gal, Kinga. 1999. Bilateral Agreements in Central and Eastern Europe: A New Inter-State Framework for Minority Protection? ECMI working paper #4. Available from: <http://www.ecmi.de/download/working_paper_4.pdf>

—. 2000. The Council of Europe Framework Convention for the Protection of National Minorities and its Impact on Central and Eastern Europe, European Centre for Minority Issues. Available from: <http://www.ecmi.de/jemie/download/JEMIE05Gal30-07-01.pdf>

Garcia, A. 2002. *Anti-Immigrant Racism and the Media.* Media Alliance. Accessed 20 August 2006. Available from: <http://www.media-alliance.org/article.php?story=20031108155709787>.

Garvis, S. 2008. Peers pair up to lift retention rate. *Guardian Messenger*, 15 October, p. 12.

Gell-Mann, M., and C. Tsallis, 2004. *Nonextensive Entropy: interdisciplinary applications.* Oxford and New York: Oxford University Press.

General, A. 2003. Iroquois Confederacy defends occupation in Red Hill valley. *Friends of Red Hill Valley Update.* 5 November. Friends of Red Hill Valley Archives (CD-ROM): 31 July 2004.

Gibbons, J. 1917. *The Faith of Our Fathers.* 83rd ed. New York: Kennedy & Sons, printers to the Holy See.

Gibson, R. 1992. Yondering—A Reading of Mad Max Beyond Thunderdome. In *South of the West: Postcolonialism and the Narrative Construction of Australia.* Bloomington: Indiana UP, 158-77.

Gieryn, T.F. 1995. Boundaries of Science. In S. Jassanoff, G.E. Markle, J.C. Petersen and T. Pinch, eds. *Handbook of Science and Technology Studies.* Thousand Oaks: Sage Publications.

Gilroy, Paul. 2004. *After Empire.* London: Routledge.

Giroux, H. 1992. *Border Crossings: Cultural workers and the politics of education.* New York: Chapman & Hall, Routledge.

Glenn, E.N. 2008. Yearning for Lightness: Transnational Circuits in the Marketing and Consumption of Skin Lighteners. *Gender and Society* 22:281-300.

Goldberg, Vicki. 1995. Looking at the poor in a gilded frame. *New York Times* 9 April. Accessed 18 June 2008. Available from:

<http://query.nytimes.com/gst/fullpage.html?res=990CE1D9163EF93 AA35757C0A963958260>
Golden, D. 1996. The Museum of the Jewish Diaspora Tells a Story. In *The Tourist Image: Myths and Myth Making in Tourism*, edited by T. Selwyn. Chichester: John Wiley & Sons, 223-45.
Goldstein, R. 2000. From old skool to no skool. *The Village Voice* 45 (47):40.
Gopinath, G. 2005. *Impossible Desires: Queer Diasporas and South Asian Public Cultures*. Durham and London: Duke University Press.
Graymont, B. 1972. *The Iroquois in the American Revolution.* Syracuse, N.Y.: Syracuse University Press.
Grbich, Judith. 2001. The Scent of Colonialism: Mabo, Eucalyptus and Excursions within Legal Racism. *Australian Feminist Law Journal* 15:121-148
Greenberg, C. 1986. *Toward a Newer Laocoon: The Collected Essays and Criticism.* Chicago: University of Chicago Press.
Greim, J.L. 1992. *Adult/Youth Relationships Pilot Project: Initial Implementation Report* (December). Philadelphia: Public/Private Ventures.
Gunew, S. 1990. Denaturalizing cultural nationalisms: multicultural readings of "Australia". In *Nation and Narration*, edited by H.K. Bhabha. London: Routledge, 99-121.
Gunkel, D.J. 2001. The Empire Strikes Back Again: The Cultural Politics of the Internet. In *Cyberimperialism?: Global Relations in the New Electronic Frontier,* edited by B. Ebo. Westport: Praeger.
Haan, R. 1980. The Problem of Iroquois Neutrality: suggestions for revision. *Ethnohistory* 27 (4):317-330.
Hage, G. 1996. *Ethnic Caging in a Multicultural Nation.* Accessed 20 August 2006. Available from: <http://wwwmcc.murdoch.edu.au/ReadingRoom/boat/Hage.html>.
—. 1998. *White nation: fantasies of white supremacy in a multicultural society*. Sydney: Pluto Press
—. 2002. Nation-building Dwelling Being. *Communal/Plural* 1 (2):73-103.
—. 2003a. *Against paranoid nationalism: searching for hope in a shrinking society*. Annandale, Victoria: Pluto Press.
—. 2003b. A viable ethics: Journalists and the ethics question. In *Remote control: new media, new ethics*, edited by E. Probyn and C. Lumby. Cambridge and Oakleigh, Victoria: Cambridge University Press.
Haggis, Jane. 2004. Beyond race and whiteness? Reflections on the New Abolitionists and an Australian critical whiteness studies. *borderlands*

e journal 3 (2). Accessed 10 January 2008. Available from <http://www.borderlands.net.au/vol3no2_2004/haggis_beyond.htm>

—. 2004. Thoughts on a politics of whiteness in a (never quite post) colonial country: abolitionism, essentialism and incommensurability. In *Whitening race: Essays in social and cultural criticism*, edited by A. Moreton-Robinson. Canberra, Australia: Aboriginal Studies Press, 48-58

—. 2007. Beyond race and whiteness? Reflections on the New Abolitionists and an Australian critical whiteness studies. In *Taking up the challenge: Critical race and whiteness studies in a postcolonising nation*, edited by D.W. Riggs. Belair, South Australia: Crawford Publishing, 307-321

Hailey, L. 2005. *Uralla Township Marketing Plan.* Uralla Shire Council, Uralla.

Hall, Stuart. 1990. The whites of their eyes: Racist ideologies and the media. In *The media reader,* edited by M. Alvarado and J.O. Thompson. London: BFI, 7-23.

Hall, S. 1997. *Representation: Cultural Representations and Signifying Practices*. London: Sage.

Hall, C.M. and H. Tucker. 2004. *Tourism and Postcolonialism—Contested discourses, identities and representations*. Oxon and New York: Routledge.

Han, C-s. 2007. They don't want to cruise your type: gay men of color and the racial politics of exclusion. *Social Identities* 13:51-67.

Hannon, K. 2002. Crean in plea to release children, *Daily Telegraph,* 26 January, p. 9.

Haraway, D. 1989. *Primate Visions: Gender Race and nature in the World of Modern Science.* New York: Routledge.

—. 1991. *Simians, Cyborgs and Women: the reinvention of nature,* London: Free Association Press.

—. 1994. Teddy Bear Patriarchy: Taxidermy in the Garden of Eden, New York City, 1908-1936. In *Culture/Power/History: a reader in contemporary social history,* edited by N.B. Price, G. Eley and S.B. Ortner. Princeton, N.J.: Princeton University Press.

Harding, P., M. Bennett, A. Draffen, and S. Webb eds. 2000. *Lonely Planet New South Wales*, 3rd ed. Footscray: Lonely Planet Publications.

Hardt, Michael. 1999. Affective Labour. *boundary 2* 26 (2 Summer):89-100.

Hartley, R. 2004. *Young people and mentoring: towards a national strategy*. A report prepared for Big Brothers/Big Sisters Australia,

Dusseldorp Skills Forum and The Smith Family, Research and Development. Sydney, Australia: The Smith Family.

Healey, J. 2005. Peer abuse as child abuse and indications for intervention in schools. *Paper presented at Symposium 30 Making a Real Difference in Educational Settings: Findings from New Intervention Research*, 7-9 June, Auckland.

Heidbreder, Eva G. and Laura Carasco. 2003. Assessing the Assessment: a review of the Application Criterion Minority Protection by the European Commission, Maastricht: EIPA working paper No. 2003/W/4.

Henrard, Kristin. 2002. The impact of the enlargement process on the development of a minority protection policy within the EU: Another aspect of responsibility/burden sharing? *Maastricht Journal* 9 (4):357-391.

Herman, J. 2007. *State of the News Print Media in Australia 2007.* Australian Press Council, Chap. 2.

Hepburn, A. 1997. Discursive strategies in bullying talk. *Education and Society*, 15:13-30.

Hetherington, K. 1998. *Expressions of Identity—Space, Performance, Politics*. London: Sage Publications

Hill, C. 2005. *Independent review of the land use strategy for certain lands at Sandon Point, Wollongong City.* Sydney: Planning Workshop Australia.

Hillier, L., C. Kurdas, and P. Horsley. 2001a. "*It's Just Easier*"*: The Internet as Safety-Net for Same Sex Attracted Young People.* Melbourne: Australian Research Centre in Sex, Health and Society.

—. 2001b. "It Made Me Feel Braver, I Was No Longer Alone": The Internet and Same Sex Attracted Young People. In *Sexuality in the Pacific,* edited by J. Nieto. Spanish Association of Studies in the Pacific.

Hillion, Christophe. 2004. On Enlargement of the European Union: the Discrepancy between Membership Obligations and Accession Conditions as Regards the Protection of Minorities, *Fordham International Law Journal* 27:715.

Hilpold, Peter. 2001. Minderheiten im Unionsrecht. *Archiv des Völkerrechts*, Bd. 39:432-471.

Hiscock, P. 2002. *Appraisal of Archaeological Studies at Sandon Point, New South Wales.* Canberra: Australian National University, unpublished.

Hofmann, Rainer. 2002. National Minorities and European Community Law. In *Baltic Yearbook of International Law Vol. 2*, edited by Ziemele. Boston: Martinus Nijhoff, 159-174.

Hoffman, D.L., T.P. Novak, and A.E. Schlosser. 2001. The Evolution of the Digital Divide: Examining the Relationship of Race to Internet Access and Usage Over Time. In *The Digital Divide: Facing a Crisis or Creating a Myth?* edited by B.M. Compaine. Cambridge: MIT Press.

Holland, W. 1996. Mis/taken identity. In *The Teeth Are Smiling: The persistence of racism in multicultural Australia*, edited by E. Vasta and S. Castles. St Leonards: Allen & Unwin.

Hollinshead, K. 1997. Heritage Tourism Under Post-modernity: Truth and the Past. In *The Tourist Experience—A New Introduction*, edited by C. Ryan. London: Cassell, 170-93.

Hollinsworth, D. 1997. *Racism and anti-racism in Australia.* Paper delivered at the Aboriginal and Torres Strait Islander Institute Conference, Canberra.

hooks, bell. 1992. *Black Looks: Race and Representation.* Boston: South End Press.

Howard, R. 2002. [Editorial] Claim has no credibility, hurts native rights' cause; Red Hill Creek Expressway: shameful. *Hamilton Spectator,* 15 April, A10.

Howard, J. (former Prime Minister). 2001. *Address at the Federal Liberal Party campaign launch.* Sydney. Viewed 1 June 2008.

Howarth, C.S. 2007. "It's not their fault that they have that colour skin, is it?": Racialisation, representation and resistance at school. In *Social representations and identity: Content, process and power,* edited by G. Moloney and I. Walker. New York: Palgrave Macmillan.

Huggins, J. 1987. Black Women and Women's Liberation. *Hecate.* 13 (1):77-82

Huggins, J. and T. Blake. 1992. Protection or Persecution: Gender Relations in the Era of Racial Segregation. In *Gender Relations in Australia,* edited by K. Saunders and R. Evans. Sydney: Harcourt and Brace Janovich.

Huggins, J. 1994. A Contemporary View of Aboriginal Women's Relationship to the White Women's Movement. In *Australian Women and Contemporary Feminist Thought*, edited by N. Grieve and A. Burns. South Melbourne: Oxford University Press.

Hughes, R. 2002. Native warns of anger over Red Hill Valley. *Hamilton Spectator,* 11 April, A4.

Hughes-d'Aeth, T. 1999. "A Prospect of Future Regularity": Spatial Technologies in Colonial Australia. In *Imagining Australian Space: Cultural Studies and Special Inquiry*, edited by R. Barcan and I. Buchanan. Nedlands: University of Western Australia Press, 47-58.

Hulley, C.E. 1999. *The Rainbow Serpent*. Frenchs Forest NSW: New Holland Publishers.

Huys, S. 2006. *Aboriginal Cultural Heritage Assessment*. Sydney: Australian Archaeological Survey Consultants.

Iedema, R., S. Feez, and P. White. 1994. *Write it Right*. Sydney: Literacy and Numeracy Research Project, NSW Department of Education.

Inspire Web page. Accessed 8 January 2008. Available from: <http://www.flinders.edu.au/careers/Inspirementor.html>

Iotzova, M. (Director). 2004. *Grass Through Concrete: the struggle to protect the Red Hill Valley* [DVD]. Canada: Maia Iotzova.

Jackson, P. and J. Penrose, eds. 1993. *Constructions of race, place and nation*. London: UCL Press Limited

Jekielek, S., K. Moore, and E. Hair. 2002. *Mentoring programs and youth development: A synthesis*. Washington, DC: Child Trends.

Johnston, C.M., ed. 1964. *The Valley of the Six Nations: a collection of documents on the Indian lands of the Grand River*. Toronto: The Chapman Society for the Government of Ontario: University of Toronto Press.

Jupp, J. 2002. *From white Australia to Woomera: the story of Australian immigration*. Port Melbourne, Victoria: Cambridge University Press.

Kauanui, J.K. 2007. Diasporic Deracination and "Off-Island" Hawaiians. *The Contemporary Pacific*. 19 (1):138-160.

Kemp, M. 2001. *Leonardo on Painting: An anthology of writings by Leonardo da Vinci with a selection of documents relating to his career*. New Haven: Yale University Press.

Kincheloe, J.L. 1999. The Struggle to Define and Reinvent Whiteness: A Pedagogical Analysis. *College Literature* 26 (3):162-204.

Kirk, M., E. Hoban, A. Dunne and L. Manderson. 1998. *Barriers to and Appropriate Delivery Systems for Cervical Cancer Screening in Indigenous Communities in Queensland: Final Report*. Brisbane: Queensland Government Press.

Kirk, M., L. Manderson, E. Hoban, C. McMichael, H. Potts, and D.C. Hill. 2000a. *Breast Cancer Among Indigenous Women Community Report*. Brisbane: Queensland Health.

Kirk, M., C. McMichael, H. Potts, E. Hoban, D.C. Hill, and L. Manderson. 2000b. *Breast Cancer: Screening, Diagnosis, Treatment and Care for*

Aboriginal Women and Torres Strait Islander Women in Queensland. Brisbane: Queensland Health.

Kismaric, Carole, ed. 1989. *Forced out.* New York: Human Rights Watch and the J.M. Kaplan Fund, in association with William Morrow, W.W. Norton, Penguin and Random House.

Kitchin, R. 1995. Creating an awareness of Others: highlighting the role of space and place. *Geography* 84 (1):45.

Kivel, P. and A. Creighton. 1997. *Making the peace: A 15-session violence prevention curriculum for young people.* Alemeda, CA.: Hunter House Inc. Publishers.

Kleinman, Arthur, and Joan Kleinman. 1997. The appeal of experience; the dismay of images: cultural appropriations of suffering in our times. In *Social Suffering,* edited by A. Kleinman, V. Das and M. Lock. Berkeley: University of California Press.

Koerner, C. and J. Harris. 2007. Inspired learning: Creating engaged teaching and learning environments for university and school students through university to school mentor programs. *International Education Journal* 8 (2):354-364.

Koerner, C., S.U. Tur, and C. Wilson. 2007. Bringing Indigenous sovereignties into community partnerships: Teaching racialisation to non-Indigenous Student volunteers in an education engagement program in school and youth services. Conference paper presented at ACRAWSA *Transforming Bodies, Nations and Knowledges Conference*, Adelaide, 10-13 December.

Korzy, M. 2002. *NSW—Injunction stops work at Aboriginal burial site,* 16 February. AAP Information Services. Accessed 11 July 2008. Available from Factiva database.

Kraack, A. 1999. *Rockhampton Women's Health Centre Evaluation.* Rockhampton: Rockhampton Women's Health Centre.

Kremmer, C. 2002a. Asylum seekers encounter new world outside fences—WOOMERA. The *Age,* 26 January, p. 5.

—. 2002b. Woomera strikers accuse guards of beatings, duress and racism. The *Age*, 25 January , p. 6.

Kremmer, C., and C. Banham. 2002. Hunger strikers deny stitching children's mouths. *Sydney Morning Herald,* 25 January, p. 4.

Kronenthal, Melissa. 2003. A Critical Assessment of EU Minority Language, Policy and Practice, Mercator Working Paper No. 13.

Kuo, A., T. Franke, M. Regalado, and N. Halfon. 2004. Parent report of reading to young children. *Pediatrics* 113:1944-1951.

LaCapra, Dominick. 2001. *Writing history, writing trauma.* Baltimore: Johns Hopkins University Press.

Lambert, A. 2000. Movement Within a Filmic Terra Nullius: Woman, Land and Identity In Australian Cinema. *Balayi—Colonialism, Law and Culture*, 1 (2):7-17.

—2005. Arresting Metaphors: Anti-Colonial Females in Australian Cinema. *Postcolonial Text [on-line journal]*, 1 (2). Available from: <http://postcolonial.org/index.php/pct/article/view/358/125>.

Land, C. 2002. Representations of Gender in EM Curr's "Recollections of squatting in Victoria": Implications for land justice through the native title process. *Indigenous Law Bulletin* 5 (19):6-9.

Lanfant, M-F. 1995. International Tourism, Internationalization and the Challenge to Identity. In *International Tourism—Identity and Change*, edited by M-F. Lanfant, J.B. Allcock and E. Bruner. London: Sage Publications, 1-43.

Le Corbusier. 1946. *Vers Une Architecture*. Trans. F. Etchells. London: The Architectural Press.

Leiper, N. 1995. *Tourist Management*. Melbourne: RMIT Press.

—. 2004, *Tourism Management*, 3rd ed. Frenchs Forest, NSW: Pearson Education Australia.

Lemorick, M. 1995. Secrets of the lost tomb. *New York Times*, 29 May.

Liebich, André. 2002. Ethnic Minorities and Long-term Implications of EU Enlargement. In *Europe Unbound*, edited by Jan Zielonka. New York: Routledge, 117.

Lippmann, L. 1994. *Generations of Resistance*. Melbourne: Longman Cheshire.

Lipsitz, G. 1998. *The Possessive Investment in Whiteness: How White People Profit from identity Politics*. Philadelphia: Temple University Press.

Little Bear, Leroy. 2000. Forward. In *Native Science: Natural Laws of Interdependence*. Santa Fe, Mexico: Clear Light Publications

Lopez, I.F.H. 1996. *White By Law: the Legal Construction of Race*. New York: NYU Press.

Lynch, P. 1996. *Minority Nationalism and European Integration*, Cardiff: University of Wales Press.

Lyotard, Jean-Françoise. 1979. *The Postmodern Condition*. UK: Manchester University Press.

MacCallum, J., and S. Beltman. 2002. *Role models for Young People: What makes an effective role model program?* National Youth Affairs Research Scheme, Hobart, Tasmania: Australasian Clearinghouse for Youth Studies.

MacCannell, D. 1976. *The Tourist—A new theory of the leisure class*. New York: Schocken Books.

—. 2001. Tourist agency. *Tourist Studies* 1 (1):23–37.

MacGregor, S. 2001. Gender, Identity, and Place: Understanding Feminist Geographies (review). *Journal of the American Planning Association* 67 (3):342-343.

Mares, P. 2000, *The New Peril: Australia's Media Coverage of the "Boat People"*. Accessed 13 March 2005. Available from: <http://www.wacc.org.uk/wacc/publications/media_development/archive/2001_3/the_media_and_asylum_seekers_in_australia>.

—. 2002. *Borderline: Australia's response to refugees and asylum seekers in the wake of the Tampa*, 2nd ed. Sydney: UNSW Press.

Marí, Isidor, and Miquel Strubell. 2002. The linguistic regime of the European Union: Prospects in the face of enlargement. "Europa Diversa", Workshop: Linguistic proposals for the future of Europe, Barcelona (Catalonia, Spain), 31 May-1 June 2002.

Marles, K. 2006. Repeat visitors to Australian caravan parks. Unpublished PhD thesis, Griffith University, Australia.

Marr, D., and M. Wilkinson. 2003. *Dark victory*. Crows Nest, NSW: Allen & Unwin.

Marschall, S. 2004. Commodifying heritage—Post-apartheid monuments and cultural tourism in South Africa. Chap. 8 in *Tourism and Postcolonialism—Contested discourses, identities and representations*, edited by C.M. Hall and H. Tucker. Oxon and New York: Routledge, 95-112.

Martin, Karen. 2007. Ways of Knowing, Being and Doing: A Theoretical Framework and Methods for Indigenous and Indigenist Re-search. In *Voicing Dissent*, edited by K. McWilliam, P. Stephenson and G. Thompson. *New Talents 21C: Next Generation Australian Studies* 76:203-214.

Martin, L. 2007. Xavier pupils suspended after bullying caught on film. The *Age*, 13 April, p. 10.

Martino, W. and M. Pallotta-Chiarolli. 2003. *So what's a boy? Addressing issues of masculinity in schooling.* Maidenhead: Open University Press.

Massey, D. 1994. *Space, Place and Gender*. Minneapolis: University of Minnesota Press.

Massumi, Brian. 2002. *Parables of the Virtual: Movement, Affect, Sensation.* London: Duke University Press.

Mattingley, C., and K. Hampton. 1988. *Survival in our own land; Aboriginal experiences in South Australia since 1836*. Adelaide: Wakefield Press.

McAllan, Fiona. 2007a. Rites of Passage? In *Law Text Culture*. Melbourne: Melbourne University Press.

—. 2007b. Australian Communities: Bound for more of the Same? In *Transforming Cultures ejournal* 2 (1).

—. 2008. Customary Appropriations. In *borderlands ejournal* 6 (3).

McLean, F. and S. Cooke. 2003. Constructing the Identity of a Nation: The Tourist Gaze at the Museum of Scotland. *Tourism, Culture & Communication* 4 (3):153-62.

McCartney, C.A., M.B. Styles, and K.V. Morrow. 1994. *Mentoring in the Juvenile Justice System: Findings from two pilot programs* (Winter). Philadelphia: Public/Private Ventures.

McClintock, A. 1995. *Imperial Leather: Race, Gender and Sexuality in the Colonial Contest.* New York: Routledge.

McConnochie, K., D. Hollinsworth, and J. Pettman. 1988. *Race and racism in Australia.* Wentworth Falls, NSW: Social Science Press.

McCubbin, F. 1904. *The Pioneer*. National Gallery of Victoria. Accessed 1 October 2008. Available from: <www.artistfootsteps.com/htm/McCubbin_pioneer.htm>

McDowell, L. 1999. *Gender, Identity, and Place: Understanding Feminist Geographies*. Minneapolis: University of Minnesota Press.

McInerny, P. 2001. Area named after the clever fella. *Illawarra Mercury,* 16 February, p. 2.

McIntosh, P. 1988. White Privilege: Unpacking the Invisible Knapsack. This essay is excerpted from Working Paper 189. White Privilege and Male Privilege: A Personal Account of Coming to See Correspondences through Work in Women's Studies. Available from: <http://www.feinberg.northwestern.edu/diversity/uploaded_docs/UnpackingTheKnapsack.pdf>

McLean, D. 1993. A Pendant of Time in Red Hill Valley. *Friends of Red Hill Valley website.* Accessed 6 March 2006. Available from <http://www.hwcn.org/link/forhv/valley/history.htm>

McNie, S. 1991. A future for the Red Hill Valley: combine nature centres with historic, native villages for a unique urban park. The *Spectator,* 6 July, A7.

Meethan, K. 2001. *Tourism in Global Society—Place, Culture, Consumption*. Basingstoke Hampshire and New York: Palgrave.

Melrose, J. 2004. *The North Coast Monthly Imag* (May). Sawtell, Tourist brochure.

Members of the Yorta Yorta Aboriginal Community v Victoria [2002] HCA 58 (12 December 2002).

Mendoza, J., and D. Reese. 2002. Examining multicultural picture books for the early childhood classroom: Possibilities and pitfalls. *Early Childhood Research and Practice* 3:1-23.

Mentoring Australia. 2000. *National benchmarks for mentoring programs.* Preliminary information.

Mercer, Kobena. 1991. Looking for trouble. *Transition* 51:184-97.

Metallic, C., and P. Monture-Angus. 2002. Domestic Laws versus Aboriginal Visions: An Analysis of the Delgamuukw Decision. *borderlands e-journal* 1 (2). Accessed 16 November 2005. Available from <http://www.borderlands.net.au/vol1no2_2002/metallic_angus.html>

Miller, J. 1985. *Koori: A will to win, the heroic resistance survival and triumph of black Australia.* Australia: Angus & Robertson.

Miller, J., and R. Miller. 2001. *Proposal for an Illawarra Regional Foreshores Park.* Wollongong: self-published.

Miranne, K.B. and A.H. Young, eds. 2000. *Gendering the City: Women, Boundaries, and Visions of Urban Life.* Lanham: Rowman & Littlefield.

Minister for Planning v Walker [2008] NSWCA 224 (24 September 2008).

Moeller, Susan D. 1999. *Compassion fatigue: How the media sell disease, famine, war and death.* London: Routledge.

mogenic. 2000-2006. Mogenic: Version Indigo. Accessed 7 November 2007. Available from: <http://www.mogenic.com/>

Molitorisz, S. 2003. *Australian Bushrangers—The Romance of Robbery.* Woollahra, Newtown, NSW.

Moore, T.G. 1997. "Radical to Conservative": An Analysis of the Establishment of a Women's Health Centre in Queensland. Honours thesis, Central Queensland University.

Moran, A. 2004. *Australia: Nation, Belonging, and Globalization.* New York: Routledge.

Moreton-Robinson, A. 1998. White Race Privilege: Nullifying Native Title. *Bringing Australia Together. The Structure and Experience of Racism in Australia.* Woolloongabba: Foundation for Aboriginal and Islander Research Action, 39-44.

—. 1999. Unmasking whiteness: A Goori Jundal's look at some duggai business. In *Unmasking whiteness: Race relations and reconciliation,* edited by B. McKay. Nathan, QLD: Queensland Studies Centre, Griffith University.

—. 2000. *Talkin' up to the White Woman: Indigenous women and feminism.* St Lucia: University of Queensland Press.

—. 2003. I Still Call Australia Home: Indigenous Belonging and Place in a White Postcolonising Society. In *Uprootings/regroupings Questions of Home and Migration*, edited by S. Ahmed, C. Castaneda, A-M. Fortier and M. Sheller. Oxford: Berg, 23-40.

—. 2004. Whiteness, Epistemology and Indigenous Representation. In *Whitening race: essays in social and cultural criticism*, edited by A. Moreton-Robinson. Canberra: Aboriginal Studies Press, 75-88.

—. 2004. The possessive logic of patriarchal white sovereignty: The High Court and the Yorta Yorta decision. *borderlands e-journal* 3 (2). Accessed on 23 July 2008. Available from: <http://www.borderlands.net.au/vol3no2_2004/moreton_possessive.htm>

—. 2005. The House That Jack Built: Britishness and White Possession. *Journal of the Australian Critical race and Whiteness Studies Association*. 1 (1):1-9.

—. 2007. *Indigenous Sovereignty Matters: Sovereign Subjects*. Crow Nest, Australia: Allen & Unwin.

—. 2007. Writing off Indigenous Sovereignty: The discourse of security and patriarchal white sovereignty. In *Indigenous Sovereignty Matters,* 86-104.

Morgan, N.J., and A. Pritchard. 1998. *Tourism promotion and power: creating images, creating identities*. West Sussex: John Wiley & Sons Ltd.

Morris, M. 1995. Life as a Tourist Object in Australia. In *International Tourism—Identity and Change*, edited by M.F. Lanfant, J. Allcock and E. Bruner. London: Sage, 177-91.

Morrison, B. 2006. School bullying and restorative justice: Toward a theoretical understanding of the role of respect, pride and shame. *Journal of Social Issues* 62:347-370.

Morrow, K.V., and M.B. Styles. 1995. *Building relationships with youth in program settings: A study of Big Brothers/Big Sisters* (May). Philadelphia: Public/Private Ventures.

Morton, Christopher A. 2006. Review of *Sahel: The end of the road* by Sebastião Salgado. *Anthropological Quarterly* 79 (1):175-7.

Morton, J. 2004. "Such a man would find few races hostile": History, Fiction and Anthropological Dialogue in the Melbourne Museum. *Arena journal* 22:53-71.

Moucheboeuf, Alcidia. 2006. *Minority Rights Jurisprudence Digest. ECMI Handbook Series, Vol. 3*, Strasbourg: Council of Europe Publishing, 750.

Moustakas, C. 1987. Cited in Jeanne P. Stubbs, *Individual Freeing in a person-centred community workshop*. Accessed 13 November 2006. Available from: <http://www.adpca.org/Journal/Vol1_1/community.htm>

Mowarljali, David. 1993. *Yorro Yorro*. Broome: Magabala Books Aboriginal Corporation.

Mudrooroo. 1995. *Us Mob*. Sydney: Angus & Robertson.

Muecke, Stephen. 1997. *No Road*. Fremantle: Fremantle Arts Centre Press.

—. 2005. *Ancient and Modern: time, culture and indigenous philosophy*. Sydney: UNSW Press.

Murray, J., ed. 1994. *Lonely Planet New South Wales & the ACT*, 1st ed. Hawthorn: Lonely Planet Publications

Myers, G.A. 2002. Colonial Geography and Masculinity in Eric Dutton's Kenya Mountain. *Gender, Place and Culture—A Journal of Feminist Geography* 9 (1):23-38.

Nagel, Klaus-Jürgen. 2004. Transcending the National, Asserting the National: How Stateless Nations like Scotland, Wales and Catalonia React to European Integration. *Australian Journal of Politics and History* 50 (1):58-75. An older version was published as National Europe Centre Paper No. 39 (2002), Australian National University.

Nakamura, L. 2002. *Cybertypes: Race, Ethnicity and Identity on the Internet*. New York: Routledge.

Nakata, Martin. 2004. Indigenous Australian Studies and Higher Education: Wentworth Lectures. Accessed July 2007. Available from: <http://www1.aiatsis.gov.au/exhibitions/wentworth/a352185_a.pdf>

—. 2007. *Disciplining the Savages, Savaging the Disciplines*. Canberra: AIATSIS Press.

Navin, K., and K. Officer. 2001a. *Sandon Point Development Area—Stages 2-6 Archaeological investigations of the area covered by the proposed Stocklands residential development at Sandon Point: A Report to Rose Consulting Group*. Deakin, ACT: Navin Officer Heritage Consultants Pty Ltd.

—. 2001b. *Sandon Point Residential Subdivision—Stage 1 Development Area—North of Wollongong, NSW: Archaeological subsurface testing program. A report to Rose Consulting Group for Stockland Constructors Pty Ltd.* Deakin, ACT: Navin Officer Heritage Consultants Pty Ltd.

—. 2001c. *Sandon Point Residential subdivision—Stages 2-6 Development Area—Bulli, North of Wollongong, NSW: Archaeological subsurface testing program and Aboriginal consultation.* Deakin, ACT: Navin Officer Heritage Consultants Pty Ltd.

Navin, K. 1993. *Further Archaeological Investigations: Sandon Point, Wollongong, NSW.* Canberra: Navin Officer Archaeological Resource Management.

Nero, C.I. 2005. Why Are the Gay Ghettoes White? In *Black Queer Studies: A Critical Anthology,* edited by E.P. Johnson and M.G. Henderson. Durham and London: Duke University Press.

Nettelbeck, Amanda, and Robert Foster. 2007. *In the Name of the Law. William Willshire and the Policing of the Australian Frontier.* Adelaide: Wakefield Press.

New South Wales National Parks and Wildlife Service 1997. *Regional Parks Policy Statement.* Parramatta, NSW: New South Wales National Parks and Wildlife Service.

Nicoll, F. 2000. Indigenous sovereignty and the violence of perspective: A white woman's coming out story. *Australian Feminist Studies* 15:386-396.

Nicoll, F. 2002. De-facing Terra Nullius and Facing the Public Secret of Indigenous Sovereignty in Australia. *borderlands e-journal* 1 (2). Accessed 16 November 2005. Available from <http://www.borderlands.net.au/vol1no2_2002/nicoll_defacing.html>

Nicoll, Fiona. 2004. "Are you calling me a racist?" Teaching Critical Whiteness Theory in Indigenous Sovereignty. *borderlands ejournal* 3 (2). Available from: <http://www.borderlands.net.au/vol3no2_2004/nicoll_teaching.htm>

Nicoll, F. 2007. "Are you calling me a racist?": Teaching critical whiteness studies in Indigenous sovereignty. In *Taking up the challenge: Critical race and whiteness studies in a postcolonising nation,* edited by D. Riggs. Adelaide, South Australia: Crawford House Publishing, 12-33.

Nordström, B. 2000. *Australien—En Guidebok (Australia—A Guidebook).* Stockholm: Bokförlaget Prisma.

Oakley, A. 1974. *The Sociology of Housework.* Oxford: Basil and Blackwell.

Officer, K. 2002. *Response to an appraisal by Dr Peter Hiscock of archaeological studies conducted by Navin Officer Heritage Consultants at Sandon Point, New South Wales.* Navin Officer Heritage Consultants Pty Ltd.

Olesko, K.M. 2006. The Century of Science. In *A companion to nineteenth century Europe 1789-1914*, edited by S. Berger. London: Blackwell, 333-344.

Ó Riagáin, Dónall. 2001. Many Tongues but One Voice: a Personal Overview of the Role of the European Charter on Lesser-used Languages in Promoting Europe's Regional and Minority Languages. In *Language, Ethnicity and the State, Vol. 1: Minority Languages in the European Union*, edited by Camille C. O'Reilly. New York: Palgrave Macmillan, 20.

—. 2002. The lesser used languages of Europe and their participation in the programmes of the European Union. "Europa Diversa", Workshop: Linguistic proposals for the future of Europe, Barcelona (Catalonia, Spain), 31 May-1 June 2002

Organ, M., and C. Speechly. 1997. Illawarra Aborigines. In *A History of Wollongong,* edited by J. Hagan and A. Wells. Wollongong: University of Wollongong Press.

Organ, M. 1990. *Illawarra and South Coast Aborigines.* Wollongong: Aboriginal Education Unit, University of Wollongong.

—. 2002. Sandon Point—No Houses: The Spirit of Sandon Point. *Honi Soit,* 19 May, pp. 12-3.

Orkin, A., and M. Klippenstein. 2003. Sacred Promise: Hamilton's Red Hill Valley expressway project violates important 1701 Crown-Iroquois Treaty rights. *Hamilton Spectator,* 13 December, F8.

O'Shane, P. 1976. Is There Any Relevance in the Women's Movement for Aboriginal Women? *Refractory Girl.* (September):12.

—. 1993. Aboriginal women and the women's movement. *Refracting Voices, Feminist Perspectives.* Marrackville, New South Wales: Southward Press, 69-75.

Osuri, G., and S.B. Banerjee. 2003. Organizing multiple spacetimes in a colonial context—Indegeneity and white Australian nationalism at the Melbourne Museum. In *Text/Work: Representing Organization and Organizing Representation*, edited by S. Linstead. London: Routledge, 138-60.

Osuri, Goldie, and Bobby Bannerjee. 2004. White diasporas: media representations of September 11 and the unbearable whiteness of being in Australia. *Social Semiotics* 14 (2):151-70.

Palermo, Francesco. 2001. The Use of Minority Languages: Recent Developments in EC Law and Judgements of the ECJ. *Maastricht Journal* 3:299-318.

Pan, Chistoph, and B.S. Pfeil. 2003. *National Minorities in Europe.* Vienna: Braumuller.

Parkes, B. 1998. Nursery children using illustrations in shared readings and re-readings. In *What's in the picture: Responding to illustrations in picture books,* edited by J. Evans. London: Paul Chapman, 44-57.

Patrick, J., A. Perry, J. McCullough, T. Jacob, and S. Patrick. 2005. When will the cycle of bullying be broken? Accessed 20 April 2007. Available from: <http://workforce.cup.edu/Patrick/4-Publications>

Payne, R. 2007. *Gay Scene, Queer Grid.* Paper presented at the Queer Space: Centres and Peripheries, UTS Sydney, 21-22 February.

Peace, W.G. 1998a. Farm, forest and freeway: the Red Hill Creek Valley, 1950-1998. In *From Mountain to Lake: the Red Hill Creek Valley,* edited by W.G. Peace. Hamilton, Ontario: The Conserver Society of Hamilton and District.

—, ed. 1998b. *From Mountain to Lake: The Red Hill Creek Valley,* Hamilton: Conserver Society of Hamilton and District.

—. 1998c. The Red Hill Creek valley: a crossroads in time and space. In *From Mountain to Lake: the Red Hill Creek Valley,* edited by W.G. Peace. Hamilton, Ontario: The Conserver Society of Hamilton and District.

Pearson, Noel. 2007. White Guilt, Victimhood and the Quest for a Radical Centre. *Griffith Review* (Winter).

Pentassuglia, Gaetano. 2001. The EU and the Protection of Minorities: The Case of Eastern Europe, *European Journal for International Law* 12 (1):3-38.

Perera, S. 2002. A line in the sea. *Race and Class* 44 (2):23-39.

—. 2006a. *Race terror, Sydney, December 2005*, Adelaide.

—. 2006b. They Give Evidence: Bodies, Borders and the Disappeared. *Social Identities* 12 (6):637-656.

Perera, S. and J. Pugliese. 1998. Parks, mines and tidy towns: enviro-panopticism, "post" colonialism, and the politics of heritage in Australia. *Postcolonial Studies* 1 (1):69-100.

Perkins, M. 2004. False Whiteness: "passing" and the stolen generations. In *Whitening race: essays in social and cultural criticism*, edited by A. Moreton-Robinson. Canberra: Aboriginal Studies Press, 164-175.

Perrottet, T. 2002. *Route 66 AD*. Sydney: Vintage.

Peters, K., and J. Poling. 1990. Province kills Red Hill expressway: won't pay for road through valley. *Hamilton Spectator,* 17 December.

Pihama, L., F. Cram, and S. Walker. 2003. Creating methodological space: A Literature review of Kaupapa Maori Research. *Canadian Journal of Native Education* 26 (1):30-43.

Piraino, A. 2002. The Northwest Block Watch Coalition: Winning the war on graffiti. *Law and Order* 50 (4):22-6.

Pitty, R. 1999. A poverty of evidence: abusing the law and history in Yorta Yorta v Victoria (1998), *Australian Journal of Legal History* 41:41-62.

Potter, E. 2002. 'How can you live in a city of monuments?': Reading Commemoration and Forgetting in Adelaide's North Terrace Precinct. *Altitude (on-line journal)*, 2 (Dreamscapes). Available from: <http://www.api-network.com/cgi-bin/altitude21c/fly?page=Issue2&n=2>.

Povinelli, Elizabeth A. 2002. *The Cunning of Recognition: Indigenous Alterities and the Making of Australian Multiculturalism*. London: Duke University Press.

Pritchard, A. and N.J. Morgan. 2000. Privileging the male gaze—Gendered tourism landscapes. *Annals of Tourism Research* 27 (4):884-905.

Probyn, Fiona. 2005. An Ethics of Following and the No Road Film: Trackers, Followers and Fanatics. *Australian Humanities Review* 37. Available from: <http://www.lib.latrobe.edu.au/AHR/copyright.html>

Pualani Louis, Renee. 2007. Can you hear us? Voices from the Margin: Using Indigenous Methodologies. *Geographical Research* 45 (2):130-139.

Pugliese, J. 2002. Migrant Heritage in an Indigenous Context: for a decolonising migrant historiography. *Journal of Intercultural Studies* 23 (1):5-18.

Pugliesi, J. 2002. *Penal Asylum: Refugees, Ethics, Hospitality, Meditation on lip-sewing*. Accessed 20 August 2006. Available from: <http://www.borderlandsejournal.adelaide.edu.au/vol1no1_2002/pugliese.html.>.

Pujadas, Bernat. 2003. The Protection of Minority Languages in the Czech Republic and in Slovakia, a Requirement for EU-Accession. *Mercator Bulletin* 53, Dossier Nr. 13.

Queensland. 1992. *Towards a Queensland Women's Health Policy—Social Justice for Women*. Brisbane: Queensland Health.

Rahn, J. 2002. *Painting without permission: hip-hop graffiti subculture*. Westport, CT: Bergin & Garvey.

Ram, Melanie H. 2003. Democratization through European Integration: The Case of Minority Rights in the Czech Republic and Romania. *Studies in Comparative International Development* 38 (2):28-56.

Rasmussen, M.L. 2004. The problem of coming out. *Theory Into Practice* 43:144-155.

Ravenscroft, Alison. 2004. The girl in the picture and the eye of her beholder: Viet Nam, whiteness and the disavowal of Indigeneity. *Continuum: Journal of Media and Cultural Studies* 18 (4):509-24.

Reinhardt, Mark, Holly Edwards and Erina Duganne, eds. 2007. *Beautiful suffering: Photography and the traffic in pain*. Williamston, MA:

Williams College Museum of Art in association with University of Chicago Press.

Revised Standard Version of the Holy Bible: Old and New Testaments. 1965. Catholic ed. Mark 9.2 and Luke 9.29. London: Catholic Truth Society, 40, 64.

Reynolds, H. 1987. *Frontier.* NSW: Allen and Unwin.

Richards, G. 2002. Tourism attraction systems: Exploring Cultural Behavior. *Annals of Tourism Research* 29 (4):1048-64.

Ridge, D., A. Hee, and V. Minichiello. 1999. "Asian" Men on the Scene: Challenges to "Gay Communities". In *Multicultural Queer: Australian Narratives*, edited by G. Sullivan and P.A. Jackson. Binghamton: The Haworth Press.

Rigby, K. 1997. What children tell us about bullying in schools. *Children Australia* 22:28-34.

Rigby, K. 2000. Effects of peer victimization in schools and perceived social support on adolescent well-being. *Journal of Adolescence* 23:57-68.

Riggs, D.W. 2003. Repressing a Privileged Location: Exploring a Place of Uncanny White Belonging. *Analysis* 12:15-27 Available from: <http://digital.library.adelaide.edu.au/dspace/bitstream/2440/37755/1/02whole.pdf>

—. 2004. "We don't talk about race anymore": Power, privilege and critical whiteness studies, *borderlands e journal.* October 3 (2). Accessed 10 January 2008. Available from: <http://www.borderlands.net.au/vol3no2_2004/riggs_intro.htm>

—. 2006. *Priscilla, (White) Queen of the Desert: Queer Rights/Race Privilege.* New York: Peter Lang Publishing.

—. 2007. Introduction: Critical race and whiteness studies in a postcolonising nation. In *Taking up the challenge: Critical race and whiteness studies in a postcolonising nation*, edited by D. Riggs. Adelaide, South Australia: Crawford House Publishing, 1-16.

Riggs, D.W., and M. Augoustinos. 2007. Learning difference: Representations of diversity in storybooks for children of lesbian and gay parents. *Journal of GLBT Family Studies* 3:82-95

Rigney, L-I. 1997. Internationalisation of an Indigenous anti-colonial cultural critique of research methodologies: A guide to Indigenist research methodology and its principles. *Higher Education Research and Development Society of Australasia (HERDSA) Annual conference proceedings; Research and development in Higher Education: Advancing International Perspectives*, 20, 629-636.

—. 1999. The first perspective: Culturally safe research practices on or with Indigenous peoples. *1999 Chacmool Conference*. Calgary, Canada: University of Calgary, unpublished paper.

—. 2001. A First Perspective of Indigenous Australian Participation in Science: Framing Indigenous Research Towards Indigenous Australian Intellectual Sovereignty. *Kaurna Higher Education Journal* 7:1-13.

Rintoul, S. 1993. *The Wailing A National Black Oral History*. Port Melbourne: William Heinmann.

Ritchin, Fred. 2004. Introduction to *Sahel: The end of the road,* by Sebastião Salgado. Berkeley: University of California Press.

Roaf, P.A., J.P. Tierney, and D.E.I. Hunte. 1994. *Big Brothers/Big Sisters: A study of volunteer recruitment and screening* (Fall). Philadelphia: Public/Private Ventures.

Rockhampton Women's Health Centre. 2002. *Annual Report*. Rockhampton: Rockhampton Women's Health Centre.

—. 2000. *Annual Report*. Rockhampton: Rockhampton Women's Health Centre.

Roderick, L.L. 2004. Fireball. *Illawarra Mercury,* 20 September, p. 1.

Rodriguez, R. 2002. *Brown: The Last Discovery of America*. New York: Viking.

Roediger, David R. 1994. *Towards the Abolition of Whiteness: Essays on Race, Politics, and Working Class History*. London: Verso.

Roger, Antoine. 2001. The influence of the European Union on political orientations of ethnic minorities: comparing post-communist Bulgaria, Romania and Latvia. Paper presented at the conference "Voice or Exit: Comparative Perspectives on Ethnic Minorities in 20th Century Europe" Humboldt University, 14-16 June 2001, Berlin

Roger, K. 1998. *"Fairy fictions": White women as helping professionals*. PhD thesis, University of Toronto.

Rojek, C. 1997. Indexing, dragging, and social construction. In *Touring Cultures—Transformations of Travel and Theory*, edited by C. Rojek and J. Urry. London and New York: Routledge, 52-77.

Rose, Deborah Bird. 1992. *Dingo Makes Us Human*. Melbourne: Cambridge University Press.

—. 2002. *Love and Reconciliation in the Forest: A Study in Decolonisation*. South Australia: University of South Australia.

Rosler, Martha. 1989. In, around and afterthoughts (on documentary photography). In *The contest of meaning: Critical histories of photography,* edited by R. Bolton. Cambridge: MIT Press, 303-42

Routt, W.D. 2001. More Australian than Aristotelian: The Australian Bushranger Film, 1904-1914. *Senses of Cinema* 18 (1). Available from: <www.sensesofcinema.com>.

Rowe, D. 1993. Leisure, tourism and "Australianess". *Media, Culture and Society* 15 (2):253-69.

Royce, C.C. 1899. *Indian Land Cessions in the United States (US Serial Set, Number 4015).* Washington: Government Printing Office.

Ruiz, V. 2000. Color Coded. *The Women's Review of Books*. 17 (5):24-34.

Said, Edward W. 1995. *Orientalism: Western conceptions of the Orient.* London: Penguin.

Salgado, Sebastião. 2004. *Sahel: The end of the road.* Berkeley: University of California Press.

Sartre, J.P. 2001. Preface. In Fanon, F. *The Wretched of the Earth.* Trans. C. Farrington. London: Penguin.

Sasse, Gwendolyn, and James Hughes. 2003. Monitoring the Monitors: EU Enlargement Conditionality and Minority Protection in the CEECs. *Journal on Ethnopolitics and Minority Issues in Europe* 1.

Schech, S. and J. Haggis. 2004. Terrains of Migrancy and Whiteness: how British migrants locate themselves in Australia. In *Whitening race: essays in social and cultural criticism*, edited by A. Moreton-Robinson, Canberra: Aboriginal Studies Press, 176-191.

Schembri, M. 2001. Ethnic Gay and Lesbian Politics: a taste of things to come. In *Queer City: Gay and Lesbian Politics in Sydney,* edited by C. Johnston and P. van Reyk. Annandale: Pluto Press Australia Ltd.

Schlögel, Jürgen. 2004. *Der Schutz ethnischer Minderheiten als allgemeiner Rechtsgrundsatz des Gemeinschaftsrechts*. Hamburg: Verlag Dr. Kovac.

Schlunke, K. 2005. *Bluff Rock—Autobiography of a massacre*. Fremantle: Curtin University Books.

Schwartz-Cowan, R. 1983. *More work for mother: the ironies of household technology from the open hearth to the microwave*. New York: Basic Books.

Sealy, Mark. 1997. Detached. In *Exodus: 50 million people on the move*, by Signum-Fotografie, M. Sealy, J. Kumin and H.C. Buch. Zurich: Edition Stemmle.

Sedgwick, E.K. 1990. *Epistemology of the Closet*. Berkeley: University of California Press.

Sekula, Allan. 1981. The traffic in photographs. *Art Journal* 41 (1):15-25.

Seldon, R. 1989. *A Reader's guide to contemporary literary theory*. 2nd ed. New York: Harvester Wheatsheaf.

Shepherd, J. 2007. Aim, shoot … miss again. *Guardian,* Tuesday, 12 June. Accessed online on 12 June 2007. Available from: <http://education.guardian.co.uk/print/0,,330003824-108729,00.html>

Shields, R. 1991. *Places on the Margin—Alternative geographies of modernity*. London and New York: Routledge.

Shor, I., and P. Freire. 1987. *A pedagogy for liberation: Dialogues on transforming education*. London: Bergin & Carvey, 180-187.

Shore, S. 2002. Pedagogy and selective amnesia: investigating the relationship between Whiteness and everyday teaching practices. Accessed 25 October 2008. Available from: <www.arre.edu.au/98pap/98218.htm>

Shuibhne, Niamh Nic. 1996. The Impact of European Law on Linguistic Diversity. *Irish Journal of European Law*, 62-80.

Shuibhne, Niamh Nic. 2002. *EC Law and Minority Language Policy*. The Hague: Kluwer.

Signum-Fotografie, M. Sealy, J. Kumin and H.C. Buch. 1997. *Exodus: 50 million people on the move*. Zurich: Edition Stemmle.

Simpson, A. 2000. Paths Toward a Mohawk Nation: Narratives of Citizenship and Nationhood in Kahnawake. In *Political Theory and the Rights of Indigenous Peoples,* edited by D. Ivison, P. Patton and W. Sanders. Melbourne: Cambridge University Press, 113–136.

Simpson, Leanne. 2004. Anticolonial Stategies for the Recovery and Maintenance of Indigenous Knowledge. *American Indian Quarterly* 28 (3&4):373-384.

Sipe, C. 1996. *Mentoring: A synthesis of P/PV's Research 1985-1995.* Philadelphia: Public/Private Ventures.

Smallacombe, S. 2000. On Display for its Aesthetic Beauty: how western institutions fabricate knowledge about Aboriginal Cultural Heritage. In *Political Theory and the Rights of Indigenous People,* edited by D. Ivison, P. Patton and W. Sanders. New York: Cambridge University Press.

Smart, B. 1986. The Politics of Truth and the Problem of Hegemony. In *Foucault: A Critical Reader,* edited by D.C. Hoy. Oxford, UK: Basil Blackwell Ltd.

Smith, David J. 2003. Minority Rights, Multiculturalism and EU Enlargement: the Case of Estonia. *Journal on Ethnopolitics and Minority Issues in Europe* 1.

Smith, L.T. 1999. *Decolonising Methodologies Research and Indigenous Peoples*, London: Zed Books.

—. 2005. On Tricky Ground. In *The Landscape of Qualitative Research,* edited by Norman Denzin and Yvonna Lincoln. London: Sage.

Smith, W.S. 1956. *Traffic and transportation plan for Hamilton, Ontario.* New Haven, Connecticut: Wilbur Smith & Associates.

Solomon-Godeau, Abigail. 1991. *Photography at the dock: Essays on photographic history, institutions and practices.* Minneapolis: University of Minnesota Press.

Somerville, M. and T. Perkins. 2005. (Re)membering in the Contact Zone: Telling, and Listening to, a Massacre Story. *Altitude (on-line journal) 6, Reading Indigenous Australian Texts Part 2.* Available from: <http://www.api-network.com/cgi-bin/altitude21c/fly?page=Issue6&n=7>.

Sontag, Susan. 1979. *On photography.* Harmondsworth: Penguin.

—. 2003. *Regarding the pain of others.* London: Hamish Hamilton.

Spearritt, P. 2003. Promoting Western Australia in Text and Image. University of Queensland, Australia, Brisbane, 3 August 2008. A revised version of the New Norcia Library Lecture, 2001. Forthcoming article in *New Norcia Studies*, on UQ eSpace. Available from: <http://espace.library.uq.edu.au/view/UQ:10917>.

Special Broadcasting Service. 2008. *Timeline: Mandatory Detention in Australia.* Viewed 18 September 2008. Available from: <http://news.sbs.com.au/worldnewsaustralia/index.php?type=category&a=timeline_mandatory_detention_in_australia_549534>.

Spelman, Elizabeth V. 1997. *Fruits of sorrow: Framing our attention to suffering.* Boston: Beacon Press.

Spivak, Gayatri Chakravorty. 1990. *The Post-colonial Critic. Interviews, Strategies, Dialogues*, edited by Sarah Harasym. New York and London: Routledge.

Steele, Shelby. 2006. *White Guilt: How Blacks and Whites Together Destroyed the Promise of the Civil Rights Era.* New York: HarperCollins.

Stewart-DeBreau, K., and J. Nugent. 1998. The Storied Past: The Red Hill Creek Valley, 1791-1950. In *From Mountain to Lake: the Red Hill Creek Valley,* edited by W.G. Peace. Hamilton, Ontario: The Conserver Society of Hamilton and District.

Stockland (Constructors) Pty Ltd v Allen Richard Carriage [2002] NSWSC 1179 (11 December 2002).

Styles, M.B., and K.V. Morrow. June 1992. *Understanding how youth and elders form relationships: A study of four linking lifetimes programs.* Philadelphia: Public/Private Ventures.

Tascon, Sonia. 2004. Uncovering Race, Returning to Origins. In *Placing Race and Localising Whiteness*, edited by S. Schech and B. Wadham. Adelaide: Flinders University Press.

Taylor, K. 2002. Ruddock removes children. The *Age*, 24 January, p. 1.

Teo, P. 2000. Racism in the News: A Critical Discourse Analysis of News Reporting in Two Australian Newspapers. *Discourse and Society* 11 (1) January, 7-49.

Tesser, Lynn M. 2003. The Geopolitics of Tolerance: Minority Rights under EU Expansion in East-Central Europe. *East European Politics and Societies* 17 (3):483-532.

Thirroul: timeline, 2008. *Wollongong City Library: Local history and information.* Accessed 1 October 2008. Available from: <http://www.wollongong.nsw.gov.au/library/thirroultimeline.asp>

Tierney, J.P., and A.Y. Branch. 1992. *College students as mentors for at-risk youth: A study of six campus partners in learning programs* (December). Philadelphia: Public/Private Ventures.

Tierney, J.P., J.B. Grossman, and N.L. Resch. November 1995. *Making a difference: An impact study of Big Brothers/Big Sisters*. Philadelphia: Public/Private Ventures.

Toggenburg, Gabriel N. 2000. Feature, "Enlargement Day". Unification via Diversification—what does it mean to be united in diversity? *EUMAP Online Journal*, 1 May.

—. 2001. A Rough Orientation through a Delicate Relationship: the European Union's Endeavours for (its) Minorities. In *Minority Rights in Europe: European Minorities and Languages*, edited by Snežana Trifunovska. The Hague: Asser Press, 205-234.

—, ed. 2004. *Minority Protection and the Enlarged European Union: the Way Forward,* Budapest: Open Society Institute. Available from: <http://lgi.osi.hu/publications_datasheet.php?id=261>

—. 2005. Who is Managing Ethnic and Cultural Diversity within the European Condominium? The Moments of Entry, Integration and Preservation. *Journal of Common Market Studies* 43(4):717–737.

—. 2007. Regional Autonomies Providing Minority Rights and the Law of European Integration: Experiences from South Tyrol. In *Tolerance Established by Law. The Autonomy of South Tyrol: Self-governance and Minority Rights*, edited by Joseph Marko et al. Leiden: Martinus Nijhoff, 143-164.

Tomopoulos, S., P. Valdez, B. Dreyer, A. Fierman, S. Berkule, and M. Kuhn, et al. 2007. Is exposure to media intended for preschool children associated with less parent-child shared reading aloud and teaching activities? *Ambulatory Pediatrics* 7:18-24.

Törnquist Plewa, Barbara. 2001. *Nationalism and Minority Questions in Central and Eastern Europe in the Context of EU Enlargement.* CFE working paper, Lund University.

Tregear, E. 1885. *The Aryan Maori.* Wellington: G Didsbury Govt Printer.

Trudgen, R. 2000. *Why warriors lie down and die: Towards an understanding of why the Aboriginal people of Arnhem Land face the greatest crisis in health and education since European contact.* Darwin: Aboriginal Resources and Development Services Inc.

Tully, J. 1995. *Strange multiplicity: Constitutionalism in an age of diversity.* Cambridge: Cambridge University Press.

—. 2000. The Struggles of Indigenous Peoples for and of Freedom. In *Political Theory and the Rights of Indigenous People,* edited by D. Ivison, P. Patton and W. Sanders. New York: Cambridge University Press.

Tur, S.U., D. Rigney, L.I. Rigney. 2003. Training Teachers for reconciliation: a work in progress. Australian Curriculum Studies Association (ACSA) Curriculum Conference. Conversations: Conversations and Actions.

Turkle, S. 1996. *Life on the Screen: Identity in the Age of the Internet.* London: Weidenfield and Nicolson.

Turner, G. 1993. *National fictions: literature, film and the construction of Australian narrative*. 2nd ed. St Leonards: Allen & Unwin.

Turnbull, D. 2000. *Masons, Tricksters and Cartographers: comparative studies in the sociology of scientific and Indigenous Knowledge.* Amsterdam: Harwood Academic.

Turner, D. 2006. *This is not a peace pipe: Towards a critical Indigenous philosophy*. Toronto: Toronto University Press.

Unaipon, David. 2001. *Legendary Tales of the Australian Aborigines*, edited by S. Muecke and A. Shoemaker. Victoria: Miengunyah Press.

unknown. 1990. Chronology. *Hamilton Spectator,* 18 December.

—. 2002a. A form guide to the players. In *The Sandon Point—A Community Bulletin for the Protection of Sandon Point*, edited by H. Brown. Bulli: Hamish Brown.

—. 2002b. Kuradji: more than meets the eye. In *The Sandon Point—A Community Bulletin for the Protection of Sandon Point,* edited by H. Brown. Bulli: Hamish Brown.

—. 2002c. Natives block expressway work. *Friends of Red Hill Valley Newsletter* (May). Friends of Red Hill Valley Archives (CD-ROM): 31 July 2004.

—. 2003. Permit granted to camp in the valley. *Friends of Red Hill Valley Update,* 7 August. Friends of Red Hill Valley Archives (CD-ROM): 31 July 2004.

—. 2007a. Red Hill Countdown: after more than 50 years of planning, the Red Hill Valley Parkway opens to traffic tomorrow. *Hamilton Spectator,* 16 November, A08.

—. 2007b. Two Row Wampum: Symbol of Sovereignty. *Indian Country Today,* 28 June, p. 1.

Uralla Visitor Information Centre. n.d.-a, *Uralla—The Meeting Place*, Uralla Visitor Information Centre, Tourist Brochure.

—. n.d.-b, *Uralla—The Meeting Place Website*, Uralla Visitor Information Centre. Accessed 10 June 2006. Available from: <http://www.uralla.com/>.

Urry, J. 1990. *The Tourist Gaze*, London: Sage Publications.

Valentine, G. and T. Skelton. 2003. Finding oneself, losing oneself: The lesbian and gay "scene" as paradoxical space. *International Journal of Urban and Regional Research* 27:849-866

Van Acker, E., and R. Hollander. 2003. Protecting our borders: Ministerial rhetoric and asylum seekers. *Australian Journalism Review* 25 (2):103-120.

Van den Berghe, Frédéric. 2004. The European Union and the Protection of Minorities: How Real is the Alleged Double Standard? In *Yearbook of European Law 2003,* 22. Oxford: Oxford University Press, 155.

van Dijk, T.A. 2000a. Ideologies, Racism, Discourse: Debates on Immigration and Ethnic Issues. In *Comparative perspectives on racism*, edited by J. ter Wal and M. Verkuyten. Aldershot: Ashgate, 91-115.

—. 2000b. New(s) Racism: A Discourse Analytical Approach. In *"Race", Racism and the Mass Media*, edited by S. Cottle. Milton Keynes: Open University Press.

Varichon, A. 2006. *Colors: What they mean and how to make them*. Trans. T. Ballas. New York: Abrams.

various. 2002. *The Sandon Point—A Community Bulletin for the Protection of Sandon Point.* Bulli: Hamish Brown.

—. 2004. *Friends of Red Hill Valley website,* July. Friends of Red Hill Valley Archives (CD-ROM): 31 July 2004.

Vassilacopoulos, George, and Toula Nicolacopoulos. 2004. Indigenous and White Australians: The Ontological Encountering and the Betrayal of Thought. In *Placing Race Localising Whiteness*, edited by S. Schech and B. Wadham. Adelaide: Flinders University Press.

Venturi, R. 1977. *Complexity and Contradiction in Architecture.* London: The Architectural Press.

Vermeersch, Peter. 2004. Minority Policy in Central Europe: Exploring the Impact of the EU's Enlargement Strategy. *Global Review of Ethno Politics* 3 (2):3.

Walker, V. 2001. Bushrangers never so popular. The *Australian*, 13 December, p. 3.

Walker v Minister for Planning. 2007. NSWLEC 741, 27 November.

Walkerdine, V. 1999. Violent boys and precocious girls: Regulating childhood at the end of the millennium. *Contemporary Issues in Early Childhood* 1:3-23.

Warrior, R. 1995. *Tribal secrets: Recovering American Indian intellectual traditions*. Minneapolis: University of Minnesota Press.

—. 1999. The Native American Scholar: Towards a New Intellectual Agenda, cited in Fredericks, B. 2007. Talkin' Up the Research, *Journal of Australian Indigenous Issues*, 10 (2):42.

Watson, Irene. 2002. Aboriginal Laws and the Sovereignty of Terra Nullius. In *borderlands ejournal* 1 (2).

Watson, I. 2005. Settled and unsettled spaces: are we free to roam? *Australia Critical Race and Whiteness Studies Association Journal* 1:40-52.

Watson, Irene. 2007. Settled and unsettled spaces: are we free to roam? In *Sovereign subjects: Indigenous sovereignty matters*, edited by Aileen Moreton-Robinson. Crows Nest, NSW: Allen and Unwin, 15-32

Watson, Irene. 2007a. Aboriginal Sovereignties: Past, Present and Future (Im)Possibilities. In *Our Patch: Enacting Australian Sovereignty*. Perth: Network Books.

Watson, Irene. 2007b. Settled and unsettled spaces: Are we free to roam? In *Sovereign Subjects: Indigenous sovereignty matters*, edited by Aileen Moreton-Robinson.

Watson-Verran, H., and D. Turnbull. 1995. Science and Other Indigenous Knowledge Systems. In *Handbook of Science and Technology Studies,* edited by S. Jassanoff, G.E. Markle, J.C. Petersen and T. Pinch. Thousand Oaks: Sage Publications.

Weisman, L.K. 1992. Discrimination by Design. *Interiors* 151 (5):10-13.

Weller, Marc. ed. 2004. Mechanisms for the Protection of Minority Rights. *ECMI Handbook Series, Vol.2*. Strasbourg: Council of Europe Publishing.

—. 2005. *The Rights of Minorities: A Commentary on the European Framework Convention for the Protection of Minorities*. Oxford: Oxford University Press.

Wiegman, Robyn. 2000. Feminism's Apocalyptic Futures. *New Literary History* 31:805-25.

Wiener, Antje, and Guido Schwellnus. 2004. Contested Norms in the Process of EU Enlargement: Non-Discrimination and Minority Rights, Constitutionalism Web-Papers, ConWEB 2.

Wigley, M. 2001. *White Walls, Designer Dresses: The Fashioning of Modern Architecture.* Cambridge, Mass.:M.I.T.

Wilson, C. 2007. Indigenous Research and Archaeology: Transformative Practices in/with/for the Ngarrindjeri community. *Archaeologies* 3 (3):320-334.

Wilson, J. 1998. The Aboriginal Presence: the Red Hill Creek valley 9000 B.C.-1615 A.D. In *From Mountain to Lake: the Red Hill Creek Valley,* edited by W.G. Peace. Hamilton, Ontario: The Conserver Society of Hamilton and District.

Winant, Howard. 1994. *Racial Conditions: Politics, Theory, Comparisons.* Minneapolis: University of Minnesota Press.

Wood, L.A. 1915. *The War Chief of the Six Nations: a chronicle of Joseph Brant,* edited by G.M. Wrong and H.H. Langton. Toronto: Galsgow, Brook and Company.

Wright, T. 1970. *The Great Unwashed: by the Journey Engineer*, 1868. London: Routledge.

Wright, Terence. 2004. Collateral coverage: media images of Afghan refugees, 2001. *Visual Studies* 19 (1):97-111.

Young, D.J.B. 2004. The material value of color: The estate agent's tale. *Home Cultures* 1 (1):5-22.

Yue, A. 1999. <interface: reflections of an ethnic toygirl>. In *Multicultural Queer: Australian Narratives,* edited by P.A. Jackson and G. Sullivan. New York: Haworth Press Inc.

INDEX